New Spaces of Exploration

TAURIS HISTORICAL GEOGRAPHY SERIES
Series Editor: Robert Mayhew, University of Bristol

Though long established as a field of inquiry, historical geography has changed dramatically in recent years becoming a driving force in the development of many of the new agendas of contemporary geography. Dialogues with historians of science, art historians and literary scholars have revitalised the history of geographical thought, and a new, vibrant, pluralistic culture of scholarship has emerged. The Tauris Historical Geography series provides an international forum for the publication of scholarly work that encapsulates and furthers these new developments.

Editorial Board:
David Armitage, Harvard University.
Jeremy Black, Exeter University.
Laura Cameron, Queen's University, Ontario.
Felix Driver, Royal Holloway, University of London.
Michael Heffernan, Nottingham University.
Nuala Johnson, Queen's University, Belfast.
David Livingstone, Queen's University, Belfast.
David Matless, Nottingham University.
Miles Ogborn, Queen Mary, University of London.
David Robinson, Syracuse University.
Charles Withers, Edinburgh University.
Brenda Yeoh, National University of Singapore.

Forthcoming in the Series:
1. *Zambesi: David Livingstone and Expeditionary Science in Africa* by Lawrence Dritsas
2. *New Spaces of Exploration: Geographies of Discovery in the Twentieth Century* by Simon Naylor and James Ryan (eds)
3. *Scriptural Geography: Portraying the Holy Land* by Edwin James Aiken
4. *Bringing Geography to Book: Ellen Semple and the Reception of Geographical Knowledge* by Innes Keighren
5. *Enlightenment, Modernity and Science: Geographies of Scientific Culture in Georgian England* by Paul Elliot
6. *Dead Sea Level: Science, Exploration and Imperial Interests in the Near East* by Haim Goren

New Spaces of Exploration

Geographies of Discovery in the Twentieth Century

Edited by Simon Naylor and James R. Ryan

LONDON · NEW YORK

Library
University of Texas
at San Antonio

Published in 2010 by I.B.Tauris & Co Ltd
6 Salem Road, London W2 4BU
175 Fifth Avenue, New York NY 10010
www.ibtauris.com

Distributed in the United States and Canada Exclusively by Palgrave Macmillan
175 Fifth Avenue, New York NY 10010

Selection and editorial matter copyright © 2010 Simon Naylor and James R. Ryan

Individual chapters copyright © 2010 Elizabeth Baigent, Christy Collis, Klaus Dodds, Felix Driver, Matthew Godwin, Jude Hill, Fae L. Korsmo, Fraser MacDonald, Simon Naylor, James R. Ryan, Nicola J. Thomas, Kathryn Yusoff

All rights reserved. Except for brief quotations in a review, this book, or any part thereof, may not be reproduced, stored in or introduced into a retrieval system, or transmitted, in any form or by any means, electronic, mechanical, photocopying, recording or otherwise, without the prior written permission of the publisher.

Tauris Historical Geography: 2

ISBN: 978 1 84885 016 3 (HB)
       978 1 84885 017 0 (PB)

A full CIP record for this book is available from the British Library
A full CIP record is available from the Library of Congress

Library of Congress Catalog Card Number: available

Printed and bound in Great Britain by CPI Antony Rowe, Chippenham

Contents

Acknowledgements		VII
Notes on Contributors		VIII
1	Exploration and the twentieth century *James R. Ryan and Simon Naylor*	1
2	'Deeds not words'? Life writing and early twentieth-century British polar exploration *Elizabeth Baigent*	23
3	Configuring the field: Photography in early twentieth-century Antarctic exploration *Kathryn Yusoff*	52
4	Explorations in the Libyan Desert: William J. Harding King *Nicola J. Thomas and Jude Hill*	78
5	Fieldwork and the geographical career: T. Griffith Taylor and the exploration of Australia *Simon Naylor*	105
6	Glaciology, the Arctic, and the US Military, 1945–58 *Fae L. Korsmo*	125
7	Assault on the unknown: Geopolitics, Antarctic science and the International Geophysical Year (1957–8) *Klaus Dodds*	148
8	'Britnik': How America made and destroyed Britain's first satellite *Matthew Godwin*	173

CONTENTS

9 High empire: Rocketry and the popular
   geopolitics of space exploration, 1944–62   196
   Fraser MacDonald

10 Walking in your footsteps: 'Footsteps
   of the explorers' expeditions and the contest
   for Australian desert space   222
   Christy Collis

11 Modern explorers   241
   Felix Driver

Notes   251
Select Bibliography   293
Index   305

Acknowledgements

This book began life as a double session at the Royal Geographical Society/Institute of British Geographers Annual Conference in 2005 on the historical geographies of exploration. We are indebted to the conference organisers, the speakers and the audience for their support in getting this project off the ground. Several people commented on the subsequent book proposal, including Mike Heffernan and Michael Bravo, and we are very grateful for their comments and suggestions. David Stonestreet of I.B.Tauris and Robert Mayhew, the editor of the series in which this book sits, have been helpful, patient and supportive throughout. Felix Driver generously agreed to supply an afterword and in doing so read the entire manuscript and provided vital encouragement. When this project began Simon was based at the University of Bristol and James at the University of Leicester, but by its close our offices were adjacent to one another at the University of Exeter's Cornwall campus. We would like to thank colleagues from all of these institutions for enabling us to see this project through to completion.

Notes on Contributors

Elizabeth Baigent is Reader in the History of Geography at the University of Oxford, UK. Her interest on polar exploration stems from her time at the *Oxford Dictionary of National Biography* (1993–2003) when she was Research Director and author of a large number of articles on explorers and travellers. Her current research interests include the life of traveller Kate Marsden (see the essay in *Geographers: Biobibliographical Studies* (London, 2008)).

Christy Collis is Senior Lecturer in Media and Communication in the Creative Industries Faculty, Queensland University of Technology, Brisbane, Australia. Collis has published on the cultural and legal geographies of the Australian deserts and the Australian Antarctic Territory.

Klaus Dodds is Professor of Geopolitics at Royal Holloway, University of London, UK. He is the author and editor of a number of books including *Geopolitics: A Very Short Introduction* (Oxford, 2007) and co-editor of *Spaces of Security and Insecurity: Geographies of the War on Terror* (Aldershot, 2009).

Felix Driver is Professor of Human Geography at Royal Holloway, University of London, UK. He is the author of *Geography Militant: Cultures of Exploration and Empire* (Blackwell, 2001) and co-editor (with Luciana Martins) of *Tropical Visions in an Age of Empire* (Chicago, 2005). He is currently working on geographical collections.

Matthew Godwin is an Honorary Research Associate at University College London, UK. He is author of *The Skylark Rocket, British Space Science and the European Space Research Organisation, 1957–1972* (Paris, 2007).

His recent research has focused on the role of Operational Research in British defence planning during the Cold War.

Jude Hill is a Research Development Manager at the University of Bristol, UK. Her research interests include historical-cultural geographies and material culture; museums, collecting and collections; medicine, health and folklore. She has published scholarly articles in a range of journals including *Journal of Material Culture* (2007) and *Social & Cultural Geography* (2006).

Fae L. Korsmo is a Senior Advisor to the Director of the US National Science Foundation, USA. Her research over the past two decades has focused on indigenous rights in the circumpolar north, polar science history, research ethics and the conduct of interdisciplinary science.

Fraser MacDonald is Lecturer in Human Geography at the University of Melbourne, Australia. His research is primarily on the historical geography and geopolitics of the Cold War. He is a co-editor (with Rachel Hughes and Klaus Dodds) of *Observant States: Geopolitics and Visual Culture*, which will be published by I.B.Tauris.

Simon Naylor is Senior Lecturer in Historical Geography at the University of Exeter, UK. He has conducted research into the geographies of fieldwork and exploration in a range of contexts, including Britain, South America, Australia and Antarctica. He is the author of *Regionalising Science: Placing Knowledges in Victorian England*, which will be published by Pickering and Chatto in 2010.

James R. Ryan is Associate Professor of Cultural Geography at the University of Exeter, UK. He is the author of *Picturing Empire* (London, 1997) and co-editor (with Joan Schwartz) of *Picturing Place* (London, 2003).

Nicola J. Thomas is Senior Lecturer in Human Geography at the University of Exeter, UK. Her research interests include the historical and cultural geographies of imperialism, biography and histories of science and exploration. She has published scholarly articles in a range of journals and books including *Journal of Historical Geography* (2004), *Cultural Geographies* (2007) and *Colonial Lives across the British Empire*, edited by David Lambert and Alan Lester (Cambridge, 2006).

NOTES ON CONTRIBUTORS

Kathryn Yusoff is Lecturer in Human (and non-human) Geography at the University of Exeter, UK. She has a broad interest in rethinking the interactions between human and physical geographies, within the context of abrupt climate change. Particularly, she is interested in how both science and visual culture observe and engage with dynamic shifts in the biophysical world. Kathryn is currently working on ideas about the political aesthetics of climate change.

1 Exploration and the twentieth century

James R. Ryan and Simon Naylor

The academic study of exploration has undergone something of a renaissance in the last two decades. While exploration has remained a strong theme for publishers and authors aiming at a popular market interested in tales of intrepid individuals venturing into perilous environments[1] it had become, by the 1960s, something of an academic backwater.[2] This state of affairs was transformed in the wake of the broad 'crisis in representation' that spread across the humanities and social sciences from the 1970s, which challenged academic disciplines to reflect critically on how their knowledge-making practices were premised upon various structures of power. Postcolonial approaches in particular took inspiration from key literary analyses of the West's relationship to the non-Western world such as Edward Said's 1979 *Orientalism*.[3] Scholars from literary studies such as Paul Carter and Mary Louise Pratt furthered this postcolonial agenda by considering accounts of European exploration as part of Western imperial discourse.[4] Rather than adopt a conventional approach of treating expedition narratives as historical records of remarkable journeys and impartial 'discoveries', such scholars teased open the strategies by which such accounts constructed an epistemological framework into which other places and peoples were relocated. In this way exploration could be regarded less as some impartial means of 'discovering' the 'unknown' than part of a powerful and enduring projection of Western imperial interests onto other parts of the world.[5]

The analysis of narratives of exploration within literary studies as part of a broader genre of 'travel literature' has thus provided some important insights into the conventional and power-laden aspects of such writings. However, as Dane Kennedy has pointed out, a narrow focus on texts and issues of textuality has limited insights into how exploration was shaped as an enterprise, distinct from other forms of travel, 'with its own scientific protocols, its own trained practitioners, and its own unique partnership with scientific societies, the state, and the public'.[6] In addition, a preoccupation with texts does little to illuminate key questions of how explorers actually performed in the field, the variety of forms of inscriptions (visual as well as textual) they deployed and, finally, how their cultural frameworks were defended and disrupted in their contact with different places and peoples. These broader kinds of questions have however assumed a prominent place in recent scholarship across a range of fields, notably anthropology, geography, history of art and history of science. In the first part of this introductory chapter we seek to situate the chapters contained in this book within this broad and interdisciplinary setting. We begin our overview of the historiography of exploration by considering four key foci of recent academic enquiry: first, exploration and the production of knowledge; second, exploration and the processes of cultural contact and exchange; third, the textual and pictorial representation of exploration; and, lastly, biographical studies of explorers.

HISTORIOGRAPHIES OF EXPLORATION

The first body of work underpinning this volume is that which takes a critical look at the relationship between exploration and the production of knowledge, particularly knowledge incorporated into Western discourses of science. This has been of central concern to historians of science and technology who have contributed much to a broader understanding of how the practices and technologies of exploration have been related to the production of various kinds of scientific knowledge.[7] A range of studies have highlighted the significance of institutional sponsors of exploration, from the British Admiralty's support of Cook's exploration of the Pacific in the eighteenth century[8] to the East India Company and British colonial Government of India, which supported terrestrial exploration and survey enterprises such as the Great Trigonometrical Survey of India.[9]

As editors situated within the discipline of geography we have inevitably approached this project with keen awareness of the work by historians of geography and science who have reconsidered practices of exploration as part of more general concerns to understand the geographical discipline's own historical foundations. Studies have shown how exploration and geographical science developed from the eighteenth century, fuelled by new technologies of navigation and cartography, new ideas and the expanding apparatus of nation states.[10] In the last couple of decades, often with interdisciplinary inspiration from the history of geography, science studies and postcolonialism, scholars have turned their attention to the complex ways in which practices of geographical exploration and knowledge making were aligned with forms of institutional and political power. Studies of nineteenth-century British cultures of exploration and empire have shown how the Royal Geographical Society (RGS) in London played a key role as a stage upon which explorers, as well as their patrons, staked their reputations and paraded their contribution to science and empire.[11] Institutions of geography and exploration throughout Europe were closely involved in the promotion of exploration as a form of national and imperial interest.[12] Geographical knowledge was thus constructed through a network that included not just individual explorers but scientific societies, government bodies, private organisations, publishers and patrons of various kinds. Geographical disputes and controversies of the age, from the source of the Nile to the location of Timbuctoo, were conducted across these spatial networks. The trustworthiness and credibility of European explorers were cultivated within such networks in a range of ways, from performances of the explorer's own body to their place within wider circles of power and patronage.[13]

The RGS was one of a number of organisations in Victorian Britain – others included Kew Gardens and the British Natural History Museum – which provided explorers with institutional support and scientific justification for their journeys and specimen gathering.[14] Such institutions not only promoted popular cultures of exploration but set important parameters for how explorers should behave, both at home and, more particularly, in 'the field'. In the second half of the nineteenth century the RGS, for example, put forward increasingly refined guidelines in its publication *Hints to Travellers*, which set out how and what explorers should observe.[15] Explorers were charged, for example, with the accurate recording of written geographical, meteorological and ethnographic observations and the collection of botanical, zoological and geological specimens. These formal duties of expeditionary work in turn necessitated the deployment of instruments, from sextants to barometers, and the development of particular technical skills on the part of their human operators. The role of instruments, as historians of science have noted, was to assist in standardisation and comparability of explorers' observations.[16] Institutions such as the RGS regarded training for explorers in field observation – both with and without instruments – as a means of protecting its reputation as the centre of authority in relation to knowledge in geographical science. However, as Felix Driver has shown, such attempts to control knowledge production were not always coherent and were fraught with 'fundamental dilemmas about the means and status of observation in the field'.[17] Recent studies of exploration, particularly those that draw on the literature in science studies, have thus paid close attention to the contextual, contingent and situated nature of knowledge. Scientific knowledge in particular, as David Livingstone has argued, also bears the marks of geography in its production and consumption across a range of sites, from the laboratory to the fieldsite.[18] This and other work has scrutinised 'the field' as a particular kind of space for the production of scientific knowledge.[19] This critical attitude to 'the field', to observation and to knowledge production informs many of the essays in this volume, from Simon Naylor's discussion of the meaning of 'fieldwork' for the mid-twentieth century geographer Griffith Taylor, to Kathryn Yusoff's analysis of how different visual and textual practices constituted 'the field' of Antarctic exploration in the early twentieth century.

The relationship between knowledge and forms of power lies at the heart of much recent work on exploration. However, this relationship is complex and dynamic. Scholars have thus begun to show the wide spectrum of philosophical frameworks and psychological motives that underpinned the ideas and actions of individual explorers operating within the context of European empire building. For Henry Morton Stanley (1841–1904), for example, exploration was a form of military conquest and geographical knowledge, a tool to the commercial and colonial exploitation of Africa. The French explorer of North Africa, Henri Duveyrier (1840–92), by contrast, embraced a Saint Simonian philosophy that rejected such aggressive colonial expansionism and practiced geographical exploration as part of peaceful commercial and cultural exchange between Europe and Africa.[20] This volume of essays seeks to examine further the relationships between knowledge and power within twentieth-century exploration practice across a range of sites. For instance, Collis's chapter analyses the recent re-enactment of Victorian imperial expeditions across the Australian deserts, insisting that imperial exploration was not restricted to the British Empire or to the nineteenth century, but that it is a significant constituent of contemporary Australian spatiality.

The second area of recent scholarship to inform this volume is that which seeks to understand exploration as a process of physical and material contact and exchange. Such work builds on the postcolonial critique of exploration practices and the epistemological frameworks that underpinned them, something of which we noted above. Mary Louise Pratt's examination of Western travel and exploration narratives thus considered processes of 'transculturation' that brought together Europeans and non-Europeans across various 'contact zones'.[21] Processes of encounter and epistemology were also central to Bernard Smith's study of early European visual representation of the South Pacific, which showed how European cultural perceptions were altered in the face of new encounters that could not be easily accommodated by existing cultural frameworks.[22]

Building upon such foundations, anthropologists and historians of anthropology have been particularly concerned to trace the physical and human spaces of cultural contact and material exchange involved in voyages of exploration. Investigation into the nature of encounters between European explorers, traders and settlers and indigenous peoples reveals how these unequal exchanges – of objects, cultures and power – could disturb perceptions and identities of Europeans as well as indigenous peoples.[23] An understanding of exploration as a process of contact and exchange is central to many of the authors in this collection. Jude Hill and Nicola J. Thomas, for example, consider how the physical geographer Harding King relied upon indigenous people in the planning and execution of his expeditions to the Libyan desert and the degree to which this was reflected in the resulting forms of knowledge. European explorers, however 'heroic' at home, were often entirely dependent upon the skills, knowledge and labour of non-Europeans in the field, and large-scale imperial surveys and expeditions could simply not have happened without the direct involvement of indigenous people.[24] Physical environments could also play a formative role in shaping explorers' ideas about nature and human identity.[25] Encounters with radically new environments – from the equator to the poles – combined with the psychological pressures of expeditionary practices could even threaten explorers' sense of rationality and consciousness.[26]

A third broad seam of scholarship that we take seriously as a backdrop to this volume includes work from a range of disciplines that seeks to move beyond the analysis solely of *written* texts. Exploration and its sponsorship by institutions of state and science from the eighteenth century onwards offered artists new career opportunities as expeditionary artists. As studies by historians of art and exploration have shown, the resulting visual records – from paintings to sketches – were located within dynamic categories of both 'art' and 'science'. Moreover, a number of expeditionary artists struggled in their attempts to use contemporary European visual conventions in the depiction of radically different environments, and developed their own representational styles in response.[27]

The making of maps and charts has, along with pictorial representations, long been central to exploration. Moreover, perhaps even more directly, cartography enabled explorers to symbolically possess the terrain that they traversed, naming places and plotting the expedition routes in a language of European cartographic conventions and spatial measurement. However, as studies of nineteenth-century cartographic endeavours have demonstrated, different kinds of survey, from the traverse surveys undertaken by explorers to the larger and longer lasting trigonometric survey undertaken by colonial states, served the interests of empire in quite different ways.[28]

As a new technology of the second half of the nineteenth century, photography was adopted with enthusiasm by explorers as a means of providing accurate and objective visual records of expeditions. However, photography was also, at least until the 1890s, an unreliable and cumbersome technology and many efforts failed through lack of knowledge or inclement conditions. Photography was certainly used on European expeditions as a means of visually mapping and colonising territory. As with painting and mapping, however, the practice of photography encompassed a broad range of skills and attitudes, each with potentially different relationships to expeditionary practice.[29] More important, as historians of science and photography have shown, the cultural currency of photography as an objective or truthful medium was culturally constructed and the use of photography as evidence in science was, from its earliest application, invariably contested.[30]

As the range of studies noted here show, visual representations, including maps, photographs and paintings, played important roles – often in dynamic relation to exploration texts – in the practice of exploration and the processes by which knowledge about non-European people and environments was assembled and disseminated. The essays in this volume contribute further to this work in their embrace of different kinds of expeditionary inscription, from the photographs of Antarctica examined by Kathryn Yusoff to the popular depictions of rocket science analysed by Fraser MacDonald, and in their appreciation of the dynamic and contested nature of such cultural objects.

The final key scholarly theme on exploration drawn upon by this volume is that of explorer biography. The renaissance in studies of exploration noted above has in many ways reanimated biographical studies of explorers. For as many recent studies of exploration have noted, 'explorers' were not born with this label; it was bestowed upon them through a complex process of cultural accretion and textual mediation. Indeed, an explorer's exploits became public knowledge not because what they achieved in the field had intrinsic value but because of a whole series of treatments and translations by other individuals and institutions. 'Acts of exploration', as Felix Driver puts it, 'are always mediated in some way, if not by the act of authorship itself, then through the labours of others – sponsors, patrons, reporters, publishers, and image-makers.'[31] As Elizabeth Baigent's essay in this volume shows, British polar explorers of the first half of the twentieth century were both 'made and unmade' as heroes and celebrities through the interpretation of the printed biographical record. Public esteem depended not just on an individual's achievements but on how their celebrity was valued as a commodity in a shifting cultural market. Social class, nationality and gendered notions of character all played a part in determining the reputations of explorers during and well beyond their own lifetimes. Explorers thus need to be situated as much in the metropolitan worlds of scientific societies, rich patrons, newspaper publishers and popular readerships as in the foreign fields in which their expeditions took place.[32]

Many biographies of explorers aimed only at a popular readership continue to tap into conventional tropes of the 'heroic' exploration genre, using them largely as mirrors for popular preoccupations of our own times. Notable here are biographies of famous explorer heroes written by today's 'explorers' wishing to take on some of the charms of their forbearers.[33] Other biographical studies have provided much more complex portraits of the often contradictory motives and ambivalent attitudes that framed the lives of explorers as well as their admirers and detractors. This is true of recent biographies of Francis Younghusband, Richard Burton and Henry Morton Stanley, for example, which pay particular attention to the historical and political contexts in which these individuals lived, revealing how attitudes to political structures of nation and empire, and social contours of 'race', class, sexuality and gender shaped the maps of their lives and reputations.[34] A number of studies have considered the construction of exploration as a distinctly masculine activity and nineteenth-century debates on whether women could qualify as reliable producers of scientific knowledge. Studies of women naturalists in the American West or women travellers in West Africa in the late nineteenth century show how, despite their often considerable achievements, women were consistently marginalised on account of both their gender and amateur status by metropolitan science.[35] Other scholars have woven together biography and detailed analysis of expeditionary practices in order to convey the material and imaginative practices through which explorers attempted to master particular spaces. For instance, Max Jones provides a critical historical analysis of Robert Falcon Scott's much celebrated but often poorly examined Antarctic expedition.[36] Similarly, Burnett's study of British explorers' searches for the legendary El Dorado shows how British surveyors and explorers – particularly the well-known Robert Schomburgk – constructed the spaces and boundaries of Britain's South American colony, Guyana.[37]

Many critical accounts of exploration have, as we noted above, evolved with postcolonial theoretical agendas and have unsurprisingly tended to focus on the European 'age of empire', for it is here that the relationships between practices of exploration and projects of European imperialism are perhaps most apparent. The relationship between exploration and empire in the twentieth century has, in comparison to that of the eighteenth and nineteenth centuries, received less critical scrutiny. However, we would suggest that examining exploration practices and politics in the twentieth century offers the opportunity to decouple the association between exploration and imperialism as either necessary or inevitable. This is not to say that the theoretical insights of postcolonialism are no longer relevant in the study of twentieth-century exploration. Indeed, the pervasive and insidious nature of imperial power, even in the absence of formal political structures of empire, demands sophisticated theoretical tools. Popular accounts of twentieth-century exploration continue to present it as a story of white Western men using their trained minds and bodies, and wielding modern technology, to overcome the obstacles of nature and penetrate new frontiers of knowledge. Much of exploration thus still seems to take place 'out there', well beyond the 'first' or developed world, and revolve around the extraction of knowledge, images, data or specimens that are 'brought home' and made intelligible through circulation within Western centres of calculation. This is notably true of national institutions of geographical science, which continue to commemorate their activities through discourses of nationalism, empire and masculine exploration.[38]

TWENTIETH-CENTURY EXPLORATION: 'GEOGRAPHY TRIUMPHANT'?

We have demonstrated a recent renaissance in scholarly writing about explorers and exploration but have also noted that the overwhelming majority of this work does not venture much beyond the first years of the twentieth century. At one level this is not surprising. For many commentators – then and now – the beginning of the twentieth century marked the end of an unalloyed era of discovery. The age of what Joseph Conrad called 'Geography Militant', supposedly characterised by a courageous quest for truthful revelation of the earth's geographical secrets – from Captain Cook's ocean voyages in the second half of the eighteenth century to David Livingstone's journeys in south and central Africa a century later – had passed. In its place had emerged what Conrad called 'Geography Triumphant', an era where the world map had few if any 'blank' spaces left to 'discover' and where the materialistic impulses of modernity and relative ease of mass travel banished forever the figure of the genuine explorer hero, motivated by a noble quest for knowledge.[39]

Conrad's lament, as Felix Driver has pointed out, was actually nothing new – such notions have long shaped both conventional and radical accounts of European exploration and encounters with the rest of the world. Whilst we agree that these boundary markers are arbitrary, the periodisation of the history of exploration that Conrad mapped out is worth reflecting upon here, not only because it pervaded the ideas of those in the business of exploration at the time but also because it has haunted the labours of explorers and historians since.

Studies of the history of exploration, including many of those already cited here, have – consciously or not – tended to emphasise Conrad's discontinuity. This is true, for example, of William H. Goetzmann's well-known trilogy examining the history of American exploration.[40] Goetzmann argues that 'the Second Great Age of Discovery' began with the South American voyages of French geographer and explorer Charles Marie de La Condamine in 1735–45 and reached its apogee in the United States Exploring Expedition of 1838–42. By 1860 Americans had not only charted their own coastline but much of that of China, Japan, many Pacific Island groups and the continent of Antarctica and were also embarking upon terrestrial exploration of the North American landmass, particularly the American West. For Goetzmann this age of science and discovery was characterised by the testing of explorers' physical and mental capacities within new human and natural environments. It ended when science was transformed from a set of disparate practices carried out in the field to something much more systematic, governed by institutions and structures, and undertaken not only in the field but also in the laboratory and museum.

Tony Rice's *Voyages of Discovery* follows a fairly familiar trajectory to other studies in the genre, beginning with the scientific revolution in Europe – in Rice's case Hans Sloane's voyage to Jamaica in the 1680s – and concluding with the apogee of European imperial power in the late nineteenth century. Rice concludes his survey with a discussion of the HMS *Challenger* expedition of the world's oceans in the 1870s (of which more will be discussed later).[41] A last example is Margaret Deacon's well-known study of the history of oceanography, which covers the period 1650–1900. While Deacon acknowledges her anxieties over where to begin her study, she expresses no such concerns over its end point. The study concludes in 1900 she states, with no qualification, because oceanography 'by 1900 was a recognised science'; this, despite her earlier discussion of the likes of Joseph Banks, James Rennell, John Lubbock and Edward Forbes as well as the work of the crew of HMS *Challenger*.[42]

The sentiments expressed by Goetzmann, Rice, Deacon and others reflect a common idea that voyages of discovery stopped being explorations when their aims were scientific rather than narrowly geographical or for personal or nationalistic ends, and that this shift occurred at the end of the nineteenth century because of the professionalisation and institutionalisation of science at that time. It is of course entirely unfair to castigate historians for setting end points to their studies, but we would argue that the overuse of the nineteenth century's end in studies of exploration unintentionally exacerbates the idea of a rupture that in many ways was a fiction. Put another way, scientifically motivated exploration extended backwards in time well before 1900, while heroic exploration traditionally associated with the Victorian era extended well into the twentieth century.

It was certainly the case that little changed in the first years of the twentieth century in terms of cultures and practices of exploration. Institutions such as the RGS – associated since its establishment in 1830 with exploration – worked hard to dispel the notion that the age of Geography Militant had passed. As Nicola J. Thomas and Jude Hill argue in their chapter in this volume, the RGS remained highly influential in the twentieth century by promoting the challenges of the 'Still Unknown', sponsoring official expeditions and giving succour to amateur enthusiasts such as William Joseph Harding King (1869–1933).

The poles in particular offered unknown frontiers to be explored, and Europe and North America focused much attention over the next two decades on reaching the poles and then over the rest of the century on the investigation of the vast icesheets around them.[43] In particular, there existed strong continuities between the gentleman hero figures of David Livingstone, who embodied the virtuous striving of the Christian colonial missionary explorer in mid-Victorian Britain and Robert Falcon Scott in Edwardian Britain. Both were also praised for their dedication to science. When the bodies of Scott and his four companions were found some eight months after their deaths, the search party noted that they had continued, despite their hardships, to carry their weighty geological collections. The search party who discovered Scott and his companions marked the burial site cross with the lines from Tennyson's poem Ulysses: 'To strive, to seek, to find, and not to yield', which perpetuated the Victorian ethos of heroic exploration. It was re-enacted briefly and on a vertical plane with the 1953 coronation conquest of Mount Everest by Edmund Hillary and Tenzing Norgay.

In terms of geopolitical frameworks for exploration, in many respects the early twentieth century saw the continuation of practices of exploration, survey and conquest that had been so well developed by European colonial powers in the preceding two centuries. Well-established geopolitical configurations such as the Great Game in central Asia continued to shape military and scientific expeditionary activity. Thus the Younghusband 'Expedition' into Tibet in 1903–4, which captured the imagination of the British Edwardian public and added Francis Younghusband to the names of famous explorer heroes, was essentially a military invasion motivated by British misapprehensions, notably on the part of Younghusband and his key patron Lord Curzon, Viceroy of India, of active Russian designs on Tibet and, by implication, British India. Few permanent British imperial advantages resulted, other than a telegraph wire and a couple of trade agents in Tibet. Patrick French suitably characterises the episode, which marked the end of the century-old Great Game between Britain and Russia in Asia, as the 'last great adventure of the Victorian age'.[44] However, from a Tibetan standpoint the 'expedition' had very real consequences, leaving almost 3000 Tibetans dead and a political vacuum into which China moved unchallenged, setting the framework for its full-scale occupation of Tibet in 1959.

Throughout the twentieth century, practices of exploration, mapping and surveying have continued to play an essential part in the strategies of national governments seeking to maintain their political claims in disputed imperial territories. This was certainly the case in the Antarctic. As Klaus Dodds argues in this volume, British civil servants used a range of such strategies to maintain a presence and stake in sovereignty in the Antarctic in the twentieth century. Despite the 1959 Antarctic Treaty and practices of international scientific cooperation, rival territorial claims from Britain, Argentina and Chile continued to infuse practices of science and exploration with contested geopolitical meanings.[45] Elsewhere Dodds has traced the way in which the British Government lent credence to its territorial claims to a slice of the continent through a programme of surveys, mapping exercises and scientific expeditions, operationalised through the wartime Operation Tabarin and later the civilian Falkland Islands Dependencies Survey.[46] As Korsmo shows in this volume, although the geopolitical situation was rather different, various governments with an interest in the Arctic also used scientific exploration to establish and justify a presence there during the Cold War.

NEW SPACES OF EXPLORATION

So far we have questioned the decision to identify 1900 as the end point of an age of exploration and have shown some of the strong continuities between practices and ideologies operating across that point in time. While we want to hang on to these arguments, it was obviously also the case that the twentieth century was marked by a series of far-reaching technological and scientific advances – from submarines to aircraft and spacecraft – and that these had profound impacts on the exploration of the Earth, its atmosphere and of outer space. The final substantive section of this introductory chapter considers some of the most notable events in the histories of science and technology as they pertained to the exploration of new spaces as well as the re-discovery of already well-trodden territory. We will also consider the geopolitical repercussions of these events. We begin with the history of hydrography and spend quite some time under the sea, if only because of the lack of a substantive chapter on this aspect of the history of twentieth-century exploration. We then take briefly to the skies and consider the significance of aircraft in the exploration of both remote and familiar territories, before moving on to look at the role of satellites in the exploration of the Earth's atmosphere and beyond. The section concludes by reflecting on motivations for exploration in the twenty-first century.

In the most general sense, hydrography refers to the measurement and description of the physical characteristics of waters and coastlines and under that definition subsumes the sciences of oceanography and limnology. However, it is often used to refer to the measurement of waters necessary for the safe navigation of vessels. The history of hydrography is as old as the history of seafaring itself, although the sixteenth century is often recognised as the beginning of modern hydrography, with concerted campaigns of coastal mapping by the English, French and the Dutch. Hydrography was recognised as a profession in eighteenth-century Europe, with the navies of various nations becoming increasingly involved in the collection of information so as to furnish their mariners with nautical charts and other documents necessary for the navigation of territorial waters and the world's oceans. In turn, they sought to gain commercial and military advantage over their national competitors. Held in tension with this, hydrography also developed as an international endeavour in the nineteenth century. In similar manner to the study of the weather, hydrography lent itself to collaborative study between nations due to the lack of national borders, the indiscriminately hostile environmental conditions and the global scope of observations.[47] In 1853 an international conference was held at Brussels with 16 maritime nations participating, to establish a common plan for the observation of winds and oceanic currents.[48] However, despite calls for greater international cooperation on the subject, it was not until after the First World War that national hydrographic offices decided that a close and permanent association was necessary. In June 1919, at the invitation of the British Admiralty, a hydrographic conference was convened in London, in which 24 nations participated. A special committee was appointed, which led to the establishment in 1921 of the International Hydrographic Bureau.

Like hydrography, oceanography – the scientific study of the oceans and seas – has a long history and one defined in part by a tension between national and international endeavours. Modern oceanography probably finds its origins in the eighteenth-century labours of the likes of James Cook, Louis Antoine de Bougainville and James Rennell, author of *Currents of the Atlantic Ocean*, published posthumously in 1832.[49] Oceanography was advanced in the first half of the nineteenth century through the work of Alexander von Humboldt, James Clark Ross, Owen Stanley and Robert Fitzroy, amongst others.[50] The steep slope beyond the continental shelves was discovered in 1849, and the laying of the transatlantic telegraph cable in 1858 confirmed the existence of a mid-ocean ridge under the Atlantic. However, the HMS *Challenger*'s 68890 mile voyage to explore the world's oceans from 1872 to 1876 was perhaps the crowning achievement of Victorian oceanography. Sponsored by the Royal Society of London and funded by the British Admiralty, the ship made use of a slew of new technologies to investigate life below the surface of the sea.[51] The expeditions gained funding because of Britain's desire to maintain its dominance of the seas. However, in the wake of the expedition, Norway, Germany, France and Russia all funded oceanographic cruises and these continued into the twentieth century. For instance, Hamblin notes that despite restrictions imposed by the Treaty of Versailles, Germany outfitted a scientific vessel, the *Meteor*, to demonstrate a German presence in foreign countries; the scientific leader of the 1925–7 expedition 'felt that Germany's destiny could be achieved by scientific greatness'.[52] However, despite these gestures, there were attempts at international cooperation. In 1902, a number of European nations with economic interests in the North Atlantic established the International Council for the Exploration of the Sea; its purpose was to encourage and coordinate oceanographic activities, especially in relation to fisheries research.[53]

* * * * *

The inter-war period saw developments in physical oceanography and in the new fields of marine acoustics and geophysics. However, it was in the aftermath of the Second World War that oceanography was able to advance materially, due to significant military funding, in turn driven by the Cold War. As Kai-Henrik Barth has shown in his study of the relationships between scientists and the US Department of Defense, scientists worked in tandem with military patrons, pursuing their own research agendas.[54] (Korsmo, in this volume, makes a similar argument in relation to the discipline of glaciology in the Arctic.) In relation to oceanography, scientists were able to guarantee funding and logistical support for their work by promising to help the Navy with the development of its submarine and nuclear programmes and the monitoring of other nations' programmes.[55] One good example of the interweaving of scientific exploration and the Cold War military is that of the investigation of ocean trenches using deep-diving bathyscaphes, submersibles able to withstand incredible pressures. The inventor of the bathyscaphe was the Swiss physicist and explorer Auguste Piccard, inspiration for the character Professor Cuthbert Calculus in the *Tin Tin* books. Piccard's initial interest was in high-altitude ballooning; in 1931, using a specially designed spherical, pressurised aluminum gondola, he reached 15785 metres and collected new data on the upper atmosphere. He then realised that this work could be applied to exploration of the deep oceans and set about designing a craft that could withstand the incredible pressures encountered underwater. Interrupted by the Second World War, Piccard and his son eventually produced the bathyscaphe *Trieste* (see Figure 1.1). It was bought by the US Navy in 1957 for $250,000 and in 1960, with Piccard's son onboard, it reached the Challenger Deep in the Mariana Trench, almost 11000 metres down and the deepest part of any ocean. However, the US Navy had other plans for the *Trieste* beyond deep sea exploration. In 1963, the submersible was sent to the Mare Island Naval shipyard and modified so that it could carry out missions related to submarine recovery – it assisted in the search for the missing sub *USS Thresher* in 1963 – and other 'black programs' (including cable tapping and espionage), uses that Piccard probably never envisaged for his craft.[56]

However, as in other fields of scientific exploration that covered vast tracts of territory, including space and polar research, oceanography did try to transcend Cold War boundaries and maintain an emphasis on international cooperation. This was especially the case during the International Geophysical Year (IGY) of 1957–8. An educational pamphlet produced by the US National Academy of Sciences at the time of the IGY suggested that:

FIGURE 1.1 The bathyscaphe *Trieste*, hauled out of the water in an unnamed tropical port by the US Navy, circa 1958–9.

> Today's oceanographic techniques are in sharp contrast with those of only a generation ago. Research vessels of many different types now range all the seas of the world. They carry elaborate equipment, which is used by trained scientists to delve further into the depths of the sea.[57]

Using technologies like Piccard's bathyscaphe, as well as magnetometers, electronic instruments similar to SONAR, deep-coring devices and deep-sea cameras, IGY scientists from a host of nations helped advance the scientific exploration of the ocean floors (see Figure 1.2 for a poster that promoted and illustrated some of these scientific technologies – small labelled photographs demonstrated particular instruments and findings). However, despite the rather triumphalist overtones of the quote above, oceanographical work during and after the IGY did not remain untainted by more worldly concerns – Walter Sullivan's semi-official account of the IGY, *Assault*

FIGURE 1.2 'Oceans', a poster from '"Planet Earth": The Mystery with 100,100 Clues'. Pamphlet produced by the US National Academy of Sciences in 1958 (courtesy of the National Academy of Sciences Archives).

on the Unknown, noted for instance that one of the main drivers of the event's oceanography programme was to investigate whether deep ocean trenches could be used as a dumping ground for radioactive waste.[58]

REACHING FOR THE SKIES

Balloons, like Piccard's high-altitude aluminium gondola, were the first vehicles that took humans into the atmosphere, as far back as the eighteenth century. Aircraft largely replaced balloons in the twentieth century, given their superior range and speed. In particular, the combination of aircraft and the camera advanced the exploration and mapping of hostile terrain – hostile both in terms of physical terrain and geopolitics. Aerial photography had been used to reconnoiter enemy positions since the First World War. What was largely a military technology became put to civilian ends in the post-Second World War period. In 1946, Britain's Colonial Office established the Directorate of Colonial (later Overseas) Survey and instructed it to map 90,0000 square miles of Africa, which it did within 10 years, using both aerial photography as well as ground surveys.[59]

Aircraft were invaluable in the exploration and mapping of remote corners of the world, most notably the polar regions. In 1926, the American Richard Byrd was the first person to fly over the North Pole and again was the first to fly over the South Pole in 1929.[60] Other explorers, such as the Norwegian-born American Finn Ronne, used a combination of aircraft, cameras and ground surveys to map portions of Antarctica and to extend understandings of the geography of the continent. During the Ronne Antarctic Research Expedition of 1947–8, he worked with British Falkland Islands Dependencies Surveyors (FIDS) to map the Antartic Peninsula and to contribute to debates about whether Antarctica was actually one continent or two.[61]

Long-range aircraft like the C-130 Hercules were also routinely used in the polar regions, both to transport scientific personnel, equipment and supplies as well as to carry out scientific observations. Advances in radio altimetry – developed in part by the US Army

Signals Corps in Antarctica during the IGY – led to a new method for sounding the ice sheet and its bed, named radio-echo sounding (RES); a technique conducted from Hercules aircraft flying above the surface. These aircraft were in effect 'airborne laboratories' and they carried a number of remote sensing and reconnaissance devices, such as radar altimeters, aerial photographic instruments, infrared sensors and magnetometers, as well as the RES equipment. Funded by the National Science Foundation and supported by US Navy aircraft, scientists were able to accumulate some 40,0000 kilometres of flight track data over the 1960s and 1970s, which in turn helped fill in and re-draw the glaciological and geophysical maps of the Antarctic ice sheet.[62]

Aircraft and cameras also combined to help re-explore familiar and well-trodden landscapes: Aerial photography transformed archaeology in the first half of the twentieth century. The earliest known aerial photograph of an archaeological site – of Stonehenge – was taken in 1906. O. G. S. Crawford, the British geographer, explorer and Ordnance Survey archaeologist promoted the use of aerial photography in archaeology, claiming in 1923 that aerial photographs 'will prove as valuable to archaeology as that of the telescope has proved to astronomy'.[63] Through the survey of the deforested regions of southern England in the 1930s, aerial archaeology, Kitty Hauser notes, 'seemed to open up an unknown country inhabiting the more familiar one, this one visible only from the air'.[64]

Technological developments in the 1950s literally took exploration to another level: outer space. As the chapter by Matthew Godwin notes, in 1957, on the eve of the IGY, Soviet Russia launched Sputnik, the world's first satellite. Although controversial objects, rockets and satellites have made profound contributions to the remote exploration of the Earth and of outer space (Fraser Macdonald's chapter in this volume extends our understanding of the former). Satellites vastly improved the accuracy of the mapping of the polar regions and of the measurements of the Earth's shape. Satellites became central to geodesy – the science of measuring the Earth – from the 1960s and from the 1980s superseded traditional methods of surveying.[65] Modern-day explorers would probably be lost without the satellites wheeling around far above them – global positioning systems, or GPS, technologies rely on them to determine their user's location.

CONCLUSION

In his book *Pathfinders: A Global History of Exploration*, Felipe Fernández-Armesto considers exploration over five millennia as a way 'to trace the laying of the infrastructure of the history of the world – the routes that put sundered peoples back in touch with each other after their long history of divergence and enabled them to exchange objects, ideas, and personnel'.[66] In his wide historical and geographical canvas Fernández-Armesto paints exploration in the period 1850–2000 as being marked by a continuation, acceleration and narrowing of well-established processes of globalisation. As 'the unknown' became increasingly diminished in the face of increasing contact and communication between people and places, 'route finding' gave way to scientific exploration or adventure as a key motive for exploration. And whilst many of the most well-known expeditions ended as episodes of heroic failure, the cumulative effect – of increasing contact, exchange and cultural convergence in a rapidly globalising world – remained. As Fernández-Armesto shows, exploration certainly did not end with the nineteenth century. Indeed, as geographical horizons narrowed, exploration diversified and evolved even more complex sets of motives, practices and power relations: 'As the pace of exploration gathered, the fronts multiplied; it is hard to keep up with them.'[67] As the essays in this volume also show, new technologies, scientific theories, geopolitical configurations and cultural values have meant that exploration has maintained a strong currency through the twentieth century and into the twenty-first.[68]

The longstanding geopolitical significance of exploration has continued apace in the light of new configurations in the global political economy, driven by the rise in demand for industrial raw materials and energy that has accompanied the growth of economies in China and India – and arguably the geographical shift of the engine of the world economy from North America to Asia. In this context, the exploration and control of new locations for resource exploitation lies at the heart of much critical geopolitical positioning. Continuities between geographical and geological exploration in the nineteenth century and today are not merely symbolic. For example, mining companies with interests in exploiting the mineral wealth of the Democratic Republic of Congo are now revisiting cartographic and geographic records of nineteenth-century explorations in what was then the Congo Free State to assist their prospecting.[69] Meanwhile, the polar regions, so strongly associated with the heroic journeys of the nineteenth and early twentieth centuries, are being re-visited in the context of various countries' attempts to extend sovereignty rights over ocean floors on adjacent continental shelves, in response to a UN commission on the delimitation of the continental shelf. Russia, for instance, claimed that the Lomonosov Ridge under the Arctic Ocean was part of its landmass, a claim that would extend Russia's seabed by 1.2 million square kilometers. In a gesture reminiscent of geopolitics from a 100 years previously, Russia planted a flag on the seabed in support of its claim. In response, Canada vowed to increase its icebreaker fleet in the region, and Denmark sent its own scientists to the Arctic to seek alternative evidence that linked the Ridge to the Danish territory of Greenland. On the other side of the world, Britain was making similar claims to a large area of the seabed around the British Antarctic Territory as well as the Falkland Islands and South Georgia.[70] Once again, scientific exploration in contested and potentially resource-rich regions of the world has taken on a heightened political significance.[71]

To conclude, we hope that the essays contained in this volume will contribute to understandings of the significance of exploration through the twentieth century and into the twenty-first. Studies range across the entirety of the twentieth century and the geographical scope is similarly expansive, although admittedly also rather biased towards polar and space exploration. We make no apologies for this; polar and space exploration were after all significant preoccupations of the age. Moreover, a comprehensive coverage of the geographies of twentieth-century exploration is not the primary aim of the book, and indeed would not have even been possible within the confines of one volume. Rather, we think that the wide range of empirical and theoretical themes raised by the authors make significant contributions to wider debates about the histories, politics and cultures of exploration, as well as to wider histories and historical geographies of the twentieth century.

2 'Deeds not words'? Life writing and early twentieth-century British polar exploration

Elizabeth Baigent

'When I went South I never meant to write a book: I rather despised those who did so as being of an inferior brand to those who did things and said nothing about them.'[1] The words of Apsley Cherry-Garrard (1886–1959), survivor of Robert Falcon Scott's (1868–1912) last expedition, seem to echo the family motto of Edward Wilson (1872–1912), who died on that expedition: *'res non verba'* or 'deeds not words'.[2] For Cherry-Garrard the ethics of autobiography changed, however, along with much else, on that expedition and he came to think instead that '[e]very one who has been through such an extraordinary experience has much to say and ought to say it'.[3] Cherry-Garrard, the independent and very wealthy landed proprietor, represents the decision to write as a private, autonomous one, determined solely by individual conscience, but in reality neither the decision to write nor the nature of the writing depended on the explorer/author alone. 'Acts of exploration do not come to us unvarnished, as it were, spontaneously and directly: they are always mediated in some way, if not by the act of authorship itself, then through the labours of others – sponsors, patrons, reporters, publishers, and image-makers.'[4] To create celebrities from explorers, image makers had to turn acts into feats and feats into commodities. The creation of heroes was yet more complex. 'It was ... the printed word which created the aura of heroism [but] this aura was dependent on the ascription of moral values by mediators.'[5] Those mediators did not have a free hand: society at large, and particularly consumers of books, films, or memorabilia, shared the business (metaphorically and literally) of making and unmaking celebrities and heroes in exploration, just as they did in the cognate fields of science, sport, and the military.[6] Since we 'father present values on past heroes', whom the public lionizes changes as societal values change.[7] To become and stay a hero then, the explorer needed not merely to excel in his calling, to handle the printed word or visual image deftly, and to provide good copy for biographers and journalists, but also to suffer his actions to be moralized and to find himself epitomizing the morality of successive ages.

This essay considers how celebrities and heroes have been made and unmade through the biographies of British polar explorers of the first half of the twentieth century. This is part of a wider consideration of how geographical knowledge and traditions are consumed, 'the changing popular view of geography, the "political economy" of geography's publications', which complements discussions of how geography is produced.[8] The focus of the essay reflects wider concerns both with popular culture as a shaper of ideology, for example the engraining of imperial ideas through images and rhetoric connected with routines of daily life,[9] and with the history of the book, which considers among other things the mediating processes by which an author's manuscript is served to its readers.[10]

BIOGRAPHY AND GEOGRAPHY AT THE START OF THE TWENTIETH CENTURY

Nineteenth-century British geography was a very mixed bag, being formed by a number of diverse traditions – literary, scientific, exploratory, educational, commercial, applied, military, and cartographic – with a number of diverse constituencies, some regionally distinct, others defined by the character of its participants. Some, but not all, of these traditions had their own institutions, but each had its distinctive way of communicating its subject matter.[11] The type of geography which is considered here, that wedded to exploration, was also bound to biography as a primary medium for communicating its findings. The Royal Geographical Society of London (RGS) declared 'GEOGRAPHY' 'a copious source of rational amusement'.[12] In early RGS proceedings analytical and synthetic contributions were rational without being noticeably entertaining, while biographical narratives captured the audience, particularly when the assembled fellows were the first to hear the narratives and knew that the writer at that moment might either have gone on to greater things or be lying in a foreign grave. Biographical narratives made the RGS a place where news as well as knowledge was made and where policy and strategy were worked out, and whose proceedings reached a wide audience.[13] The first committee of the RGS did not discount 'speculative geography' (theories about how land masses might look or where rivers might originate), and such geography continued to lead and mislead exploration, but the committee expected the society to be primarily concerned with 'actual observation' by explorers who reported their observations through autobiography.[14]

Autobiography by explorers had always been contentious, and it continued to be so in the first half of the twentieth century, after press sensationalism was entrenched but before satellite navigation could verify claims. Was the autobiographer (like Frederick A. Cook (1865–1940) and Robert E. Peary (1856–1920), dubious claimants of the north pole in 1908–9) lying?[15] Or if not lying then at least, in the words of Roald Amundsen (1872–1928), who considered himself free of the charge, 'romancing rather too bare-facedly'?[16] The influence of the sensationalist press on polar life writing is well established, but such sensationalism was never universal and those who promoted rational entertainment gave scope for biography without sensationalism.[17] John Murray, the highly influential publisher of travel books, dropped writers if they 'appeared to stray into the world of romance', and autobiographical reports in the proceedings of societies such as the RGS or Royal Central Asian Society were generally sober.[18] Arthur Robert Hinks (1873–1945) was the RGS secretary from 1915 to 1945. His interest in exploration stemmed from his expertise in geodesy and surveying, and the entertainment offered by the society was always rational on his watch.[19]

By the early twentieth century more fundamental a problem for biography than sensationalism was the question of whether even the best autobiographical record could constitute science. As early as 1888 Richard Strachey (1817–1908), speaking to the RGS as its president, stated, 'Accounts of personal adventure will always add to the interest that attaches to the exploration of unknown countries, but from the point of view of geography, the mountains, the deserts, and the seas are the main objects of consideration, rather than the fatigues and perils encountered in crossing them.'[20] This was perhaps not surprising, coming as it did from one of the most prominent advocates of reform in the RGS's brand of geography, but even the old guard recognized that biography and science writing had moved apart. Writing only 10 years after Strachey delivered his address, Clements Markham (1830–1916) insisted that 'true deeds of knight errantry ... are recorded of our geodesists and ... surveyors', but conceded that it was only 'When the *stories* of the Ordnance Survey in Great Britain and of the Trigonometrical Survey of India are *fitly* told, [that is in biographical accounts, separate from the existing scientific ones] [that] they will form some of the proudest pages in the history of our nation.'[21] What constituted fit telling was contested. Since 'exploration required not only a journey into an unknown land, but also a journey into the self',[22] the content and style of explorers' accounts were both scientific and literary. Rigorous observation, systematic measurement, and careful inference of connections between newly observed facts and existing knowledge were juxtaposed with descriptions of physical struggles, outpourings of emotion, and reflections on spiritual matters: but such a combination looked increasingly old fashioned. In the early twentieth century, British expeditions still combined exploration with science: Britons famously, if unjustly, contrasted Amundsen's 'dash for the pole' with Scott's scientific expedition in which speed and priority had, it was claimed, taken second place to the pursuit of knowledge.[23] But though tales told by twentieth-century explorers, including Amundsen's *Sydpolen* (1912), had meteorological, geological, and other scientific sections, the latter were generally appendices to the exploration narrative and often separately authored. A few polar scientists mastered both genres: scientific reports by Frank Debenham (1883–1965) and Raymond Priestly (1886–1974) commanded specialist respect, whilst Debenham told his *Stories of Scott's Last Expedition* (1952) and Priestley's autobiographical *Antarctic Adventure* (1914) was successful enough to warrant a 1974 reprint (unlike his autobiographical account of life as a vice chancellor). But the genres themselves were by this time quite different in tone, audience, and usually authorship.[24] This reflected the split within the RGS between the new (academic) geography and the old (exploratory) geography, begun in the 1870s (though this trajectory was not characteristic of all British geographical traditions). Whilst explorers discovered the particular, new geographers sought general explanations. Whilst explorers provided rational entertainment, new geographers were useful.[25] Whilst explorers ranged the globe in the service of empire, new geographers built empires at home, projecting geography in the disciplinary jostle for attention in the school and university curriculum and in professional scientific circles.[26] The founding of the Institute of British Geographers (IBG) in 1933 further distanced new from old geography.[27] By excluding exploration from its *Transactions* the IBG ousted biography too.[28] Narrative in general was too chronological for a geography which wanted synoptic maps and models, and biographical narrative in particular was too idiosyncratic for geography conceived as a law-making science, too accessible for professional geography which wanted its own specialist language, and too lowbrow for a university discipline. Biography was banished from university teaching as well as from university research. H. Yule Oldham, the RGS lecturer at Cambridge from 1893, disquieted the RGS and university authorities with 'his discourse – racy, anecdotal, scarcely perhaps by modern standards systematic enough to pass as academic [although it] kindled an interest in ... the story of the sailors and explorers who opened up the New World by their curiosity and courage'.[29] Even had it been rational rather than racy, such biography was out of place in scientific geographical teaching.

Exploratory biography does share distinctive media, notably maps and charts, with academic geography. Pencil additions to a chart of the South Polar Sea used by Ernest Shackleton's (1874–1922) Ross Sea party, for example, are quiet, poignant autobiographies, showing how the desperate men plotted their route and marked the positions of the dépôts they left for a party which never arrived.[30] Printed maps and charts, mediated by publishing houses and others, are more strident, laying claim to land by delineating and naming it. Twentieth-century place naming in uninhabited polar areas escaped the controversy attached to giving European names to places long lived in and named by local people, but it might still be tied to empire building.[31] 'There will be islands and mountains and lands to name with British names', declared Shackleton as he strove to muster support for his transantarctic expedition.[32] But place names tell not only a nation's life story: they 'carry with them a record of history, of priority in the field' and 'situate [each successive explorer] in relation to a previous history of endeavour and commemoration'.[33] Conventionally, place names are biographical, not autobiographical. An Antarctic glacier was named after Victor Campbell (1875–1956), 'though not by Campbell of course', his biographer and editor briskly remarks.[34] Place names flatter, and while the poles show an 'embarrassment of royalty', such as King Edward VII Land, named by Scott in the National Antarctic Expedition of 1901–4, commercial patrons outstripped royalty for twentieth-century British explorers, who left a 'scattering of trade names over … polar regions'.[35] Thus Shackleton memorialized his Antarctic patrons, Glasgow engineer William Beardmore (1856–1936) and Dundee jute manufacturer Sir James Caird (1837–1916), in the Beardmore Glacier and the Caird Coast.[36] William Bruce (1867–1921) memorialized his patrons, threadmakers James and Andrew Coats of Paisley, in Coats Land.[37]

Place names become autobiographical when they record the daily routines, not merely the existence, of their namers, and these names speak to modern readers more eloquently than do names of royalty or businessmen, though they comparatively rarely reach the gazetteer. Campbell's diary, for example, records workaday names such as Back Door Bay, Front Door Bay, and Butter Point, but few such reached the map.[38] Place names as autobiography record the vulnerability more often than the vainglory of their namers. On the British Antarctic Expedition of 1907–9 Shackleton named Mount Hope, which guarded the entrance of his route to the pole.[39] On Scott's last expedition his northern party overwintered in a tiny snow cave in unspeakable conditions on Inexpressible Island; over Warning Glacier clouds signalled the approach of southerly gales; Safety Camp was a backup dépôt; and at Relay Bay the northern party had to relay the sledges, retracing their steps repeatedly because sledge loads had to be lightened before they could be pulled.[40] These understated place names are an autobiographical record of the feelings of men at the edge of endurance and fully aware of the precariousness of their situation.

Maps and charts and the place names on them might be distinctively geographical media for recording explorers' lives and deeds, but narrative, sketches, and photographs, with their accessibility and relative cheapness, were central to geography as rational entertainment, if treated warily by scientific geography. As Joseph Conrad wrote, 'No doubt a trigonometrical survey may be a romantic undertaking ... but its accurate operations can never have for us the fascination of the first hazardous steps of a venturesome, often lonely, explorer jotting down by the light of his camp fire the thoughts, the impressions, and the toil of the day.'[41] Moreover, narrative, sketches, and photographs because of their cheapness and accessibility were central to the *business* of exploration. On the Imperial Transantarctic Expedition of 1914–17, his ship *Endurance* having been beset and crushed, Shackleton performed his most celebrated feat by sailing 800 miles in an open boat through treacherous seas to secure help. More than half of his parting note to Frank Wild (1873–1939) written before he set off on a venture whose most probable outcome was death, dealt with the rights to publicize the results of the voyage. 'I wish you, Lees and Hurley to write the book. You watch my interests. In another letter you will find the terms as agreed for lecturing you to do England, Great Britain & Continent. Hurley the USA.'[42] The scene was being repeated on the other side of the continent in a party whose survival looked still less likely. Captain Æneas Lionel Acton Mackintosh (1879–1916), realizing that physicist Richard Walter Richards (1893–1985) had not signed the customary agreement governing what members of the expedition might publish on their return, immediately drew up a contract and had it signed and witnessed.[43] If Richards thought this bizarre, Shackleton knew that money for exploration depended on capturing the public mood, and this in turn hinged on speed and priority of publication. During his homeward voyage after the British Antarctic Expedition, Shackleton worked with a literary assistant so that his *Heart of the Antarctic* (1909) could be published as soon as possible. After the transantarctic expedition he dictated its more exciting episodes to his assistant lest he die in the First World War.[44] Shackleton 'hated anything in the way of heroics', yet had to project and cultivate his public image to raise funds for the exploration at which he excelled.[45]

While geographers by the early twentieth century retreated to academic seclusion, explorers courted publicity. While geography spurned narrative, explorers knew they must make their immediate mark through stories, not maps or place names. While geographers disdained biography, explorers, for all their talk of science, continued to embrace it as their means to fame, social elevation, and, if not fortune, then at least financial solvency.

MAKING CELEBRITIES, MAKING HEROES

The discussion of how British polar celebrities and heroes of the early twentieth century were made and unmade has since the late 1970s focused on the controversy over Scott, and then on Shackleton *versus* Scott, and most recently on Shackleton *and* Scott. Enduringly fascinating though the two are, this narrow view has kept the debate focused on Great Men, and often fails to make connections with the historiography of other specialist fields.[46] To enrich and broaden the debate, this essay, while not ignoring Scott or Shackleton, considers the lives and afterlives of a wide variety of British polar explorers and compares the historiography of exploratory heroes with those of related fields such as sport, science, and the military.

'The hegemonic ideal of the gentleman amateur' dominated early British exploration, as it did the fields which underlay it: sport, the military, and science.[47] The classic Victorian and Edwardian hero was conceived as a gentleman amateur who was to carry his success lightly and see his actions as a public calling and part of a national and imperial vision.[48] This vision excluded from the pantheon of heroes working men, professionals, women, and foreigners, including 'natives', and was shaped by and buttressed the prevailing rhetoric of imperialism, masculinity, and racial superiority. Gradually the establishment's grip on what constituted heroism loosened; audiences without classical educations and with different ideas of gentlemanliness, and therefore heroism, came to dominate. Gentlemanliness gradually came to be ascribed not to rank but to innate moral qualities – the courage and character of Samuel Smiles' *Self Help* (1859) heroes – and the path to gentlemanliness and heroism was open to professional men of lower-middle- or working-class origins, and eventually even to foreigners and to women. Professional heroes had to combine prowess with decency, suggesting that they were ordinary men who happened to be extraordinarily good at their calling. The rise of the professional was by no means straightforward as competing professions jostled for priority, and the amateur culture, with its ideals of class, classics, and character, proved remarkably resilient, putting the onus on professional heroes in exploration, as in sport and science, to act the amateur gentleman.[49] The establishment's grip on print and celluloid was so strong that as late as the Second World War it was the officers who became heroes ('the dashing young fighter pilot, fresh from public school or Oxbridge, with silk scarf, sports car, good looks, and raffish charm – an image epitomized on the silver screen by David Niven'), while their lower-class peers, however deserving of celebration, faded from view.[50] But in the history of exploration, as in military history, lower-class men are being recovered for the historical record, while some gentlemanly heroes find themselves debunked, not chiefly because of individual failings, but because the ideals they personified have fallen out of favour.[51]

The Royal Navy had claimed polar exploration as its prerogative since the end of the Napoleonic wars, when exploration provided fitting employment for the service in peacetime. The Royal Navy claimed that it alone had the required institutional professionalism for polar exploration, but individual naval officers (gentlemen by virtue of their service rank, though on entry they were a much more mixed bag socially than their army counterparts) were necessarily amateur explorers, since their professional duty, irreproachably aligned with patriotic interest, lay elsewhere. The RGS, as co-sponsor of many polar expeditions staffed by naval men, similarly claimed professional scientific knowledge as an institution, but many of its individual fellows were gentlemen amateurs as geographers (unlike the academic geographers who later formed the IBG who were professionals and often of lower social class than their RGS equivalents).[52] The pluck and manliness of the gentleman amateur, combined with duty to science and empire were means and end for naval officers who were thus uniquely well placed to become heroes of exploration. Their line stretched from Cook through Franklin to Scott, their service rank guaranteeing them gentlemanly status whatever their social origins (very lowly in Cook's case for example). Naval officers dominated the historical record, and service rank determined eligibility for hero status: of Scott's polar party, for example, the *Dictionary of National Biography* (*DNB*) memorialized two officers but not the petty officer.[53]

As well as naval officers, the scientists – 'University men' – were also eligible to become heroes. With the exception of the antipodeans, scientists were generally from Cambridge or Oxford, the latter being described as 'the apotheosis of the amateur'.[54] They were undoubtedly gentlemen, and, whatever their academic qualifications, they were generally polar amateurs: 'You can rest assured that I will have sufficient trained men besides the University men', wrote Shackleton to his wife, acknowledging the University men's lack of professional competence in anything, especially sailing and polar travel, which might be of practical use on the expedition.[55] Scientists could become heroes: Cheltenham and Cambridge educated Edward Wilson, for example, was acclaimed a hero as soon as it became known that he had died with Scott on his way back from the South Pole.[56] On the whole, however, scientists were judged to lack the manly virtues of naval officers (the shore party, including all the scientists, on Shackleton's transantarctic expedition, for example, were labelled 'the FuFu gang' by the hardboiled ship's crew)[57] and they less often reached the status of hero. The dedication of naval officers to science (at which they were amateurs) increased their nobility and materially increased their chances of becoming heroes, but it did not do the same for professional scientists.

Officers who were made heroes in part because of their rank were not required as individuals to be flawless: indeed saintliness was deprecated. Jones suggests that Scott, who 'never went into a church' and travelled with Darwin rather than the bible, deferred to 'the will of providence' in his last message as a 'deliberately crafted appeal to a domestic Christian audience'.[58] While sermons declared Scott's party 'true Christian gentlemen',[59] in the expeditions themselves and in polar biographies, religion was largely confined to public observation of conventional religion. 'Divine service' or 'church' on polar explorations kept up naval discipline and usefully marked the passage of the weeks, but was not the place for personal display. Victor Campbell was only half in jest as he described the 'terrible ordeal' when he and Murray Levick were the only two left 'singing' an unfamiliar hymn.[60] The 1933 and 1937 biographies of Edward Wilson by Revd George Seaver (*b*.1890), dean of Ossory, stressed Wilson's religion so much that those close to Wilson thought he appeared offputtingly priggish.[61] Later treatments have been happier to stress Wilson's artistic talents and love of nature.[62]

Polar heroism is said to have advanced secularization in Britain: even religious writers for whom suicide was technically both crime and sin claimed as heroes both Lawrence 'Soldier' Oates (1880–1912), who 'gallantly overtook death' by walking out into a blizzard to die, and Henry 'Birdie' Bowers (1883–1912), whose musing about using pickaxes as a means of suicide is still rather disconcerting.[63] Secular heroes were not required to be flawless. Image makers at the time of Scott's death had derived from their classical educations a 'rich ... and deep' conception of the hero and judged that, like Greek heroes, Scott died because of his human flaws, but died well. An early account of the last expedition was written by 'Caesar' whose pseudonym set the classical framework in which the tragedy was to be understood.[64] Editorial changes to Scott's journal were relatively minor such that *Scott's Last Expedition* (1913) was no whitewash, as later critics have alleged, but rather revealed someone who was complex as both man and leader but who none the less performed heroic feats.[65] Cherry-Garrard's *Worst Journey in the World* (1922), written at some distance from the events described, was still less hagiographic: George Bernard Shaw, who encouraged Cherry-Garrard to write and helped him to shape his thoughts, commented that 'bringing a hero to life always involves exhibiting his faults as well as his qualities'.[66] In Shaw's eyes Cherry-Garrard painted a more compelling portrait of the hero by showing his flaws. It was only after the publication of Roland Huntford's *Scott and Amundsen* (1979) that Scott's personal failings appeared to a modern audience to undermine his heroic status. Moreover, Huntford's picture did not perform some Dorian Gray type transformation of Scott, making him awe-inspiringly vicious – a villain of heroic proportions – , but instead made him appear 'a boring and nasty little man' – an antihero in fact.[67]

If being of the right class helped a man to celebrity or heroic status, as the examples above show, it did not guarantee it. Some, like Arctic explorer Reynold Bray (*d.*1938) (Harrow and Balliol), died young (aged 27 years), and, like fighter pilots who died before their time, unknown outside specialist circles.[68] Other officers were of the wrong personality. 'Birdie' Bowers, who died with Scott, was too 'perfectly simple' to be enduringly interesting.[69] Moreover he wrote selflessly, to please his mother and sisters, not, as did Scott, to impress a public. Private recollections of intimate domestic moments like singing Moody and Sankey hymns together, punctuate Birdie's letters, while Scott's mind is always on a wider stage. After they had been beaten to the South Pole, the profound disappointment which impelled Scott to fine rhetoric drove poor Bowers to the banal. Trying to salvage something from the situation for his mother and sisters who he knew would rather have him safe at home, he wrote: 'You will be glad to hear I have been to this spot I am sure.'[70] His writing reached the public only indirectly, notably in Cherry-Garrard's *Worst Journey in the World*; he left no autobiography, and biographers have been attracted to him not as an individual, but as a type: in 1938 as a fellow Christian gentleman and in 1999 as a man overlooked.[71] His writing has most recently attracted the attention of those looking for another type – the male imperialist – for his view of man-hauling: 'it will be a fine thing to do that plateau with man-haulage in these days of the supposed decadence of the British Race'.[72] Much more characteristic is his writing as a devoted son: 'Although the end will be painless enough for myself, I should so like to come through for your dear sake', he wrote poignantly in his last letter.[73] Bowers' moment of heroism was brief and collective: he was never debunked though he has been stereotyped, but his utterly straightforward character meant he never secured a position as a household name.

If officer rank could not guarantee elevation to celebrity or heroism, it was a long time before lower ranking men could aspire to hero status. The working man of Scott's polar party was Petty Officer Edgar Evans (1876–1912). Included in that party largely as a representative of the lower deck, he was later spurned by the *DNB* in part because of his rank. He was the first of the party to die and early accounts attributed his 'failure' to his class. His moral fibre and intellectual resources – products of his birth – proved inadequate. Petty Officer Evans was the drag on the party; officer and gentleman Oates sacrificed himself for others.[74] Typically for a working man, Evans left no autobiography or journal to allow him to vindicate himself and found no contemporary biographer to defend him.[75] A rarely heard working-class voice in 1973 calls into question the allegedly unanimous contemporary acclaim of Scott's men: 'I did not much like Scott and most of his brother officers and gentlemen after reading the socially superior explanation of Petty Officer Evans' collapse.'[76] An analysis of 1974, which suggested dehydration, malnutrition, incipient scurvy, and anthrax, rather than class, as likely causes of death, set the scene for biographies which celebrate Evans precisely because he was an outsider.[77] In 1995 the council of his home town claimed him as *Swansea's Antarctic Explorer*, defying his national reputation,[78] and a still more recent treatment presents him as isolated amongst unsympathetic and unfeeling officers.[79]

Petty Officer Thomas Crean (1877–1938) typified his class in leaving no autobiography and attracting no contemporary biographer, despite his importance on Scott's *Discovery* expedition and final journey, and Shackleton's transantarctic expedition, three of the most widely recorded polar expeditions in history. Moreover, his Royal Naval service record has him dying on 17 February 1912, the day Petty Officer Evans died, bluejackets being interchangeable in the eyes of some contemporaries.[80] As the concept of heroism expanded to include working men, Crean secured his first biographical article in 1985, a full-length biography (tellingly entitled *An Unsung Hero*) in 2000, and his place in the *DNB* in 2004.[81] Like Evans's biographers, Crean's celebrate his distance from the establishment and from the traditional idea of hero as martyr: he was instead 'a great Irishman who didn't have to die to become a hero'.[82]

Chief Stoker William Lashly (1867–1940), with Scott on two expeditions including his last, still awaits inclusion in the *DNB*, though unusually for a bluejacket he left a diary and letters.[83] His prose gives glimpses of the Book of Common Prayer (he was a devout churchman) but is mostly that of the man who left school at 13: his entry for 13–17 October 1902, for example, starts majestically: 'Now comes the hour of our hardship', before descending into unconscious bathos with 'which lasted longer than any of us expected'. His view of the landscape is that of the countryman (he describes one moraine as 'a splendid place for growing spuds'), not that of the gentleman artist, like Wilson, or the literary gentleman, like Scott. As he faced death on 10 February 1912 he records simply, 'Things don't look any too bright for us.'[84] The diary was the private work of a working man, not self-consciously written for publication. It was published, but not in the way a lettered man's work would have been. Selections appeared in *Worst Journey in the World* (1922). Others were privately published in an edition of

75 copies (School of Art, University of Reading, 1938–9), as a vehicle for artist Robert Gibbings and his students. In his introduction, officer E. R. G. Evans (1880–1957) pigeonholes Lashly as a class type: 'one of the Yeomen of England'. The most recent selections, published in 1969, have Lashly *Under Scott's Command* and that of his upper middle-class editors.[85] Vivian Fuchs claims that Lashly's diary shows the support of the lower deck for the scientific aims of the journey. This is true (Lashly dutifully did everything he was asked to, including scientific work), but only up to a point (he dumped his geological samples when lives depended on shedding weight, while the pole party's retention of theirs became a talisman of their martyrdom to the cause of science). Declaring 'It was the combination of great leadership [Scott's] and loyal support which added an epic to our history', Fuchs co-opts Lashly in defence of Scott.[86] Though Lashly was unrelentingly deferential (styling officers 'Mr' even when writing in the face of death), his diary has little to say about Scott's leadership. With similarly little evidence, editor Commander Anthony Ellis co-opts Lashly to argue that Royal Naval discipline had given the expedition its successes (although Ellis's editing was itself rather heroic as he fought off blindness to finish the work). But the fact that Lashly's journals were published at all shows the changing conception of gentlemanliness and heroism, and a reviewer noted that 'These modest records ... will inspire admiration for a very brave and gentle man, in the true sense of the word'.[87]

The gentleman hero's transition from amateurism to professionalism is as hard to date in British Antarctic exploration as it is in science or sport, but it is closely linked to the involvement of antipodeans, renowned for their lack of deference, as explorers and as writers on exploration. Douglas Mawson (1882–1958) is on the cusp of change: British-born but living in Australia; born into trade, but dying a knight; a professional geologist whose expeditions nonetheless had territorial aims, declining a place on Scott's last expedition because its science was not clear enough, yet hailed a hero.[88] Antipodean influence is perhaps best seen in the events and recent reappraisals of Shackleton's transantarctic expedition. This expedition culminated in British popular memory with his spectacular rescue of all his men after the open boat journey described above.[89] In fact, however, three men from the expedition's Ross Sea party died. They were Revd Arnold Patrick Spencer-Smith (1883–1916), Æneas Mackintosh, and

Victor Hayward (*d.* 1916). Their story was told at the end of Shackleton's *South* (1919), but in a way a later editor describes as 'curious' and designed to give the impression 'that this was a separate expedition outside his control [a tactic which allowed him to] perpetuate the myth than he "never lost a man"'.[90] The story then passed to antipodean non-commissioned officers (NCOs) and civilians Ernest Joyce, Richard Richards, and Lennard Bickel.[91] Joyce's journal was published early (1929), and consequently suffered from middle-class mediation. 'The reader need not look for literary graces or journalistic effusion in this story, for it is told by a man of deeds and not of words', warns Hugh Mill of the RGS, but he cannot disguise Joyce's insubordinate tone. Joyce explains bluntly that command passed from gentleman but polar amateur Mackintosh (Captain of *Aurora* and Lieutenant in the Royal Naval Reserve) to himself, because he was more experienced, professional, and competent (and more than happy to say so). Though not altogether in agreement with Joyce's account, Richards relates Mackintosh's errors of judgement with similar dispassion and notes wryly when they enter Scott's hut that the 'men' (his inverted commas) had less space than the officers.[92] Bickel tells 'the story of ordinary men who rose to extraordinary heights of courage, determination, and endurance' and, disdaining gentlemanly dissembling about science, states: 'There was no romance in this venture; the only prize was achievement.'[93] The narrators accord no privilege to social or service rank, but only to courage. The exhausted men rescue the ailing Mackintosh not because of a duty to an officer, but because of loyalty to 'our lonely mate' and 'our comrade'.[94] Mackintosh and another man then walk to their death against their rescuers' advice. There is none of the Soldier Oates about this. Mill glosses their 'tragic death' as 'a bold attempt to reach Cape Evans over the still insecure sea-ice'.[95] But Joyce bluntly describes the venture as 'foolish'; Richards suggests that Mackintosh went out because he could no longer bear conditions in the hut where they had taken refuge; and Bickel quotes Richards: 'We'd worked our guts out to get them into the safety of the hut, so there was some bitterness in seeing them go out against advice.'[96] In his intended farewell note, officer Mackintosh cultivates a heroic tone: 'I feel glad to say that [the men's plight] has not been due to any lack of organization. ... I leave it on record that all have done their duty, nobly and well. The rest of our simple adventures can be explained by this note, also by other members of the party ... if it is God's will that we should have given up our lives then we do so in the British manner as our tradition holds us in honour bound to do. ... I feel sure my dear wife and children will not be neglected.' This is obviously modelled on Scott's 'Message to the Public' and last journal entries; but Mackintosh's 'rough notes', unlike Scott's, really were rough, and they were set before the public by a working-class professional who had no time for amateur heroics.[97] But the criticism is of poor judgement, not class *per se*, so all narrators mourn the death of the uncomplaining padre, ex-prep school master Spencer-Smith. He was a gentleman by birth, brought along on the expedition as an amateur photographer, and sustained by the language of the public school amateur: 'It's all in the game. Play on', he wrote on the flyleaf of his diary.[98] However, it is neither his gentlemanliness nor his amateurism which shaped the way his companions (preponderantly working-class men and Australian) responded to him. They described him on his memorial cross not as the 'gallant gentleman' of Oates's memorial, but simply as 'A brave man', just as they referred to him as 'Smithy' rather than 'Mr Spencer-Smith' in their diaries, and had recalled his concern, *in extremis*, for the 'stranded' on London's Embankment.[99] The narrative of the expedition, shaped in the antipodes and on the lower deck, is of character irrespective of class. This reflects the now-emerging facts of the Ross Sea party during which antipodeans and NCOs proved themselves remarkably undeferential, and gentlemanly codes of conduct were abandoned. This was shockingly obvious to British contemporaries such as John King Davis, captain of the vessel sent to relieve them, who wrote in 1919: 'Mackintosh was a sahib and the rest ... apparently did not understand the rudiments of playing the game.' He attributed the party's troubles in part to insubordination – to misrule which simply did not recognize the authority of the 'sahib' as unquestionable, or the endeavour as a public school game.[100] The antipodeans of the party and later antipodean and American commentators disagree: leadership determined by class not character or competence was the problem, and the professionalism of the ordinary men was the party's salvation. King and other contemporaries such as Hugh Mill voiced their views privately, leaving the later narrators to make heroes of the professional men, not amateur gentlemen.[101]

Working-class men who joined Royal Naval or related expeditions have more easily entered the polar pantheon than have mercantile polar professionals. Professional merchant mariners, particularly whalers and sealers, who explored polar waters, and the traders of the Hudson's Bay Company, who opened up the Canadian Arctic landmass, were suspect from the start because trade was neither gentlemanly nor amateur.[102] This affected the history of exploration (in 1896 the whiff of trade alienated Markham from one of Carsten Egeberg Borchgrevink's (1864–1934) projected voyages south[103]) and especially its historiography. Many merchant mariners waited long before finding a biographer in Godfrey (A. G. E.) Jones (1914–2002), who dedicated his life to wresting the glory of polar exploration from Royal Naval officers and their historian John Knox Laughton (1830–1915).[104] Jones's successors include Don Arlidge whose *Rescue of Captain Scott* (1999) records how Captains Harry Mackay and William Colbeck (1871–1930) freed *Discovery* in 1904 with ice blasting techniques developed by whalers. Its blurb declares it a 'study in myth making', contrasting the 'false heroics' of the Royal Naval men with the 'patient progress in getting the job done' and the 'supreme seamanship' of the whalers, and the book in effect discounts suggestions that Scott did not need rescue, that *Discovery* (built in Dundee) leaked, and that the sudden warming of the weather freed the ship.[105] Arlidge and the curators of Dundee's *Discovery* museum acclaim the professionalism of the local Dundee shipbuilders and whalers, contrasting it with the antics of the gentlemanly Markham and Scott, who were busy cultivating national and imperial fame. This parallels a trend in Canadian research, where much research questioning the reputation of British Arctic explorers has sought to bring out the perspectives of professional fur traders as well as of aboriginal peoples.[106] But while specialists and local readers celebrate the hunting professionals (and while their Scandinavian hunter-explorer peers are hailed by their less squeamish compatriots), modern Britons consider such bloody trades too ungentlemanly to look to them for heroes.[107]

There were some true amateurs in polar exploration: yachtsmen Benjamin Leigh Smith (1828–1913), Sir James Lamont (1828–1913), and Lord Dufferin (1826–1902), for example, made significant Arctic discoveries – but Leigh Smith left no autobiography, and Lamont's *Seasons with the Sea-Horses* (1861) and *Yachting in the Arctic Seas* (1876), and Dufferin's *Letters from High Latitudes* (1857), written with the easy grace of the amateur, seemed mere travel books. The men's achievement was underplayed in a contemporary British polar narrative which rested on the endurance of manly naval officers in the face of privation, and though they have attracted modern biographers, notably again Godfrey Jones, their enjoyment of hunting makes them ungentlemanly and unheroic to wider modern audiences.[108] Apsley Cherry-Garrard, neither officer nor scientist, but an amateur dabbler with a large private income, won fame as a writer on other people's Antarctic achievements, but his own doubts about his part in Scott's final journey (could he have relieved the desperate pole party if he had pressed on to meet them?) spilled over into his public reputation as someone rather ineffectual, and he had to wait until 2002 to be memorialized in his own biography.[109]

'Those who are ... enshrined in the collective memory are only those who succeeded in personifying the cultural identity *of an area*.'[110] Thus Britons remember Britons, Scandinavians Scandinavians, and French French.[111] Edwardian Britons were suspicious of foreign polar explorers, regarding them as ungentlemanly because they were professional and hence unsporting. This suspicion transcended class: Lieutenant Bowers found Amundsen 'a back handed, sneaking ruffian'; the establishment RGS treated Amundsen and Borchgrevink shabbily, considering them ungentlemanly; and Petty Officer Joyce's highest compliment for a companion was 'He is a Briton'.[112] Borchgrevink was half English, but could not overcome British prejudice against his being half Norwegian, having been born in Norway, living in Australia, and having a Russian-sounding name. Although his most famous expedition, the British Antarctic Expedition of 1898–1900, sailed under a British flag and with an English patron, Britons hesitated to claim him and his significant achievements. His autobiography, *First in Antarctica* (1901), was dismissed as journalistic (that is, not gentlemanly) and sold poorly. The British *DNB* still has no place for him, despite the importunate Godfrey Jones, though its Australian counterpart does.[113] Norwegian Tryggve Gran (1889–1980), Scott's ski instructor, wisely published his account of Scott's expedition in Norway rather than Britain.[114] British public opinion had difficulty looking even as far as Scotland for celebrities. William Bruce led the Scottish National Antarctic expedition (1902–4), in the *Scotia*, supported by the Scottish Geographical Society and

Scottish subscribers, and staffed primarily by Scots. Bruce was honoured primarily by Scottish societies;[115] Bruce and Borchgrevink's contemporary obscurity to Britons at large was due in part to Markham's fear of anything which might steal the limelight from Scott and his *Discovery* expedition of 1901–4, but largely to his and his compatriots' mistrust of non-Englishmen.[116]

This mistrust rested on different national conceptions of explorer heroes. Scandinavian polar heroism, for example, was based on success: Scandinavian polar failures (such as that of balloonist Salomon August Andrée (1854–97))[117] were an embarrassment, while the British 'elided material failure [such as Franklin's and Scott's] with the pursuit of higher goals'.[118] Scandinavian heroism rested on professionalism and a long-established (indeed native) mastery over Arctic regions, while British polar heroism was based on amateurism, a public school sense of adventure, and being 'uniquely unprepared for the job'.[119] Despite the proven tragic consequences of this fondness for adventure, British explorers still feel the need to cultivate it in public even, or perhaps especially, when they are professionals in all senses of the word. To take a recent example from Everest – referred to in the heroic phase of exploration as the 'third pole', that is with the north and south poles, the earth's third great challenge awaiting conquest – Stephen Venables (*b*. 1954, Charterhouse and Oxford) could say in 2007 of his expedition: 'We had a feeling that this would be a great adventure. We had no idea if we could pull it off.'[120] By contrast, as early as 1919 Icelander Vilhjálmur Stefánsson said of Arctic exploration, 'Having an adventure is a sign that something unexpected, something unprovided against has happened; it shows that someone is incompetent, that something has gone wrong.'[121] The point is not, of course, to impugn Venables's proven professional competence, but to show that explorers need to play to a British public which still thinks of exploration in a tradition of amateur adventure, something Scandinavians have long found unfathomable. A Scandinavian tradition based on success and professionalism could claim as a hero Norwegian Otto Sverdrup (1854–1930). Between 1898 and 1902 he charted more Arctic land than had been mapped in the previous 50 years. But to the British 'he seemed to have had no adventures. His account made his four years seem too easy, and gave visions of men in comfortable settings, well-fed, and able to enjoy their leisure. ... That was neither what the [British] public wanted to hear nor what the [British] press wanted to publish. He was ignored by both.'[122] It is not only in the matter of adventure that national sensibilities vary between Britain and Scandinavia. The suspicion that Amundsen was no gentleman was bolstered by his autobiography which seemed, in its recounting of the group's actions at the pole, for example, to show unseemly haste and gratuitous tastelessness. The planting of the flag at the pole is a solemn moment (though Britons could not comprehend quite how much it meant for newly independent Norway), but Amundsen describes how the party very briskly and matter-of-factly moved on to other things. 'Hanssen set about slaughtering Helge ... his best friend ... an uncommonly useful and good-natured dog. ... Helge was portioned out on the spot, and within a couple of hours there was nothing left of him but his teeth and the tuft at the end of his tail.'[123] Britons, who share Scott's squeamishness about dogs, needed no further confirmation that Amundsen was a bounder, though the book worked (and still works) in Norwegian and for Norwegians. Writing about Scott, Max Jones argues that 'the network of geographical societies sustained a heroic language of exploration across national boundaries', and it is true that the RGS, allegedly a bastion of British imperialism, often honoured foreign explorers and even indigenous people who accompanied British explorers or, as in Tibet, went on their behalf to places they could not go.[124] The wider public, however, had narrower views and, with a few exceptions such as Scott's, reputations were local, national, or imperial rather than international. This has changed little. Huntford debunked Scott, but, despite his alleged 'hero-worship' of Amundsen, did not make him a hero in British eyes, while Tryggve Gran's biography took 70 years to reach an English public, and then only a specialist one.[125]

If other white men were suspect, non-Europeans were usually invisible. Indigenous peoples are systematically written out of much exploration narrative, in the Arctic as elsewhere, because they are so inconveniently present in the areas which Europeans are discovering.[126] In their final assaults on the North Pole Cook took two Inuit and Peary took African American Matthew Henson (1866–1955) and four Inuit. In the controversy over who, if either, out of Cook and Peary reached the pole, contemporaries deplored the absence of other white men who could substantiate their claims. Peary's and Cook's choice of companions also ensured that they reaped most of the profit from their feat.[127] Henson published *A Negro Explorer at the North Pole* (1912), but died a retired messenger 'boy' rather than a manly hero.[128] Britons were fatally suspicious of 'native' clothing (generally preferring western materials to furs), of 'native' methods of transport (dogs, skis, and the kayaks used to good effect by Borchgrevink's *Southern Cross* party), and of 'natives' themselves (Borchgrevink set no precedent by taking Sami (Lapps) to Antarctica).[129] (Britons preferred horses to dogs not just because the latter were 'native', but for reasons of class: 'gentlemen used horses'.)[130] It was only the language of race which entered the British Antarctic narrative. Scott regarded man-hauling as a test of racial, not simply national or individual, or even class-bred stamina.[131] The purifying whiteness of the South Pole contrasted with tropical putrefaction.[132] Ernest Joyce admires his Antarctic comrades: 'they are White men'; 'A Whiter man never existed'.[133] 'Niggers' were relegated to the men's comic minstrel shows, the names of a dog on Shackleton's Ross Sea party and the ship's cat on *Discovery* on Scott's last voyage, and, once, to themselves when they 'worked like niggers' doing the unheroic if necessary work of loading their ship.[134] Dock labour (exhausting and commonplace) made 'riggers' of the explorers, while manhauling (exhausting but distinctive) made them true British heroes.

Women were the inspiration to distinctively male achievement in Victorian and Edwardian Britain: the separation of spheres which was central to anti-feminism demanded spaces reserved for male derring-do, and none better than Antarctica which was to be conquered by manly physical and mental (scientific) exertion.[135] In particular, RGS president Clements Markham fixed 'on a grand Antarctic expedition [by men] to reconcile the warring factions and restore the Society's reputation' after the debacle over women's admission as fellows of the society.[136] British women's exclusion from Antarctica in a practical sense rested on their exclusion from the Royal Navy, RGS, and Royal Society, which largely controlled British polar exploration; on the absence of colonial administrators and diplomatists who elsewhere were used by their female friends and relations to gain access to places and official papers and thereby to become both explorers and writers on exploration; and on contemporary views on camaraderie, decency, and women's strength. Man-hauling was just that. Though American Josephine Diebitsch Peary (1863–1955) accompanied her husband Robert to the Arctic and published her memoirs (1892, in which the men become her 'boys'), British wives were left at home.[137] Mesdames Scott, Evans, and Wilson who steamed to the antipodes to see off the *Terra Nova* on Scott's last expedition were thoroughly resented: 'the wives are much in evidence', noted Cherry-Garrard testily, while even Wilson commented, 'I hope it will never fall to my lot to have more than one wife at a time', though the women provided some entertainment when they forgot they were ladies. ('Mrs Scott and Mrs Evans have had a magnificent battle, they tell me it was a draw after fifteen rounds. Mrs Wilson flung herself into the fight after the tenth round.')[138] Moreover, if the companionship of women was problematic for officers, it was doubly so for less well-bred men. Scott meant sex as well as drink when he reported to the admiralty that, in the junketings which surrounded the ship's departure on his last expedition, the ratings 'have been feted, and made much of, and fully exposed to all the temptations which so frequently demoralize men of their class'.[139] Shackleton flatly turned down the 'three sporty girls' who volunteered for his transcontinental party.[140] In a self-reinforcing argument women were deemed unfit to explore and became redundant to it and a distraction from it: 'our two "Launcelots" are still deeply engrossed with the cloud of ladies', complained one of Shackleton's men as the more conscientious men struggled to fit out their ship in little time.[141] Women entered polar exploration in the feminine nicknames surprisingly often given to men ('Penelope' and 'Marie' were among those on Scott's last expedition), though not in an obviously sexual way since such names did not connote effeminacy and since the men were living in a hut which Cherry-Garrard described as 'Virtue Villa'.[142] Women also entered the language of polar exploration when the explorers fell short of manly ideals. When Edgar Evans became incoherent and incapable, Oates wrote dismissively, 'he ... behaves like an old woman'.[143] When Shackleton dithered, his surgeon Eric Marshall (1879–1963) called him a 'little old lady'.[144] Women properly appeared at the poles occasionally in the names of places or vessels: one of Shackleton's boats, for example, was named after his patron Janet Stancomb-Wills (1853–1932), and all vessels were referred to as 'she'. More famously women appear as addressees, silent in one-sided correspondences: Scott's and Wilson's wives, Bowers' and Oates' mothers and sisters became icons of purity, fortitude, and idealized domestic life as the private words of their husbands and sons hit the public press.[145] Left at home women were to be patient when appropriate (or devotedly importunate like Jane Franklin, agitating for the rescue of her husband), to mourn their loss when necessary, and, like Kathleen Scott, to cultivate the reputation of their men. If they had doubts – and Caroline Oates had profound misgivings about the amateurism which killed her beloved son – they were to keep them to themselves. Mrs Oates sought private satisfaction: it was only much later that her son's biographers made her doubts public.[146]

The concept of gentlemanliness gradually widened to include women, helped by the loosening of the grip of the classics on education which in both science and exploration had helped to keep heroism essentially male.[147] Women entered both exploration and its history, but not unproblematically. On Everest, the 'third pole', mountaineer and explorer Joyce Dunsheath (1902–76) staked her reputation on her gentlemanliness. Warning of 'the dangers of professionalism' she wrote: 'There are those today who climb to make a name, to get money from books and lectures, to earn a living. This is not the right approach to mountaineering.' Her solution was the admission of women to the Alpine Club to restore the spirit of gentlemanly amateurism.[148] Women entered the historiography of polar exploration late but professionally. Meteorologist Susan Solomon used her professional expertise to show Scott's complaints about unusually bad weather to have been scientific observations, not mere gripes.[149] Ann Savours is a seasoned polar historian. Elizabeth Chipman, in another challenge from the antipodes, revealed that *Women* [had been] *on the Ice* since the eighteenth century, but shared the class-based neglect suffered by their merchant mariner husbands.[150]

The changing understanding of professionalism and gentlemanliness are exemplified in the afterlives of Herbert Ponting (1870–1935), Scott's photographer, and of Frank Hurley (1885–1962), Shackleton's and Douglas Mawson's (1882–1958). The photographers' work was popular with contemporaries, but they themselves were not particularly. They presented themselves to their contemporaries in now wholly outmoded terms: Hurley's *Southward Ho! with Mawson* (1930) recalls Charles Kingsley's muscular Christianity; his *Siege of the South* (1931) was 'An Epic of Man's Glorious Struggle with Nature in the Frozen South'; while his *Argonauts of the South* (1925) recalled classical heroes. The photographers also strove to fulfil the old wish to unite science with entertainment. It was claimed that 'exploring, thanks to photography, will be transformed into an exact science',[151] and in the Antarctic photographers recorded new landscapes and newly discovered wildlife.

They also entertained with animal sketches and human portraits. Modern audiences, however, to whom the landscapes and wildlife are now well known, value the images for their aesthetic not their scientific qualities and find the animal portraits rather kitsch. They admire instead the dedication with which the photographers pursued their art, their professional competence, and their eye for telling 'everyman' shots of football games and (apparently) unguarded moments. There is now a rash of books and articles on Ponting and Hurley.[152] Though Wilson's watercolours of Antarctica are still valued particularly by specialists, they lack the appeal of the photographic image for a wider public. The old-fashioned amateur accomplishment gives way to the modern professional skill.

Shackleton similarly epitomizes the changing understanding of gentlemanliness. He was a 'player in gentleman's clothing', a professional merchant mariner who took out a commission as sub-lieutenant in the Royal Naval Reserve to acquire a veneer of gentlemanly amateurism.[153] Contemporaries did not recognize as a gentleman the brother of a criminal, an outsider whose expedition lacked official sponsors, a man who went back on his word and used 'Scott's' area of Antarctica in 1907–9. Edward Wilson declared, 'I consider he [Shackleton] had dragged polar exploration generally in the mud of his own limited and rather low down ambitions.'[154] Shackleton's ambivalence towards money betrays the tension between amateurism and professionalism. If he had a clear sense of the money to be reaped from writing and lecturing on the professional circuit, he gave much of the resultant income to relatives and charities, behaving with a gentlemanly liberality he could ill afford.[155] He undertook various unsuccessful business ventures 'in his persistent dream of making a [gentlemanly] fortune with which to endow his family'.[156] He did not become an unalloyed hero until he had rescued his men in the transantarctic expedition, but his star rose as Scott's sank, as the moral lessons which can be drawn from Shackleton's actions aligned much more closely with the priorities of the later twentieth and twenty-first centuries than those which can be drawn from Scott's. Shackleton is celebrated for having foregone the pole in 1909 to bring his men back alive, and for not resting after the transantarctic expedition until his men were safe. If Scott won his place in the pantheon as 'a suitable hero for a nation in decline',[157] then Shackleton gained his as Britain began to feel comfortable with itself again, in a process which had remarkably little to do with the men's competence. Shackleton had flaws very similar to Scott's. In the transcontinental expedition, for example, he proceeded south against the advice of professional Norwegian whalers; failed clearly to demarcate responsibilities or ensure stores were adequate; landed in a place which endangered the ship; tried out new (useless) motor sledges; could not handle and underestimated the value of dogs and skis; was preoccupied with the public representation of his expedition; and underplayed in print the misfortunes of his men, to such an extent that even the sympathetic Hugh Mill thought that 'the full tale had better remain unpublished for some time to come'.[158] Yet Shackleton is now a hero. The moral lessons he presents to a modern audience range from determination to survive, which is attractive in modern business climates, to solidarity with his men, which is attractive to ordinary people in a democratic age.[159]

Of all polar reputations Lawrence Oates's has best weathered the changing conception of gentlemanliness, 'gentleman' being the 'word which was to define ... Oates's values and behaviour throughout his life' and his afterlife.[160] He was a gentleman by birth, his father being simply styled 'gentleman' on Lawrence's birth certificate. After Eton, Lawrence Oates was commissioned into a cavalry regiment, where his interests ranged from polo to hunting with hounds to yachting but not much further.[161] Contemporaries recognized a gentleman by class-based character: Tom Crean wrote to Oates's sister, 'oh! he was a gentleman, quite a gentleman, and always a gentleman!'[162] Scott wrote of his death, 'it was the act of ... an English gentleman';[163] and his memorial cairn testifies: 'Hereabouts died a very gallant gentleman' – a designation echoed in the title of his first biography *A Very Gallant Gentleman* (1933).[164] As amateurism came to appear ridiculous rather than heroic to a later public, Oates consolidated his reputation as a professional and gentleman by character and remained a hero, despite an effort to recast his death as suicide to avoid further pain and another to suggest he fathered a child with an eleven-year-old girl.[165] He was utterly professional with the ponies, and scathing when Scott overrode his professional judgement. He admired the professionalism of the Norwegians: 'If it comes to a race, Amundsen will have a great chance of getting there as he is a man who has been at this kind of game all his life and he had a hard crowd behind him while we are very young.'[166] For

Oates, amateurism was not redemptive: after he knew of his party's defeat in the race to the pole he commented that Amundsen's party seemed 'to have had a comfortable trip with their dog teams, very different from our wretched man-hauling'.[167] He refused to see Amundsen's professional determination as morally reprehensible: 'They say Amundsen has been underhand the way he has gone about it but I personally don't see it is underhand to keep your mouth shut.'[168] His nickname 'Soldier' (in fact used to distinguish him as an army officer from the officers of the Royal Navy and Royal Indian Marine) now has an 'everyman' quality, its American usage as a way of addressing common soldiers ('privates' in British English) now being familiar to Britons through war films. The name 'Soldier' also evokes admiration for a man who soldiered on through his pain. A modern public, though in some ways far more swayed by celebrity culture than were previous generations, understands his scorn for 'little putty heroes' who strut before their public: 'we have made far too much noise about ourselves all the photographing, cheering, steaming through the fleet etc etc is rot and if we fail it will only make us look more foolish'.[169] Readers warm to Oates's apparent spurning of class convention; Crean reported being baffled by the figure who turned up in a worn mackintosh and battered bowler hat on the back of his head: 'we never for a moment thought he was an officer, for they were usually so smart. We made up our minds he was a farmer.'[170] A regimental friend visiting Oates in London docks as *Terra Nova* was loaded describes their 'munching huge slices of bread and jam and drinking coffee out of ½ inch thick mugs, with the people ... wondering who in the world we were'.[171] On board, Oates dined with the bluejackets on his watch: 'they were very shy at first but soon warmed up ... I have never sat down with a finer looking lot of men and they are capital chaps'.[172] Such comments have prompted suggestions that he disdained class,[173] but in fact he had an old-fashioned squire's disdain for the bourgeoisie and their conventions, and found that the men shared his admiration for 'sportsmanship'.[174] His treating the men as equals did not mean he expected them to treat him as an equal: 'you can treat them as equals without their presuming on it'.[175] If he turned up in an old mackintosh it was an Aquascutum, and if he failed to wear morning dress to the races he nonetheless wore a Norfolk jacket.[176] He despised army reforms which sought to turn cavalry officers, characterized by the 'individual vigour of the amateur and the sportsman' into middle-class professionals; he distinguished 'gentlemen' (officers) from bourgeois 'scientists'; and he castigated Scott's bourgeois behaviour: Scott 'would fifty times sooner stay in the hut seeing how a pair of Foxs spiral puttees suited him than come out and look at the ponies legs or a dogs feet'.[177] Oates the gentlemen by birth and the amateur could be a hero to contemporaries of all classes, including working-class critics of his bourgeois companions,[178] and Oates the gentleman by character and the professional could be a hero to later audiences. Similarly Edward Wilson, praised by contemporaries as Scott's loyal follower and by Bowers as the 'beau-ideal of an English gentleman', now finds approval as a gentleman by character who combined scientific professionalism with personal qualities of peacemaking and calmness.[179]

CONCLUSION

The polar hero then is complex: a personality created by himself, but also a commodity for sale in the market of the moment, and a moral exemplar fitted to the spirit of the age. But 'heroes were not just "made" or "constructed" by the media...they had to give a live performance'.[180] The integrity of hard-won excellence makes accounts of exploration enduringly attractive, and dictates that, though those accounts collectively may overlook explorers who deserve admiration, they cannot create explorer heroes out of nothing. Moreover, some argue that first-hand experience of polar regions itself bestows authority in heromaking: Wheeler uses her Antarctic experience to judge whether Cherry-Garrard's winter journey really was *The Worst Journey in the World*, and concludes that it was quite extraordinary.[181] Fiennes and Solomon challenge Huntford's view of Scott on the basis of professional knowledge gained in, not just of, the Antarctic. They echo Ernest Joyce's and Cherry-Garrard's disdain for the 'easy' judgements of civilization.[182] Regardless of whether we accept the argument that only polar explorers or polar professionals are fit judges of their fellows, Fiennes supports Young's view that Huntford's ungentlemanly sniping was possible only because he failed to live up to professional historical standards. Huntford's amateur performance as an historian, they suggest, makes him an inadequate judge of Scott's professionalism as an explorer.[183]

As business writers adopt explorers as role models, buoyed up by beliefs that qualities of leadership transfer across fields and that it is the heroic individual (almost invariably male) who determines collective fortunes, malleable notions of gentlemanliness remain useful. Shackleton, nicknamed 'The Boss', becomes a business role model in part because he was not obsessed with rank or class (gentlemanliness in the old sense), but instead treated his men of whatever rank as professionals who commanded respect. Poor Scott, nicknamed 'The Owner', has overtones of the rentier capitalist to add to his shortcomings, which include a class understanding of gentlemanliness which led to his stress on naval rank.[184] But whomever we acclaim as a polar hero and for whichever qualities, the process of polar heromaking continues unabated. The observation that 'Success ... is short-lived, however hard-won' seems to apply more to the lives of polar explorers than to their afterlives, as the making, unmaking, and remaking of polar heroes is seemingly endless.[185] The opening of Dundee's *Discovery* museum in 1993, the present Shackleton boom, and the recreations in 2006 and 2008 of Scott's and Amundsen's polar journeys testify to the continuing attraction of polar heromaking, and numerous recent biographies attest to the important, if not unrivalled, part that that medium still plays in the process.[186] If the polar pantheon has opened to some previously neglected types, there has been no loss of interest in those, especially Scott, whose heroic status is now questioned. In this boom, geography is often ignored and sometimes disparaged: the *Discovery* museum presents Clements Markham and the RGS as cut off from the realities of Antarctic conditions. Shackleton seems the more admirable, especially to antipodean and American commentators, because his expeditions are independent of the RGS: 'free from the institutional control that had allowed Markham's prejudices and outmoded ideas to stifle innovation and talent'.[187] In 2007 the *Oxford DNB* memorialized polar explorers Duncan Carse (1913–2004) and Virginia Fiennes (1947–2004), while geography was relegated to excerpts in the life of David Woodward (1942–2004), historian of cartography.[188] The RGS's sesquicentennial volume of 1980 celebrated the acts of exploration, not the scientific results of it, still less academic geography.[189] All of these tacitly acknowledge the perspicacity of the RGS's founders in forging an exploratory geography with enduring popular appeal, a geography which could legitimately be entertaining as well as rational, a geography whose practitioners could be raised to iconic status through biographical narrative.[190] Yet, just as it is questionable, how feasible is a wholesale return to such a geography, forged in the field, as advocated by for example David Stoddart and as exemplified by the Scott Polar Research Institute (and the idea that geographers might become heroes on a large scale is in any case absurd), so it is questionable whether such a geography and its counterpart, the new, academic geography, are more caricature than historical reality.[191] Just as a focus on the British regional geographical societies reveals a tradition of academic geography which flourished before, during, and after the much vaunted RGS split, tracing the historiography of polar heromaking through biographical narrative shows a tradition of exploration which is 'precisely not clear cut'.[192] There seem instead a multiplicity of exploratory traditions, partly at least having geographical roots: the Scottish tradition represented by Bruce and the Dundee whalers; an Irish strand, represented by Shackleton, Crean, and Arctic explorer Francis Crozier (1796–1848), who in a more settled Irish political climate can be celebrated in Ireland despite their service in British and sometimes British imperial ventures;[193] a Welsh strand ready to rehabilitate Edgar Evans; and an antipodean contribution reflected not just in the long-acclaimed Mawson, but also in a restive history and historiography of other ventures. Traditions were shaped by popular culture as much as in august institutions, rooted in material culture as well as ideology, and responsive to the change of cultural norms across time periods and from country to country. This essay, then, is a step towards the writing of 'a genealogy of [geography's] traditions in [un]familiar terms'.[194]

3 Configuring the field: Photography in early twentieth-century Antarctic exploration

Kathryn Yusoff

Our eye finds it more comfortable to respond to a given stimulus by reproducing once more an image that it has produced many times before, instead of registering what is different and new in an impression.[1]

Above all, a gaze that appears to see not a third of what it takes in.[2]

For the observer, there was no Antarctic interior before it was photographed. There was the Antarctic 'coast', an arbitrary line at best within the continuum of expanding and contracting ice. There were many other sketches and more detailed sightings drawn of the coastal regions of the Antarctic – of landfalls, barriers, icebergs and ships in ice – but these were all of the continental edges. Inside the Antarctic there were no cave paintings to attest to humankind's tentative emergence among the beasts, no early architectural ruins, no paths worn into the landscape and no human signature to inscribe matter before the arrival of the camera. Even the first Antarctic painting by a notable artist, William Hodges (on Captain Cook's 1772 voyage to the southern ocean), was only recently discovered because he had painted over it, presumably deciding that this field of ice failed to distinguish itself in the manner befitting a subject.[3]

The first photograph taken on the Antarctic continent was of a British flag, hoisted by Carstens Egeberg Borchgrevink, on 2 March 1899. Taken at the turn of the century by Louis Bernacchi, the photograph authenticated landfall and made a geographical possession on behalf of the British crown.[4] Shortly after this inaugural moment, Robert Falcon Scott led the first extensive interior exploration on his *British National Antarctic Expedition* of 1901–4. On this expedition Ernest Shackleton was raised 750 feet off the ground in a hydrogen balloon to take the first aerial photograph of Antarctica (see Figure 3.1).[5]

* * * * *

Since these tentative inaugural moments, the practice of photography in Antarctica continued apace with developments in the technology, expanding into colour, film, photogrammetry and trimetrogon photography through to the satellite maps that are in use today.[6] However, what marked the immense power of the photographic medium in the

FIGURE 3.1 Ernest Shackleton, *Practice on skis, Ross Island*, 1902, Antarctica, National Antarctic Expedition 1901–4 (courtesy of the Royal Geographical Society, image: C48J/19-SL86).

Antarctic was the exclusive technical coupling of this new technology to the discovery of the continental interior itself. Antarctica, in short, had no pre-photographic moment.[7]

Making an argument about the historical importance of configuring the Antarctic field through photography necessarily requires a detailed examination of how the 'field' is formed through photography and how this visual field affects both subjectivities and historical memory. As Felix Driver has noted, fieldwork is constructed from multiple forms of spatial and temporal inscriptions, including the traversing and embodiment of the material terrain, as well as the academic labour in the epistemological or ontological field. Driver comments, 'If we think of geographical knowledge as constituted through a range of embodied practices – practices of travelling, dwelling, seeing, collecting, recording, and narrating – the subject of fieldwork, its geography and its history, becomes more difficult to escape. In this context, the "field" may be understood as a region that is always in the process of being constructed ...'[8] In the construction site of the field, the role of new technologies in mapping, marking and manipulating the spaces of exploration are paramount to the way in which history was made and how it was perceived as historical. Vision is inseparable from time, and with the use of visual technologies such as the camera, new forms of temporality were mobilised that both affected the formation of subjectivities in the field and structured new forms of visual memory of that field *into* place. For Jonathan Crary, 'vision is always multiple, adjacent to and overlapping with other objects, desires, and vectors',[9] and the visual 'field' is multiply sited across interlocking practices and sites, which included the embodied seeing subjects of the Antarctic field (the 'explorers'), but extended through the financial, material, historical and imaginative networks of knowledge production. What distinguishes the emergence of the Antarctic visual field in the twentieth century was its lack of any prior interlocking visual cultures. There were multiple forms of visual practices that accompany the use of photography, such as cartography, painting, observational drawing and sightings, and the use of visual technologies such as sextants, prismatic compass and theodolites, but none that had such a profound and powerful relation to mimesis and modernity as the camera.

The 'discovery' of the interior of Antarctica through multiple expeditions in the early part of the twentieth century coincided with the extensive use of field photography, which became a critical technology of polar exploration, in both cultural and scientific terms. Culturally, the photographic method allowed Antarctica to be recorded and transmitted in a recognised format to audiences 'back home'; scientifically, it enabled the rapid identification of geographical features that could be recorded, identified and possessed. Opening up the territory of Antarctica to the popular geographical and scientific imagination, photography instituted a particular historical *field of vision*, configured through the limitations and possibilities of this medium. Yet, we might ask, what is interesting about this field of vision compared to the photographic work done in other continental 'interiors', such as Africa, India or the tropical jungles of the Americas? First of all, to see this lack of a pre-photographic moment as important, we would have to ask whether there is 'anything peculiarly "photographic" about photography – something which sets it apart from all other ways of making pictures?'[10] We might further ask whether the photographic medium was distinct from other forms of geographic representations. If we contend for the time being that there was something very important about the lack of a pre-photographic Antarctic moment, we might proceed to ask questions about the forms of observation and observing subjects that emerged through the camera. Thus, we might question: what forms of witnessing did the photographic field establish? What is the role of the photograph as a document to secure geopolitical power? How did the desire for the Antarctic photographs fund exploration? What are the tensions between the technics of photography and the Antarctic landscape? How did the presence of a professional photographer affect the embodiment of the field and forms of self-witnessing?

Questions of the historical *place* and cultural *effect* of visual regimes and new technologies require detailed attention. In this chapter I will look at two case studies to illuminate some of the issues at stake in the emergence of the Antarctic field and photography. Concentrating on two historic photographic moments, or what Crary calls 'points of emergence'[11] in the history of vision, in early twentieth-century Antarctic discovery, I will discuss some of the themes and questions that arise out of the unique coupling of continental discovery and the camera. These two points of emergence – *Terra Nova Expedition* of 1910 and the *Imperial Trans-Antarctic Expedition* of 1914–16 – are characterised by the fact that a professional photographer was integral to both expeditions, and consequently their practice had a profound effect on the configuration of the Antarctic visual and experiential field. Crary suggests that by outlining some of the 'points of emergence' of a modern and heterogeneous regime of vision, he could simultaneously address the related problem of 'when, and because of what events', ruptures occurred in models of vision and of the observer. His rationale for this approach is to shift the focus from *representational* forms and conventions into a consideration of 'a massive reorganization of knowledge and social practices that modified in myriad ways the productive, cognitive, and desiring capacities of the human subject'.[12] Thereby, Crary suggests a way of seeing change in vision and visuality as something not simply configured around new technologies, but implicitly embedded in distinct moments that reconfigure entire fields of knowledge practices.

This chapter begins with an initial discussion that establishes the importance of Antarctica's lack of a pre-photographic history and the implications of this for establishing the power of the photographic medium in Antarctic histories. The first point of emergence will examine the relationship between the discovery of Antarctica and time, specifically with recourse to perceptions of Antarctica being in and out of the time of modernity. I will argue that while the 'Heroic Era' (1890s–1910s) of Antarctic exploration was perceived as an antiquated form of exploration, it was the very modernity of photographic practice that gave these expeditions an unprecedented visibility and circulation on the global stage. It was this coupling of the supposed timelessness of the Antarctic with the timely reproduction of the photographic capture that presented the pursuits of explorers 'in time' within a narrative of scientific– technological – imperial advancement, which would come to characterise activities in the Antarctic continent. The utilisation of photography served as a narrative tool that brought Antarctica within the globalising drive of twentieth-century modernity, even as it seemed to observe a very 'un-modern' subject operating in primitive conditions. The discussion of this first case study focuses on the circulation of Herbert Ponting's *chrono*photography (or moving photographs, later known as film) from the Cape Evans expedition hut, Antarctica, to its subsequent showings in London and the Western Front. In contrast to the circulation of Ponting's *chrono*photography, Robert Falcon Scott's automated pole photograph, taken on the same *Terra Nova* expedition, is considered in relation to the anxieties of geopolitical possession. It was photographic practice, I will argue, that organised the landscape and its explorers into an image that was able to circulate as an intimate window into the culture of exploration and the making of empire. These images then redefined the very possibility of expeditions to the 'furthest south' through their circulation in expanded cultural and financial networks.

* * * * *

While particular equipment was taken, viewpoints were chosen, focal points and positions were enacted, there was nothing inevitable about the photographic forms of Antarctic (re)production. The second point of emergence – the *Imperial Trans-Antarctic Expedition* 1914–16 – addresses the distinct incompatibility between the Antarctic landscape and photography, which thwarted the configuration of the 'field' into such a coherent landscape. While the photographic medium was acutely sensitive to light variations and could be utilised for scientific observations, it was not yet able to adequately configure the 'depth of field' to capture the vastness of the Antarctic landscape into anything beyond a blank excess of whiteness. And so, prior to the use of photography as an aerial cartographic tool (in the mid-twentieth century), Antarctic exploration was characterised by a 'close-up' engagement with human and animal subjects (see Figure 3.2). Without the existence of indigenous peoples on whom to focus an observing optic and in the absence of conventional landscape scenes, the explorers themselves became the subjects of exploration.

In this sense, we see in early Antarctic exploration an unprecedented ethnographic focus on the everyday activities of exploration and explorers. While written diaries gave a fairly robust account of continuous drudgery and hardship, the camera offered the capture of extraordinary moments of engagement – football games in the snow, hammy rehearsals of putting up a tent, gramophone records played to penguins, men with dogs, men with ponies, men with men, and finally

FIGURE 3.2 A. H. Ninnis, *Untitled* (Expedition members taking photographs), Imperial Trans-Antarctic Expedition (Ross Sea Party) 1914–1916 (courtesy of the Royal Geographical Society, image S0011377)

men in pieces. This second 'point of emergence' will then discuss the work of the professional photographer Frank Hurley and his intimate inscriptions of expedition life in relation to concepts of subjectivity and documentation. In conclusion, I will consider the legacy of those initial photographic moments of discovery for the configuration of the Antarctic visual field.

THE PRE-PHOTOGRAPHIC MOMENT IN THE 'MOMENT' OF DISCOVERY

> We could not function within this teeming multiplicity without some ability to skelatize it, to diagram or simplify it. Yet this reduction and division occurs only at a cost, which is the failure or inability of our scientific, representational, and linguistic systems to acknowledge the in-between of things, the plural interconnections that cannot be utilized or contained within and by things but which makes them possible.[13]

Imagine, upon first encounter, no human signs marked or ordered the space of Antarctica. Ice was uninterrupted and surrounding. Extreme cold and the dynamics of ice were the only force. What happened here, the moment of discovery, had to be made from scratch. Never before had an encounter been made with a whole continent without indigenous people and human history. This was the cold, hard fact of *terra nullius,* rather than the fiction of such a desired imperial territorial form. In terms of nomination, Antarctica was a metaphoric blank page on which the markings of empire could be writ large. The 'teeming multiplicity' was skelatized by the 'moments' of discovery, where human presence brought Antarctica into the world, into meaning and into history.[14] The pre-photographic referent literarily did not exist nor proceed this moment of discovery. But, how does the 'moment' make and mark the time and space of Antarctica? No doubt this discovery was a form of spatial and temporal inscription, but how did the technics of photography transform this inscription?

Thinking with photography required no great adaptation for the explorers, as they had come from and were already embedded in a relation to photography and the photographic potential of their expeditions. The sale of image rights that acknowledged the entertainment value of the technology even more than its scientific potential had funded the expeditions.[15] The then-new visual technologies of the photograph and *chrono*photography did not necessarily change the representational strategies of older technologies of vision, such as the genres of landscape depiction, but they introduced a specific relation to time into the equation. Visual technologies, Crary argues, incorporate historical processes of looking. Yet, as he suggests, each technology is a historical process and is embedded in a much larger collective assemblage of events and knowledge structures.[16] Further, as Joel Synder exemplified in his discussion of the genre of landscape photography, the compositional conventions of print media and painting were initially continued by photographic practice, rather than radically restructured.[17] A historically reproductive viewpoint (in the case of landscape depiction) goes some way to explain how the 'field' may be configured compositionally (which was certainly the case with Herbert Ponting's landscape photography), but for a discussion of a field that was not yet designated as such, it does not touch upon what was most singular about this engagement – that was the photograph's relation to time.

The emergence of the field through photographic practice installed a particular temporality into the field. Walter Benjamin makes clear that the essential relationship was between the photographic image and time (specifically modernity's time), and argues that being modern is inextricably linked with our conception of history as understood through a photographically-entangled perception. This perception, for Benjamin, was characterised by a discontinuous process of history marked by interruption, or arrest.[18] Benjamin's 'now' of the photographic moment implicitly suggests that the specific formation of history that was manifest in photography could not exist without the photograph. He argued that the photographic moment was *the* moment of coming into modernity. Outside of the advent of photography and its 'arrests' was pre-modern history.[19] Moreover, Benjamin suggests that this was how history was made: in the imagistic capacity for arrest, analogous to the photographic method. It was the mimetic relation between the nature of history and 'the dynamite of the tenth of a second'[20] that was photography, which for Benjamin secured this entanglement between photography and modernity. So, we might ask, what does it mean to discover a continent in the 'dynamite of the tenth of a second'?

Initially, what may seem to mark the photographic moment in the Antarctic as problematic was the disjuncture between the tenth of a second (or in Benjamin's terms, the conscription into modernity's time) and Antarctica's seemingly ahistorical geological time (as a continent devoid of and unable to sustain human life). Antarctica, before its 'discovery', was without the anthropomorphic time that characterises a 'naturalised' (or normative) notion of history, secured through a human centre. It was specifically the camera that brought Antarctic into time (in the tenth of a second). This is to say that what establishes the power of photography in the Antarctic was that time went from the ahistorical or geologic to the photographic, and it was this sudden rupture and bursting into time that made these images so distinct and historically laden. While this photographic inscription had none of the cultural overwriting that characterised much colonial ethnographic photography, it did establish a persistent imaginative occupation that has yet to be challenged by any other significant mode of visuality. To address Antarctic visual culture you must address Antarctica's relation to photography.

How photography makes history in the Antarctic is embedded in multiple material practices and activities of place making (such as the use of huts that facilitated the establishment of dark rooms), and the very specific challenges of making photographs in freezing conditions (frostbitten plates and frozen film). The 'opening up' of Antarctica through the photographic image to audiences was a form of production contingent on the technologies of photography, which include the chemical, classificatory and circulatory processes that constitute its cultural form (which I will discuss later). What is crucial here was that photography was a modality of seeing, installed in the Antarctic from the moment of its continental discovery, and that moment was made in photography's reproductive, circulatory, affective, chemical, subjective and temporal capacity.

As a dissecting optic on the teeming multiplicity of the Antarctic, the camera transformed Antarctica into an object of intelligence and – more importantly for the expedition's sponsors – an object of intelligibility (the photograph) that could be understood in places far from Antarctica. The ability of photographs to circulate and be reproduced (in newspapers, magazines and in theatres) was crucial to its commodity form. Discovery is less about practices *per se* than transformations that are an effect of those practices, a taking and making of the world (which facilitated implicitly geopolitical aspirations). The photographic moment in the non-represented field was a state of transformation, what Elizabeth Grosz calls 'a conscious rendering'[21] of matter as thing, and thus characterises the architecture of that space. In this way, Grosz argues, matter is rendered as humanised space through a prosthetic technology (the shift was from an observing subject to observations made through prosthetic technologies, which was situated in a wider shift in the rendering of observable phenomena in imperial practices and the natural sciences), but simultaneously, matter was supplemented by a human signature as a form of prosthetic to make this matter necessary in some way (be that psychically, scientifically, culturally, imperially or some assemblage of these).

Antarctica's coming into existence was held in the photographic frame even before the explorers arrived. The camera transformed their actions in that space, actions that had been sold in advance to newspapers, advertisers and film distributors. This technology transformed the explorers as subjects (or as forces that shaped the environment and as prosthetic extensions of that technology) while also transforming the spaces of possession (see Figure 3.3).

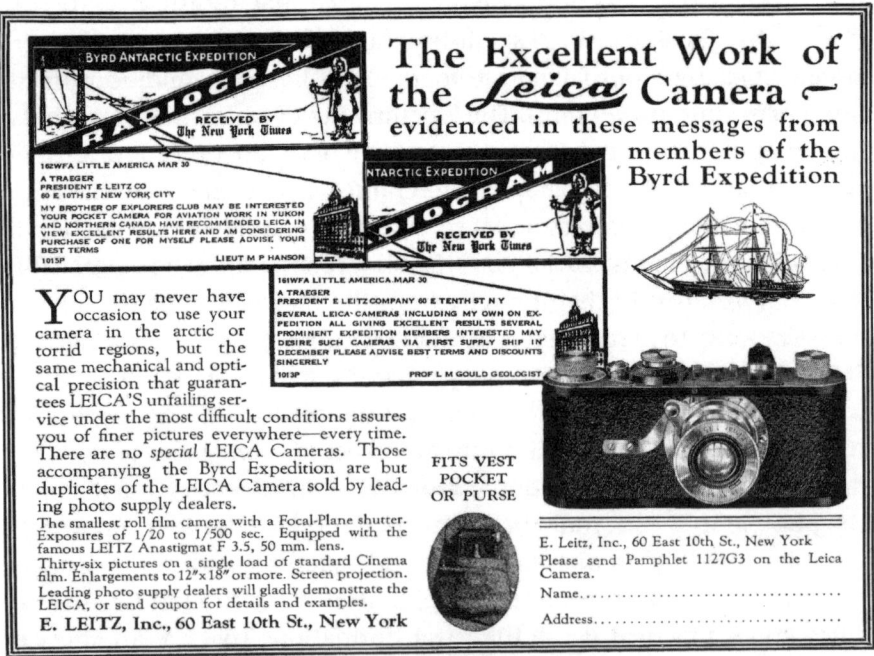

FIGURE 3.3 Advertisement for Leica cameras from the *Bryd Antarctic Expedition*, *National Geographic*, 1957.

The co-joining of photography with the discovery of the Antarctic interior produced an optical unconscious inflected through a photographic optic that effected and configured the perception of subjects as well as matter.

* * * * *

The importance of photography as a prosthetic device for resolving the irresolvable dilemmas of inhabitation in an uninhabitable and uninhabited continent is vital to forms of self-witnessing as a historical process. In Antarctic discovery, the photograph and the photographed merge are inflected as modalities of seeing. The camera reassures and configures moments of discovery by making the explorers the predominant actors, securing their purpose in an icy, cold environment and ensuring the legacy of that-which-has-been. What purpose, we might ask, would their being there otherwise have? At the most intimate level, representational practice is intimately bound up with the possession of places and of self or other. The photograph lent intelligence to man-hauling countless miles, on the brink of starvation and death to reach an abstract point in the snow. The powerful geographic imaginary of a flag at the axis of the world alleviated the lack of conventional or rational meaning their presence might otherwise have had. While discovery in Africa and Asia was characterised by the curiosity and wonder that new flora and fauna brought, in Antarctica the landscape was unremitting ice, punctuated by disorientating optical phenomena.[22] Thus, the photograph frames a space out of the chaos of ice storms and frigid matter to give Antarctica an architecture that it otherwise lacked. Yet, what became apparent was that what was framed in the Antarctic – the teeming white space – was discontinuous with the mimetic realism that bound photography so intimately to nineteenth- and twentieth-century urban space. That is to say, the rectangular frame of the photographic plate seemed arbitrary when faced with a 360-degree horizon, thousands of miles of ice, not a vertical bisecting line to be found, a sun that went round in circles and a night that lasted for six months.

Benjamin's maxim about the relationship between the camera and the modern world illuminates some of the traverse connections between modernity and photography; but in the case of Antarctica it was the very disconnections between the medium and the environment that lent Antarctic photographs such a curiously antiquated appeal (and arguably obscured what was so interesting about that pre-photographic moment). Antarctic photographs had the appearance of a pantomime, where men were dressed up in funny suits, playing with penguins, playing with snow; or men in what seemed like exaggerated forms of action (Figure 3.4). As the photograph of the men in bear suits promoting Shackleton's bioscope film typified (bioscope was a form of *chrono*photography), exploration in the far south was something of a joke, but entertaining and profitable none the less.[23]

* * * * *

The photographic whitewashing of the landscape into white space (caused by the lack of perceptible definition that ice presented to the camera) both produced and reinforced this perception of Antarctic exploration as performative.[24] Photography structured the multiplicity of the Antarctic environment; yet this rendering was made at the cost of

FIGURE 3.4 Men dressed in explorers' furs advertising one of the lantern lectures by Sir Ernest Shackleton, December 1909 (courtesy of the National Maritime Museum).

understanding this space as profoundly other and potentially disruptive of normative regimes of European vision. It is in this interplay between the cultural and the pictorial void (as a mimetic doubling of that space) that I situate this discussion of the following historical *points of emergence.*

FIRST POINT OF EMERGENCE: LANDSCAPES IN TRANSMISSION

> Antarctica / burrs into life / on a patched sheet / somewhere in France. British tracks / dawdle the white / screen and country / No mud in sight! The arc lamp spits / the smoky air, / bold ghosts wave / and disappear into a blizzard / where clean fun binds / the living and dead / one more time Smokers' coughs, / farts, nose blowing / punctuate / a repeat showing of all that broke / and crashed and fell / in Gallipoli / and Flanders fields.[25]

In 1915, 'in response to an appeal from the Front', the expeditionary photographer Herbert Ponting gave sets of his Antarctic films (later released as the *Great White Silence* then *90° South*) 'for the benefit of our soldiers in France'. The films were 'shown to more than 100,000 officers and men of the British Army'.[26] The intended resonance between the narrative of Scott's dead pole party and the sacrifice being enacted on the battlefields in the name of empire was not subtle. Rev. F. I. Anderson, Senior Chaplain to the forces, sent a letter to Ponting praising the inspiring qualities of the film. Directly relating the Antarctic journey to their present situation in wartime, he wrote:

> The splendid story of Captain Scott is just the thing to cheer and encourage out here.... The thrilling story of Oates self sacrifice, to try and give his friends a chance of 'getting through' is one that appeals so at present time.... We all feel we have inherited from Oates' and his comrades a legacy and heritage of inestimable value in seeing through our present work. We thank you all with grateful hearts.[27]

The focus on Oates' 'thrilling' sacrifice (or suicide) is a telling aspect of the emotional reverberations that the film was expected to generate in its audiences on the Western Front. The expectations of national subjectivity meant sacrifice, contextualised within the domestic relations of gentlemanly conduct, whether in Antarctica or at the front. More importantly, the narrative of Scott responded to anxieties about death and colonised the domain beyond the reaches of life as an example of how to die in a particularly 'clean' way, far removed in geographical distance, but present in a complimentary ideology, amongst the slaughter of the battlefields. A thread of 'English-ness' that Scott had claimed to pick up in his infamous last 'letter to the public' was extended, and ran through as a 'legacy and heritage of inestimable value' to the 'comrades' on the Western Front – because it served 'in seeing through our present work'. As thousands of troops sat through the projection of this Antarctic encounter in France, Ponting, having secured the rights to the film, lectured daily in London for ten months in 1914 (later touring on the Western Front).[28] At a time when the death of men was a growing concern to soldiers abroad and civilians at home, the film bound 'the living and dead / one more time'.

On the film's first screening in London, on 20 October 1911, it received quite a different reception. The *London Standard* reported:

> in a cosy little darkened room just off Piccadilly Circus, last evening, a special company of about forty persons sat and watched a small band of men fighting their way over mountains of ice towards the South Pole ... No previous Polar expedition has had such 'live' chronicles taken of its life among the snows.[29]

Unaware of Scott's death, and the disjuncture between 'live' images and dead subjects (or that live images must be paid for by life), the audience, including Mrs Scott, had sat in a little darkened room and watched images that appeared comical and endearing. As Ponting writes to Scott:

> the picture of you getting into your sleeping bag. That one always brings down the house ... it makes them all laugh, because Birdie goes through such funny antics; that, and the film of you & Co doing the sledging, are always voted by everyone the best things in the show.[30]

Watching this image on a white screen somewhere in a tent on the Western Front, the response was markedly different – with death pressing so close, who would dare to laugh as Scott struggles into his sleeping bag? Yet, in the Antarctic, knowing well that death was a distinct possibility, they have rehearsed this performance of making camp many times for Ponting's camera. Acting for the camera and for each other at the Royal Terror Theatre[31] was part of their expeditionary culture captured by the camera. The chaplain stated that 'the intensity of appeal is realised in the subdued hush and quiet that pervades the massed audience of troops while it is being told.'[32] In an environment where death was a real and imminent possibility, the preparation for sacrifice that the images portrayed was not comical, nor devoid of the intended symbolic reverberation.

Further away from the intensity of death, in London, a curious postcard advertising daily showings of the film at the Philharmonic Hall was footnoted with a quotation from the *Daily Telegraph*, 'Scene after scene of inimitable comedy'. On the reverse side of the card the *Sunday Times* was quoted as saying, 'There is nothing in the theatres of London to approach this drama. There is no comedy so amusing, no play so poignant, no tragedy so heart rendering as this tale in pictures.' The *Daily Sketch* proposed that 'To see Mr Ponting's historic film and hear his brilliant lecture is to realise what being an Englishman should mean.' The *Daily Mirror* was more insistent and suggested that 'people should be made to see it'.[33] The King hoped that Britain's children would see the film and that it 'would help promote the spirit of adventure that had made the Empire'.[34] The performance of images and narratives of Scott's death became cultural capital that could be drawn upon to validate, inspire and consolidate the practices of empire and the demands of imperial masculinity. The *London Times* wrote that the value of the expedition lay in proving that the practice of Empire-building could be continued by the present generation:

> It is proof that in an age of depressing materialism men can still be found to face known hardship, heavy risk and even death, in pursuit of an idea. That is the temper of men who build empires and while it lives among us we shall be capable of maintaining an Empire that our fathers builded [sic].[35]

The aestheticisation of the 'pursuit of an idea' was a crucial aspect of empire building; conceptually and physically it becomes a justification for the act itself. Framing empire as 'an idea', and an idea worth dying for, was an essential aspect of separating the imagination from the body, and the afflictions the body might have to face in the service of the idea. As Rosalyn Deutsche and Cara Gendel Ryan comment, the three tenets of domination and possession are *mapping, mythologising* and *aestheticising*.[36] The 'moving' photographs of Scott in the Antarctic provided a corresponding modern aesthetic for the performance of this idea on the Western Front.

Alongside audience responses, the financial fortunes of Ponting's photographs provide a useful insight into the economic production of the photography within expeditions. Unaware of the pre-expedition deals Scott had set up without his knowledge, Ponting wrote a recriminating letter to him about image rights, to berate him for the lack of financial benefit he was able to reap from the photographs. As Ponting laments:

> words utterly fail to express my disappointment and chagrin, as though the work I have done in the South is the most difficult, and perhaps the most valuable that I have ever done, from a Geographical standpoint, yet I am unable to reap any benefit from it.[37]

Ponting continued to clearly point out to Scott that Mr Amundsen's arrival had been instrumental to the lack of popularity and financial backing that the films had so far received. He indicated the financial implications of not coming first. Ponting notes:

> To get back to the films ... you may, I think, safely figure on another two or three thousand pounds ... you ought to get something like £6/7000, perhaps more. If Mr Amundsen had not turned up, there is no doubt that the sum I have always named you, £20,000 might well have been reached.[38]

The hoped-for sums that Ponting had envisaged were never fully realised. Ponting bought out Gaumont's rights to the film after Scott's death and released a feature-length silent film called *The Great White Silence* in the 1920s. In 1929, the Duke of York formally took possession of the film and its negatives, passing them on to the British Empire Film Institute to be held on behalf of the nation; but after 1918 audiences were considerably reduced for the film. Presumably the story of 'heroic' death no longer held popular or cathartic appeal. In 1933, Ponting put in another £10,000 of his own money to re-release the film once again, under the title, *90° South*. However, the film was not a commercial success, and Ponting died bankrupt.

The photographic vision of early Antarctic exploration had a considerable afterlife in other imperial spaces, yet to render Antarctica solely as a scene to a larger imperial narrative neglects the imaginative work that photography produced in the field of exploration itself. The oscillation between imagined audiences and the practices of photography, and the conflicts suppressed in the process of signifying practices remained deeply ambiguous, located in the uncertainties of real encounters. One of those encounters on the *Terra Nova Expedition* was a photograph taken at the South Pole with a hand-held camera automated by a piece of string.

The camera and explorers had arrived too late to be the first to mark this pre-photographic moment. Another photograph had already been taken in this very place by the Norwegian explorer, Ronald Amundsen, with a cheap brownie camera (the official camera having broken). The first photograph at the South Pole was an unremarkable unfocused photograph of shadowy figures by a flag, but it did the work of authenticating presence. The camera's temporal and circulatory capacity transformed the abstract point, 90° south, into a historic space. Aware of the importance of photography for authorising and authoring time and place in geopolitical possession, it was this spatial enclosure that Scott had to step into, to be pictured, belated, and in defeat.

* * * * *

Observing himself as a photographic subject engaged in 'making history' that would travel through the spaces of empire, Scott shuffled through the frames (with three frames taken just in case) (Figure 3.5). The other expeditioners changed places through the photographic frames but remained still, in deference to the role of the camera, but Scott did not know quite how to position himself in this most historic of frames. He moved from the right, eyes to the front, to the right again, side view, and then to the left, eyes to the right. By this point in the expedition, Scott already knew himself from the outside, as an image for the public, caught in the flickering light of Ponting's lantern displays that had been projected to the explorers in the hut through the previous winter's night. How much did the explorers themselves see their actions projected onto the mimetic stage of history? Scott had spent his spare time practicing photography in the darkroom at Cape Evans and watched Ponting conjure photographs of 'the explorers' – their shadowy shapes emerging from the chemical bath of his developing tray. The photograph of exploration had to possess this hallucinogenic quality if it was to communicate beyond the moment of its taking to the now of seeing, and so the explorer had to absorb and embody the spectre of his life existing beyond that moment, and ultimately beyond his death. After that photograph was taken, the Antarctic weather would overwrite their bodies into irreversible immobility, and it was uncertain whether the photograph would ever be found. Susan Solomon argues that the ten days of blizzard

FIGURE 3.5 Camera activated by string by various members of the expedition, South Pole, Terra Nova Expedition, 17 January 1912 (Lot 175, Herbert Ponting, Christie's *The Polar Sale* catalogue).

that Scott claims kept the explorers in their tent was a meteorological impossibility. She suggests that either Scott lost track of time or that the blizzard outside abated, but by then it was too late for Scott (who could not walk due to frozen feet). She concludes, 'if his companions could not carry him and told him it was not possible for them to leave, then it might as well have been blowing a hurricane'.[39]

Tragic comedy in tents on the imperial periphery coupled with the recasting of Antarctic fieldwork (and its photographer) into the battlefields of the First World War attest to the power of photography, not just to join imperial spaces, but to act as a connective tissue between extremely disparate landscapes and experiences. The time of the photograph was productive of the time of the subject, as a mass subject, available to be viewed at all times. Photography not only seemed to offer an intervention in time, but also a bounded space of representation that allowed the subject photographed to be *read* in an entirely different manner. Productive of modern time, photography also instituted a globalised time of landscape – as a telepresent terrain – where even the 'ends of the earth' could be made available to vision. The smooth progress of this visualising technology *across* space allowed the Antarctic field to have 'meaning' in radically differentiated ideological and physical fields. The use of these photographic technologies and professional photographers projected the expedition beyond the walls of the expedition hut, to France and to London and into the future, giving their polar expeditions an unprecedented visibility in history.

As the recording of historical geographical journeys created an external visibility of explorers around the world, the technology was also distributed internally as a form of experience constitutive of subjectivity. In the tripartite image of Scott at the pole, the double bind of photography as externally and internally constituted emerges. Here, we can view the unprecedented possibilities of photography to be present and to address the anxieties of the moment of 'discovery'. In defeat, no longer able to regard himself in the historical moment of claiming the South Pole, the photograph of Scott performs an uncomfortable presence-ing through the frames of time. Akin to the *chrono*photographic images of Edward Muybridge or Dr Charcot's *Iconographie photographique de la Salpêtrière*,[40] photography, read as a diagnostic time-based tool, allows us to concentrate on the moment of discovery itself articulated within time. Ponting's over-determined performance (of camping) is too intentional and too rehearsed in its presentation of an historical event to disturb us. The other photographs, that do not see the light of day as a triptych till the Christie's *Polar Sale* in 2001,[41] brought the process of making a discovery to the fore, that is, as a shifting, uncertain practice, imbued with anxiety and the ambiguities of presence.

SECOND POINT OF EMERGENCE: CLOSE UP AND ETHNOGRAPHIC

The lack of an accurately perceptible 'depth of field' in the Antarctic for both human sight and the camera lenses used in early exploration led to sighting problems across the field of embodied exploration and photographic reproduction. Stated simply, there was too much indistinguishable white space that lacked contrast and too much light that caused photographic plates to be overexposed. Hence, that teeming multiplicity of ice recurrently became a pictorial void organised by the explorers' activities. This pictorial action creates positive and negative spaces that are separated by conditions of time, in which the Antarctic is brought *into* time through the action of the explorer and his incision in the pictorial space. This slice of action through an exterior space establishes the active explorer and the event of his discovery as the formative act in defining the ahistorical void. Thus, the camera and the explorer co-constitute the possession of Antarctica. The subject's translation of the spatial into the temporal (a space of human time) makes, what Richard Serra called, an 'anti-environment'. The anti-environment has, he says, 'the potential to create its own place and space and to work in contradiction to the spaces and places where it is created ... to divide or declare its own area'.[42] This declaration of Antarctic white space amounts to the creation of the environment as an atemporal (and thus ahistorical) 'other'. The point here is that such isolation or division of subject and environment was a pictorial conceit that could only occur in the Antarctic photograph.

The contemporary photographer, Ed Osborn has demonstrated quite clearly how this led to extensive cropping of photographs through his work in the Canterbury Museum Antarctic archives.[43]

He investigated the various conditions of the suppression of spatial openness as a psychic and practice-based transaction. Using examples of cropped archival photographs he explored the repeated removal of 'white space', which he comments 'look less like simple framing devices than visible artefacts of the limits of what is comprehensible'.[44] Human subjects anchored and gave meaning to the vast expanse of non-human space. This practice was a crude form of arrest that stemmed from the expectations of making photographs that could circulate as intelligible images. But something else was at stake in the editing of 'white space' that indicated a more profound inability to perceive of, or mechanically reproduce, Antarctic space as anything other than the blankness depicted by conventional globes and cartographic projection.

The marks of human presence in the Antarctic multiplied unabated at the beginning of the twentieth century, in no small part due to Frank Hurley's extensive photographic practice (on *the Australasian Antarctic Expedition*, 1911–14, and *the Imperial Trans-Antarctic Expedition*, 1914–16). As has often been remarked, while Ponting's work was characterised by the method of 'To Pont', which translated as the excessive formal arrangement of frames and subjects, Hurley's photographic methods are decidedly more ethnographic. Accepting the problematic of the lack of a depth of field the subsequent displacement of the landscape into white space, Hurley perused a different methodology in his photographic practice. Realising the compelling subject of the Antarctic to be both the human subjects and in-between-ness of their environmental interactions, Hurley produced an extraordinary catalogue of the *force* of both humans and ice in the Antarctic. For Hurley, authenticity was located in the experience of the viewer not in the pictures themselves, which made him actively montage and edit plates where necessary to tell his story of embodied experience in place (much to the chagrin of contemporary commentators who have called his photographs 'fakes').[45] Moreover, he understood that the lack of a depth of field confined his practice to close-up shots of seemingly 'ordinary' activities of the expedition: the respite of smoking, football games on ice, newborn pups, chippy's cat, ship life, lectures, cooking hoosh, the weather written in the faces of men, the social lives of men and animals, washing, camping, tents.

The density of this pictured expedition life made Antarctic exploration into a very social scene that concentrated on ordinary practices in an extraordinary environment. The concentrated gaze on explorers as the anthropological other in the landscape not only provided an observation of Antarctic social history, but a spectacle of imperial place-making that constructed memory-images of a clean national endeavour in far away places. Although the compositions have all the traits of documentary observation, they were aimed at producing a specific response: constructing the explorer as a heroic actor in the conquest of a remote and challenging landscape. Yet, to see Hurley's work as simply constructing a quest narrative would miss the intensity and pull of his photography, which established the Antarctic environment as an extraordinary force in reorganising subjectivity. Such inhabitation, interaction and integration between ice and men had not been seen before. It was a picture of intensity.

From one intense environment to another, on return from the Antarctic, Hurley and other men from the expedition went straight to the Western Front. Rather than staging performances of the Great White War in the South (as Shackleton had reframed their expedition), Hurley went to the front in 1917 as a war photographer with the Australian Imperial Forces and produced some of the most extraordinary bleak landscapes of the battlefields ever imaged (and the only colour plates of the Great War). His pictures of men picking their way through the muddied duckboards of Ypres (*Battle of Menin Road*, 1917–18) captured an alien, inhuman landscape decimated by the activities of war. Not unlike the desolation photographed in Antarctica, Hurley made deeply humanist landscapes defined by the presence of men in bewildering and hostile environments. In his depiction of the battle of Passchendaele, rather than try to hold the intensity of the battlefield in his frame, Hurley concentrates on the intimate stories of *How I did it* (1917) – one man recounting his story to his comrades. This photograph is directly paralleled in its composition to the night watchman's vistas: Hurley's image of the nightwatchman on *The Endurance* recounting stories as they watch for signs of change in the ice. Akin to the visually incomprehensible landscapes of Antarctica, the landscapes of war frustrated Hurley's enframings (he could not 'contain' events within the frame of a single negative). His response, as in Antarctica, was to think about the 'truth' of the observing subject in the experience of war rather than a truth that was concerned with historic reliability, and so he produced montages that captured the enormity of the space of conflict.

Hurley and other amateur expeditionary photographers of early Antarctic exploration were instrumental in configuring the density of Antarctic space through a concentration on the 'close up' ethnographic practices of exploration, thereby rendering a distinctly humanist conception of place out of a vacuum of non-human space. It was not until the advent of an aerial optic and the trimetrogon photograph (a composite photograph of three photographs taken simultaneously with three cameras) that the humanist centre that had characterised Antarctic visual culture shifted. Whereas human embodiment had been a prerequisite of geopolitical claims made on the skeletal areas of coast and pole, aerial photogrammetry was essential for establishing large-scale territorial claims in preparation in the 1930s–50s, prior to the International Geophysical Year (1957–8). The American, Richard E. Byrd, had pioneered techniques in aerial photography and he flew over the South Pole with a mapping camera in 1929. As much as 700,000 square miles were 'discovered' via the flying camera, and 40 per cent of the coast was charted (using some of the 65,000 aerial photographs).[46] The US programme, codenamed *Operation Highjump* (1946–8) that included 4,700 personnel, 13 ships and 19 fixed-wing aircraft, performed extensive aerial photogrammetry. The primary remit of the expedition was to test personnel and equipment in frigid zones in preparation for polar engagements. However, one of the (now declassified) aims was 'To consolidate and extend American sovereignty over the largest practical area of the Antarctic continent', and this was achieved through large-scale aerial trimetrogon photomapping[47] and sustained airdrops of national claim sheets. The historic geographies of vision in the Antarctic began with portraiture and ended in higher and higher optical verticalities, from aerial to satellite. Despite differences in subject focus, these fields of vision were always tied to forms of geographical possession, first by establishing embodied presence and later through the reproduction of vast tracts of ice. What remained, as the problematic in the configuration of the Antarctic visual field, was how to address adequately the disjunction of this vast space within the capacity of the available technologies and the more profound matter of how to adequately make meaning in the void.

CONCLUSION: DARK ROOMS, WHITE SPACE AND FIELDS OF VISION

Photography and embodied exploration co-constituted the interior of Antarctic discovery. Photography was not just the dominant 'scopic regime' of the Antarctic visual field, overlapping with other competing visions of place, but *the* scopic regime. There was no perception of the Antarctic interior prior to the photographs of it. Despite the modern photographic technology that the explorers carried with them on expeditions, the blank white space of cartographic absence never entirely went away. The pre-photographic moment was a void that returned to haunt the subsequent photographic formations of the landscape as 'white space'. The use of photography and the employment of a professional photographer on two important early expeditions created two distinct 'points of emergence' in polar exploration that led (to reiterate Crary) to a massive reorganisation of knowledge production and the social practices of expeditionary life, which in turn modified the observation, perception and aspirations of the human subject in Antarctica. What is important to note here is that it was

FIGURE 3.6 Herbert Ponting, Interior of darkroom, 24 March 1911 British Antarctic Expedition 1910–13 (courtesy of the Royal Geographical Society, image S0004276).

the constellation of new technology, discovery, dark rooms, professional photographers, commercial appetite and photography as part of expeditionary social life, a medium that could document geographical possession and authenticate presence, that made photography the dominant inscribing technology (see Figure 3.6). In particular, the emergence of modernity's time through the photographic method propagated Antarctic exploration as a meaningful enterprise able to travel – materially, commercially and ideologically – across the spaces of empire. Thus expeditionary photography not only configured the Antarctic field, but also was a form of fieldwork in its own right. The photographs traversed the spaces of communication between empires and constituted how history was made and perceived as 'historical'. Antarctica was brought into time through the photographic method and thus its history is configured through that optic, in frozen, arrested moments of human activity that existed in the first part of the century alongside the white space of environmental time.

4 Explorations in the Libyan Desert: William J. Harding King

Nicola J. Thomas and Jude Hill

> *It is often said that the day of geographical discovery is drawing to its close, and, indeed, that there no longer remains any part of our globe's surface, except for the circumpolar regions, where the explorer can hope to reveal important facts wholly unsuspected or unascertained. Another Alexander, he sighs for new worlds to conquer, cries for the Moon – et sic itur ad astra! But why should the explorer despair just yet? There lurks unseen in the world enough to last his time and, withal, his son's; and the Royal Geographical Society, which has done so much to encourage him in the past, now proposes to offer him renewed incentive by patronising a series of summary discourses on the Still Unknown.*[1]

Those members of the Royal Geographical Society (RGS), London, who feared that exploration and 'geographical discovery' was at an end in the beginning of the twentieth century, were offered reassurance through a series of lectures delivered between 1908 and 1911 titled 'Problems in Exploration'.[2] Launching the series D. G. Hogarth told his audience that the 'Still Unknown' of continental interiors offered opportunities and suggested 'The explorer is perhaps suffering from nothing worse than reaction after a day of great things ... we may be nearing a day of lesser things, but the day of little things is still far off'.³ Although Hogarth's own lecture was concerned primarily with opportunities open to explorers in Western Asia, it is notable that his opening remarks concerned Africa, the continent that had become such an iconic part of the culture of exploration encouraged by the RGS in the nineteenth century. Hogarth noted (using a familiar metaphor) that although Africa was no longer the 'Dark Continent' it was, nonetheless, 'guarding jealously at this moment some very dark spots'.⁴

Given the central role the RGS played in the cultures of British exploration in the nineteenth century, it is unsurprising that the Society should sponsor this series of lectures. In so doing, the RGS positioned itself at the forefront of a new century of geographical discovery, informing some of its varied membership about the stake they could still hold in travel and exploration.⁵ Whether all the membership found succour in the lectures is open to question; however, for the armchair explorers who enjoyed reading the narratives of discovery in *The Geographical Journal*, the days of 'Geography Militant' were not lost and for those whom the society might encourage to travel in a purposeful manner the opportunities were clearly presented.

Indeed, the RGS's continued support and encouragement of exploration can be charted in these early years of the twentieth century through people such as William Joseph Harding King (1869–1933). In 1907, Harding King followed the advice of the Society's Secretary, John Scott Keltie, and began planning a series of explorations in the Libyan Desert which he undertook in the years leading up to the outbreak of the First World War. At the very time Hogarth was asking his audience, 'who has followed Rohlfs down the line of Senussi oases?' Harding King, on the advice of Keltie, was already tracing the footsteps of the German explorer.⁶

Harding King's decision to explore the Libyan Desert was guided by advice from the RGS. He had originally wished to return to Algeria (a region he had visited as an independent traveller a few years previously) with the intention of undertaking triangulation work across the Sahara to Timbuktu and completing a systematic survey of the region. His stated purpose was to observe 'the density and distribution of vegetation and the fauna and on the salinity, depth of the wells etc. so as to make the maps as much practical value as possible'.⁷ Replying to a letter written by Harding King to the RGS about his proposed trip, Keltie indicated that although Harding King could obviously write a popular book about such a trip, given the French survey activity in the region he would be better off devoting his energy for 'original exploring including careful mapping and a study of everything that comes within the Geographical sphere' in another location.[8] Keltie went on to suggest that if Harding King wished 'to carry out a Geographical expedition, and want to break into as much new ground as possible, why not try the Libyan Desert or better still endeavour to get into the Tibesti mountains, in the South-Eastern Sahara'.[9] For both Keltie and Harding King the lure of this area was its 'unexplored' nature; in Keltie's words 'a region likely to yield more original results' than the Algerian Sahara. Harding King, keen to cement his reputation as an explorer, was more than willing to be directed to a fruitful site.[10]

Harding King was a member of the English upper-class elite who was educated at Jesus College, Cambridge and then graduated to work in the Law at the Middle Temple in 1893.[11] His travels to the Algerian Sahara in 1900 sowed the seed for his later ambitions, and we can see outputs from his earlier travels marking him as a purposeful traveller with ambitions to publish work and establish a reputation for himself.[12] Following his father's death in 1903 it would appear that Harding King had sufficient independent means to support his family and fund his own expeditions. However, his ambitions for further travel were delayed until 1907 when he first contacted the RGS with his intentions, requesting advice and support.[13] The distinction that Keltie drew between 'popular' and 'scientific' travel was one that Harding King identified with immediately; he clearly wished to position himself as a 'scientific' traveller who would undertake 'practical' activities, whether surveying unmapped land, undertaking systematic descriptive observations of areas through which he travelled, or developing scientific experimental work – in Harding King's case on sand movement. Although the distinction that Keltie made between 'scientific' and 'popular' travel appears clear cut, the difference between categories of travellers (from tourists to explorers) was, as Felix Driver has noted, open to negotiation, with the boundaries between different types of 'scientific' traveller being hotly contested.[14] For those keen to undertake a journey with a scientific purpose, guidance from institutions such as the RGS, alongside instructional manuals, offered clear advice on how to go about undertaking one's activity.[15]

The decision to 'explore' the Libyan Desert was by no means an innocent act. As Ryan and Naylor remind us in the introduction to this volume, exploration, empire, commerce and power remained entwined in the early twentieth century, and Harding King's activities in the Libyan Desert resonated with the British colonial imperatives of the time.[16] Harding King undertook surveying and mapping work, arguably fulfilling his own desire to 'tame' an unknown space; however, his activities were attentive to the needs of the time. For those concerned with security and potential threat from outside interests, the desert regions of colonial territory and surrounding regions were inadequately surveyed. However, as Collier and Inkpen demonstrate, the type of survey to be undertaken was a controversial topic in the late nineteenth and early twentieth century, with the different needs of naval and army personnel coming into conflict. For the Army and professionals within organisations such as the Survey of India, importance was placed on the collection of systematic knowledge which would result in detailed topographical survey.[17] In their discussion of the disputes surrounding the correct method of survey and the training of surveyors by the RGS from 1870–1914, Collier and Inkpen illustrate the ways in which institutions such as the Survey of India and figures within the RGS were instrumental in determining the type of survey that an explorer such as Harding King would produce and the ways in which subsequent survey and maps would be valued. From Harding King's discussion of his surveying activities in the field and the circulation of his findings in map and discussion form, we can address contemporary debates that circulated around who was trusted to map imperial territory and what type of information was valued in this exercise.[18]

David Livingstone has called for greater attention to be paid to the geography of scientists' lives and findings, specifically using biography as a methodological approach to enable a closer understanding of the 'making of science and scientist'.[19] For Livingstone the geography of a scientist's life is important and issues such as where scientists did their work and who they interacted with in different spaces, alongside the place in which their work was judged and how it was received in specific locations, are central. A critical, contextual and biographical approach enables a more nuanced understanding of the individual and the discourses and networks in which they circulated. As Felix Driver has demonstrated, attention to individual lives enables us to explore the 'unfamiliar histories' of ideas and institutions.[20] Rather than use a biographical approach to recover 'heroic' explorers or travellers, isolating their achievements and placing them on a celebratory plinth, paying attention to individuals, the places and spaces of their lives and the network of people, institutions and ideas they negotiated enables us to pay attention to the nuances of the 'making of science' in all its varied forms.

In this chapter we draw on the records of Harding King's explorations, including his letters, field notebooks, photographs, books, journal articles and reviews, to unpack the cultures of desert exploration in the early twentieth century. Through these documents we address debates around the increasing professionalisation of both science and colonial survey at the turn of the twentieth century and the role the RGS played in policing the boundaries between professionals and amateurs, and between science (whether surveying or field science) and popular travel.[21] As a man of independent means, Harding King was something of an outsider. He was neither a trained surveyor nor a member of the Department of Egyptian Survey whose task it was to survey the territory under British control in Egypt and neighbouring territory as required. He was neither a member of the Army, whose interests lay in seeing the desert region from a strategic standpoint, nor a colonial administrator, who might undertake the sort of investigations that Harding King did as part of his duties or general interests. Alongside this, Harding King was also not a professional academic geographer working within a University department, something that was increasingly common in the early decades of the twentieth century.[22] Harding King's independent position and the resulting fight for recognition within the geographical establishment is thus revealing of the professionalisation of exploration and geographical science in the early twentieth century.

* * * * *

Harding King spent three main field seasons in Egypt and the Libyan Desert. The first (1909) and third (1911) seasons were regarded by Harding King as the most successful in terms of the 'unknown' territory he travelled through (see Figure 4.1). During his time in the

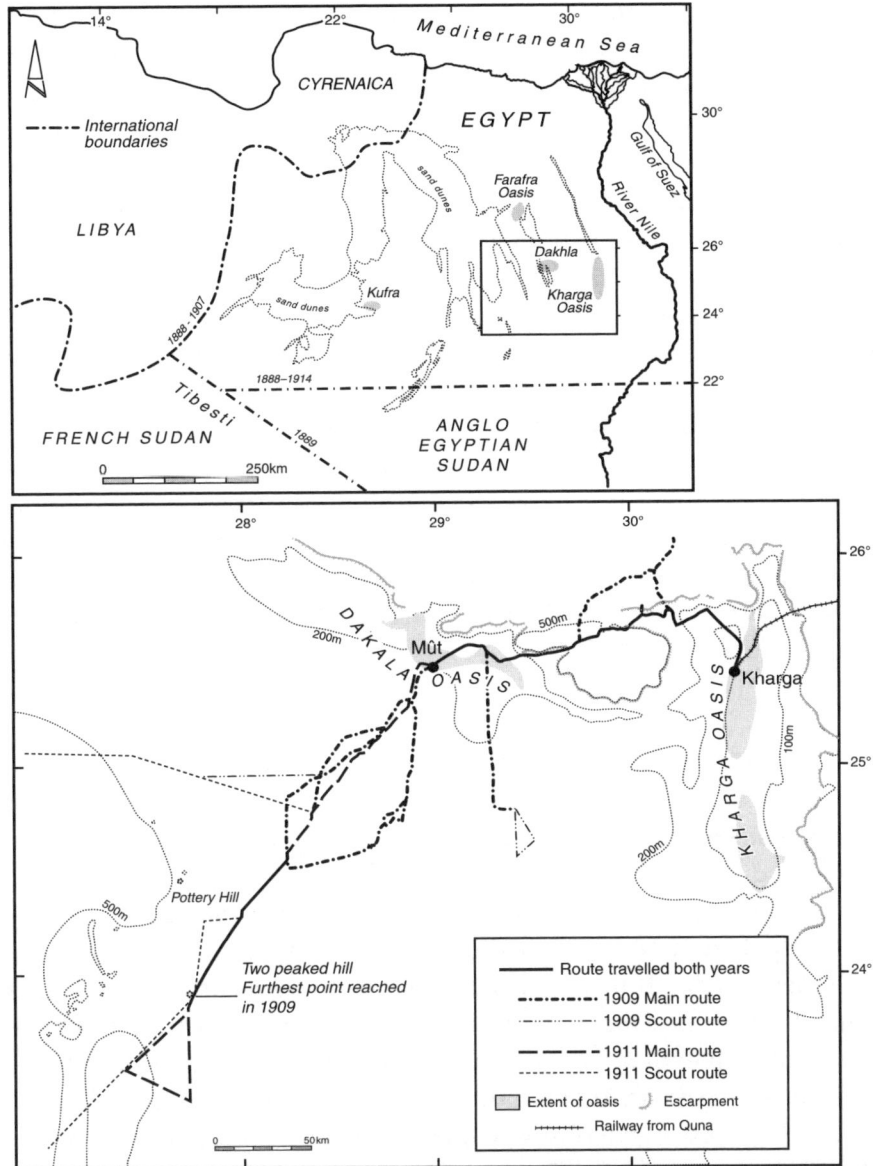

FIGURE 4.1 Map of routes taken on 1909 and 1911 expeditions by Harding King and his accompanying staff.

field Harding King demonstrated his eclectic range of interests. At the beginning of the first season, whilst acclimatising and establishing the route and organising the caravan for his journey, he undertook a series of scientific investigations concerned with the movement of sand and dune morphology. He developed this work in his second and third seasons, publishing his findings and engaging in a series of debates with academic geographers in Britain working in the burgeoning field of desert morphology.[23] The reputation he gained in this area resulted in his return to Egypt in 1913–14, employed by the Egyptian Government to apply his understanding of dune processes to the protection of the Cairo Sewage Works. Although Harding King clearly made a name for himself in connection with this work, his own primary purpose for going to Egypt was for the exploration he would undertake – the surveying and detailed observation of the people, places and environments through which he travelled, which had a 'sternly practical' colonial purpose.[24] In the discussion that follows we outline the reasons why surveying the Libyan Desert in all its 'geographical spheres', as Keltie described the totalising activity of Harding King's task, was a colonial imperative. We also chart the ways in which Harding King made sense of the desert and the debates that emerged as he disseminated his findings and attempted to make his reputation amongst the geographical establishment in Britain.

THE GEOPOLITICAL CONTEXT OF THE LIBYAN DESERT

In his first letter to Keltie indicating his desire to undertake observational and survey work, Harding King presented his prime purpose as one of creating a map with as much 'practical' information as possible. As Edney demonstrates, the cartographic survey was a critical imperial tool that enabled British imperial interests to be secured, if only for a limited period of time.[25] The British occupation of Egypt in 1882 and the establishment of Anglo-Egyptian Sudan in 1899, alongside nationalist pressures within Egypt and Italian and French ambitions in northeast Africa, set the geopolitical context of Harding King's travels. While the margins of the Libyan Desert were clearly recognisable within Western cartographic conventions and parts had been subject to survey by colonial officers working for the Department of Egyptian Survey, the relatively unknown interior had greatly attracted Harding King. Information about the interior of the vast desert sea was sparse, but the colonial European will to know and control this area was intense. For those indigenous groups who lived and operated in this space – particularly the political-religious order of the Senussi who maintained strong resistance to European colonial presence in the Libyan Desert – it was highly desirable that this space stayed beyond Western cartographic convention and control. As Harding King discovered, this resistance limited his ability to fulfil his own ambitions as his work unfolded.

Having been directed towards the Libyan Desert by Keltie, Harding King responded to the suggestion enthusiastically:

> I am very much taken with the idea of the Libyan Desert. I know at present very little about it, but I have been reading up during the last day or two and there is evidently a great deal of unexplored ground in the southern part ... There are also reported to be a number of oases that are as yet undiscovered. ... I will read up the subject of the Libyan Desert more thoroughly and then, if you could spare me the time, I would like to consult you as to the best place to go to.[26]

As the days progressed Harding King corresponded with Keltie about his proposed journey, and these letters reflect the constraints that he had to negotiate: an unwillingness to travel to the Tibesti region owing to the cost of such a journey and concerns for his safety travelling through Senussi-controlled territory. Although unwilling to take the more challenging option, Harding King identified that he could make a contribution to the production of practical knowledge about the more marginal areas of the Libyan Desert. Harding King's letters to Keltie reflect the relatively limited knowledge of the desert interior that was available at the time. Indeed, the majority of the reading he did would have illustrated the peculiar status of this region as a stubbornly unknowable space, with an imagined geography that was imbued with a romance of mystery; explorers were lured to find the 'lost oases of Zerzura' and Ptolemy's 'lake of mud tortoises'.[27] Prior to his departure Harding King consulted maps made by D'Anville (1697–1782), particularly his 1766 *Mémoires sur l'Egypte*, and also reviewed the travels of the German explorer and geographer Gerhard Rohlfs (1831–96), who had travelled into the Libyan Desert in the early 1870s.[28] Like his contemporaries, Harding King drew on a broad range of sources when attempting to understand and navigate its geography. It is of note that for those exploring the Libyan Desert in the first half of the twentieth century, discussion of 'older' classical European cartographers and geographers' work – Ptolemy in particular – remained strong. Harding King also referred to antiquarian manuscripts such as *The Book of Hidden Pearls*.[29] Although popularly associated with folklore, myth and intrigue, such books were scoured for geographical information that might be verified through careful survey and exploration work. As the hunt for the 'lost oases of Zerzura' took hold, such manuscripts were given greater prominence for the hints they might have given of places in an otherwise unknown space.[30]

Although presented as 'the unknown' at the time of Harding King's expeditions, the need to map and survey this region was already fully appreciated by the British Government, with members of the Egyptian Survey Department actively undertaking this task. The publication of *The Cadastral Survey of Egypt, 1892–1907* by the Survey's head, Captain H. G. Lyons, reflected the work that had been completed by his department.[31] The need to disseminate knowledge about the region was certainly felt by Lyons, who encouraged the launch of a new publication called *Survey Notes,* later to become the *Cairo Scientific Journal*, in 1906. This publication was designed to 'enable an outlet for members of his staff to publish their findings and observations about their work for the survey, enabling cross department communication', and it became the in-house journal for the Survey Department.[32] In the first editorial of the journal it was hoped that if members of the Survey shared their findings the Department would 'escape the famous satire of Swift, who observed of some primitive survey of this continent:

> So geographers, in Afric maps,
> With savage pictures fill their gaps,
> And o-er uninhabitable downs,
> Place elephants for want of towns.'[33]

The work of the Egyptian Survey Department, similar in purpose to the legendary Survey of India, harnessed both professional surveyors working for the department, alongside Army personnel sponsored under their auspices, to undertake surveys of the British-Egyptian interests. Surveys were not simply designed to secure colonial boundaries; they were required for administrative and cadastral purposes and to provide strategic information linked to the development of commerce and the maintenance of security from threats, hence the need for detailed topographic maps that would be of use to those travelling over land.[34] Surveys therefore incorporated geopolitical, economic and administrative intentions and information. However, one of the main challenges to the Colonial Office was the shortage of skilled surveyors to undertake the activity. The RGS emerged in the nineteenth century as a key provider of survey advice and training for students, prospective colonial officers and private individuals.[35] The encouragement and sponsorship given to Harding King by the RGS to undertake survey work in the Libyan Desert was indicative of the role the Society played in training suitable candidates, but also points to the shortage of professional surveyors during that period.[36]

Harding King's goal to undertake trigonometric survey, alongside the collection of 'practical' information, reflects his participation in the geopolitical discourse of surveying. Harding King also described the topography he saw on his journeys, detailing in particular the type of sand underfoot and the difficulty of the terrain. Such topographical information on maps was critical for land travellers, both in terms of the terrain to be covered and also for the location of resources to replenish supplies. Thus Harding King placed great emphasis throughout his travels on the identification of oases and water supplies and often supervised his staff digging holes to discover the height of the water table.

Harding King's efforts to identify water sources and useful strategic information led him to exert considerable effort collecting what he called 'native information': knowledge held by local people about water sources, desert roads, topographical features and the days and direction it would take to get to certain points. Such information was to form a useful basis for future mapping exercises of a more systematic nature. In addition to his mapping-related survey work Harding King undertook a wide variety of collecting and observational activities throughout his travels. He collected head measurements and ethnographic data of people 'who have not I think been done before', alongside oral folklore, songs and population data.[37] In addition, he made botanical, zoological and geological collections; copied rock inscriptions; noted camel brandings; and made descriptions of settlements and dwellings and the encounters he had with people in them. From Harding King's eclectic collections and interests we can see several threads that were of colonial importance, from the production of maps that would aid the Army in securing Egypt's borders to the commercial interests of those involved in agriculture.

Harding King's work in the Libyan Desert was made possible not only through the backing of institutions such as the RGS, but also from local employees whom he hired to guide and support his journeys. Although these men are rendered anonymous in his writings in *The Geographical Journal*, they played a central part, as named individuals, within Harding King's more popular travelogue, *Mysteries of the Libyan Desert* (1925), where their participation within the expeditions was discussed at great length, sometimes with ambivalence, at other times with great affection, but always set against an airy, authoritative, objectifying colonial discourse. Harding King maintained some staff throughout his different seasons' work. His cook and interpreter, Dahab, and two camel drivers, Abd er Rahman and Ibrahim, were all highly trusted and performed multiple functions within the party. Each acted as scouts or guides and alongside their main duties kept watch for the security of the party during sleeping hours. Harding King employed two principal guides: Qway, the principal guide for Harding King's first and second seasons, and Qwaytin, the guide for his final expedition. The importance of these members of his staff is conveyed by Harding King's photograph of them together (see Figure 4.2).

* * * * *

Jane Camerini has highlighted the crucial role played by local employees in the efforts of Europeans working overseas, and Harding King is no exception.[38] His dependency on others was always highly visible in the letters he wrote to Keltie and is also apparent from his book. This was particularly of note with reference to the role of the guide who would ultimately be responsible for keeping the party safe within the desert region. Harding King describes his exhaustive but often unsuccessful attempts to hire guides with first-hand local knowledge and experience of travelling the routes he intended to take. Moreover, Harding King trained his guides in the use of the survey equipment and used them to help his survey of the desert region that they crossed. The guides would scout routes and undertake visual surveys of areas that Harding King did not get to, which were duly recorded. In addition, Harding King would question his guides about their own local knowledge, recording the observations they made. Although attracted

FIGURE 4.2 Harding King, photograph of expedition guides Qway and Qwaytin

by the language of venturing into 'the unknown', Harding King was well aware that he was following familiar paths for those living in the region, and while he might be the first to map the region, he was by no means a lone explorer penetrating 'virgin' territory.

MAKING SENSE OF THE LIBYAN DESERT

On arrival in Cairo in 1908 Harding King sought local expertise to assist the planning phase of his expedition. Following a discussion with Captain Lyons, Director of the Egyptian Survey, Harding King reported his planned intentions to Keltie at the RGS:

> I propose to ... start from the pyramids and strike across country to Dakhla or Farafra, that what appear to be unsurveyed portion of the desert and then to start from one of these oases off westwards into the dune belt to try and find any oases, routes or wells there may be there and if possible to find a road right across. I cannot make any definite plans as the whole of this country appears to be entirely unexplored.[39]

The exact plan for Harding King's first journey kept changing as he discussed his intentions with people on the ground in Egypt, particularly members of the Egyptian Survey Department such as John Ball who had experience of the sort of desert expedition that Harding King was proposing. Writing to Keltie from Cairo, Harding King reported:

> My plans with regard to Libya are rather unsettled at present. It is a much more difficult job than I expected. I had not realised that all the dunes between Egypt and Kenya are probably longitudinal; i.e. at right angles to the E/W route. These dunes from what I hear, if they extend for any distance, would be almost impassable for a laden caravan, as the camels have to be helped up the slopes and they can't stand the strain for long ... I have not of course seen these dunes yet, so cannot form an opinion myself. I don't much believe in 'impossibilities' but I can see that is going to be a very difficult job – and I expect I shall make two or three bad shots before I pull it off.[40]

Harding King's discussions with Ball certainly resulted in him making a less ambitious journey, taking the newly opened railway to the Kharga oases on the desert margins and starting his surveying expedition from there. Following the completion of his first field season in early August 1909, Harding King reported triumphantly to Keltie:

> I have covered altogether something over 1000 miles, nearly all of which was over unsurveyed and most of it over unexplored ground, but I am afraid you will think my 'bag' very disappointing, as I have not found a single oasis. I kept up a prismatic compass survey, checked by astronomical observation nearly all the way. ... The farthest point

I reached was only about 150 miles SW of Dakhla. I had hoped to get very much farther but really the work is rather difficult. I suppose this is the least known part of Africa. The maps are all blank and I could get no definite information at all from the natives.[41]

The first season that Harding King spent in Cairo and the Libyan Desert established the purpose for the remaining travels he would make and resulted in an increased awareness of the utility of his survey work. Reflecting on his first season Harding King responded to the political context of his travels and placed geopolitical concerns at the centre of his subsequent journeys. For Harding King the continued security of Egypt required strategic control of the desert regions, including detailed knowledge of roads and resources to traverse the desert. The desire and search for this knowledge brought him into conflict with members of the Senussi whom, Harding King noted disingenuously: 'it would be useless to tell ... that I had come out in the interests of abstract science'.[42] Reporting to the RGS following his first season, Harding King's communication was reflective of his perception of the geopolitical context of his work:

> Having found a fairly easy sand free road between Dakhla and Kufra will probably be useful later on. The Senussi are said to have designs on Egypt and there was a report in Dakhla when I was there that the Senussi Makdi was going to reappear and proclaim a jehad if things got really serious in Turkey. It was really in consequence of this that I went out for my last trip. I had not intended to spend the Khaussin in the desert and my food had come to an end, but I thought I had better see if there was any sand further out than I had been[,] to prevent the Senussi coming in, in force, to Egypt via Dakhla.[43]

In his second season, Harding King desired to extend his first journey and intended to 'push as far as possible along the old road to the south-west of Dakhla, that we had already followed for about 150 miles, hoping to find an oasis'.[44] His hope was that he might continue his journey into the French Sudan. One of the geopolitical aims of this trip was to see if the route was still usable and, if not, whether it could be made so through the digging of new wells. The aim he professed would be to get 'a considerable hold over the inaccessible tribes of the interior and at the same time be a severe blow to the Senussi'.[45] Harding King's incursions into the borderland of Senussi territory did not go unnoticed. Although Harding King had asked the

RGS not to publicise his first journey in the newspapers in an attempt to be incognito, he noted in his letters that this approach backfired and local suspicion about his intentions was rife. Certainly Harding King seemed to be more fearful and cautious about the Senussi in this journey, and his handling of the men in his camp indicated his unease. In later reflections on the second season, Harding King put the plentiful disasters firmly at the door of the Senussi, from his difficulty in buying barley for the camels' feed ('the barley boycott that the Senussi had engineered against me') to the 'tampering' of his trusted guide Qway, resulting in the spoiling of water and food supplies in the desert, which was a near-fatal incident. Due to the problems encountered on the way, the second season did not go well and Harding King ventured no further than he had done in his previous expedition. Commenting on this he noted: 'The Senussi had certainly won the first trick in the game.'[46]

Harding King's final season saw him change track and, accepting that crossing the desert into the French Sudan was impractical, he instead 'set out to explore as much as possible of the unknown parts of the eastern and western side of the huge depression in which lies the oasis of Farafra'.[47] Although a change of direction, Harding King's designs on thwarting the Senussi were still uppermost in his mind and he later described one of the objects of this journey as being 'to score a trick of the Senussia [sic] by making a dash into the dunes to the south-west of Farafra and locating the oasis of Dendura that was used sometimes by them as a half-way house when travelling from Egypt to Kufra'.[48] To assist him in finding practical information on this trip, he hired a local guide, Qwaytin. Harding King quickly realised that Qwaytin could impart a considerable amount of information about unknown parts of the desert 'when he was inclined to be communicative'. However, Harding King's intention to 'pump Qwaytin as dry as I could of the information he would give me' met with resistance; Harding King recorded his irritation as Qwaytin gave erroneous information, or refused to talk when he took his notepad out and started writing.[49] Undeterred, Harding King described the ways in which he tried to trick Qwaytin into providing him information and how he asked questions a few days later to corroborate what he had been told. It would appear that Qwaytin had ulterior motives for travelling with Harding King, who recorded that after a few days into their journey Qwaytin had revealed a book that purportedly recorded a site where treasure had been hidden. Resigned to the inevitability that this would change his objectives, Harding King made the most of his guide's desire for treasure seeking and followed him to a place called Bu Gerara where, as it was reputed to be a fertile spot, Harding King got his men to dig a hole, not for treasure but for water. They found neither.

Harding King's dealing with members of his staff, the Senussi and the inhabitants along his route, reveals much about the politics of encounter and exchange within exploration and travel. We can see Harding King appropriating local knowledge into his work, but while he did so he also acknowledged its origin, and his openness of the source of his information (whether Qway or Qwaytin) was clearly expressed. This was, however, an exchange that both Harding King and his staff continuously negotiated, with varying dimensions of power being held at any one time by each party. Although Harding King was the colonising subject, his position was at no point uncontested by those he travelled amongst in the field. In his final field season Harding King reported that his guides and caravan were infiltrated by Senussi ideas at one of their stopping points, which came to a head when, as Harding King described it, he walked into a 'Senussi trap' and struggled to avoid mutiny with his men in the caravan.[50] The event clearly left him feeling very insecure and resulted in a hasty (and sleep-deprived) retreat to safety during the five-day journey from Bu Mungar to Dakhla. Indeed, he noted 'it was not until we got to Mut that I felt I could trust my men enough to risk being caught asleep[,] even while inhabiting the old store, Dahab and I took it in turns to keep watch during the night'.[51] This was the last expedition of this nature that Harding King undertook.

MAKING REPUTATIONS

David Livingstone has noted that 'the circulation of scientific knowledge was an inescapably *social* affair involving judgement about people'.[52] While planning his journeys and undertaking his work in Egypt and the Libyan Desert, Harding King had gained the support of key institutions (such as the RGS) and individuals (for example John Ball) that was required to enable him to undertake his work with credibility. On his return home, he was judged not by his enthusiasm for the work, but by the value of the knowledge he had collected. David Livingstone has noted the importance of asking how knowledge moves 'from the peculiarities of the site of its production to communal exchange'.[53] In Harding King's case this is a pertinent consideration as the value of his knowledge and his position within the academy were often contested. The tensions and anxieties he experienced in terms of making a positive reputation for himself as a scientific explorer can be charted in the documents associated with his subsequent publications. Harding King's position outside of the Egyptian Survey, the British Army and academic geographical establishment meant he was forced to build and defend his reputation without the associated credibility that others gained from their position within such institutional networks. Individuals concerned with the Libyan Desert who questioned his work included Captain Lyons, the Director of the Egyptian Survey Department, and Vaughan Cornish, one of the early British academic arid zone specialists. However, Harding King did enjoy greater credibility with other figures familiar with the Libyan Desert region, such as Ralph Bagnold, N. B. De Lancey Forth and John Ball. Harding King's reputation was bolstered by the support of officials within the RGS, particularly Keltie's successor as Secretary, Arthur Hinks. However, the RGS also became the site where some of the most prominent negotiations over Harding King's reputation were played out. On the whole, Harding King was promoted within the Society as a specialist in the region, long after he had finished travelling in the area, and was generally to be found on the panel of discussants at evening meetings of the RGS when a lecture on the region was under discussion.[54] Although Harding King published some of his work shortly after his expeditions, he extended the use of his data until his last publication in 1931.[55] Although he acknowledged the 'historic' nature of his material, it did not prevent him from presenting papers for publication to the RGS, and the appearance of these in the Society's *Geographical Journal* reflects both the continued support he had from the Society and the apparent relevance that his work continued to have long after his field seasons. Some of the tensions that surrounded the reception of his work long after the completion of his field activities were due to his status as an armchair expert amongst those who were actively working in the field and reviewing his work.

Following his first two field seasons, Harding King submitted a paper and map titled 'Travels in the Libyan Desert' for publication in *The Geographical Journal*.[56] The editor of *The Geographical Journal*, John Scott Keltie, requested peer review comments on submitted articles and then fed back comments to the author, identifying the reviewer by name. The correspondence between Harding King, the editor and the reviewers indicated the tensions around the value of the knowledge that Harding King claimed to have produced. Harding King emerged as an author who was highly sensitive to criticism and would defend himself against an unfavourable review with dogmatic belligerence. We see this attitude in his response to the comments made by Lyons when asked to review Harding King's paper. Although reviewed in haste shortly before a return journey to Egypt and without reference to the map that Harding King had enclosed with the paper, Lyons' comments point out the level of activity in the region and the competition that Harding King faced in his work. Harding King took offence to Lyons' review, which started with the opening statement: 'I suppose this is a summary to be printed much fuller as it cannot represent the results of 2 winters travel.'[57] Harding King clearly felt this was a 'low blow' and made great pains to find out if Lyons had seen his maps with the full extent of his travels in reviewing his article. Overall, Lyons felt that the paper was scant, failed to compare adequately Harding King's findings to others' work in the region, including members of Lyons' own survey team such as H. J. Llewellyn Beadnell, and failed to place the journey in the context of existing knowledge from earlier travels. Review comments that Harding King took badly included: 'Seems a bold assumption on slender evidence'; 'is this the road I followed from Mut?'; 'But this scarp has been surveyed so appearance here not much value'; 'this is new and should be very fully described – not enough altitudes given'; and 'I found the eastern boundary on Mut-Ferfawt road so by comparison of all data a closer description could be made.'[58] It would appear that a letter sent by Harding King immediately after receipt of the review contained a rather personal attack on Lyons in response to his comments, and the ensuing correspondence over the following months escalated the normal review process into something of a controversy.[59] Reflecting on his heated response some months later Harding King commented, 'I must admit I was badly annoyed at being told I had been trying to palm off other men's work as my own' and that Lyons' commentary 'claimed to have first surveyed ground already done by himself or his dept, when it was only necessary to compare our routes to prove that this is not the case'.[60]

These exchanges clearly positioned Harding King as a man defending his reputation against the might of the Egyptian Survey. Keltie tried to calm the debate by reminding Harding King that Lyons had not seen his map and that he only saw the paper the night before he left 'so of course he read it hurriedly. He did not see your map at all. I shall of course let him see that when he returns.'[61] However, Harding King had clearly been affronted and requested that 'it would be much more to the point if he either proved his criticisms to be correct or withdrew them, which he could do at present – without the slightest loss of prestige. Surely he must see this is necessary.'[62] A bemused Lyons, and a rather despairing editor, responded to Harding King's defence of his reputation by soothing his brow. Lyons stated that he had not seen the map and that he simply thought with a little more detail the paper 'could easily be enlarged and improved so as to be a valuable addition to desert geography'.[63] Meanwhile, Keltie declared that Lyons was not being personal and that Harding King should not be so sensitive to criticism, adding 'Capt Lyons is one of the most courteous and considerate men that I know and is incapable of any such animus as you seem to attribute to him.'[64] The matter was finally laid to rest ten months after the initial review, following a meeting between Lyons and Harding King of which the latter reported: 'there seems to have been a good deal of misunderstanding' and having discussed the matter thoroughly 'we understand each other perfectly'.[65] The beleaguered paper went to press in February 1912.

Harding King's sensitivity to criticism was a recurrent feature of his dealings with the RGS, to the extent that Harding King framed a paper he submitted in 1913 with the comment: 'May I hear any criticisms directed to the map and paper I left today? I do not want to involve you in any dispute that may occur about it, but if this paper is criticised in the way my last two were I shall take steps that will I think effectively prevent anything of the kind in the future.'[66] As the years passed subsequent correspondence between King and the editor drew attention to the problems of wartime publication. Harding King appeared to have seen it as his duty to support *The Geographical Journal* during this time, submitting many short papers on his work. Harding King even gave the impression that his contributions to the journal amounted to his own war effort, as, much to his annoyance, he had been rejected from taking part in active service. Furthermore, it was also helpful for Harding King that he could publish his papers as his planned book on his travels was held up due to the war.[67]

In 1919 Harding King was awarded the RGS Gill Memorial for his investigations of desert conditions in Northern Africa.[68] He was nominated by Hinks, Secretary of the Society, and the minutes of the awards meeting noted he had contributed several papers over the years linked to desert science. Given the company that Harding King kept during that year's medal ceremony (the highly esteemed physical geographer William Morris Davies was the Victorian Gold Medal holder), it is of note that the RGS drew attention to Harding King's scientific work on 'sand dunes and sand motion', rather than his more descriptive articles that had given fodder for *The Geographical Journal* in the war period.[69] The RGS also used Harding King as a reviewer for others' work. In 1921 the RGS approached him in a deferential way 'as an experienced desert traveller', asking for his opinion on Rosita Forbes' paper of her travels in the Libyan Desert.[70] Harding King offered an enthusiastic response to her paper, but noted in a light-hearted aside: 'I suppose the lady members are now going to take on all this kind of work and the mere men will be reduced to mapping alterations in the British Coast line!', a reminder of the contested debates around the inclusion of women within the Society and their position as legitimate travellers that had dogged the RGS in previous decades.[71]

Harding King's correspondence with the RGS reflects the fact that he kept continuously up to date with activities in the Libyan Desert, responding to articles in the *Times* and *The Geographical Journal*, and in personal correspondence with people who were active in the region. Harding King maintained a close eye on his own reputation in the 1920s. He continued to feel his work had currency, and that the explorations that were being undertaken were only starting to touch what he regarded as the ground-breaking work he had undertaken over a decade before. It was perhaps something of a thrill for him to consider that members of the British Army were finally making headway, using more advanced technology, such as vehicles with caterpillar tracks, than he had been able to use, and were finally filling in the gaps he had identified.⁷² Although fascinated by the emergence of new knowledge, he was also anxious to maintain his reputation, and pounced on articles that he felt covered his findings. Such an example is a paper by Sarsfield Hall published in 1920 that presented a way of accurately mapping 'native information', a specialism that Harding King felt to be his own. Hinks – clearly used to Harding King's approach – refused to allow a controversy to escalate, pointing out the difference between Sarsfield Hall's work and his own.⁷³ On this occasion, Harding King submitted and replied in a self-deprecating manner, declaring: 'I doubt if much good would come by raising the question of those papers of mine on the Libyan Desert now, as they are getting to be such very ancient history.'⁷⁴

Although dated, the years did not stop Harding King from publishing new material based on his travels. Indeed his work had currency as a new generation of explorers were making use of such material to make further incursions into the Libyan Desert.⁷⁵ Harding King was in a position to capitalise on this renewed activity in the region and sustained another decade of publications on the back of it. A paper titled the 'The Dakhla – Owenat Road' published in 1925 is reflective of the work that Harding King presented for publication in this period.⁷⁶ Illustrated with images from his expedition previously lodged with the RGS (see Figure 4.3) he based this article on work he had undertaken in 1909 and wrote to the RGS pointing out: 'I wish someone would try for Owanat from the East – from what I heard, there are several places waiting to be found there.'⁷⁷ It is interesting to reflect on Harding King's motives here, in publishing dated material framed in a way that suggested both his research and the area was still worthy of further consideration. In response Hinks thanked Harding King for his paper, noting that 'I believe that John Ball and his Egyptian Prince are going to tackle it this Spring in a caterpillar car.'⁷⁸ John Ball was someone with whom Harding King kept in touch, and it is entirely plausible that Harding King was cementing his prior claims to knowledge through this paper.

* * * * *

Although the editors of *The Geographical Journal* turned a blind eye to the dated nature of Harding King's journal articles, others in the field

FIGURE 4.3 Harding King, 'Remains of the Dakhla – Owenat Road' (courtesy of the Royal Geographical Society, image S0015289).

were less forgiving to the delayed outputs. Despite referring to his own work as 'antiquated' Harding King secured a book contract and brought together his work on the Libyan Desert for publication in 1925, romantically titled *Mysteries of the Libyan Desert*.[79] The book generated discussion amongst those exploring the area. Francis Rodd requested the book prior to its publication and Douglas Newbold wrote to Rodd asking 'Have you seen the petroglyths in the appendix to Harding King's book *Mysteries of the Libyan Desert*, an exasperating book, but with points of great interest?'[80] Rodd went on to write a review of the book for *The Geographical Journal* in which he opened with the dismissive line: 'Mr Harding King has at last given us an account of his journey before the war in the Libyan Desert' and ended by telling the readers 'In conclusion, it is only fair to state that had fortune been kinder to Mr Harding King he would have rendered geography a much greater service than he was able to do in the course of his journeys, which, through no fault of his own, were not productive of sensational results.'[81]

Rodd's principal complaint was that Harding King had presented his book as an account of his scientific explorations, but that it failed to fulfil this claim, offering instead a lively, popular travelogue. In turn, Harding King was incensed by Rodd's review and a full file relating to the 'controversy' that ensued can be found in the RGS's archives. From Rodd's perspective Harding King failed to negotiate the path between sensationalism and science and noted that had it been 'a superficial book of a sensational or sporting character, I should have refrained from this criticism'.[82] However, the presentation of scientific work within the book warranted, in Rodd's view, a critical review for a journal coming from a scientific society such as the RGS.

Harding King responded to Rodd in deeply personal tones, arguing that his book had been taken out of context. His arguments linked to this point are interesting in terms of how he perceived the value of his work:

> Mr Rodd, perhaps naturally, does not at all realise the pre-war conditions in the Libyan Desert. The Senussi had an extraordinary influence then, hardly a native would go against them. They *only* knew the desert beyond the frontier and were extremely secretive. Guides to show one anything there were consequently unprocurable. The map was a sheet of blank paper, so there was no known objective. In my last year I was able to get a lot of information (almost entirely from one man) upon which I could have acted, if I had had it earlier – but it came too late. The Senussi from the background did all they could to hamper one and I was told that not even moslems [sic] could go to Kufra, unless they conducted them there. How in these circumstances could I be expected to get 'one exact description' of their secret roads to Kufra! No! Rodd expects too much.[83]

Such reflections are revealing of the role that local informants played in allowing Western travellers like Harding King access to the desert, and the agency that others exerted in controlling their movements. We are reminded again of Harding King's reliance on indigenous people for knowledge of the desert, but also his sense that others were using their knowledge of the locality to defy him or hamper his activities.

Harding King was deeply upset by the RGS, noting that he had given them all his best scientific material, leaving little for the book, and felt a sense of injustice that they should have done his book such a great disservice as to publish a poor review. Rodd responded to Harding King's concerns in a letter to Hinks pointing to the fact that reviews in

The Geographical Journal were not meant to be marketing material and refused to give in to Harding King's viewpoint, noting:

> I am as convinced that his book is superficial as he is convinced that my review is superficial. My feelings are of disappointment that a book which has been delayed for over ten years from appearing should contain so much lack of scholarliness. However I have no intention of labouring the matter.[84]

In extended exchanges of points (sometimes labouring 17 points in a single letter) Rodd and Harding King battled out the detail of Rodd's critique. Although these exchanges reached farcical proportions neither Harding King nor Rodd were willing to concede. As Hinks tried to bring the controversy to a close, Harding King continued to provide evidence to refute Rodd's claims and undermine his lack of position as an authority, drawing on others such as John Ball (who was by that time Director of Desert Surveys, Egypt) to bolster his position. Drawing attention to private correspondence he had received from Ball, Harding King noted to Hinks:

> I cannot publish the information as it is in a private letter but I heard a few days ago from John Ball that on a car journey he recorded some relics of Rohlfs' from the middle of the dune field west of Dakhla. He also says 'you were right about a lot of the dunes ending at your scarp' so I am not at all anxious on this point! With Prince Kemal el Din and his cars, he has reached Owanat from the East and found that place, Merga, I said was there.[85]

The controversy linked to the *Mysteries of the Libyan Desert* eventually petered out, and in the final years of his life he continued to play a prominent part in discussions linked to the Libyan Desert at the RGS. This gained pace as the hunt for Zerzura occupied the years of desert exploration at the end of the 1920s into the 1930s. Harding King followed the activities of the Army desert explorers and official surveyors of the time, corresponding with some, reading commentary in the newspapers about others. He used correspondence with the RGS Secretary to convey his opinions on their explorations, noting where his own activities bore relevance and proffering advice, clearly assuming that the RGS would pass it on to the relevant people. Harding King continued to publish articles from his own work which had currency and gained a public accolade for his pre-war survey work from John Ball, Director of Egyptian Survey in 1927, who praised the quality and geopolitical significance of his work.[86] As the hunt for the lost oasis of Zerzura gained prominence, he contributed an article to the discussion titled 'The Lost Oasis of the Libyan Desert'.[87] In 1929 Hinks sought his assistance in publishing a collection of papers for *The Geographical Journal* titled 'The Zerzura Problem' and, perhaps characteristically, Harding King reviewed papers on the results of survey, together with Johnson Pasha's discussion of the likely whereabouts of Zerzura based on an Arabic manuscript.[88]

CONCLUSION

Although his reputation was contested, Harding King managed to maintain his authority as a 'desert expert' long after his travels had ended. Clearly the role of the RGS and latterly the support of John Ball were critical in legitimating his position. However, the diverse membership of the Society at the time enabled him to be treated with respect when he did not tread too deeply in unfamiliar waters. It is notable that the aspects of work in which he continued to be active were those connected to his surveying and exploration, rather than those linked to scientific experiments on sand movement. While he had published credible papers in this area and would later be noted for his pioneering studies by Bagnold in his seminal 1941 work *The Physics of Blown Sand and Desert Dunes*, Harding King was unwilling or unable to engage with areas of geographical science that had become highly professional during the years since his field studies.[89] Ultimately, Harding King could maintain a reputation in an area that was less fiercely defended by members linked to the academic geographical establishment, and was in a position to garner support from members of the Society who had engaged in exploration and surveying in a similar fashion to his early expeditions. The division reflected the growing schism in the RGS as it sought to satisfy an increasingly diverse membership of academic and amateur geographers in the first half of the twentieth century.[90]

It is also worth remembering that it was the location in which Harding King travelled that shaped this uneasy negotiation of nineteenth- and twentieth-century science. The Libyan Desert was an inhospitable region for a traveller on a camel (or indeed the snowshoes that Harding King experimented with on occasion) in the early twentieth century. The environment and technologies of travel limited the production of knowledge, and would do so until there were major advances in technology – notably aerial surveying and, in the second half of the twentieth century, remote sensing. Harding King's work in the early twentieth century was that of reconnaissance mixed with rough trigonometric survey work, which would enable others to follow and complete more accurate surveys. His position outside the formal structures of the Egyptian Survey clearly irked Captain Lyons, although it must be noted that Harding King used the services of the Survey to help compute measurements and was directed by their advice. Harding King was simultaneously supported and subdued by the same colonial institution. These politics of place and knowledge were played out at many levels, whether between Harding King and his staff, the national level politics of the Senussi experienced first hand by Harding King, or the institutional politics of the RGS.

Harding King's activities reveal the attempts he made to travel with a scientific purpose, conforming to the expectations of a geographer at the time. His attempts to work in a systematic way, directed by Keltie to collect all things that come into a 'Geographical sphere', resulted in what seems – certainly to a twenty-first century audience – an extraordinarily wide range of interests and information. His publications ranged from popular travelogues, descriptive accounts of his journeys, to precise topographical discussions linked to surveys and discussions of modelling sand movement processes. Although encouraged by influential RGS figures such as Keltie and Hinks, this eclecticism ran counter to the growing specialism of academic geography at the time, and his writing lacked the scientific objectivity and rigour that professionals in the sphere were looking for. Harding King is thus a revealing figure through which to explore the tension between professional and amateur, and the different distinctions and privileges given to those travelling and working in colonial spaces such as Egypt in the early twentieth century.

Harding King enjoyed a long career out of a limited number of field seasons and he was fortunate that the region in which he travelled remained so current throughout his life owing to the slow advances in desert exploration and European colonial geopolitics. Although he enthusiastically followed advances in knowledge that were reported, Harding King also mourned the passing of the particular mode of exploration that he had enjoyed. The preface to his book *The Mysteries of the Libyan Desert* reflected his nostalgia and the lure that the desert continued to hold over him:

> The Libyan Desert, that in the past has to a great extent defied the efforts of all its explorers, is bound before long to give up its secrets. Suitably designed cars, accompanied perhaps by a scouting plane, are enemies against which even the most avid desert is defenceless, though one cannot but regret the necessity for such prosaic mechanical aids, they unquestionably afford an ideal method of conducting long pioneer explorations in a waterless desert. But these things have only recently been invented, and there are still many problems that remain unsolved as to 'what lies hid behind the ridges' in the vast area that we know as the Libyan Desert, and speculation is so full of fascination, that it seems almost a pity that those problems should ever be solved.[91]

The role of the RGS in supporting exploratory work did not end in the first half of the twentieth century. Indeed, Harding King is one of the many figures who were supported by the Society. Although the discourse of 'exploration' subsequently shifted to that of 'expedition', the RGS continued to sponsor individuals and groups wishing to undertake travel with a purpose (as it continues to do today). Indeed, it is poignant to end this discussion with a letter written to the Secretary of the Society in 1939 by Harding King's son, requesting the Society direct him in the right way to obtain experience so he might 'follow in his [father's] footsteps'. The acting Secretary replied to this letter:

> Before being able to join an expedition it would probably be necessary to have some specialised knowledge of survey or other field subject and I suggest you might come into the Society's house and consult Mr Flower our Instructor in Survey.[92]

5 Fieldwork and the geographical career: T. Griffith Taylor and the exploration of Australia

Simon Naylor

For the likes of the Halford Mackinder and Joseph Conrad, the early twentieth century was witness to the passing of the era of geographical discovery. For Mackinder, Reader in Geography at the University of Oxford, the 500-year period of 'Columbian' exploration reached its conclusion in the first years of the century. Meanwhile, Joseph Conrad suggested in an article in the *National Geographic* in 1924 that the era of 'Geography Militant' – the quest for empirical knowledge about the earth through voyages of exploration by sea and land – was superseded by 'Geography Triumphant' – 'the irreversible closure of the epoch of open spaces, the end of an era of unashamed heroism'.[1] As the other essays in this book demonstrate, this attitude was by no means held by everyone. Indeed, Conrad's own essay was included alongside articles documenting various forms of geographical and anthropological exploration and discovery. The announcement of the passing of Geography Militant was therefore, Driver notes, somewhat premature.[2]

Geographical institutions like the Royal Geographical Society, the Société de Géographie of Paris, the Scottish Geographical Society and the American Geographical Society continued to promote exploration as their *raison d'être* well into the twentieth century; their meetings and journals replete with records of the recent exploratory endeavours of their members. Forms of geographical education, from schools to universities, also promoted the subject as training in exploratory skills – practical skills that were necessary for the furtherance of empire and the colonisation and settlement of land.[3] This chapter examines the arguments for precisely this sort of geographical education, by one of the most important figures in the geographical discipline in the first half of the twentieth century: T. Griffith Taylor – leading proponent of 'environmental determinism' and the holder of university positions in three different countries and the founder of geography departments in two of them. Throughout his career Taylor promoted fieldwork, travel and exploration as foundational elements in geographical education, and as the only proper bases for any theorisation concerning natural or human processes. Indeed, it was the geographer's ability to operate properly and effectively in the field that lent them the authority to speak of the things witnessed there and so too to gainsay the contrary claims of others.

In considering Taylor's claims over the centrality of exploration and fieldwork in the geographical discipline in the 1920s, the chapter contributes to a wider set of debates concerning the history of fieldwork. Although historians of biology like Robert Kohler have highlighted the increasing dominance of the laboratory over the fieldsite by the late nineteenth century, geography, along with subjects like anthropology, geology, ecology and archaeology, continued to place great emphasis on the study of phenomena *in situ* and in all its messiness.[4] Historians of science over the last decade or so have devoted considerable effort to understanding the histories and cultures of these 'practices of place', to use Kohler's term.[5] In the introduction to their volume, *Science in the Field*, Kuklick and Kohler have laid out an agenda from which any history of the field might orient itself:

> We must attend to the exigencies of getting to and staying in the field; to the affective aspects of natural places; to the heterogeneity of field science workers and tasks; and to the chronic issues of status and credibility that derive from the social and methodological tension between laboratory and field standards of evidence and reasoning. We must see how practitioners deal with the difficulties

of bringing some order to phenomena that, far more than those of the laboratory, are multivariate, historically produced, often fleeting, and dauntingly complex and uncontrollable.[6]

Questions of authority and claims to truth; of morality, movement and heroism; and of method, measurement and representation have preoccupied those who have attempted to provide robust histories of fieldwork and exploration. Historians have shown that fieldworkers gained the ability to make convincing truth claims through their exhibition of certain social and moral characteristics and the practice of a variety of scientific procedures. In relation to the former, the fieldworker tended to base their reputation as a reliable source on their social position – up to the mid-nineteenth century as the leisured gentleman but increasingly as the trained professional – as well as on their moral attributes: gendered attributes such as manly heroism, valour, physical robustness, fortitude and the eschewal of extravagance.[7] The reputations of polar explorers, as Baigent shows elsewhere in this volume, relied on precisely these moral attributes to lend credibility to their claims, alongside those operating in other demanding environments such as mountains, deserts and the tropics.[8] Unlike their equivalents cosseted away in the laboratory, explorers overcame geographical trials by getting to, operating in and extricating themselves from the field, and in so doing lent themselves – in their own eyes at least – a certain moral superiority.

While the explorer's recourse to moral attributes as the basis of their ability to make truth claims was often a defensive reaction to an alternative moral position put forward by laboratory scientists, their reference to forms of method and measurement were quite the opposite – attempts, in fact, to turn the fieldsite into a laboratory in its own right. Historians of science have traced the variety of ways in which fieldworkers have attempted to replicate laboratory conditions in the singular and irreducible spaces of the field.[9] Scholars have examined the use of various forms of transportation in the field, whether the ship, the airplane, the car or the bicycle.[10] They have highlighted the increasing reliance on a plethora of technologies for the observation of fleeting phenomena – the deployment of recording technologies and practices of description and dissemination, not to mention the correct performance of certain field methods.[11] It was through the correct use of these technologies and techniques that scientific explorers were able to counter claims by laboratory scientists that fieldwork was always necessarily dogged by idiosyncrasy and irreproducibility, and at the same time to distinguish themselves from others they were forced to share the field with, such as the journalist, the tourist and the adventurer.

This chapter engages with a range of these issues in the context of Taylor's exploration of Australia in the 1920s, during his tenure as Professor of Geography at the University of Sydney. For Taylor, fieldwork was the most important means by which geographical knowledges of both people and place could be acquired. This is discussed with reference to Taylor's exploration of northern Queensland and the Northern Territory in 1922. For Taylor, fieldwork was also important as an arena in which one learnt geographical skills – practices of movement, observation and subsistence. It also lent the fieldworker the ability to speak authoritatively about place and place-based processes. Taylor's disagreement with the claims of another explorer, Vilhjalmur Stefansson, upon his visit to Australia in 1924, is used to illustrate this. The chapter concludes with a consideration of fieldwork's place in the history of the geographical discipline.

FIELDWORK AND THE GEOGRAPHICAL CAREER

By any measure Griffith Taylor was a significant figure in the history of the geographical sciences. He founded two geography departments, first at the University of Sydney in 1920 and at the University of Toronto in 1935, and in between held an appointment as a Professor in the Geography Department at the University of Chicago.[12] During that time he published extensively on a range of geographical themes, such as migration, race, settlement, political and cultural geography, the city and geographical methods; his ideas were summarised in books such as *Environment and Race* (1927), *Australia, A Geographical Reader* (1931), *Environment and Nation* (1936), *Environment, Race and Migration* (1937), *The Geographical Laboratory* (1925), *Our Evolving Civilisation* (1946), *Canada* (1947), *Urban Geography* (1949), and the edited volume *Geography in the Twentieth Century* (1951). Indeed, the combined eminence of the contributors to the last-named volume – which included chapters by Isaiah Bowman, Ellsworth Huntington, Stephen Visher and L. Dudley Stamp – is testament to the editor's standing in the field. It is also surprising when we consider that Taylor had not actually been trained in geography – he had received a BSc from Sydney University in 1904 with Honours in Geology and Physics and then attended the University of Cambridge on an 1851 Exhibition Scholarship to study geology, particularly the Cambrian corals from the Flinders Range. However, when he later took up his position as McCaughey Associate Professor in Geography at Sydney University, he did not feel that his education constrained his ability to perform the new role:

> my not inconsiderable practical experience in the fields of Geology and Climate, not to mention ten years' scientific travel, had certainly provided me with a basis for geographical teaching; and I have discovered that students are less impressed by lectures based upon the published works of others than by information derived from a teacher with personal and firsthand knowledge of his subject.

For Taylor, geographical training involved exposure to and the study of various social and natural processes and phenomena *in situ*. Despite not having taken a degree in geography his extensive experience working in the field more than qualified him to lead Sydney's new Geography Department. For Taylor, what made a good geographical researcher and lecturer was first-hand empirical experience of the world; his experiences were certainly extensive, including a period spent in Antarctica (see Figure 5.1 for a caricature of Taylor as worldly explorer).

*****

While studying for his PhD in geology at the University of Cambridge, Taylor undertook some teaching in geography and physiography, which brought him to the attention of the geographers A. J. Herbertson and William Morris Davis.[13] Davis invited him to join an expedition to the European Alps, which he accepted – the study of glaciated topography accelerating Taylor's shift from geology to geography.[14] Taylor's association with Archibald Geikie, then president of the Royal Society of London and a member of the Advisory Committee of the British Antarctic Expedition, helped him secure a place on Scott's Terra Nova expedition to Antarctica. As leader of the Western Geological Party, Taylor supervised the survey of the coast of Victoria Land, which

FIGURE 5.1 Pencil caricature of Griffith Taylor by the cartoonist Leonard Reynolds, 1919. (courtesy of the National Library of Australia)

included geological and physiographical reconnaissance of an extensive glaciated terrain. The work largely involved the collection of observations, although Taylor did attempt to draw some more analytical conclusions, relating to climatic drivers of erosion and to glacial processes and landforms. He was subsequently awarded a DSc by Sydney University in recognition of this exploratory work.[15]

Upon his return to Australia, Taylor took up a position as physiographer to the Weather Service. This was an appointment that had been negotiated prior to the Terra Nova expedition and which enabled him to travel extensively across Australia and to take part in some of the earliest meteorological studies by air. His work for the Australian government – the Weather Service came under the control of the Department for Home Affairs – enabled Taylor to develop his ideas about the relations between resources and settlement. As Powell has noted, this work lacked 'the romance of the heroic treks' of the Terra Nova expedition, but it nonetheless helped Taylor develop a reputation as an expert in Australian exploration and surveying.[16] He carried out work in the Mount Field National Park, Tasmania, in 1919, for instance around Canberra and in the Nullarbor-Lake Eyre region. He also managed to fit in numerous other overseas travels, to Britain, South Africa and to South East Asia, all prior to taking up his post at Sydney in 1921. Although Taylor was already 40 years old when he took up the position of Head of Geography at the University of Sydney, he had in fact followed a fairly conventional career-path for the professional geographer.

It was common in the first decades of the twentieth century for university geographers to serve an informal apprenticeship in the field, whether as part of a scientific expedition, a governmental or imperial survey, or by conducting resource assessments for a commercial company. For instance, before taking up academic posts in geography and geology at Rangoon University and then in economic geography at the London School of Economics, T. Dudley Stamp worked as a geological surveyor for the Yomah Oil Company in Burma. Whilst there he conducted research into climate and ecology, noting that 'My previous training in Science and in Geographical methods has accustomed me to the recording of the necessary observations.'[17] Meanwhile, Alan G. Ogilvie, future Professor of Geography at the University of Edinburgh, accompanied the American Geographical

Society's Transcontinental Excursion of the USA in 1912 and worked on their Hispanic America survey programme in the 1920s.[18] As a last example, Isaiah Bowman acted as geographer and geologist on the Yale South American geographical expedition in 1907, the Yale Peruvian expedition in 1911 and led a third expedition to the Central Andes for the American Geographical Society in 1913, before becoming Director of the Society in 1915.[19]

Although the security of an academic position could have dampened his enthusiasm for hazardous or uncomfortable travel, Taylor's position at Sydney did not seem to curtail his ability or desire to conduct field research. To the contrary, his role as head of Sydney's Geography Department actually motivated him to continue his travels. For instance, he claimed that his decision in 1922 to survey the glacial topography of Mount Kosciusko in New South Wales (NSW) was 'for the benefit of students'.[20] Taking with him Dr W. R. Browne, a geologist, and Mr Jardine, his senior geography student, Taylor set about surveying Kosciusko by 'prismatic compass, aneroid, and Abney level', and using photographs and sketches.[21] Whilst the measurements were to help in the construction of a three-foot model of the Mount that students could then use in class, the survey also resulted in the naming of a moraine a mile from the summit after the geologist H. I. Jensen; the discovery of several cirques that were hitherto unmapped; and Taylor's use of the Mount's glaciological features as evidence of the effects wrought by a temporary Ice Age.

Although Taylor conducted a number of excursions overseas during his tenure at Sydney, most notably to the Philippines, Japan and China in 1926, the focus here is on his expeditions within Australia itself. He conducted fieldtrips to the north west of Queensland and the Northern Territory in August 1922, to northern inland NSW in January – February 1924, to its north coast in August – September of that year and then to Western Australia in December 1924. Each of these trips were documented using field notebooks and photography, through letters home to Taylor's wife Doris, in newspaper reports – Taylor wrote numerous articles for papers like the *Sydney Morning Herald* – as well as in academic journals and monographs. The letters to Doris, written during periods of repose while travelling, are particularly interesting as they gave Taylor the opportunity to provide his brief and disjointed fieldnotes with a much stronger narrative flow and to make connections between field observations and his more general theories and preoccupations.[22] These letters were in fact Taylor's preferred way of communicating his findings to his family, friends and colleagues, and indeed important as a resource he himself could later refer to. He routinely made carbon copies of his field letters and on one occasion when he failed to do so – his trip to Ballina on the coast of NSW – he explicitly requested that the recipient, his wife, should retain the letter for him.[23]

Taylor's Australian fieldwork was important for two main reasons. First, time in the field enabled him to collect empirical geographical evidence that could support his more general theories about the effects of the natural environment on human settlement and economy. Secondly, fieldwork provided an arena for the training of the geographer – indeed, the foundation for any geographical claim to truth.

FIELDWORK AND GEOGRAPHICAL KNOWLEDGE

The importance of the field as a site for the collection of geographical knowledge and for the development of geographical theories is perhaps best illustrated by Taylor's expedition to northern Queensland and the Northern Territory during August – September 1922 (see Figure 5.2 for a map of the region). The journey first involved a long trip north up the Australian east coast to Townsville, somewhat south of Cairns. There Taylor paid a visit to Dr Anton Breinl, the inaugural Director of Townsville's Institute of Tropical Medicine – although at the time of Taylor's visit in 1922 he had resigned from that post and was running his own private medical practice in the town.[24] While Breinl hoped Taylor would stay in the town for a few days and visit the area, Taylor himself was keen to continue west into the interior and his fieldwork.[25] That said, he did not waste his brief visit to Townsville – as well as accompanying Breinl on his rounds he also ascended Castle Hill, which provided a 'profitable view' of the town and coast and which Taylor later turned into one of his famous 'block diagrams' (see Figure 5.3 for an example of this sort of diagram). This epitomised a common stance taken by the geographer during this period: the assumption of an elevated position so as to describe and comprehend a geographical region – what

FIGURE 5.2 Taylor's map of northern Queensland and the Northern Territory; part of his article, 'Tropical Problems', in *The Argus* newspaper.

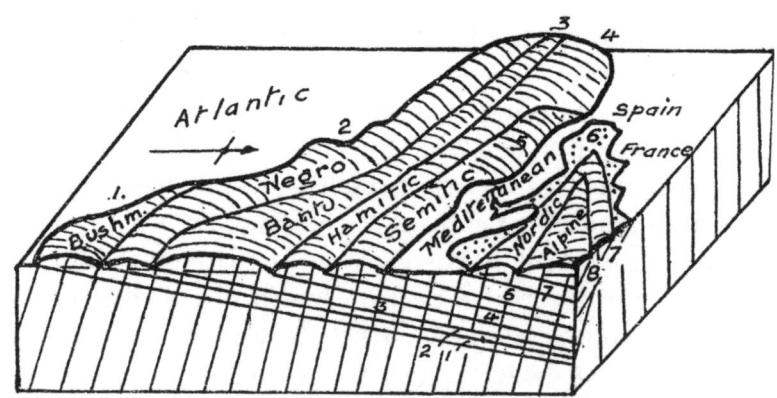

FIGURE 5.3 An example of Taylor's block diagrams 'illustrating the Migration Zones from Cape Town to Russia, and showing the order of "strata" submerged by later migrations'.

Matless has termed an 'outlook geography'. This position is shown, even if perhaps in gentle parody, in the Reynolds' drawing of Taylor in Figure 5.1.[26]

* * * * *

The railroad took Taylor west from Townsville into the interior of Queensland and to Cloncurry and then Duchess. From there he went by motorcar in a loop that extended as far west as Avon Downs in the Northern Territory and Camooweal in northern Queensland, before heading east to Calton and then south, back to Duchess and the train home. Whether travelling by train, by motorcar or on foot Taylor obsessively took notes on the landscapes he was travelling through. His field notebook was filled with a constant stream of words, phrases and sketches recording his observations, and his lengthy letters to his wife placed these into a wider narrative on the human and physical geographies of the region. Like his geographical contemporaries elsewhere in the world, Taylor documented the topography of the region, its geology, vegetation, wildlife and climate. He also considered the morphology of the towns he stopped in and the living conditions of the inhabitants, as well as the main industries of the region, particularly mining and agriculture.

This travelling accumulation of landscape observations was invaluable in the production of wider geographical ideas. Nothing was irrelevant to the geographical gaze. Upon spending all day travelling at around 30 mph on the train 'over dead level plains covered with dried Mitchell grass 8" high', Taylor noted that 'It's the least scenic ride in the world but interesting to the geographer.'[27] In particular, the trip enabled him to develop on a number of his suppositions about Australian topography and the Australian environment. For instance, his railroad traverse across Queensland effectively confirmed his views on prevalent cartographies of the region:

> One of my theories is proved. There's no range of mountains where they put the Great Dividing Range at Burra. The feeble little engine romped up without knowing it![28]

The data Taylor collected on geology, climate, industry and settlement contributed to other theories of his, particularly to those on the relations between environment and human settlement. This was an area that he had been writing on for some years now and that he felt particularly strongly about – in his opinion it was one of the key geographical questions of the age, alongside exploration.[29] In his capacity as physiographer to the Australian Commonwealth Weather Service, Taylor had taken a strong interest in the continent's weather patterns and their relation to settlement, with a particular focus on temperature, humidity and rainfall.[30] He then expanded his considerations to include other environmental factors – topography, drainage, vegetation, natural resources and health, for instance.[31] Taylor based his thinking on what he termed 'the fundamental law controlling settlement – that no one will occupy distant and unfamiliar regions who can gain a satisfactory living under more attractive circumstances'.[32] Taylor argued that environmental factors could be effectively weighted in terms of their effects on settlement possibilities and then regions awarded a particular cumulative score. These scores could in turn be mapped using contours – what Taylor called 'isoiketes' – so as to represent 'degrees of "habitability"',[33] or, elsewhere, a 'discomfort scale'.[34] (Figure 5.4 provides an example of this kind of map.) Taylor's theories had some influence on the development of the geographical discipline, and perhaps most notably on the thinking of the American geographer Ellsworth Huntington, who wrote to Taylor in 1921 to tell

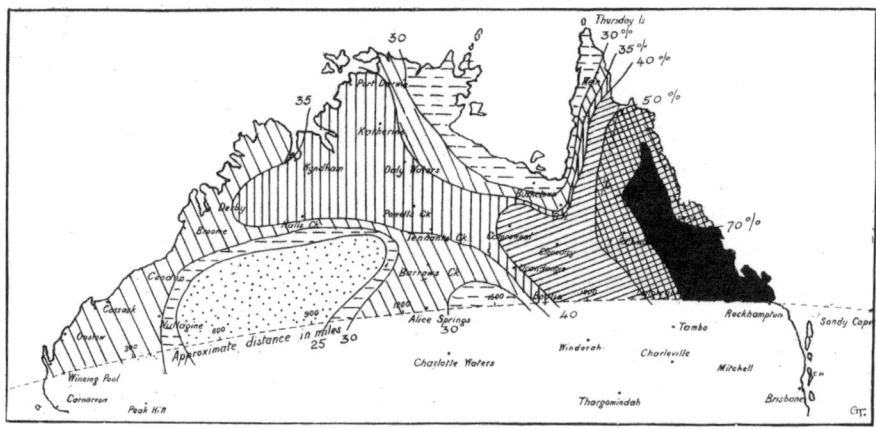

FIGURE 5.4 Taylor's map 'Potentialities of Moderate Settlement in Tropical Australia', from Taylor, 'Geographical Factors Controlling the Settlement of Tropical Australia', *Proceedings, Queensland Branch, Royal Geographical Society of Australasia*, 32–3 (1917), p. 66.

him that the latter's work on climographs and settlement had 'deeply impressed' him.³⁵ Indeed, both geographers made extensive use of maps to convey their theories of climatic effects on settlement – what Livingstone refers to as a 'rhetorical device of persuasion'.³⁶

* * * * *

The 1910s and 1920s were marked by much optimistic writing on the potential for agricultural, mining and settlement schemes in Australia, perhaps best summarised in Edwin James Brady's 1918 *Australia Unlimited*.³⁷ Taylor came to quite the opposite opinion, using his isoikete maps and his wider environmental determinism to argue for the very *limited* settlement and agricultural possibilities of much of Australia. His general maps of the continent carried a very stark message: the centre of Australia was uninhabited and uninhabitable. It was ringed by an area suited only for pastoral land, whilst the south west, the south east and east coast of Australia were the only areas that promised good agricultural and settlement opportunities. The prospects for what Taylor called 'Tropical Australia' were particularly poor (see Figure 5.4).

Taylor's theories were understandably unpopular with many Australians. He was ridiculed in the press for his views, whilst one of his books, *The Geography of Australia*, was actually banned in the schools of Western Australia.³⁸ However, Taylor's fieldtrips, such as the one he undertook in 1922, provided him with the empirical evidence with which he could counter the claims of his many detractors. In his map of Tropical Australia Taylor had identified the region containing Camooweal, Cloncurry and Urandanji as possessing between 40 and 50 per cent potential of moderate settlement (whilst an area – like Australia's interior desert – with no possibilities of settlement was anywhere below 25 per cent). Taylor's cartographic claims could finally be proven through first-hand experience. As Lorimer and Spedding argue regarding the history of geomorphological fieldwork in the Scottish highlands, 'it was the effort of ground coverage that authenticated knowledge'.³⁹

In his fieldwork Taylor made a number of observations pertinent to his theories of environmental influence on human affairs. For instance, in the area around the border with the Northern Territory

Taylor noted the unpredictable agricultural conditions, where rain at the wrong season could rot off any hay produced from Mitchell grass. He recorded the decline of the town of Duchess upon the working out of the town's mine: 'The picture show is departed. Houses have been removed and the Duchess is despoiled of her comforts.'[40] He also discussed the high temperature and its effect on people's health and well-being, reporting the testimonies of numerous residents of the region. Of four young women he spoke to he noted: 'They don't like the life at all – and I don't blame them a bit.'[41] Near Barclay, south of Camooweal, he drew attention to the grave 'where a man died of thirst lately',[42] whilst he said that even 'Dr Breinl couldn't restrain his muse (at lunch) from saying that Townsville was awful in the summer.'[43] All these observations enabled Taylor to later make the following general conclusion: 'A striking feature of this drier region is that in which Geology controls vegetation, and therefore economic occupation.'[44] Taylor's fieldtrip to northern Queensland and the Northern Territory was instrumental in the formation of his wider theories about the way environment determined the limits of human settlement. The expedition also confirmed his views about the marginal nature of settlement potential in the region.

A GEOGRAPHICAL PERFORMANCE

Fieldwork enabled Taylor to make truth claims about the nature and potential of settlement in northern Queensland, his observations combining recursively with his earlier and highly visualised settlement predictions as Weather Service physiographer. But time in the field did not serve only to produce a suite of geographical observations. It was also a geographical performance in itself. Taylor was careful not only to record the objects of his landscape study but also the more practical and mundane acts of doing work in the field. Although this aspect of Taylor's travels rarely made it into his research reports and newspaper articles, they were nonetheless crucial in the justification of his claim to be a reputable geographer and scientist. As we saw earlier, by the late nineteenth century travel was a necessary but still insufficient means of acquiring geographical knowledge – knowledge was only useful and truthful once the traveller had learned what and how to observe in the field.[45]

Taylor's field diaries and letters were full of commentary on the pragmatics of fieldwork. He described eating and drinking routines, the various sorts of accommodation he stayed in, the contingencies of travel and transportation, issues of data recording, the use of particular research methods, fieldwork objectives, travel companions, and the other activities he partook of during his trips. Fieldtrip accommodation varied widely, from the hotels in the more affluent towns and the houses of families he knew to the meagre tin huts on cattle stations and the improvised campsites. Meals followed accordingly. If at a hotel or as the guest of a local family, meals were fairly grand affairs and Taylor would describe their contents to his interlocutors.

There was a sense though in which Taylor felt that such accommodation and food was morally not quite appropriate during field research. He wrote of the expense of staying in hotels during research, and spoke highly of camping as the preferred mode of accommodation and simple meals as the best form of sustenance. In his published guide, *Scientific Travel in Australia*, Taylor stated that during fieldwork the Australian 'almost invariably uses a tent and "fly"', made using an oblong piece of canvas suspended on a rope lashed between two trees.[46] Meals were similarly uncomplicated, involving no more than bacon, eggs, chops, or steaks, whilst tea was 'the universal beverage, boiled in a tin "billy" over the camp fire' (ibid.).[47] The tacit assumption that anything more than a campsite or a tin hut was morally inappropriate for fieldwork was epitomised in Taylor's complaint to his wife that, after weeks of steak and billy tea, the porridge and eggs served at the hotel in Duchess had brought on his 'dippepsia' [sic].[48]

Like his improvised campsites Taylor took some pleasure in documenting his resourcefulness as a traveller. Taylor's fieldtrips regularly combined a range of forms of conveyance, including train travel, steamer, motorcars, hiking, bicycling and even – during his work with the Weather Service – airplanes. As Powell has noted, for Taylor fieldwork should be 'energetic', although his attempts to travel over the Antarctic sea ice on a bicycle, Powell claims, nearly killed him.[49] As noted earlier, much nineteenth- and early twentieth-century fieldwork has been marked by a masculinist imperative to bodily conquer space – to prove the intellectual veracity of the fieldworker through corporeal hardships. This was certainly the case with Taylor. He would routinely conduct extensive geographical surveys by foot, even during the full heat of the day. He often chose not to take the comfort of a sleeper on long train journeys and instead preferred to doze in his seat. Beyond the railroad Taylor recounted adventures by motorcar. 'The vast level stretches of arid Australia', he claimed in his *Scientific Travel*, 'offer unique facilities for transport by strong motor cars'.[50] That said, tyres routinely 'blew out' and Taylor and companions were often forced to improvise repairs,[51] although these moments provided further opportunities for the performance of field competence and heroic endeavour.[52]

Whilst the train provided a fairly good viewing point from which to collect field observations, the motorcar gave much more immediate access to the landscape and added an obvious flexibility to the journey. After claiming to have covered 650 miles in six days Taylor reported that he had nearly filled up his notebook and taken 8 spools, or 48 photographs. There were disadvantages though:

> It's hard work sketching in a motor going 30 mph. You only get two looks at a thing and its [sic] left far behind – and the joggles are disconcerting too![53]

The usefulness of photography and the motorcar to the geographical fieldworker combined to perhaps best effect when Taylor finally reached the Northern Territory: 'I reached my goal at 11.45 and got a photo of the car ½ in and ½ out of the Territory.'[54]

CONTESTING SCIENTIFIC EXPERTISE

The combination of extensive travel, the performance of a particular set of fieldwork practices, the extensive recording of a suite of landscape observations, and the proper application of wider geographical theories gave Taylor the licence (in his eyes at least) to declare himself 'the world authority' on northern Queensland upon a month's fieldwork there.[55] I want to end this chapter with a consideration of the way in which such declarations of geographical competency produced from fieldwork were always open to contestation – to illustrate in other words the politics of geographical knowledge in the field. To do so I will focus on the controversy surrounding the visit to Australia of the Canadian explorer Vilhjalmur Stefansson.

In May 1924 Stefansson arrived in Sydney. He was an acknowledged expert on the Arctic and well known for the popular books and lectures that were based on his travels there.[56] As Powell notes in his discussion of Stefansson's 1924 visit, the latter's publications 'promoted the idea of extensive mining and commercial grazing prospects of the Northern "wastelands", waxing eloquent on the Arctic Ocean as a veritable Mediterranean spatial system, unified by over-ice and submarine transport and flights over the pole'.[57] In other words then, Stefansson's views on the settlement possibilities of the world's desert regions were diametrically opposed to Taylor – he was the possibilist to Taylor's determinist.[58] Central to Stefansson's motivation to visit Australia was the search for proof that, like the Arctic, the Australian desert could be conquered by human ingenuity.

Taylor became aware of Stefansson's visit when Isaiah Bowman, the then President of the American Geographical Society, wrote to him in January 1924 informing him that Stefansson planned to write a book on the continent 'and one of his purposes in taking this journey is to gather material to this end'.[59] Bowman went on to list the explorer's credentials – a gold medallist of the American Geographical Society, President of the Explorer's Club, an LLD from the University of Michigan – and competencies: 'He is, as you know, of an investigative turn of mind and has quite original powers of observation and expression.'[60] Considering Stefansson's reputation Bowman thought it only proper that the Australian government offer him transportation facilities to support his travels. Australian bodies – its scientific societies, government departments and press – were certainly keen to promote Stefansson and his views on the possibilities of opening the Australian interior. His fieldtrip north into the MacDonnell Ranges was even supported by a fleet of Dodge cars.

Stefansson's press reports were predictably optimistic about the Australian interior. The scenery was varied and beautiful and the dry air 'as exhilarating as champagne'. In short the Australian interior was 'far less forbidding than the "real" deserts of California' and could be opened in the same way as that state, Arizona and Colorado.[61] Taylor had graciously met Stefansson upon his arrival in Sydney and assisted him during his trip, even if this had more to do with his desire to fulfil Bowman's request than to help the explorer with his research.[62] Taylor nonetheless was damning of Stefansson – whom he referred to as a 'thorn in the flesh' – and his opinions and methods.⁶³ In particular, Taylor and his colleagues' criticisms centred on Stefansson's competence as a fieldworker and geographer.

Shortly after Stefansson's arrival in Australia, Bowman wrote a second letter to Taylor regarding the Canadian explorer's work. In direct contradiction to his previous letter to Taylor, Bowman roundly criticised Stefansson's abilities as an explorer. In reference to his views on Arctic habitability Bowman noted that an expedition Stefansson had sent to Wrangel Island had all died, and that the explorer was reported as saying he 'will not return for further exploration in the Arctic because if he lost his life it would tend to diminish the force of his theories'. With this sort of expeditionary incompetence in mind Bowman 'tremble[d] to think of the possibilities of mischief' that Stefansson could get up to in arid Australia.⁶⁴ Taylor confirmed Bowman's misgivings upon the completion of Stefansson's trip. In response to the explorer's claims as to arid Australia's settlement possibilities, Taylor was quick to point out that he had failed entirely to actually visit the region: 'Stefansson ... had kept almost exclusively to the belt of sparse Stock Country, situated between the large Western Desert and the smaller Eastern, or Arunta, Desert' and had not entered the region Taylor, in a 1925 article in the *Sydney Morning Herald*, had labelled 'Almost Useless'.⁶⁵

As well as questioning Stefansson's choice of route and fieldsite, Taylor was critical of the quality of the observations taken and ensuing reports. He noted dismissively that Stefansson's articles 'dealt mainly with incidents of his journey, with the vivid colourings of the rocks and vegetation he had seen' and failed entirely to consider the crucial geographical questions of rainfall or patterns of settlement.⁶⁶ Huntington, responding to Taylor's complaints about Stefansson, confirmed his friend's opinion, noting that in Stefansson's field reports 'the mere details of travelling receive the emphasis, whereas with us, the emphasis is more on scientific observation'.⁶⁷ Taylor claimed that 'he lacks a sense of proportion – or of comparative geography – or some attribute that makes a useful scientist',⁶⁸ whilst Bowman conceded he had some expertise in anthropology, but 'is very deficient in geography'.⁶⁹ Keith Ward, a friend of Taylor's and the government geologist assigned to accompany Stefansson on his fieldtrip, noted damningly in a letter to Taylor that 'He is in my judgement not a scientific man at all, in spite of all the claims that he makes to be regarded as such.'⁷⁰ Ultimately then, Stefansson's status as a geographer and scientist was called into question, a deficiency highlighted and justified by his untutored visual apprehension of Australia's natural landscapes.

Criticism of Stefansson's fieldwork in Australia – his problematic field observations and dubious credentials – was often linked to his career as a journalist. Bowman, Huntington and Ward all questioned Stefansson's scientific objectivity in the face of his need to sell stories of his travels to the press and to attract audiences to his talks. Taylor's silence on this matter is telling. Taylor had himself made extensive use of the press to disseminate his views. He also appeared to have financed his fieldtrip to northern Queensland at least in part from the five reports he wrote on the region for the *Herald* and *The Argus*, published September – October 1922.[71] Meanwhile, his five-week fieldtrip to Western Australia in late 1924 was financed by the army authorities, who employed Taylor to write the economic and topographical sections of a military handbook,[72] while his trip to visit the aboriginal reserves in north coastal NSW was actually conducted as part of a lecture tour to various towns in the region, where Taylor spoke of his travels in Antarctica, Java and tropical Australia.[73] In many ways then, the differences between Taylor and Stefansson were ones of degree not of kind. Whilst it was difficult for Taylor to criticise his adversary on the basis of his career or motivations, the quality of his fieldwork presented much firmer grounds on which to exert geographical authority and to claim the right to speak for a territory. Taylor's field practice – his relatively frugal lifestyle, his oft-expressed resourcefulness, masculinity and grasp of the pertinent geographical questions – was an effective counter to the excesses of Stefansson's own manner of travelling and ignorance of geography. Taylor's field methods and geographical understanding effectively exposed him to the landscapes under examination; Stefansson's more regal entourage of local dignitaries, business magnates and government 'boosters' clouded his vision as to the true nature of arid Australia.

CONCLUSION

Although it is beyond the scope of this chapter, it is worth recording that Taylor also conducted scientific travel, as he referred to it, in his study of 'racial geography'.[74] He conducted several trips in the 1920s to research the effects of racial inter-breeding between settlers and aborigines. Taylor's controversial views on race and settlement eventually led him to leave Australia for North America in 1928, where he took up positions at the University of Chicago, USA, and then the University of Toronto, Canada. Once there he continued to travel extensively, ensuring that he was personally acquainted with his new home. He noted that:

> The writer has had the interesting experience during the last two years of investigating the fundamental topographic features of a second great section of the British Empire [Canada]. For twenty years he carried out similar investigations in Australia. A comparison of the two studies, which deal with very different environments, has but confirmed the conclusion reached in Australia, that Man's material progress is the product of his environment.[75]

In conclusion, Taylor is a good example of a more general geographical figure in the early twentieth century – that of the scientific traveller. He, like his geographical contemporaries – Bowman, Huntington, Stamp and others – placed exploration and fieldwork at the very heart of their nascent discipline. Periods of research in difficult environments, whether in the Australian outback, in the Yukon or the Andes, were essential for the production of meaningful geographical and anthropological knowledges. It was *also* central to any geographical education and the basis for any geographical career. Not only did it provide the student with a regional or topical specialism, it also conferred upon them certain moral attributes – of endurance, courage, fortitude, resourcefulness and organisation. It is worth noting that despite the emergence of spatial analysis in the 1960s, and of remote sensing and geographical information systems even more recently, fieldwork continued to form an important part of any geographical degree throughout the twentieth century, a legacy that owes much to the arguments put forward by the likes of Taylor at the beginning of the century. For the geographical discipline, perhaps more than any other then, fieldwork and exploration are inexorably bound up in the constitution of proper scientific knowledges and proper scientific practice. It is incumbent upon us as historians of geography and exploration to give fieldwork due credit in our interpretations of geography's history.

6 Glaciology, the Arctic, and the US Military, 1945–58

Fae L. Korsmo

The melting of glaciers and the decrease of sea ice in the Arctic made it into the headlines of the American media in the last several years. As a geographic space, the Arctic appears to be losing the descriptors that set it apart from the lower latitudes. 'Change' has become the watchword for the Arctic; a major US research program is called the Study of Environmental Arctic Change (or SEARCH).[1] The idea that what was once frozen and solid for much of the year, such as the vast expanses of tundra, is now sodden and unstable more often than not, may yet be an abstract notion to inhabitants of America's 'Lower 48,' as the Alaskans refer to contiguous, continental United States. To Northerners, however, particularly the indigenous communities that have been living in the Arctic and sub-Arctic for thousands of years, the dramatic change is a threat to continued existence. Extractive oil, gas, and mineral industries in the North have also realized that the pace of environmental change is potentially devastating to existing infrastructure.

This is not the first time that decision-makers in the United States have seen Arctic environmental change as a potential threat. The warming of the first half of the twentieth century alarmed military planners who were counting on the frozen expanses for operations. Not only was the Arctic a relatively unknown frontier, but it seemed to be a frontier in motion as glaciers and sea ice coverage diminished.

By the early years of the Cold War, immediately following the Second World War, the Arctic took on new importance for the US military as a remote region for testing and developing equipment and vehicles, detecting possible threats from the Soviet Union, and building air bases and landing strips. Yet, as Paul Siple of the US Army lamented, scientific and engineering knowledge of the North lagged behind the area's increased strategic importance. The United States, having acquired the non-contiguous territory of Alaska in the late nineteenth century, was hardly an Arctic nation. Arctic expertise there consisted of former explorers, such as Viljalmur Stefansson, and a handful of geographers, meteorologists, glaciologists, and geophysicists. Some worked collaboratively across national boundaries and expressed impatience with the secrecy and bureaucracy associated with military patronage; others felt at ease asserting national interests.

Elsewhere I have described the US military's approach to the Arctic in the years 1945–50.[2] In this chapter, I focus on two geographers whose organizational work exemplifies the context in which US Arctic glaciology and exploration was approached from the end of the Second World War up to and including the 'assault on the unknown' represented by the International Geophysical Year (IGY) of 1957–8.[3] The time frame witnessed debates among Arctic experts on how best to plan and carry out exploration: secret versus open, focused versus comprehensive, comparative and international versus mission-oriented and limited to strategic concerns. Barnes and Farish argue that the field of geography made a transition during this time period from a natural history approach (descriptive, field-based, and relying on the observations of lone scholars) to a more model- and machine-based theoretical, abstract, and instrumental tool to achieve functional objectives.[4] Certainly this tension characterized the Arctic debates, although the transition was far from complete.

An important intersection of natural history and model-based approaches could be found in glaciology. In the process of understanding the Arctic and correlating the climate-related phenomena found in high latitudes with high altitudes, the discipline of glaciology emerged. The first volume of the *Journal of Glaciology* appeared in 1947. This emergent science of snow and ice facilitated Arctic exploration by introducing the discipline of the laboratory to compare glacial advance and retreat across the continents. Micrometeorology was used to take the glaciers' temperatures at various depths and establish baselines for longitudinal study. Two US geographers were key to organizing the transition from expeditionary natural history to comparative, quantitative science of glaciology, although each had different motives. For Paul Siple, the Arctic represented an important challenge for the US military, one that required extensive engineering and applied science to overcome. For William Field, the Arctic represented a laboratory for experimentation in circumpolar glaciology and climate studies, a necessarily international approach. Both Siple and Field saw the Arctic as a frontier for exploration, but also a natural laboratory for experimentation, whether it was a less-than-controlled experiment on ice sheet dynamics or the human factors testing of clothing, equipment, and techniques. This new way of looking at the Arctic brought the Arctic and glaciology into the IGY of 1957–8 as a subject of study.

The US IGY glaciology program led by William O. Field encompassed mountain glaciers and ice sheets from Greenland to Antarctica, including North and South America, Eurasia, and Africa. Expeditions to Greenland and Antarctica enabled the development of ice coring and the ability to map the history of extreme events and shifts in climate. The IGY glaciology program emerged in the context of Cold War science and the tensions between nationalist and international aspirations. Both competitive and collaborative elements shaped the US interest in the role of glaciers and ice sheets in understanding polar environments.

THE ARCTIC AND THE US MILITARY

During and immediately after the Second World War, the military was the main, if not the only, source of funding in the United States for Arctic research. Farish raises the question of what influence this had on the science agenda.[5] Doel notes that military patronage in environmental sciences, generally, focused more on the physical sciences rather than the biological sciences.[6] There is no question that the instrumentalist, functional approach of the US military was to know as much as possible about the physical environment of the Arctic in order to operate there. Yet within the military and the circle of military patronage that extended to universities, there were striking differences in the latitude given to researchers to define the scientific questions and the methods of carrying out the work. The Office of Naval Research, for example, offered open-ended grants to universities for basic research in a variety of sciences, including geography and glaciology. Other services focused on engineering or technical solutions to practical problems: the best place to build an air field, the best site for a Loran tower, the best materials to use in winter clothing. Combinations of basic science and applied technology were not unusual; if the Office of Naval Research was supporting a descriptive study of glaciers in Alaska, it might be the Air Force that dropped the equipment and the Army that supplied the ice drill developed at its Snow, Ice, and Permafrost Research Establishment laboratory.

Coordination of such projects took place in the US Joint Army – Navy Research and Development Board. Renamed the Research and Development Board under the National Security Act of 1947 (the same legislation that separated the Air Force from the Army and established the Department of Defense, the National Security Council, and the Central Intelligence Agency), the Board consisted of a civilian chairman (Vannevar Bush, President of the Carnegie Institution of Washington, who had led the Joint Committee on New Weapons and Equipment during the war) and two representatives from each service: the Army, Navy, and Air Force. The Board reported to the Secretary of Defense. Its primary duties were to prepare an integrated military research and development program, advise on scientific research trends relevant to national security, coordinate research and development among the services and allocate responsibilities for programs, formulate Defense Department policies on non-Defense Department R&D, and advise the Joint Chiefs of Staff on the interaction of R&D and strategy. The Board conducted its work through committees, and the committees formed panels and working groups. Each committee, panel, and working group comprised military and civilian members, thus in total providing hundreds of forums for civilian – military interactions on science. While the committees varied in size and scope over the R&D Board's short history (it was dissolved in 1953, with its functions absorbed by the Assistant Secretary for Research and Development under the Department of Defense), together they encompassed all sciences and engineering that had a bearing on military operations and strategy.[7]

In the R&D Board's Committee on Geographical Exploration, the Army proposed to set up its own program to coordinate all snow, ice, and permafrost research. Not surprisingly, the Navy objected. The ensuing battle and compromise gave the Navy responsibility for sea ice and beneath, while the Army held responsibility for the land-based snow and permafrost. The questions of responsibility, funding, and programmatic plans forced both the military and civilian members to take stock, share knowledge, and develop inter-service collaborations on projects such as ice coring.

The panels created under the Committee on Geophysical Sciences and Geographical Exploration (renamed Geophysics and Geography) included meteorology, oceanography, seismology, atmosphere, geology, hydrology, geodesy, terrestrial magnetism and electricity, instrumentation, and snow, ice, and permafrost (referred to as glaciology under the IGY). It was this committee and its panels that set the US research agenda for the exploratory aspects of the IGY well before IGY planning started in 1953. Thus the US military was poised to participate in international science, particularly in polar environments. The more the military knew about ice, snow, and climate, the better their planes, submarines, and troops could function in strategic regions such as the Arctic.

PAUL SIPLE AND THE POLES

Geographer and Antarctic explorer Paul A. Siple of the US Army General Staff was an active member of the R&D Board and an advocate for Arctic exploration. He noted, 'The Arctic affords a straight line attack to the Eurasian centers of our potential enemy, and because of that if for no other reasons, we must give full consideration to the best exploitation of the polar regions.'[8] Siple was well aware of the fact that the Army was behind the Navy and the Air Force in knowledge and experience of remote northern regions.

It was the Army that seized upon the problem of snow, ice, and permafrost during the Second World War. During the war, the US forces built weather stations and airfields in Greenland and the Canadian North and constructed a highway from Dawson Creek, British Columbia, to Big Delta, Alaska. The Army Corps of Engineers had the job of building airfields in Alaska. To understand how to build on frozen ground, the Army Corps asked the US Geological Survey to do field studies in Alaska and learn from the considerably more extensive Russian literature on construction in the Arctic and sub-Arctic.[9]

After the war, the Army called on experts such as Henri Bader of the Swiss Snow and Avalanche Research Institute to assemble and disseminate what was known on snow and ice mechanics. In addition, the work of Hans W. Ahlmann came to the Army's attention through meteorologist Carl Gustav Rossby. The Swedish-born Rossby recommended that the War and Navy Departments take advantage of Ahlmann's 1947 speaking tour (Ahlmann was going to visit Johns Hopkins University, Yale University, and Rossby's own University of Chicago) to send officers to study glaciology with him at the University of Stockholm.[10]

Siple, a seasoned Antarctic explorer who had served in the US Army during the Second World War and in 1946 became a civilian scientist in the Army Chief of Staff's Office of Research and Development, responded enthusiastically to Rossby's invitation. By then defense interest had turned to the Arctic and Siple's suggestion 'that the blank map areas in the Arctic basin be filled in' resulted in an aerial reconnaissance program.[11] Thus began the Army Air Force flights to the North Pole. Much was unknown about the Arctic. Ahlmann was a prominent glaciologist who was sounding the alarm about glacial retreat in his own Sweden and neighboring Norway. Comparative studies in Iceland and Greenland led him to conclude that a great deal of work was needed to study the relationship between the climate warming observed in the first half of the twentieth century and glacial shrinkage. Ahlmann's approach was a systematic comparison of glaciers and ice sheets in order to determine the effects of local climate and general circulation of the atmosphere on the glacial regime (i.e., quantitative determinations of accumulation and ablation).[12]

In Ahlmann's view, as he expressed it in a lecture delivered at the Scott Polar Research Institute in Cambridge, England, in 1948, the work that he and others had done on mountain glaciers needed to be conducted on the great polar ice sheets: Greenland and Antarctica. In his many publications, Ahlmann detailed the methods of measuring accumulation, ablation, and regime (the grand total of a glacier's entire accumulation and net ablation), and recommended simultaneous measurements in different climates. At the Scott Polar, he called for exact measurements to be made on the ice sheets: temperatures at different depths, seismic methods to compute thickness, and detailed observations of stratification of annual layers. The only way to do this systematic comparison in different parts of the world was through international cooperation. It is fitting that Ahlmann labeled his lecture, 'The Contribution of Polar Expeditions to the Science of Glaciology'. He was encouraging polar explorers to take a much more systematic approach and emulate the precision and exactitude of a controlled experiment. The expeditions would bring back more than complete field reports, in the style of natural history; they would contribute to a growing databank of comparable measurements. Ahlmann's frequent calls for this style of comparative work eventually led to the Norwegian – British – Swedish Antarctic Expedition of 1949–52, the first scientific traverse in the Antarctic interior. Included in the program were seismic sounding, the determination of snow accumulation rates through stratigraphy, and measurements of temperature at different depths in the snow. This traverse served as a model for the IGY expeditions to Antarctica.[13]

Siple's primary interest in Ahlmann's work was the potential for predicting winter trends, trends that 'might conceivably alter the entire character of war,' such as the warming of the Arctic.[14] Unlike Ahlmann, Siple focused primarily on winning the Cold War, arguing for more resources devoted to snow, ice, and permafrost science as a means to this end. In this way, Siple, at least during this period, and Ahlmann represent two divergent motivations for focusing on the polar regions: national security versus international cooperation in science.

In his 1959 account of his Antarctic adventures, Siple praised the international cooperation accomplished by the IGY, but also emphasized the national achievement of the US presence on the frozen continent.[15] As a 19-year-old, Siple was chosen by the Boy Scouts to accompany Commander Richard Byrd on his 1928–30 Antarctic expedition. Byrd had just returned from his famous flight over the North Pole and decided that the South Pole would be his next destination. Having proved himself to be a worthy expedition member contributing to Byrd's success in reaching the South Pole, Siple, by then a college graduate, was invited to accompany Byrd's second expedition in 1933–5. In 1939 Siple earned his PhD in geography from Clark University. He would return to the

Antarctic several times, but also found the Arctic an important target for exploration.

Siple saw polar exploration as a source of national pride. Siple's focus on national goals can be seen in his reaction to the criticism of the Army's cold-weather endeavors bluntly leveled by polar explorer Vilhjalmur Stefansson. Siple had been trying to get the R&D Board leadership to focus on the Arctic, when the R&D Board's civilian chairman, Vannevar Bush, met Stefansson in the spring of 1947 at the Cosmos Club in Washington, DC. There, Stefansson had brought up the issue of cold-weather clothing, an interest of his prior to and during the war. Stefansson had admired and adopted the warm, lightweight garb of the Inuit in his arctic travels and recommended that the Army learn from the Inuit in their cold-weather operations. After the war, he saw the R&D Board as the logical place to take up the issue of developing a new material 'light and insulating as cork but also as soft and flexible as velvet.'[16] There is no indication that Bush took any interest in the Arctic as a result of Stefansson's or Siple's advocacy.

A year later, in March 1948, Stefansson wrote to Bush, prompted by an article in *The New York Times* indicating that the Army's cold-weather operations were disastrous. According to the article, wrote Stefansson, 'the Army, instead of starting afresh on arctic clothes, is thinking of surrendering.'[17] In the article, Hanson W. Baldwin, journalist and military affairs reporter for *The New York Times*, cited interviews with senior US military leaders who observed and participated in cold-weather exercises that showed 'the extreme and almost insurmountable difficulty of conducting large-scale military operations by surface units in the Arctic or sub-Arctic.'[18] Problems of food, clothing, and shelter were cited as major obstacles. This struck Stefansson as bewildering news, given his 'experience of ten winters of living on northern lands and on the drifting ice beyond the lands.' Stefansson called the Army's attitude toward the Arctic 'defeatist.'[19] Bush found Stefansson's letter interesting and assigned the R&D Board staff to look into the matter.

Paul Siple already had been grappling with the problem of Army defeatism in the Arctic. When asked to comment on Stefansson's letter, Siple produced a seven-page memorandum for Vannevar Bush with a briefing he had written earlier for the R&D Board's Committee on Geographical Exploration. Stefansson's letter gave Siple the opportunity to renew his call for enhanced understanding of the arctic environment. Siple's analysis revealed his concern for national security.[20]

Siple began his analysis by encouraging the R&D Board to look into cold-weather clothing, noting that the Army Quartermaster Corps and the Canadians already were making progress but could benefit by enhanced R&D Board action. Having disposed of the clothing issue, Siple moved quickly to a more important topic, military preparedness in the Arctic. He wrote that the overall defense plan placed the Army as a 'stepchild' (or 'foster child' as he described it in the earlier R&D Board briefing) in the Arctic program. The Air Force had become an independent service in 1947, leaving the Army responsible for land-based operations. Unlike the Navy or the Air Force, the Army was land-bound and, according to Siple, incapable of Arctic travel. (Ironically, personnel in the Army's Corps of Engineers Snow, Ice, and Permafrost Establishment often worked with their counterparts in the Air Force and the Navy.) When invited to observe Navy or Air Force operations in the Arctic, the Army was forced 'to sit and watch and not take part.'[21] Joint operations involving all three services were needed to force the Army to learn to function. As Siple put it:

> The Air Force and Navy have been able to carry out exploration of new areas which fall into the Arctic Defense zone because they have planes and ice breakers. The Army has been restricted to forays near Fairbanks, Alaska, Ft. Churchill, and a few other spots to try out their pitifully inadequate surface transportation in local bad spots but without appreciating the full scope of their problem.[22]

And why was the Arctic so important? After all, General Jacob L. Devers, Army Ground Forces Commander, had told *The New York Times* reporter that the Arctic or sub-Arctic would not likely be a major theatre for ground troops. Siple did not disagree. He saw any future fighting in the Arctic as primarily an air activity, with the field soldier in a support role. Arctic footholds would be places for bombers, not masses of troops. In the atomic era, that meant possible destruction of cities in Canada and the United States unless the US forces could repel initial attacks in Greenland or Alaska. Siple urged the use of the Greenland Ice Sheet as a natural landing field and possible refueling site for US bombers. Not that Siple sought war. On the contrary, he believed that 'if we showed great polar strength, the Russians who pride themselves as superior in that sphere will realize that they must talk with us rather than fight.'[23]

Finally, Siple discredited Stefansson as a promoter, an unreliable arctic authority whose knowledge was not up to date and whose loyalty to the United States was uncertain. As Siple noted, Stefansson was a controversial figure by this time, shunned by the Canadian government for prior expeditions that had gone awry, and distrusted by some in US government circles for his entrepreneurial wartime consulting.[24] To Siple, Stefansson represented the old-fashioned explorer, an individual whose insights about the North were no longer useful to the modern military in the atomic age.

Siple renewed his call for Arctic research in the fall of 1949, after the extensively planned Antarctic expedition, Operation Highjump II, was canceled. Highjump I took place in 1946–7, a US Navy undertaking with Admiral Richard Byrd as the Officer in Charge and Captain Richard Cruzen as Commander of the Operating Task Force. The purpose of the operation was to establish a new base and build an ice strip for reconnaissance planes. Siple served as Byrd's Scientific and Polar Advisor and Senior War Department Observer. Regrettably, Siple recalled that while many scientists accompanied Highjump I, Cruzen considered them superfluous. The aerial reconnaissance proved useful, however, by providing the first nearly complete map of the coast of Antarctica.[25]

For Highjump II, planned for 1949–50, Siple was the Army's representative to the Naval Forces, Antarctica, courtesy of Admiral Byrd's suggestion to the Navy. Byrd argued passionately for the expedition on the basis of national security and scientific quality, the latter endorsed by the R&D Board. The Secretary of the Navy canceled it, however, for budget reasons.[26] Siple's explanation, however, was based on the powerful personalities in Washington. President Truman had been arguing with Admiral Byrd's brother, Senator Harry F. Byrd of Virginia. Quoted by a newspaper as saying 'There are too many birds (Byrds),' the President did not approve the Admiral's expedition.[27] Turning to the Arctic and perhaps fearing a similar fate for Arctic research, Siple wrote an impassioned plea for basic research leading, not following, strategic planning.[28] For Highjump II, the Navy had proposed an aggressive plan to explore, occupy, and develop the Antarctic continent to strengthen the position of the United States in the face of competing claims to Antarctica.[29] Scientific justification came later. Siple may have had this in mind when he wrote 'Research and development generally must precede rather than serve or be steered by so-called strategic guidance,' since strategic guidance depends on the political conditions of the moment.[30] Again, as he had in 1948, Siple appealed to the need for military superiority in the Arctic to spur research and development.

Siple was not the only one in the United States calling for military superiority in the Arctic. By the early 1950s, the United States was constructing Thule Air Base in Greenland. As glaciologist Carl Benson recalled, 'They were putting up, basically, a building every day.'[31] There was no radar station, however, and no anti-aircraft facilities; nor were the runways large enough to take the bombers that the Air Force wanted to base there. So the Air Force contracted with glaciologists and with the Army Corps of Engineers Snow, Ice, and Permafrost Research Establishment (SIPRE) to study the physical characteristics of the ice sheet.[32]

While Siple argued on the basis of national security, he was open to international research collaboration as long as the United States held a leadership role. By 1953, Siple had laid the groundwork for the glaciology program of the IGY, envisioned to take place in 1957–8.[33] He then handed off the responsibility for the IGY glaciology program to William O. Field of the American Geographical Society. From the beginning, the IGY was to include Antarctic exploration, and the international tensions surrounding national claims – including the claim of the Soviet Union – virtually guaranteed US interest in linking Antarctica to scientific exploration. Field was known to Siple, since he had made several presentations to the R&D Board on his glaciological research in the late 1940s. He was firmly in the internationalist, comparativist camp of field science and maintained a collaborative relationship with Ahlmann. Field was a geographer interested in glaciology, but had two additional traits that made him well suited for the job. First, he was a synthetic thinker, integrating meteorology, geology, and botany in an ecosystem approach to his Alaskan glacier studies. Second, he knew how to plan, organize, and carry out expeditions in alpine and high-latitude locations. He cobbled together financial and logistical support from the Navy, Air Force, and Army, and kept the R&D Board informed of results. While Siple was part of the US government's national Antarctic program, Field was not employed by the US government and retained the detached stance of an independent scientist.

WILLIAM O. FIELD AND THE IGY

Siple's 1953 proposal to the US National Committee for the IGY emanated not only from his experiences in field science in the Antarctic but also from his familiarity with studies written or inspired by Ahlmann. Ahlmann's colleague, Sverre Petterssen, suggested that if the warming trend continued we might see an ice-free Arctic basin in 50 years.[34] Both Petersson and Ahlmann had been invited by the American Geographical Society and the US Air Force to Alaska in August 1952. There they visited the Lemon Creek Glacier to observe ongoing studies similar to those conducted in the Scandinavian north.[35] On the basis of their findings, Siple proposed a sweeping climate change study that would include measurements of glacial changes, aerial photography of as many glaciers as possible, a worldwide network of observing stations, tree ring analyses to understand past climate, as well as hydrology and meteorology.[36]

Wallace W. Atwood, Jr., a professional geographer and the son of Siple's former professor and mentor at Clark University, showed a keen interest in Siple's proposal. Atwood, too, had been on the R&D Board, staffing the Committee on Geophysics and Geography. Atwood later became the Director, Office of International Relations, at the National Academy of Sciences. It was Atwood's office at the Academy that initially organized US participation in the IGY. Atwood championed the inclusion of climate and glaciology in the IGY science program. He showed Siple's climate change proposal to botanist Donald Lawrence of the University of Minnesota. Lawrence had worked with William Field on an earlier study of Alaskan glaciers and glacial environments.[37] Lawrence's main criticism of Siple's ideas was the lack of an ecosystem approach; too much emphasis was placed on the influence of climate on vegetation. Lawrence wrote:

> One must not assume that changes in position of vegetation boundaries result solely from climatic changes. Any change in boundary may result from any one factor or combination of factors in the whole ecosystem involving animal populations, fire, competition with new plant species, and susceptibility to new diseases as well as to climate.[38]

Lawrence drew upon his conversations with glaciologists and meteorologists to propose an expansion of Siple's climate study to measure on a worldwide basis the carbon dioxide content of the atmosphere and the sea, noting that even slight changes in the carbon dioxide content of the atmosphere resulting from burning of fossil fuels would influence the heat balance of the earth.[39]

While Lawrence's ambitious suggestion did not turn IGY into a climate change program, many of the geophysical research areas covered by IGY had significant implications for understanding climate. Importantly, the longitudinal measurement of carbon dioxide and ozone that became so crucial in the latter half of the twentieth century indeed began during IGY.[40] Glaciology itself remained on the agenda of the IGY, largely through the interest and diplomacy of Atwood, Joseph Kaplan, Lloyd Berkner, and William Field.

While the record is not entirely clear on how Field became involved in IGY, as early as January 1954, Field sent Siple a draft glaciology program for IGY. In his letter, Field wrote:

> I envision this IGY program as a possible shot in the arm in helping to get established in this country a practical long-term glaciological program. First of all, some study must be given to how glaciology can be of more practical application to students of climatic change.[41]

It seems logical that it was Siple himself who encouraged Field to take the glaciology program forward. Certainly Atwood, in charge of the National Academy of Sciences' Office of International Relations and an acquaintance of both Siple and Field, made sure that glaciology – and thus the Arctic – was included in the IGY science agenda. But among the international organizers of IGY, only the Anglo-Americans considered it a priority, for IGY initially focused on the upper atmosphere and Antarctica.[42]

Field later recalled that UCLA geophysicist Joseph Kaplan, Chair of the US National Committee for the IGY, told him 'Field, I think glaciology is going to be a sleeper. I think it's going to have a lot of support and be very interesting.' Field mused, 'I don't think he'd ever considered it before.'[43]

Indeed, prior to the logistics-intensive ice sheet traverses of the early 1950s, glaciology was a small-scale enterprise involving field camps on individual mountain glaciers. The IGY would involve both types of glacial exploration. No doubt Kaplan understood that glaciology would help the organizers of the IGY sell the program as a human interest story, since glaciology resembled nineteenth- and early twentieth-century heroic expeditions to cold, forbidding places rather than the modernity of ionosphere-probing rockets.

Field was enthusiastic about leading the US glaciology effort in the IGY, particularly the fact that IGY programs were to be open, civilian, and international. He had organized one of the Greenland Ice Sheet expeditions of the early 1950s, Project Mint Julep, and found the strictures of the Air Force contract, including secrecy and classification, far less conducive to science than the less restrictive Office of Naval Research funding arrangements.[44]

THE IGY AND THE COLD WAR

The IGY originally was envisioned as an upper atmosphere program, with an Antarctic component. Lloyd Berkner provided the initial inspiration. Berkner had been a member of the scientific staff on the first Byrd Antarctic Expedition in 1928–30. As an expert in ionospheric physics and telecommunications, Berkner also figured prominently in the post-Second World War R&D Board. The story of Berkner's involvement in international relations and science policy during the Cold War is told by historian Allan A. Needell.[45] Physicist James Van Allen recalls that it was Berkner who suggested in April 1950 that it was time for another polar year. The first polar year took place in 1882–3 and the second polar year in 1932–3 as designated periods of coordinated expeditions to the polar regions. By 1950, Berkner and others were interested in new scientific frontiers, particularly the upper atmosphere. Van Allen, who worked on rockets and their instrumented payloads to understand the properties of the ionosphere, gathered a few geophysicists for dinner, including Berkner and Sydney Chapman. Van Allen recalled that:

> The dinner conversation ranged widely over geophysics and especially geomagnetism and ionospheric physics. Following dinner, as we were all sipping brandy in the living room, Berkner turned to Chapman and said, 'Sydney, don't you think that it is about time for another international polar year?' Chapman immediately embraced the suggestion, remarking that he had been thinking along the same lines himself. The conversation was then directed to the scope of the enterprise and to practical considerations of how to contact leading individuals in a wide range of international organizations

in order to enlist their support. The year 1957–8, the 25th anniversary of the second polar year and one of anticipated maximum solar activity, was selected. By the close of the evening, Berkner and Joyce had agreed on the strategy for proceeding.[46]

The polar year became the geophysical year in the process of discussions with both international and national organizations. By the time of the first meeting of the US National Committee for IGY in March 1953, Berkner was ready with a plan to take to the special international IGY committee (known as CSAGI after the French initials) in July of the same year. At the first US National Committee meeting, all sorts of questions arose about whether the Soviet scientists would participate, the then common practice of classifying all high-latitude ionospheric data, and the disadvantages of top – down, large-scale science programs. Berkner had answers for every question and every doubt, expressing optimism that the Soviet Union would join IGY.[47]

In 1954, the Soviet Academy of Sciences accepted an invitation to participate in both the International Union of Geodesy and Geophysics meeting and the CSAGI meeting that would follow, both meetings taking place in Rome. By 1954, glaciology was on the US and international IGY agenda, but the small delegation sent by the Soviet Academy did not include glaciologists.

Field, drawing on Siple's original proposal, wrote a comprehensive plan for the US glaciology program under IGY in May 1954 and submitted a shorter version for the international meeting in Rome. Field's plan portrayed glaciology as a young science full of potential for an interdisciplinary understanding of the earth. Throughout the world, IGY's synoptic measurements of glaciers and ice sheets – area, volume, accumulation, ablation, thickness, surface, and sub-surface characteristics – combined with meteorological observations would provide correlative and comparative data as a basis for studying and predicting change. Why, for example, were some Alaskan glaciers advancing when most were retreating? What would be the effects on sea level should the inland ice of Greenland and Antarctica begin to melt more rapidly?[48] The US plans for glaciology fieldwork concentrated on Alaska, the Greenland Ice Cap, and Antarctica, but cooperation with other nations would be necessary for a truly global program. The Soviet Union, with its large arctic expanse, would be a crucial participant in any comparative study of snow and ice.

By 1955, the Soviet Union established a larger official IGY presence at the CSAGI meeting in Brussels, and the delegation included a prominent glaciologist, Professor G. Avsiouk (also spelled Avsjuk). The US National Committee approached the Brussels meeting with great anticipation: what would the Soviet Union bring to the table? All three US armed services were required to attend the Brussels meeting. Invitations went out to high-ranking officials. The world had changed; Soviet scientists were now at the table. The US delegation numbered 39, and all participants received instructions and briefings on how to conduct themselves. In addition, the leaders for the various sessions were asked to describe the Soviet science plans and compare them to those of the United States. Questions included:

> What is your impression of the overall Soviet IGY program when compared to that of the US?
> Is the USSR program larger and better organized than the US program?
> Do you consider the Soviet program more advanced and comprehensive than that of the US?
> Which particular phases of your specialty having possible strategic applications to military problems are the Soviets working on?
> What is your most recent information regarding possible Soviet IGY plans in rocketry and radioactivity of the air?[49]

In response to the questionnaire, William Field reported that the USSR glaciology program was comprehensive and conformed in the main with the international program already developed by CSAGI, but that the main object of USSR investigations in glaciology was to study the processes of accumulation, formation, and ice expenditure on the earth's surface. Permafrost and other frost phenomena should be considered a form of glaciation, according to the Soviet proposal. Additionally, the USSR recommended observations of avalanches and ice-melt flows or glacial runoff.

After listening to the Soviet proposal, Paul Siple suggested that the IGY produce a broad inventory of all known glaciers, recording as a minimum location and elevation, name, approximate area, estimated volume, photographs, measurements of activity, and other observations of glaciological and meteorological value. The glaciology working group agreed to forward this recommendation to the main international IGY committee (CSAGI).[50]

Avsiouk, the Soviet delegate in glaciology, had been stationed in the Tien Shan mountains in Central Asia for 10 years and also worked in the Pamirs and in the Arctic. Field appears to have been impressed with Avsiouk's knowledge of glaciology both inside and outside of the USSR. As Field put it, 'Prof. Avsiouk knew a good deal more about glaciological developments outside the USSR than is known in the US about what goes on in the USSR itself,' probably because the Soviet science establishment took more pains to translate foreign material than did their counterparts in the United States.[51]

Field also understood the reasons for the comprehensive nature of the Soviet program:

> It should be pointed out that the study of glaciers in the Soviet Union has always been of much more direct economic importance than in this country. Glaciers in the Caucasus bear somewhat the same relationship as in the Alps to the local economy. Similarly, in Central Asia, glaciers of the Pamirs, Tien Shan, and other mountain ranges exert a considerable influence both as barriers and as means of access to mountain passes of economic and military significance. The runoff from glaciers in the ranges of Central Asia is also important in providing water to the adjacent arid areas of the USSR and northwestern China. In the Soviet Arctic the major concern is with navigation. More studies are made of floating sea ice than with glaciers or ice bergs, but some attention has been given to the ice caps on Novaya Zemlya, Franz Joseph Land, and Severnaya Zemlya. Here data on the variations of glaciers and the relationship to climatic change would play an important role as in the regions to the south. ... The inclusion of permafrost and other forms of frost phenomena is a logical one.[52]

Field himself had been in the Caucasus in the 1920s and was familiar with Russian geography. His report is the most comprehensive and analytical of all the US delegates' answers to the questions about the Soviet IGY program. He not only reported the content of the Soviet program and the ways in which it agreed with or differed from the US and CSAGI programs, but also offered reasons why the differences might be expected. In response to the Soviet plans, the working group on glaciology agreed to observations on runoff but added that measurement be extended to the transportation of solid load, since this is an important aspect of erosion and deposition by glaciers. With regard to permafrost and other frost studies, the working group recommended leaving it up to the member countries but suggesting such observations where feasible.

Soviet participation in IGY influenced the science programs of the United States. For example, Soviet plans for the Arctic included two drifting stations in the Arctic Ocean. Until the Soviet announcement at the 1955 Brussels meeting, the US IGY national committee had no plans for ice islands or drifting stations;[53] nor did the National Committee have a separate committee or working group for the Arctic as a region (as opposed to the Antarctic). The Brussels meeting inspired the creation of the US Ad Hoc Arctic Committee chaired by J. C. Reed of the US Geological Survey. N. C. Gerson, Air Force Cambridge Research Center, and executive secretary of the US National Committee, served as vice-chairman. The membership overlapped partially with the glaciology working group. The committee proposed two drifting stations in the arctic ice pack and asked that the USNC chairman 'emphasize to the appropriate Department of Defense official the possibility and desirability of expanding the US IGY geophysical program in the Arctic, based on the more complete revelation of other nations' arctic IGY programs at the Brussels meeting ...'[54] The Department of Defense charged the Air Force to establish and maintain the facilities for the drifting stations.

In late 1955, then, the Arctic acquired the same degree of geopolitical importance as the Antarctic in the US IGY agenda. For the military, the Arctic had been a subject of secret reconnaissance operations as well as of glaciological studies for the last decade, but now civilian science, which would be open, shared, and international, called upon US military support and logistics. Sea ice studies now joined land-based glaciology as an essential part of a regional Arctic science program.[55]

To better coordinate the various national arctic programs, CSAGI convened a special conference in Stockholm, 22–5 May 1956. Attended by delegates from Finland, Norway, Sweden, Iceland, Denmark, Canada, Germany, Poland, England, the United States, and the USSR, the Stockholm conference resulted in a proposal by a Soviet delegate, Dr V. F. Burkhanov. Dr J. C. Reed of the US delegation expressed an interest in obtaining continuous and consistent aerial photographs at regular time intervals to examine in detail the movement of the arctic ice. He outlined the US plans for flights from Fairbanks, Alaska, and in return Dr Burkhanov outlined the Soviet plans for flights originating in Murmansk. Burkhanov then suggested that the US and Soviet flights alternate, covering the same area between Fairbanks and Murmansk. The US delegation did not have the power to accept or reject this offer and simply recorded it in the minutes of the conference. However, notes of the US delegates indicate that they would have liked to accept the idea. After the Stockholm conference they were asked to record their impressions of their encounter with the USSR scientists, just as they were after the Brussels meeting. Every US delegate reported positive interactions and impressions. Formerly classified Russian volumes on geomagnetism were shared, although one delegate noted some of the pages had been cut out. The spirit of cooperation seemed to guide the conference, and everyone agreed on the necessity of exchanging publications, correspondence, and data. On the US side, the Soviet proposal for mutual overflights went to the State Department for a decision.[56]

Just three months earlier, President Eisenhower canceled Project Genetrix, a program of launching high-altitude photo-reconnaissance balloons over the USSR. In early 1956, the Strategic Air Command had launched 516 of them from Western Europe and Turkey, but was able to retrieve only 44 of them. At the same time Eisenhower approved an Air Force project to fly SAC reconnaissance aircraft over and around the Soviet North, mapping it completely. Project Homerun launched the flights from Thule, Greenland, between 22 March and 10 May 1956. The planes flew almost daily over the North Pole to cover the entire northern slope and interior portions of the USSR, from the Kola Peninsula to the Bering Strait.[57]

The USSR protested the American overflights, and on 28 May 1956, Eisenhower met with top administration officials to prepare a response. The following July, a U-2 plane flew a first mission over the Soviet Union and drew another protest. In December, three bombers outfitted for photo-reconnaissance took off from Japan for the Soviet Far East, again drawing a Soviet protest. Eisenhower ended the US military flights a few days after receiving the Soviet note (CIA overflights continued periodically).[58]

These flights were highly classified. The object was to determine whether the Soviet Union had long-range bombers at its northern bases. The purpose of recounting the program here, in connection with IGY, is to show that while the spirit of scientific cooperation reigned at the Stockholm conference, tension between the two countries was at an all-time high. On 20 September 1956, the US State Department issued a note to the Soviet Embassy offering an arrangement whereby the Soviet and American planes would make alternate flights between Murmansk and Nome, a small town on the coast of Alaska that was far from the strategic site of Fairbanks, 'along routes and under such operating conditions as agreed upon by our two Governments.'[59] In November the Soviet Union replied that the Soviet Air Force would take care of the aerial photography of the ice on the Soviet side of the Pole, and the proposal for alternate missions disappeared.[60]

While the US military was directly involved in the IGY as a logistics provider and research supporter, and secret programs, such as the use of submarines under arctic sea ice, co-existed with the open IGY programs, it was understood that research results from the IGY would be freely available and shared across national borders. To be sure, the IGY programs were mostly conducted on a national basis. Yet agreement by the national programs to share data through a system of World Data Centres marked the IGY as a triumph of science over secrecy.

GLACIOLOGY, THE ARCTIC, AND THE IGY

The Arctic as well as the Antarctic provided platforms for IGY research that included but was not limited to glaciology. Likewise, glaciology was done outside of the polar regions on mountain glaciers in Africa, North and South America, and Eurasia. The mass balance of glaciers, the relationship of glacial variation to changes in solar radiation, and variations in atmospheric circulation were some of the main questions that glaciologists sought to answer during the IGY. Methods included photogrammetry and mapping, calculation of accumulation and ablation through isotope studies and stratigraphy, and observations/calculations of radiation and albedo (percentage of incoming radiation that is reflected off the surface).[61]

A major emphasis of the IGY glaciology program was deep ice core drilling in Greenland and Antarctica, drilling that eventually led to an understanding of past climate change. The geophysics of snow and ice demonstrate the overlapping interests of military and civilian science. The properties of ice on sea and land determined whether planes could land, submarines could surface, and technology could be used to detect or avoid detection. For the civilian scientists, innovations in equipment and instrumentation yielded new methods and observations of earth system history.

Of the 67 countries that participated in IGY, about 15 had active glaciology programs. The two countries with the most extensive programs in terms of coverage and geographical distribution were the United States and the USSR. As Field wrote in 1962:

> Communications established for the first time in the IGY have been maintained. The system of World Data Centres A, B, and C in the US, the USSR, and the UK have continued to function. Furthermore, in line with the trend toward internationalism, the British Glaciological Society early in 1962 changed its name to the Glaciological Society. In 1960 at Helsinki the Commission of Snow and Ice of the International Association of Scientific Hydrology, IUGG [International Union of Geodesy and Geophysics], elected for its officers a President from the USSR, a Secretary from the UK, and three Vice-Presidents from France, Italy, and the US.[62]

Glaciology during IGY led to heightened efforts to coordinate measurement on a worldwide basis. UNESCO launched the International Hydrological Decade (IHD), 1965–74, to enable countries to assess their water resources. Leading up to the IHD, Peter Kasser of the Swiss Federal Institute of Technology conducted a study of glacier fluctuations for the International Association of Scientific Hydrology, incorporating data from the IGY and from the earlier reports of the International Commission of Glaciers.[63] As a result, UNESCO produced for the IHD data compilation and other guidelines for international studies of perennial ice and snow masses, glacial variations, Antarctic glaciology, and mass balance at selected glacier basins.

The technology emanating from IGY – the rocketry and satellites, drilling equipment, and cold-adapted instrumentation – enabled glaciology to become a much more exacting science. The science of overflight, observation, and detection that emerged in part from national interests in winning the Cold War became a means to understand the earth's past as well as predict future change. Major syntheses of continuous observations and study, such as the Arctic Climate Impact Assessment, point to the importance of internationally coordinated long-term observation systems and process studies.[64]

The scientists who first proposed an international polar year in 1950 (which later became a more encompassing geophysical year) debated among themselves whether the Soviet Union would participate. After Stalin's death, it seemed more likely. When the Soviet Union did accept the invitation, western scientists caught a glimpse – in many cases, for the first time – of the instrumentation, facilities, methods, and products of their Russian counterparts. For the relatively small and unorganized field of glaciology, the IGY enabled researchers to coordinate their measurements and methods to provide comparability over vast geographical regions and set the stage for longitudinal studies of climate. Despite the Cold War and the fact that a great deal of polar research remained classified, the glaciology program of IGY demonstrated that open, civilian science on a worldwide basis is not only possible, but highly desirable in times of political tension.

The same individuals who had been carrying out glaciology research under US military programs during and/or immediately after the Second World War continued to do research during the IGY. This chapter has focused on two of them, Paul Siple and William Field. Siple represented the pre-IGY national mission of understanding and functioning in extreme environments for the purpose of maintaining national superiority in wartime situations. Yet Siple as a scientist was able to adapt to and even help establish the research agenda of an open, civilian, and international program. Field was less comfortable with nationalism and much more at home with sharing methodologies, theories, and data among interested scientists for the purpose of understanding glacial environments in different parts of the world. Both Siple and Field were drawn to the Arctic and sub-Arctic as a relatively unknown region. For them, exploration was of the scientific as well as geographic frontier.

After the IGY, the Cold War continued and the Arctic remained a contested territory (not the least by indigenous peoples who pressed their claims through courts and legislatures), but it was no longer an unknown frontier. It was both a laboratory and a strategic space where field work and military exercises took place simultaneously, sometimes using the same platforms and means of transport. For example, use of US Navy submarines and hydrophone systems in the early 1990s allowed scientists to study the ocean depths. As the Cold War came to an end, and the US military interest waned, scientific interest in the Arctic remained.

What then is the role of exploration? The emergence of glaciology as a means of understanding the development of ice-covered environments such as the Arctic relied in part on technological progress in transportation and deep drilling. In the years following the IGY, getting to the field and back became less arduous for the individual scientist than the analysis of the massive amounts of data that could be collected from a short time in the field or from automated instruments left in the field. The post-IGY transition from natural history to model-based knowledge of the Arctic and its role in climate change has meant that knowledge of the Arctic no longer requires exploration. To develop a sense of stewardship and a commitment to the Arctic, Matthew Sturm encourages us to impart the history of Arctic exploration and scientific research to our students.[65] As the effects of rapid environmental change, including the possibility of an ice-free Arctic, once again mobilizes national security concerns, commitment to the Arctic as a region rather than a means to national security requires the openness of an IGY.

7 Assault on the unknown: Geopolitics, Antarctic science and the International Geophysical Year (1957–8)

Klaus Dodds

Is there one big Antarctic continent, or are there two Antarctic landmasses cemented by an ice cap of unknown depth? The geographer wishes to know ...[1]

No longer does an expedition venture into the unknown knowing that for the rest of the world, it will be unseen and unseeing, unheard and unhearing for an indefinite period until its returning ship touching at some New Zealand port, bring to the world views of the drama of the past months or years.[2]

This chapter is concerned with an extraordinary episode of international scientific endeavour – the International Geophysical Year (IGY) of 1957–8. The *New York Times'* science journalist, Walter Sullivan, rightly described the IGY as an 'assault on the unknown'.[3] Notwithstanding the accumulation of geographical knowledge since the eighteenth-century crossing by Captain Cook of the

Antarctic Circle, the Antarctic was still comparatively unknown when considered alongside the Arctic, the Equatorial jungles and high mountains such as Everest. It continued to defy cartographers and geographers eager even to trace the outline of a continent let alone explore and research the polar interior. While the quest for the South Pole in the early twentieth century aroused further passion, limited funding meant that exploratory and scientific work in the inter-war period was sporadic at best. Paradoxically, the onset of the Second World War galvanised many countries including Argentina, Britain and New Zealand to initiate new polar expeditions, which carried out detailed mapping and surveying of parts of the polar continent and sub-Antarctic islands such as Auckland and Campbell.

The IGY was, therefore, an ideal opportunity for polar scientists to accumulate new knowledge about the Antarctic. Specific practices and disciplines such as mapping and geophysics were vital accomplices in the search for a greater understanding of the southern continent. Even though the IGY encompassed other parts of the Earth's surface as well as outer space, attention was devoted to the Antarctic.[4] Over a period of 18 months, 12 countries and 5,000 scientists from the United States, the Soviet Union, Japan, Britain and eight others established over 50 research stations in order to, *inter alia*, further explore and investigate the geophysical qualities of the Antarctic continent and the electromagnetic properties of the earth. Seismic soundings accompanied by geographical traverses of the polar icecap were critical in generating a more nuanced physical sense of Antarctica, one in which icecap thickness and continent integrity prefigured.[5] Scientific stations were, during this period and thereafter, intended to be information colonies tasked with importing ideas and energy and exporting raw data for further analysis.

The research generated in the Antarctic was intended, therefore, to connect up with scientific research of the earth as a whole and outer space. As Harry Wexler, one of the chief scientists attached to the US-IGY Antarctic programme noted, 'the adjective geophysical is substituted for "Polar" [he was referring to earlier International Polar Years in 1882–3 and 1932–3] because of the emphasis on the study of the earth as a whole'.[6] The poles were an important element in this global enterprise and their scientific importance was further enhanced by geopolitical considerations. The Antarctic, although comparatively poorly mapped and studied, underwent a fundamental re-evaluation. If eighteenth- and nineteenth-century writers and poets were fixated with the thought that the Antarctic might harbour monstrous ice and repressed terror, others were prepared to consider the possibility that a southerly paradise awaited the brave and the intrepid.[7] By the twentieth century, the Antarctic was still poorly understood but new ideas and practices were being deployed in an attempt to impose scientific and political order on this unruly space. This transition from mythological and romantic understandings of the polar continent to more scientific and systematic was not smooth, however. Even in the 1940s, some elements within German Nazism were dreaming of the Antarctic as a physical platform for a new Aryan civilization.[8]

The onset of the Cold War in the late 1940s had a paradoxical effect on the Antarctic. On the one hand, changing technologies such as the long-range bomber aeroplane and ballistic missile were eroding senses of distance and remoteness. The United States and geographically proximate states such as Argentina, Chile, South Africa, Australia and New Zealand were re-assessing their geopolitical and strategic priorities with regard to the Antarctic.[9] Research by American scientists unquestionably benefited because successive administrations were eager to invest in the creation of knowledge, especially if offered some measure of strategic advantage over the Soviets and their allies. On the other hand, this meant that ideas about the Antarctic as a place also changed. In a curious return to some of the earliest debates about the possible existence of a southerly continent; the lure of gold and other mineral resources alongside fears of unknown strategic activity on and beneath the ice co-existed uneasily with more sombre discussions about the continent's geophysical connections to the globe.

Given that the IGY occurred in the midst of a Cold War between the United States and the Soviet Union and their respective allies, exploratory and scientific activities were even more geopolitically embedded, especially in the aftermath of the 1950–3 conflict on the Korean Peninsula. This conflict was catalytic in the sense of persuading military and intelligence agencies to expand their involvement in scientific communities for the purpose of improving offensive and defensive capabilities. More generally, Simon Leslie and John Cloud are surely right when they note, albeit in different scientific contexts, the existence of a Cold War military – industrial – academic complex.[10] In post-war United States, as other historians of the earth and geophysical sciences such as Ronald Doel have concurred, the intelligence agencies, the armed forces (in the case of the Antarctic, the US Navy (USN)) and scientists were frequently drawn to one another whether they wished it or not.[11] As Alan Hemmings has noted, there was no shortage of what might be described as military-utility research.[12] The emergence of the Soviet Union as an atomic power helped many American scientists and others to rationalise the need for those networks and relationships – the ideological context of the Cold War and the necessity of the confrontation with the Soviets, was as a consequence, part of a taken for granted life-world. As Doel and Needell have concluded, 'By the time the Korean War broke out in 1950, most American scientists regarded the Soviet Union as a credible threat to American national security, and accepted that Communist Party interference was distorting the Soviet scientific community.'[13]

The participation of the Soviet Union in IGY-based research greatly concerned political leaders and journalists in the United States and its southern hemispheric allies such as Australia and South Africa – albeit for different reasons.[14] In the case of the United States, the Eisenhower administration was worried that the Soviets were developing a substantial and intimidating scientific-technological capacity.[15] The high-profile launch of Sputnik in October 1957, during the IGY itself, provided apparently ample evidence for such a judgement.[16] Their exploratory and scientific plans in the Antarctic elicited further anxiety as the Soviets established a base at the Pole of Relative Inaccessibility. Figure 7.1 illustrates how the Soviets and Americans in particular located their scientific bases all over the polar continent. While justified in ostensibly scientific terms, their geographical distribution was also judged to be invaluable if, and when, it was necessary to press a territorial claim to the region.

Given the prevailing Cold War, the Soviet bases were perceived to be a direct challenge not only to the United States' role as a global leader in exploration, science and technology but also to their traditional position of reserving the right to make a substantial claim to Antarctica, on the basis of previous American episodes of exploration and settlement activity. There were, by the time of the IGY, unquestionably two large powers that possessed the capacity to establish bases

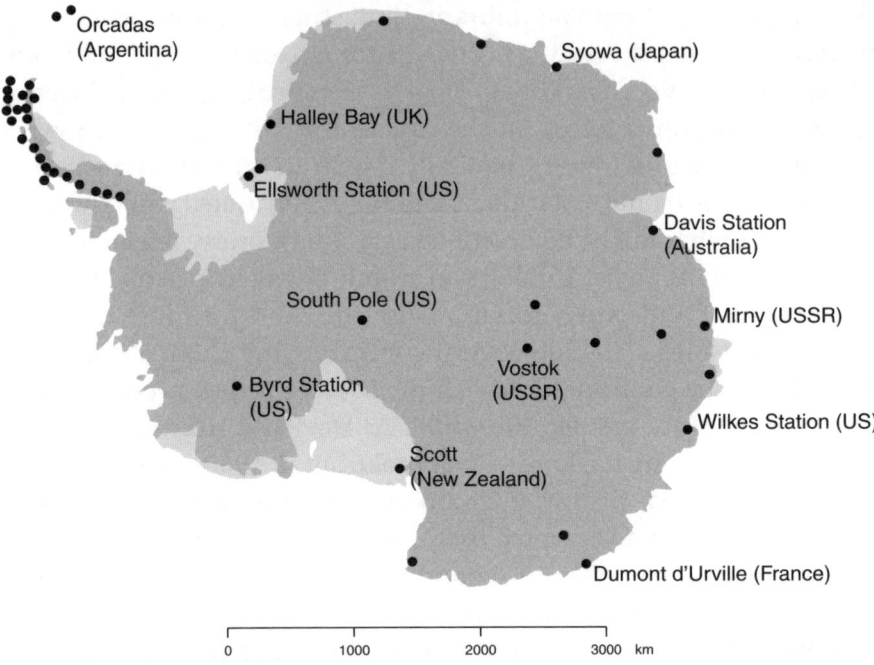

FIGURE 7.1 Map of the major scientific stations on Antarctica during the IGY. Lighter shading indicates floating icesheet.

across the Antarctic continent. Ten years earlier, the United States and its allies had hoped that they could exclude the Soviet Union from a condominium designed to manage the political affairs of the continent. Soviet participation in the IGY demonstrated how untenable that aspiration now was.[17] In 1949, the All Soviet Geographical Society reiterated its commitment to pursuing studies of the Antarctic and the Stalin government, in less than a year, confirmed its intention to strengthen its interests in the polar region.[18]

For the duration of the IGY, seven claimant states including the three counter-claimants Argentina, Britain and Chile were sharing the polar continent with five non-claimant states including the two superpowers. In 1956, in a move that only complicated Antarctic geopolitics still further, India raised the issue of the Antarctic at the United Nations and questioned whether the polar continent should be managed in the wider interests of the international community. At the same, one claimant state, New Zealand, raised the possibility of renouncing its territorial claim in the belief that might encourage further co-operation in the Antarctic. Both proposals did not proceed beyond public discussion and thus were never implemented. Ultimately, the pioneers behind the IGY hoped that this complex legacy of territorial and counter-territorial claims would not hamper international scientific co-operation, and for much of the period in question scientists and the militaries that provide logistical support were able to co-exist with one another. As American scientist, Ronald Potts recollected in June 2000, 'I cannot recognise many accounts of the period because they leave out the spirit of co-operation fostered by the IGY.'[19] During the IGY, he has worked with Soviet scientists in the Antarctic. The spirit of co-operation and scientific exchange, moreover, did not suddenly terminate with the ending of the IGY as British, American and Australian scientists continued to work with their Soviet counterparts.[20]

The changing geopolitical condition of the Antarctica is only one aspect of this momentous era. Arguably, the IGY contributed not only to new stores of scientific knowledge but also to a different set of geographical understandings about the polar continent. Antarctic science, as with other areas of scientific activity in remote spaces such as the ocean basins, was entering into a decisive phase aided and abetted by higher levels of funding, co-operation with military and intelligence communities, state-sponsored logistical support and, where appropriate, a wider network of scientific stations.[21] Antarctica was arguably little different from other areas of Cold War scientific endeavour. As Ronald Doel has claimed, 'US geopolitical strategy involving Antarctica was furthered by allowing this continent to be "constituted for science"'.[22] One of the most decisive developments was the use of seismic sounding and long-distance traverses, which helped to enhance understanding of the Antarctic landmass and icecap thickness.

This chapter is organised into three further sections. First, the contested geopolitics of the Antarctica is considered because it had a critical impact on twentieth-century exploration. For example, Britain's Falklands Islands Dependencies Survey (FIDS) carried out little mapping and surveying outside the country's claimed sector because there was neither the resources nor the strategic rationale to do so. Non-claimant states such as the United States felt no such constraint and thus devoted resources and personnel to explore and investigate the entire Antarctic continent. Second, the IGY and its relationship to Cold War science is reviewed with particular attention being devoted to the role of the United States' IGY programme and the USN therein. Institutions such as the USN were critical in facilitating the implementation of scientific research and their presence greatly extended the geographical remit of scientists. It also meant that science, exploration and the geopolitical priorities of the US military were co-joined in a latter-day Faustian pact. The final substantive section considers how new forms of research especially in the form of seismic sounding and geographical traverses generated a different sense of Antarctica, which bore little resemblance to at least a thousand years of speculation about a southerly world filled either with monstrous ice or unimaginable wealth. Scientists could, for the first time since ancient Greek geographers speculated on the existence of the Antarctic, talk confidently of a polar continent composed of an icecap extending well over 10,000 feet (c. 3000 metres) in thickness.

THE ANTARCTIC PROBLEM: EXPLORATION, GEOPOLITICS AND TERRITORIAL CLAIMS

By the time the first territorial claim was pressed by the British in 1908, knowledge of the Antarctic continent and Southern Ocean was fragmentary. Coastlines had been barely mapped and awareness of the continental interior was highly circumscribed, as the 1896 International Geographical Congress had recognised.[23] Exploration remained also a highly seasonal affair and largely restricted to the summer season (October – March). Ironically, dog sledging during the summer season was often carried out 'at night' because the ice was firmer. During the polar winter, personnel were largely restricted to their bases and those that did undertake exploration and travel, in the midst of the perpetual darkness and unforgiving blizzards, became the stuff of legends.[24] Whatever the time of year, exploration and discovery, as Captain Scott and his team discovered in 1912, could be fatal in the Antarctic.[25] The blueprint for a British Antarctic Empire was not realised in part because of appalling weather and geographical inaccessibility. Even for those who survived in the polar region, the liveliness and sheer unpredictability of the continent was never far from their minds let alone bodies. Bases were consumed, aircraft grounded, ships were trapped and the ice occasionally killed men.[26]

These kinds of physical constraints did not hinder ever more elaborate so-called 'ceremonies of possession' designed to incorporate Antarctic territory into the national jurisdictions of claimant states.[27] Resource exploitation especially whaling provided a lucrative incentive to assert control over Antarctic territory and the surrounding ocean. Prior to the Second World War, whaling and private expeditions dominated the region's human activities. While explorers and scientists were, in some cases, required to undertake formal claiming ceremonies, others were expected to combine the roles of scientist, postmaster, magistrate and even Justice of Peace.[28] Between the first territorial claim (1908) and the IGY (1957–8), seven countries namely Argentina, Australia, Britain, Chile, France, New Zealand and Norway made such claims to polar territory. Argentine, British and Chilean claims to the Antarctic Peninsula and surrounding islands overlapped with one another. This contributed to what one contemporary observer called 'the Antarctic problem'.[29] Others such as the United States and the Soviet Union reserved the right to make a future claim and categorically rejected the legitimacy of existing claims. By the 1940s only one part of the Antarctic continent remained unclaimed – the so-called Pacific Ocean sector (see Figure 7.2). Arguably the most remote and least accessible part of the polar environment, Britain and its Commonwealth allies hoped, without success, that the United States would eventually press a formal claim. Successive American administrations were, however, reluctant to restrict their potential territorial jurisdiction to one specific sector because their extensive record of exploration and discovery would mean that any claim could be far greater than merely the 'Pacific Sector'.[30]

This evolving territorial tapestry had several implications for Antarctic exploration and science. First, the geopolitics of the region placed important restraints on the nature and scope of activity. In the case of a claimant state such as Britain, the main agency responsible for polar science was exclusively charged with mapping and surveying 'British Antarctica'. Created in 1945 and managed by the Colonial Office, the FIDS (as the name suggested) was concerned with producing reliable maps of the region for the explicit purpose of strengthening British claims in the face of South American opposition. This did not mean that British Antarctic scientists were unable to co-operate with colleagues from different countries as witnessed by the 1949–52

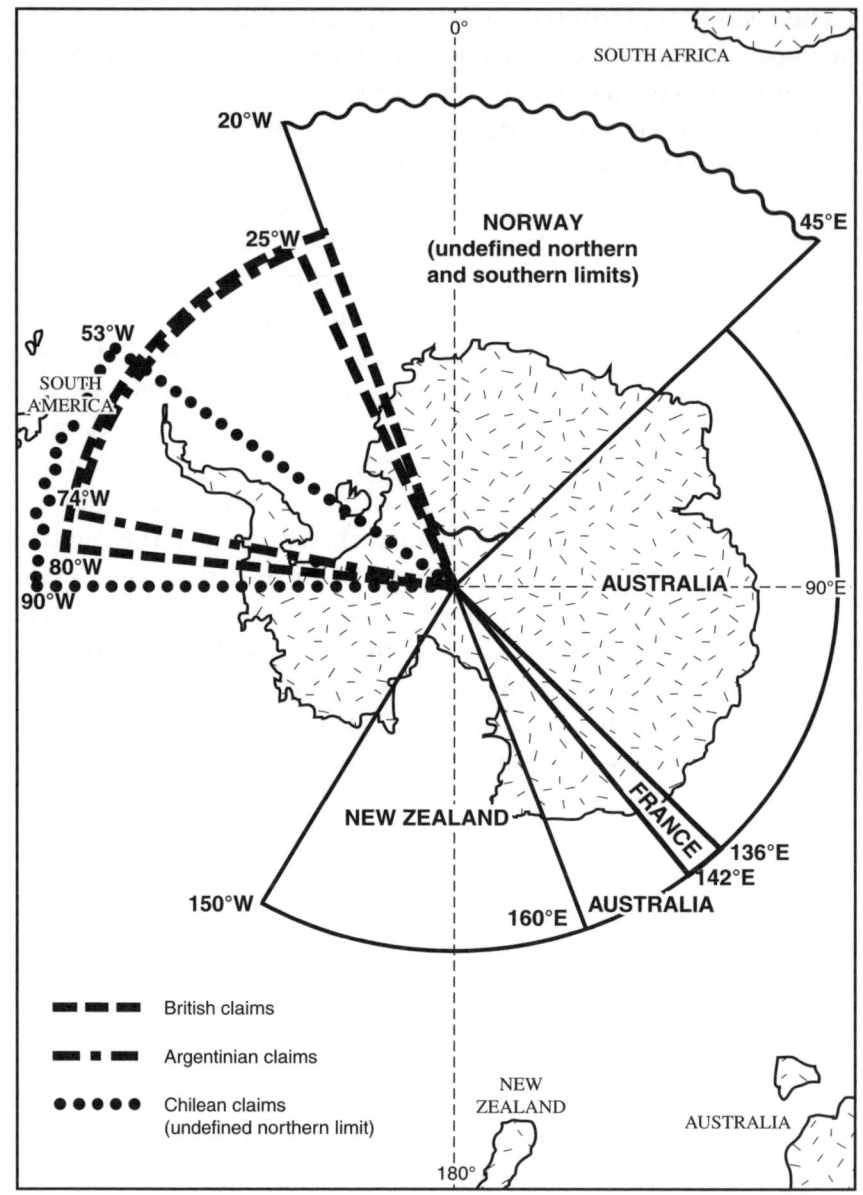

FIGURE 7.2 National claims to the Antarctic.

Norwegian – British – Swedish Antarctic Expedition (which occurred within the Norwegian sector) and acts of co-operation with American polar counterparts in the late 1940s. However, the perceived need to scientifically service the British Antarctic sector was considered overwhelming. If this servicing was not done to a satisfactory standard as measured by map production or scientific output, then FIDS staff frequently faced criticism from polar administrators in Whitehall and threats of funding cuts. As a consequence, exploratory activity was geographically targeted and areas such as the Antarctic Peninsula and outlying islands such as Deception were considered to be a priority because of counter-claimants and the comparative accessibility of this part of the Antarctic to other visitors such as the USN and individual explorer-leaders such as Admiral Richard Byrd and Captain Finn Ronne. Importantly, the Royal Society-sponsored IGY research station, Halley Hay, had its eventual location determined by more overtly scientific rather than geopolitical criteria.

Argentina, Britain and Chile were engaged in a mapping war, which led to the respective authorities sending one another their updated maps and charts for the purpose of demonstrating cartographic chutzpah.[31] The British frequently worried about the quality of the Argentine polar maps and vice versa. As one official attached to the Directorate of Overseas Surveys acknowledged to a colleague in the Foreign Office in February 1958, 'Most of the detail is obviously taken from air photographs, the coastal detail is very convincing and the inland detail, though stylized, has also a fairly authentic appearance. Certainly these [maps] are a great improvement.'[32] Preparations for the IGY only produced additional pressures as none of the participants could be certain what would happen either during this period or the immediate aftermath. Conflict was not out of the question as the British and Argentines had already clashed over Deception Island in 1953.[33] Shots were fired, plaques and flags destroyed and rival parties threatened with a dousing of ice-cold water.

Second, as a consequence of the first factor, funding for scientific exploration and investigation was better financed and organised in the immediate post-war period. Funding for FIDS was increased and the number of bases and summer-only stations increased particularly in the Antarctic Peninsula region.[34] The Colonial Office was responsible for FIDS but worked closely with other agencies including the Foreign Office, the military and the Governor of the Falkland Islands. Other countries such as the United States deployed their naval forces and newly created agencies such as the National Science Foundation

(NSF, 1950) sponsored continental wide exploration and mapping. The NSF established a government-funded model of polar activity based on congressional appropriations. In 1953, a grant of $5000 was awarded for IGY preparations but by 1956 that had been transformed to $40 million. The decision of the Soviet Union to resume interest in the Antarctic was critical and indeed US Antarctic science was a major beneficiary as a consequence. The well-connected geophysical scientist, Lloyd Berkner, was able to persuade the Eisenhower administration to restore in addition the science attaché programme at the Department of State.[35] Science in general, especially in the United States, was enjoying higher levels of funding and political exposure with the onset of the Cold War and the Antarctic was not isolated from this general development.

By the time the IGY was initiated, the United States and the Soviet Union were operating polar stations littered across the entire continent and in so doing provoking unease on the part of the claimant states, in particular Britain, Argentina, Chile and New Zealand. Likewise, the growing presence of the Soviet Union caused discomfort to the Australian authorities, who were eager to ensure that the Soviets understood that they were formally operating in Australian Antarctic Territory (AAT). The Australians, for instance, offered to issue radio licences to the Soviet Antarctic programme operating in the AAT, but the Soviet planners simply ignored the gesture.[36] At the heart of the matter were two rather different sorts of models of Antarctic exploration. The first was geographically selective (all claimant states and smaller polar operators such as the South Africans) and the second was geographically expansive (the United States and the Soviet Union) with correspondingly different levels of funding and attitudes towards territorial claims. American over-flights (supported by the US armed forces) were helping to generate a far more comprehensive sense of the scale and extent of the polar continent than ever before. New maps, produced by the American Geographical Society, also played a critical role in presenting for wider audiences the achievements of American explorers and naval officers such as Admiral Byrd.

Third, and closely linked to the aforementioned factors, different kinds of agencies and individuals were beginning to exercise control over Antarctic exploration and scientific activity. Within Britain, new figures such as Brian Roberts of the Foreign Office and the Scott Polar

Research Institute at Cambridge became the key players shaping British Antarctic policy.[37] In Argentina and Chile, the military were the most important shapers of polar expeditions and, in the United States, a civil – military relationship was critical in determining the scale and extent of polar exploration. Lloyd Berkner was again instrumental in calling for an enhanced role for scientific expertise in American foreign policy making. The creation of the NSF was, according to his vision, just one element in this strategic enhancement of science. He was also content to liaise closely with the military and worked for the Joint Research and Development Board (JRDB) and the Pentagon. In general terms, most of the countries active in the Antarctic in the 1940s and 1950s were creating new government agencies for the purpose of professionalising Antarctic activities, and the United States was leading the way in embedding the military in logistical and developmental activities.

Finally, Antarctic exploration and scientific investigation was becoming increasingly visible within the public cultures of claimant and non-claimant states alike. While the Antarctic must have felt as remote as the moon for many newspaper readers in the northern hemisphere, a new breed of polar explorers (both civilian- and military-based) was beginning to emerge which helped to develop a sense of immediacy. Individuals such as Admiral Richard Byrd and later Sir Ed Hillary became American and British/Commonwealth household names from the 1940s onwards. One important feature of the IGY was the presence of journalists such as Noel Barber (*Daily Express*) at Antarctic stations who helped to publicise the achievements of scientists as opposed to explorers. Other journalists such as Walter Sullivan of the *New York Times* were catalytic in this popularisation of Antarctic science and exploration. This is not, of course, to underestimate the role played by print media in sensationalising earlier acts of polar endeavour, rather it is to acknowledge that exploration and scientific investigation alongside the changing geopolitics of the Antarctic was inviting ever more newspaper column inches, radio commentaries and filmic treatments.[38]

Some of the reporting was unquestionably spirited, in the sense that some journalists and academic commentators adopted the role of Cassandra and predicted that the polar continent would become a scene of discord. In the 1958 edition of the *American Mercury*, journalist

Ray Cromley warned readers that the United States needed to consider making a claim to the polar continent because:

> It might be very useful for missile or atom bomb testing The Antarctic has great strategic value ... The Antarctic also has minerals ... The Antarctic is probably the best place in the world to track and record messages from satellites revolving around a north – south orbit ... We may not have much time left. Some dedicated Americans, are pushing hard behind the scenes, to get United States actions [sic] before it is too late.[39]

Very few highly placed individuals interested in the Antarctic such as Admiral Richard Byrd believed that the forthcoming plans for the IGY, even if they provided a temporary sovereignty freeze, would remove the need for the United States to think carefully about its strategic and political interests in the region. He also concluded that the potential resource value should not be under-appreciated: 'As we recklessly squander our natural resources in this country [i.e. the US] we will need these new resources. It is imperative that they do not fall into the hands of a potential enemy.'[40]

Science, exploration and geopolitics were perceived by many political leaders and journalists to be a dangerous if necessary cocktail, which had to be handled carefully especially during the Cold War. In November 1956, on the eve of the IGY, a secret Australian paper prepared for their Joint Intelligence Committee summed up the collective zeitgeist of the English-speaking participants such as Britain and the United States. Entitled 'The strategic value of Antarctica to the Communist Bloc and any threat which might arise to Australia from their use of bases in Antarctica up to 1958', it noted that the Soviet Union would gain valuable oceanographic, climatic and geomagnetic information which would be vital to the future development of missile systems and their navigation.[41] Antarctic exploration was seen to have a dual function. Both scientists and military operators from the Soviet Union and elsewhere in the Communist Bloc would unquestionably benefit. Australia, however, as with the United States and its other allies would simply have to ensure that it derived maximum advantage from this period of international collaboration. The Australians also hoped, somewhat optimistically, that the Soviets might be persuaded to leave their bases in the aftermath of the IGY. By February 1957, it was conceded by all the Western allies that the Soviet Union were firmly entrenched in the region and unlikely to depart in the aftermath of December 1958. Despite the soothsayers predicting Soviet territorial claims being pressed either during or immediately after the IGY, no such development occurred.[42]

US SCIENCE, THE IGY AND THE COLD WAR

Most historians of post-1945 US science concur that the Cold War marked a major turning point in the funding and organisation of physical and life sciences.[43] The development of the Manhattan Project and the post-war development of the nuclear bomb provide just one illustration of many of how science, in this case nuclear physics, became a critical element in security planning, military operations and claims to national prestige.[44] Later serious consideration was given by scientists such as Edward Teller and military personnel to using nuclear explosions for the purpose of 'geographical engineering' in apparent remote spaces such as the Alaskan Arctic.[45] In the case of the Antarctic, Walter Sullivan noted in the journal *Foreign Affairs* that some discussion had also occurred regarding the use of atomic energy in order to melt away the Antarctic ice sheet so that it might be easier to exploit any minerals buried under the ice.[46]

Although a great deal of credit is given to the co-operative spirit that prevailed throughout the IGY, James Spiller has rightly noted that 'President Dwight D. Eisenhower's security and foreign affairs advisors endorsed the Antarctic, component of the IGY for a narrow, geopolitical reason.'[47] The United States wanted to reduce international tension over the Antarctic, while at the same time obtain geophysical and atmospheric data deemed vital for national security planning. In this respect, the Eisenhower administration marked a shift away from President Truman's aspirations for a humanitarian form of science and the role of the United States as a provider of scientific and technological knowledge to 'under-developed' areas.[48] President Eisenhower recognised that America's scientific capabilities could be used to influence US relations with not only European allies but also third-world states in Latin America, South Asia and Africa. Securing scientific co-operation in the Antarctic would enable the United States to concentrate its energies elsewhere in the world.

Within the physical sciences, disciplines such as geodesy, cartography and geophysics also emerged as strategically significant. The geophysicist and engineer Lloyd Berkner played a key role in promoting major scientific programmes, which would have a direct benefit to the United States and its pre-eminent role in global exploration and data collection. Berkner, having been Executive Secretary of the JRDB's Policy Council, had extensive experience of liaising with national government departments.[49] The Secretaries of War and Navy created the JRDB in 1946 for the purpose of facilitating the input of scientific research into national security planning.[50]

Two basic trends contributed to the rise of the physical and life sciences during this period. First, growing international interest in the Antarctic, the ocean floors, deserts and the consequences of nuclear testing reinforced the perceived need to have extensive information about these environments. Second, as noted earlier, military interest in ballistic missile systems and anti-submarine warfare meant that it was judged critical to have an understanding of specific operating environments including the Antarctic. New geophysical and oceanographic institutions were created as a consequence in the United States and institutions such as the Mapping and Charting Research Laboratory at Ohio State University became major centres of geodesy, for example. As John Cloud has noted, these organisations were central in enhancing models of the figure of the earth so vital for the determination of positions and distances.[51] Global sharing of data was considered critical by scientists as they strove to enhance understanding of ocean floors and remote terrestrial environments such as the polar regions.

In April 1950, Berkner and other scientists such as James Van Allen and Sydney Chapman proposed an IGY because new information was needed about the earth and its upper atmosphere in order to assist the further development of rockets, radars and missile instrumentation.[52] While aware of the military application of this research, these scientists were also eager to stress the benefits of developing international co-operation in the physical environmental sciences. The United States did not have the resources and logistics to explore and investigate all the world's extreme environments. The idea for an IGY was submitted to the International Council of Scientific Unions (ICSU) for consideration and subsequent approval in 1952. The period 1957–8 was proposed because it coincided with maximum solar activity and gave participants the opportunity to plan for a programme of exploration and research lasting 18 months. In the case of the Antarctic this would embrace two polar summer seasons and allow for 12 months of research in more benign conditions. As Vice-President of the ICSU (1957–9) and a member of President Eisenhower's Scientific Advisory Commission, Berkner was to be at the epicentre of America's endeavours during the IGY. The British glaciologist Sydney Chapman was elected President of the ICSU, a particularly suitable choice given his prior involvement in the 1932–3 International Polar Year.[53]

Antarctica had been identified by the planners of the IGY as a major area of geophysical interest. Knowledge of the polar continent and its upper atmosphere remained fragmentary. Exploration of the continental interior remained piecemeal and little was known of the depth of the polar ice mass and possible connections to global weather systems. If scientists were frustrated by these gaps of knowledge, so too were the military. In the early 1950s, the Arctic and Antarctic were emerging areas of strategic interest to the United States. Wartime experiences in both Polar Regions had already demonstrated that enemy forces were quite capable of traversing ice and frigid water in order to attack shipping and/or installations in places such as the Aleutian Islands off the Alaskan Peninsula and the Southern Ocean. Demands for new maps and surveys intensified with the onset of the Cold War, as it became clearer that the United States and the Soviet Union were only separated by the Bering Strait and the larger Arctic Ocean. As missile technology improved and the flight paths of bombers expanded, the apparent shrinking of distance generated new sets of anxieties and fears about the capabilities and intentions of the other side. Maps had to be improved and higher resolution aerial photographs were considered essential, especially those to be obtained later by U2 spy planes over the Soviet Union. In order to process this new data, the Eisenhower administration created major mapping facilities at the Army Map Service in Bethesda and enhanced the Naval Hydrographic Office at the Naval Yards close to Washington DC.[54]

This geopolitical atmosphere led to new investment in those environmental sciences deemed relevant to a new Cold War theatre, which was genuinely global in scope. Geography, cartography and geodesy were major beneficiaries in terms of funding and logistical support. Even if the polar continent was somewhat remote in terms of the prevailing US – Soviet confrontation, leading figures such as Admiral Byrd were convinced that the Antarctic's strategic importance was likely to increase in the post-1945 period. As with the Arctic, the Antarctic became a geopolitical and scientific frontier for the United States and other interested parties.[55] In 1946–7, the USN participated in Operation *Highjump*, which witnessed the dispatch of 13 ships and over 4,000 personnel including scientists to the Antarctic. Three main groups (Eastern, Western and Central) were created for the purpose of instigating extensive aerial and land-based exploration of the polar continent. It was also a major opportunity for the military to engage in cold weather training with the Antarctic functioning as an analogue environment for the militarised Arctic.

The following year, the USN launched Operation *Windmill* and this time helicopters were deployed for the purpose of transporting surveyors around the Antarctic landscape in an attempt to establish ground control with reference to the aerial photography. While the weather intervened to disrupt proceedings, the two operations provided a model of future Antarctic operations. As Aant Elzinga concluded, 'The mapping done in both the north and south poles shortly after the war by the US was a way of de-scaling the wartime build up, and testing equipment and personnel in order to combat a new "enemy"; one that boasted polar lands and experience.'[56] This operational experience was invaluable for pre-IGY planning especially when the 1955 CSGAI conference in Paris envisaged a network of research stations scattered across the Antarctic for the purpose of co-ordinating continental-wide scientific activities involving the United States and 11 other parties.

The USN later provided extensive logistical support (under the guise of successive Operation *Deep Freezes*) for scientists at the same time as other military objectives were pursued in theatre. As Walter Sullivan concluded, 'The Cold War had given special importance to the Arctic, which lay between the chief antagonists, and United States military leaders were interested in a large scale military exercise in a polar area sufficiently removed from the Soviet Union to avoid charges of sabre-rattling. The answer was Antarctica.'[57] In short, the Antarctic provided a geographical context for naval officers, scientists and political leaders to pursue their own particular goals albeit shaped by Cold War tensions, intellectual curiosities and territorial advantage.

By the time the IGY was initiated, therefore, the United States' Antarctic programme was well and truly geopolitically embedded. Science, exploration and the military were no strangers to one another. While the National Academy of Sciences sponsored and housed the US National Committee for the IGY and the National Science Foundation funded the programme, the USN provided logistical support. In so doing, this well-established model of polar exploration and scientific activity stood in stark contrast to the British endeavours, which were not only managed by civilian operators throughout but also geographically concentrated in the British Antarctic sector. Given the scale and intent of the US-IGY programme, it was perhaps inevitable that the military were vital in delivering the proposed research programme.

While these military – scientific dimensions were important throughout the IGY, it would be unfair to neglect the endeavours of the American political and scientific community to inform the general public about the exploratory and scientific rationale behind this multinational and multi-disciplinary research programme. As Fae Korsmo has demonstrated, the US National Committee for the IGY developed a series of films on each of the IGY topics such as glaciology and cosmic rays for the classroom and the wider viewing public.[58] While the process of initiating filming was not unproblematic, the films were also intended to show how the objective of scientific achievement was helping to reduce international tension. They were, ironically enough, finally released in November 1960 under the title 'Planet Earth' and thus due to funding problems, managerial changes and creative differences of opinion were not available during the actual period of the IGY. However, public interest in science and the IGY was excited, even if the Soviet launch of Sputnik in October 1957 stimulated some American newspaper editors to fear that its Cold War rival was overtaking the United States.

NEW VISION FOR ANTARCTICA: GEOPHYSICS, SEISMIC SOUNDING AND OVER-SNOW TRAVERSES OF ANTARCTICA

One of the claims often made about the IGY is that it signalled a shift from exploration to scientific activity in the Antarctic environment. As part of Antarctica's discursive transformation, it was increasingly imagined as a 'laboratory' for science rather than either an unexplored frontier or arena for persistent political intrigue.[59] The analogy with the laboratory was significant for at least two reasons. First, it conveyed a sense that Antarctica was now an orderly space capable of hosting experimentation supported by permanent communities of scientists.[60] Second, it was used discursively to signal a fundamental change in the nature of human activity in Antarctica. It was hoped for the sake of international co-operation and peace that scientific activities would enable previous episodes of intrigue, exploratory competition and occasional conflict to be contained. Such an impression, however, of clear-cut change was misleading. While knowledge of the polar continent was greatly enhanced from the era of so-called 'Heroic Age' exploration, a great deal remained to be discovered. In particular, very little was known about the thickness of the Antarctic ice sheet and the continental interior had been barely mapped or surveyed beyond that provided by aerial photography. Moreover, as one contemporary publication noted with reference to the purpose of the IGY, 'the Antarctic was no more familiar to us at present then the visible side of the moon'.[61]

The technique of seismic soundings and later radio-echo sounding (RES) was used to explore the boundaries between ice and rock and ice and water. Seismic sounding played an essential role in determining ice thickness and in so doing the nature and extent of the Antarctic landmass. After its use by the pioneering Norwegian – British – Swedish expedition of 1949–52 and the 1957–8 Trans-Antarctic Expedition, seismic sounding and traverse work was greatly extended during the IGY, as US naval planes and overland snow-cats in particular crossed the continent taking soundings.[62] American and British colleagues worked closely with one another and the Scott Polar Research Institute at the University of Cambridge emerged as the major hub for the collection and exchange of data derived from seismic soundings. The creation of World Data Centres (WDC) in 1957 was, therefore, seen as a vital outcome to ensure that the results generated from the IGY were collected and available for worldwide scientific consultation. The two major hosts were the United States (WDC A) and the Soviet Union (WDC B).

In the area of glaciology, American scientists Albert Crary and Charles Bentley were at the forefront of exploratory-scientific research. They organised soundings and over-snow traverses that encapsulated huge geographical areas such as the Ross Ice Shelf and the Ellsworth

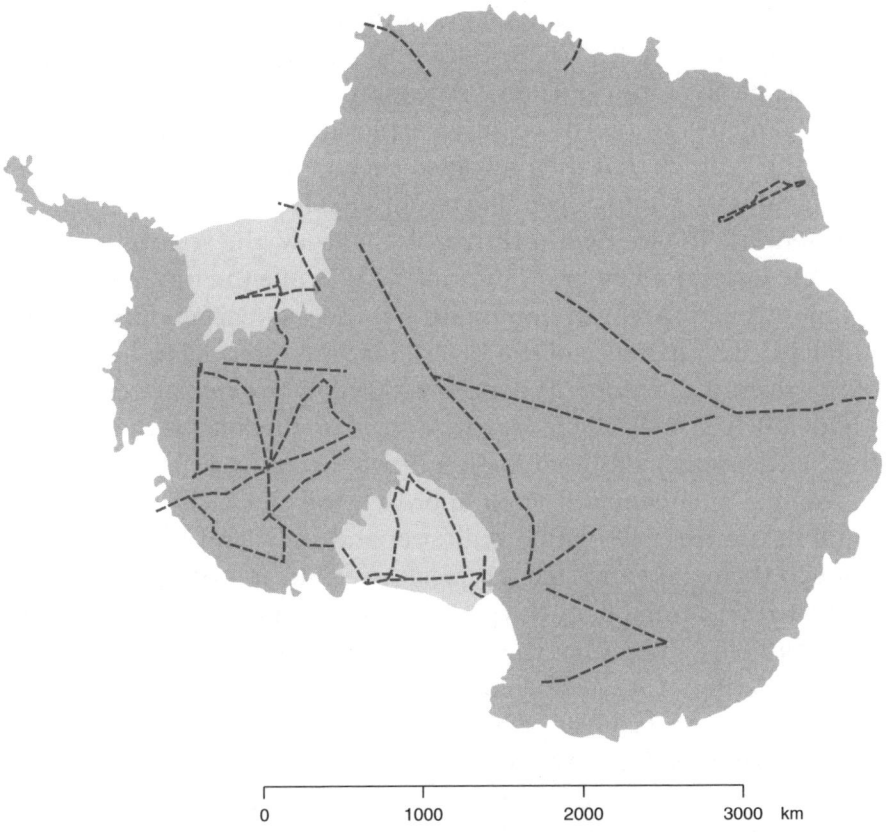

FIGURE 7.3   Overland snow traverses during the IGY.

Highland. As Figure 7.3 shows, US scientists and naval personnel travelled over the ice and used a series of seismic recorders, which determined ice thickness by measuring the time taken by sound waves travelling from a surface explosion to the underlying rock strata. The traverses were essential to construct a detailed record of the geographical profile of icecap thickness

The seven major IGY bases established by the United States provided vital hubs for a detailed network of traverses.

Memorably, in January 1957, Charles Bentley and four other scientists spent two months carrying out a traverse from Little America station to Byrd Station for the purpose of further calculating the submerged topographies of Antarctica. The distance involved was over 650 miles and the US Army had earlier marked up a potential route for his three Tucker Snow-Cats with the aid of flags every half a mile and oil drums that were placed every three to five miles. As the convoy travelled along the ice, one scientist would drill a hole and place sound explosives into it. Then a seismograph cable would be attached 200–300 metres away. The resulting explosion sent sound through the ice to the bedrock that then reflected back to sensors, which recorded the signal onto photo paper. The results enabled the team of scientists to determine the ice depth. During the journey, the scientists discovered the lowest known point in Antarctica. While the traverse was tremendously significant in illuminating those sub-glacial aspects of the Antarctic, the assistance of the US military was essential to the success of this scientific venture. As Bentley recalled, 'The extensive crevassing was nearly insurmountable for the Army team that blazed the first trail from Little America to Byrd Station. It was an Army team with lots of experience in Greenland. Their approach was not to go around, but to fill in the crevasses with a bulldozer and snow and to make a trail through them. It seemed like a typical American approach.'[63] The team depended on a number of Navy planes for the duration of the traverse and clearly benefited from the Arctic experience of the US military.

The sharing of traverse data later became a critical issue for military personnel and civilian scientists alike. As leading scientists such as Lloyd Berkner and Harry Wexler noted, new models of data sharing were needed in an era of Cold War intrigue and suspicion. The USN wanted access to the data protected because it was believed that Antarctica might contain strategic reserves of uranium while at the same they were anxious to ensure that the Soviets did not develop some kind of geopolitical advantage in the region. But as American scientists such as Wexler also recognised, sharing data was vital to the ethos of the IGY and to ensure that American scientists had access to a network of global geophysical data including that accumulated by other scientists operating in Antarctica such as the British, French and Soviet IGY parties. Moreover, the sheer physical enormousness of the polar continent meant that no one party, not even the US-IGY programme, could hope to accumulate sufficient data without research partners. As Wexler concluded, 'Some of the nations [working in Antarctica during the IGY] willingly transferred their planned stations to new sites to fill in gaps in the observing network, and all nations agreed to exchange freely all information on logistics and scientific matters.'[64] This led to the United States favouring a polycentric model of data access,

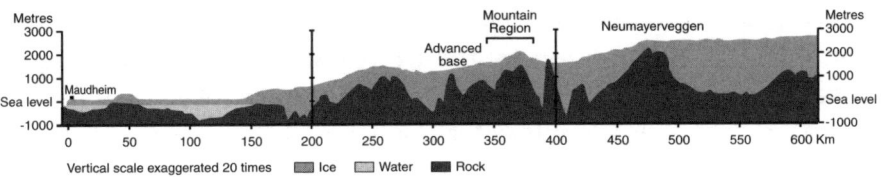

FIGURE 7.4 Sub-glacial Antarctica.

which sought to maximise the strategic value of scientific information through international co-operation and scientific exchange, which did prevail throughout the IGY and beyond.[65]

These kinds of activities led to the emergence of new three-dimensional sub-glacial maps.[66] Figure 7.4 provides one such illustration of how the Antarctic was being mapped in fundamentally different ways from earlier representations, which had imagined Antarctica as an all-encompassing white blanket. It was now possible to differentiate and discern the varied morphology of the Antarctic.

As a consequence of the seismic soundings and traverse research, Antarctica was now shown to be one continent albeit composed of two distinct geographical entities – East Antarctica, a continental shield, and West Antarctica, an archipelago with large areas of ice – rock contact. Snow accumulation maps of the polar continent were also prepared with the help of information generated at various research stations. Exploration of a more vertical type was helping to generate new glacial geographies of the polar continent.[67]

New knowledge while exciting and intellectually rewarding for the geophysicist brought renewed pressures to bear on those charged with maintaining geopolitical order. As Wexler noted:

> Although we did not go to the Antarctic as prospectors, the IGY program will undoubtedly bring nearer the day when Antarctica will begin to yield its geological treasures. Who can say what the Antarctic will be like in the Age of the Atom with prospects of practically unlimited heat or energy for ships, aircraft, camps or machines.[68]

The prospect of Antarctica as a future treasure house was not an appealing one for those men and women intent on finding a solution to 'the Antarctic problem'. Any form of mineral exploitation inevitably raised questions of ownership and the superpowers might have felt compelled to press territorial claims at the end of the IGY in order to secure future prospecting rights for minerals such as Uranium.

While scientists only had a patchy appreciation of Antarctica's mineral potential, the decision by the United States to host an international conference on the future of Antarctica in October 1959 proved critical in providing a context for resolving (at least for the duration of any resulting treaty) some of these tricky issues such as sovereignty claims. The IGY had shown that co-operation was possible and that science could have a palliative effect. However, scientific activity during the IGY also provided a platform for national rivalries and controversy regarding the location and purpose of scientific and exploratory research. While such rivalries existed well before the IGY, it did point to the rhetorical limits of international scientific co-operation and the Antarctic *esprit de corps*. Even when there was talk of abandoning stations such as Halley Bay in the Falkland Islands Dependencies in the aftermath of the IGY, the prospect of offering it to another country's scientists seemed unthinkable. As Sir David Brunt of the Royal Society in London noted to a colleague in the Foreign Office:

> If I was free to take such action, as I would like to, I should prefer to blow the Halley Bay station sky high with a powerful dose of high explosive rather than to leave it to either one of those three nationalities [Argentina, the Soviet Union and or the United States].[69]

CONCLUSION

Using the IGY as a backdrop, this chapter has considered how the Antarctic was transformed by the intersection of scientific practices, exploration, geopolitics and ideas about the Antarctic. The 1950s marked a fundamental transformation in human understanding of the southerly continent. Thanks in the main to geophysical research and specific activities and techniques such as the over-snow traverse and radio echo sounding, a vertical view of the polar continent was derived. Military and geopolitical factors unquestionably contributed to this newly found knowledge of the Antarctic and its place within global geophysics. This informational and representational transformation was never entirely straightforward, however. Long-standing fears and fantasies concerning the Antarctic were not banished by the scientific gaze. Throughout the 1950s, there was still much debate about what lay beneath the ice and the possible usage that might be made of this ice-filled kingdom. In 1956, on the eve of the IGY, non-participating countries such as India raised the Antarctic as an issue for potential discussion within the United Nations. Concerned about the possible usage of the polar continent, the Indian government sought guarantees that the proposed IGY would be entirely peaceful and non-threatening to the global community. While India was later persuaded to withdraw its call for further discussion about the future of the UN, it did point to a growing interest about the future of the Antarctic and the role of exploration and science in enhancing human understanding of this southerly continent.

The IGY unquestionably provided the foundation for the subsequent conference at Washington in October 1959. Science was co-opted in order to shape the future political and territorial management of Antarctica.[70] On the one hand, it became an instrument of power projection especially amongst the superpowers that used their technological and logistical advantage to create a network of bases across the continent irrespective of any sensitivity that might have been touched upon within the existing club of claimant states such as Britain, New Zealand and Argentina. As Aant Elzinga has noted, 'modern science has therefore shown itself to be a useful surrogate instrument for underpinning territorial claims'.[71] On the other hand, scientific research into sub-glacial Antarctica produced revolutionary views of the polar continent and revealed a subterranean world of ice and rock, which contributed to a more holistic view of the region. Those territorial claims looked, in the aftermath of the IGY, even more artificial as it was clear that further scientific understanding of the Antarctic ice mass would require scientists to continue to work across those boundaries. But for states such as Argentina, Australia and Chile those lines were deeply embedded in the national DNA and there was no reason to assume that they would resist pressure to think differently about the polar continent just because the United States was eager to find an international solution in the aftermath of the IGY. There was also no basis to the belief that the Washington Conference would automatically conclude with a settlement for resolving competing territorial claims and establish a new modus operandi for science and peaceful co-existence. Notwithstanding 18 months of prior discussion to the Washington Conference, little could be taken for granted.

In December 1959, the Antarctic Treaty was signed and in so doing a new political architecture was created. While it was ultimately unable to agree to the dissolution of those existing territorial claims as some parties such as New Zealand had suggested, it cemented a rather different view of Antarctica nonetheless. All parties, including claimant states such as Britain and non-claimants such as the United States and the Soviet Union, committed themselves to the promotion of international scientific collaboration alongside respecting the status of the Antarctic as a zone of peace. Exploration and science continued albeit under a different kind of remit; but it would be wrong to conclude that they had become geopolitically disembodied. The key article of the Antarctic Treaty (Article IV) states that all the varied political and legal positions on territorial claims affecting the polar continent are frozen for the duration of the treaty. While most observers hope that the Treaty will prevail, scientific exploration and investigation remain as politically sensitive today as it did in 1957–9. Such recognition sits uneasily with a more geographical let alone geophysical vision of the Antarctic. As the then Director of the British Antarctic Survey recognised in June 2006:

> The planet does not recognise the geographic boundary delimiting the jurisdiction of the ATCM [Antarctic Treaty Consultative Meeting]. Since a major task of the ATCM, through its Committee for Environmental Protection, is to protect the Antarctic environment from damage, the interconnected nature of the Earth system will increasingly present a challenge. The outcomes of the IPY [International Polar Year] will provide [a] sound scientific basis to address this significant issue.[72]

8 'Britnik':[1] How America made and destroyed Britain's first satellite

Matthew Godwin

As the Cold War matured over the course of the 1950s with the introduction of the hydrogen bomb, it became increasingly impossible for the rival blocs of East and West to face each other militarily. To do so would have lead inexorably to nuclear annihilation. This meant the ideological struggle had to be played out in other ways, leading to a host of more minor confrontations in various forums. Perhaps the most notable of these is the space race, the ostensible scientific exploration of space which turned into an increasing show of one-upmanship.

The birth of the space race is usually dated 4 October 1957. That autumn day marked the shock launch of the Soviet Sputnik satellite which became not only a scientific and technical feat of great magnitude, but also an unrivalled propaganda coup. As such it was seen in the West and especially in America as a demonstration of the USSR's military might and ascendant geopolitical power. America was caught completely off guard and struggled to re-capture the initiative, dogged by an embarrassing series of rocket explosions during its attempts to launch its own satellite. However, this standard account has recently been revised and expanded. Recent scholarship has begun to shed intriguing new light on American policymaking in the lead up to Sputnik. The pioneering work of Rip Bulkeley and other scholars has done much to illuminate the early phases of the space race to take the story beyond just an account of the 'Sputnik shock'.[2] Using British official records, I seek to take the analysis into the post-Sputnik period by looking into the United States' interest in bilateral collaboration with its allies, in particular Britain. While my main aim is to present an interesting episode in Anglo-American scientific space exploration, I also highlight the differing conceptions of space centring on the widely noted central dichotomy of many fields of Cold War science, that is between scientific exploration and military utility.[3]

'SPUTNIK SHOCK'

The Sputnik satellite was launched as the Soviet contribution to the International Geophysical Year (IGY), an international scientific programme to study various characteristics of the Earth which ran during 1957–8. The concept of the IGY was not an entirely novel idea and in fact dated back to two earlier International Polar Years which had concentrated on the polar regions during 1882–3 and 1932–3.[4] The first proposals for the IGY are generally considered to have originated in a meeting between American scientists, notably including technocrat Lloyd Berkner, and also the British geophysicist and polar explorer Sidney Chapman in April 1950. At this stage it was still a proposal for a further Polar Year or IPY3, but the idea for an expanded event was quickly taken up in scientific circles with the various international scientific unions such as the International Union of Geodesy and Geophysics and the International Astronomical Union, all expressing an interest and accepting the proposals. By 1952 the event had been expanded to become the IGY and was formalised with the establishment of the International IGY Organising Committee, the CSAGI, with Chapman as its president.[5]

However, the motivation and further development of the IGY had come about for a number of reasons. First, there were concrete scientific grounds for wanting a world-wide study during 1957. It was forecast that the period between mid-1957 and late-1958 would be a year of intense solar activity, making an intensive study very desirable scientifically.[6] Second, in connection with this, the development of rocket technology during the Second World War meant that the exploration of the atmosphere with adapted rockets was a new and exciting possibility.

The interest here lay in the physics of the atmosphere, notably its composition and structure of which relatively little was known. This was important basic research, which also had significance for meteorology and the earth sciences as well as implications for technologies such as radio. Previously only balloons had been available for conveying experiments into the atmosphere.[7] Now scientists with rockets could probe the previously unobtainable upper atmosphere and fringes of space. This at least was the scientific case. However, other motivations existed. The atmospheric physicists, who, in the late 1940s, had been working with a finite supply of captured V2 rockets, were on the lookout for new rockets and new funding streams. The IGY therefore offered a potentially useful opportunity to highlight their field (and also its military significance) to national governments.[8]

This was made easier by the contacts that scientists had within government. In particular Lloyd Berkner, a radio engineer and ionospheric physicist by profession who was present at the 1950 IGY meeting, was also appointed as deputy president of the CSAGI. This appointment placed Berkner at the heart of the IGY preparations. Intriguingly, Needell's biographical account of Berkner suggests that he was in fact the one who had first suggested the IPY3 proposal and therefore the originator of the whole idea.[9] Indeed, Berkner, who is known as one of the leading technocrats of 1940s/1950s America, had just completed a report for the US Secretary of State entitled 'Science and Foreign Relations'. Berkner's IGY plans were therefore undoubtedly all part of his technocratic manoeuvres for which he was ideally placed. He held an integral position in the growing 'big science' infrastructure in the United States following his war-time work, and had direct contacts in national science, intelligence, and military and political institutions.[10]

By 1954 Berkner was recommending that America develop a satellite as part of its contribution to the IGY. Prior to an IGY planning meeting, Berkner discussed the political aspects of a satellite programme with his US colleagues, and in particular stressed that, even at this early stage, there was a sense of competition with the Soviet Union which was known then to be considering entering the IGY.[11] Needell speculates that Berkner may also have been aware at this time of a RAND report which discussed the merits of a reconnaissance satellite.[12] By January 1955, however, the situation was complicated. Berkner knew well that the only satellite project then under active consideration was a military project. This was potentially awkward as the presentation of the satellite development and launch was the key to its success.[13] In a review written by a CIA official this dimension was made clear:

> If the United States successfully launches the first satellite, it is most important that this be done with unquestionable peaceful intent. The Soviet Union will undoubtedly attempt to attach hostile motivation to this development in order to cover her own inability to win this race. To maximise our cold war gain in prestige and to minimise the effectiveness of Soviet accusations, the satellite should be launched in an atmosphere of international good will and common scientific interest. For this reason the CIA strongly concurs in the Department of Defense's suggestion that a civilian agency such as the US National Committee of the IGY supervise its development and that an effort be made to release some of the knowledge to the international scientific community.[14]

These points were clearly taken on board, the President and interested agencies all agreeing that the United States should submit to the CSAGI its intention to develop a satellite for the IGY. The public relations exercise regarding this was carefully orchestrated with Berkner announcing that the United States had 'stated its willingness to carry out this important program of research on behalf of all nations'. Further, 'it is a matter of gratification to scientists and people of every nation that American foresight and leadership will make it possible to discover the new knowledge of our planet that the Earth satellite vehicle will disclose'.[15] Therefore the satellite is presented in these terms not as a military device but simply as a means of generating scientific knowledge, opening up the previously uncharted sphere of space for exploration and data collection. Of course, in the event the Soviet Union beat them to it. News that the Soviets were planning their own satellite launch during the IGY had been circulating in 1956 and a formal announcement was made in June that year.[16] This obviously implies some kind of failure on the part of the Americans. As noted, the US government knew the kind of propaganda coup that would result from being first in space. How the Soviets came to beat the Americans in this respect is difficult to determine, but almost certainly it centred on an under-estimate of Soviet technical ability and an over-estimate of US technology.[17]

Despite being beaten into space, what all this highlights is in fact a very sophisticated development of space policy on the part of the Americans. In particular, in no small part through the co-ordinating role of Lloyd Berkner, the interests of various national bodies were combined into a technocratic blueprint over the course of the 1950s. This is seen in the US attitude to the IGY, when ironically the USSR's success surely highlighted for the Americans the validity of their own early policy ideas on space and international science. Indeed, the success of Sputnik highlighted for many countries the new significance of space, not only as a field for further scientific exploration, but also as a military stage. Conceptions of space turned on this dichotomy between exploration and military utility. This was acutely realised by the Americans and Western powers, for Sputnik demonstrated the viability of placing satellites in orbit (be that for scientific exploration, espionage or communications) and also highlighted the capability of Soviet inter-continental ballistic missiles (i.e., if you can launch a satellite into space, you can also use the same rocket to launch a nuclear warhead at long range). Sputnik was also a technological marvel which clearly captured the imagination of the world's public. As a result, immediately after the IGY, various countries moved to organise themselves for space activities on a national and international basis. Calls were made to institute a legal framework for space, a natural parallel being drawn with Antarctica where various countries had territorial interests.[18] However, the move to create national and international bodies to facilitate national space policies provided new opportunities for space exploration, and also for space exploitation. As IGY planning in the West had been based on American technocratic synergies, the post-IGY period continued this trend. For example, while the establishment of the National Aeronautics and Space Administration (NASA) seemingly opened up co-operation with other countries, in practice the nature of co-operation was controlled by the Americans.[19] In addition, US military policy towards space was such that commitment on specific elements of international space regulation was, for some time, lacking.[20] The case of Ariel demonstrates these strands, highlighting a particular instance where the careful and deliberate planning associated with the IGY gave way to a more ruthless approach in the United States in which military and scientific interests were less well co-ordinated in presentational terms.

THE ORIGINS OF ARIEL

Once Sputnik was in orbit, the Soviet Union followed up with a series of dramatic space records – first animal in space, first human in space and first space walk. Not to be outdone, the Americans succeeded in launching its own satellite in 1958, and, indeed, in 1961 President Kennedy pledged that his country would land a man on the moon by the end of the decade. However, the exploration of space and the space race itself were not limited to the bold technological gesturing associated with manned missions and projects with a clear military significance. Rather the space race could be run in other ways. One effect of Sputnik was to highlight space as an area for fruitful collaboration. One country that took particular advantage of this was Britain.[21]

The United Kingdom had received news of the Sputnik satellite with comparative calm. In part this was very deliberate. Minutes from the Foreign Secretary at Cabinet sum up the British view that the Soviet Union was:

> seeking to focus world opinion on the military implications of the earth satellite which they had recently launched. It was undesirable that we should appear to be unduly concerned about these implications; and our attitude should, therefore, be primarily one of welcome to a notable scientific contribution to the International Geophysical Year.[22]

An assessment was made of Sputnik and its implications by the Ministry of Defence and the Joint Intelligence Committee (the senior co-ordinating intelligence body in the British State). This centred particularly on the reasons why the Soviets might have made what appeared to be such rapid technological progress over the 1950s.[23] However, while the United States had entered into a period of urgent reassessment in order to try and catch up with the Soviets, the British government felt no such compulsion. Indeed, even British scientists were happy at first to simply monitor the path of Sputnik as it circled overhead. The British interest was more oriented to what benefit could be obtained from the United States in foreign and defence policy terms. Britain had suffered a long period of isolation from America on matters relating to nuclear co-operation. In 1946 the American administration had passed legislation, namely the McMahon act, which forbade the exchange of nuclear information with any other country, including Britain. This was despite Britain's wartime co-operation with the United States in the Manhattan project. Although there were indications that the regulations might be lightened, in large part the United Kingdom had been denied access to American nuclear technology.[24] To British officials the effect of Sputnik in the United States looked like a golden opportunity to tap into American concerns and win greater co-operation. Prime Minister Harold Macmillan remarked that the Americans 'need Pearl Harbours [sic] from time to time, and perhaps it is just as well that the Russians are capable of delivering them in this relatively harmless way'.[25] Indeed, channels of communication were soon opened, and, after the awkwardness of relations following the Suez Crisis, the US authorities eased the restrictions on nuclear co-operation. Britain's use of Sputnik shock in this way was therefore successful, but this appeared to be where the British interest stopped. However, in time Britain's own scientists began to consider the benefits of a British satellite.[26]

In October 1958 the United States formally created NASA, an intentionally civilian agency with a very deliberate mission to embrace international co-operation in space.[27] At almost the same time the US government issued a document which outlined the advantages of international co-operation in space exploration. In particular, the report had cited Britain as the most developed European space power and one ideally suited for collaboration.[28] This sits very well with what we know about earlier American space policy and US policy in the run-up to Sputnik, and in particular about strengthening science in the West. International science and its diplomatic and political benefits were an important motivation in American technocratic thinking.[29]

The report was followed in March 1959 by an American announcement at COSPAR, the International Committee on Space Research which had been set up after the IGY to co-ordinate scientific space research. The Americans put forward an invitation for interested countries to submit experiments for launching inside US satellites. This invitation came at a time when the United Kingdom, like many countries, was considering its first space policy. At that time Britain had only one real space project, the Skylark sounding rocket, which had been launched as part of Britain's contribution to the IGY. Skylark, which although unsung, was one of United Kingdom's most successful space projects and was designed as a means of conveying physics experiments into the upper atmosphere.[30] However, by 1959 British scientists were keen on the idea of using a satellite along similar lines, that is as a way of transporting experimental devices into space in order to record the physical characteristics of the upper atmosphere.[31] The US invitation was therefore viewed with interest, especially as there was little political desire at this stage for an entirely British satellite programme. Thus, in his announcement of the United Kingdom's first space policy in May 1959, Macmillan outlined only modest proposals, centred on a continuation of the Skylark rocket project and for co-operation on satellites with the United States.[32]

Following this announcement Sir Harrie Massey (a leading space physicist and adviser to the government) led a small scientific team to America to discuss the possibilities for satellite development. The proposals arising from this were for an Anglo-American programme in which the United States would supply the rocket (the then new Scout rocket still in the development phase) as well as the satellite engineering itself, although for later satellites the United Kingdom would take on more of this work. The United Kingdom would provide the experiments to go into the satellites and there would be three satellites at intervals of around one a year.[33] It was stipulated that the experiments had to be of mutual interest to NASA and for the first satellite in the series were primarily concerned with measuring the composition of the upper atmosphere at altitudes of between 400 km and 1200 km. They were designed and built by Birmingham University, University College London, Leicester University, and Imperial College London and focused on a number of atmospheric characteristics such as electron density and temperature.[34] It should be emphasised that at this time there was still a lot to be uncovered about the earth's atmosphere. As a consequence, experiments like these were at the forefront of the new field of scientific space research and were a necessary step towards further space activities. Furthermore, the success of this Anglo-American satellite held the potential promise of further space collaboration with the United States, not only for Britain but also for other European countries. A name was clearly needed for the satellite. It is not clear at what point the name 'Ariel' was given to the satellite, but Massey and Robins record that the name was suggested by the wife of Roger Quirk, the then senior official in the Office of the Minister for Science. Convention meant that the name Ariel would be applied to the satellite only once it was in orbit. While still on the ground, the satellite was named S-51.[35]

The Anglo-American agreement was first announced in Parliament through a written answer by the Minister of Supply, Aubrey Jones. The civil nature of the project was emphasised, along with the affirmation that 'British science will be able to play its own part in the advancement of scientific knowledge of our planet and its environment.'[36] The press in Britain received the news enthusiastically, although in several cases it noted the comparative low cost of the programme when compared to the whole of the American space effort. The *Manchester Guardian* described the Scout as the 'Poor man's rocket', and certainly it was a lot cheaper than other US rockets such as the Atlas and Thor (although these rockets had distinct military associations: the Atlas was known to be designed for carrying a nuclear warheard, as was the shorter range Thor).[37] Despite these remarks, a Whitehall official writing to Henry Billingsley, the foreign relations officer at NASA, commented that 'now that we have launched our sputnik in the press, I thought I would send you a line to say that things went more or less according to plan here ... I am glad to say that the press references have been entirely favourable'.[38]

Certainly, the arrangement was viewed very favourably by British officials and by the scientists involved. From January 1962 a special publicity committee was formed in the Office of the Minister for Science with representatives from the Foreign Office, Central Office of Information, Department of Scientific and Industrial Research (DSIR) and Royal Society. The committee was tasked with co-ordinating publicity for the project both in the United Kingdom and the United States. Special interviews, television programmes and news broadcasts were planned, with much emphasis being laid on the project as the first 'international satellite.' The Canadian government questioned the correctness of the title as in fact they had launched one of their own experiments in an American satellite in June 1960. British officials argued that 'the UK view was that the two projects were not comparable', and so Britain stuck to the title.[39] NASA was also known to be taking the project seriously, a sense emphasised in reports by the UK project manager, Malcolm 'Mac' Robins. In comments which he flagged as strictly his own personal impressions, Robins commented:

> There is every indication that NASA regard this, their first international satellite, as of the greatest importance and urgency and one cannot fail to be impressed by the amount of design and development effort going into the satellite and its auxiliary services. The NASA management appear to be giving us high priority in their programme

at Goddard Space Flight Centre and the engineers concerned are most co-operative and helpful. In some areas of work additional manpower is being hired, and overtime is regularly worked.[40]

All appeared to be going well, although there was one minor set-back. It became clear that the Scout rocket would not be ready for some time, leading NASA to decide to opt instead for the more expensive Thor-Delta rocket.[41] This could only be launched from Cape Canaveral in Florida rather than from the Wallops Island base where the Scout operated from. With all this duly arranged, and after one aborted attempt, the Thor-Delta rocket, carrying the satellite with its British experiments, was finally launched successfully on 26 April 1962.[42] British Minister for Science, Lord Hailsham, had sent a telegram with his congratulatory text on 6 April to be ready for passing to the US authorities. It read:

> I send you my fullest congratulations on our first joint satellite. We owe you a great debt of gratitude for this opportunity; it will add immensely to the warmth of Anglo-American relations, and sets an example to the world in international co-operation in scientific space research.[43]

The successful launch was clearly a significant event. However, after it had been in orbit for only two months, the Americans effectively destroyed Ariel (Figure 8.1).

'STARFISH' AND THE NUCLEAR DESTRUCTION OF ARIEL

In May 1962 the US government announced its intention to conduct a series of very high-altitude nuclear tests in the Pacific over Johnston Island. The announcement was controversial, especially given that the highest blasts would take place on the fringes of space. This news was quickly acted on by a number of British scientists, in particular Sir Bernard Lovell, the director of the Jodrell Bank Observatory at Manchester University which had famously tracked the Soviet Sputnik. Lovell's fears centred on the impact this series of explosions would have on the makeup of the atmosphere, notably on the then newly discovered Van Allen belts.[44] Lovell also criticised the unilateral way in which the announcement had been made without reference to international scientists, commenting that 'the much-vaunted dedication of the United States to the peaceful

FIGURE 8.1 Political cartoon of Ariel in Orbit (with the face of Harold Macmillan, orbiting around the Earth, which has the face of JFK), published in *Reynolds News*.

use of extra-terrestrial space will now be seen as a veil which can be torn asunder at the convenience of the American militarists and their attendant scientists'.[45] The situation had the potential to be embarrassing to the British government which had given its support to the tests along the lines that 'we have based our support on the great importance of these tests to our defence'.[46] The British Prime Minister Harold Macmillan became the recipient of a series of letters from Sir Harry Legge-Bourke, an MP in the

House of Commons, who was very much opposed to the American tests and who was in touch with Lovell.[47] Consultation with the government's main space advisor, Sir Harrie Massey, showed that he too was not happy with the unilateral way in which the United States had acted. In particular no approach had been made to the international space science community through COSPAR ahead of the American announcement.[48]

Condemnation also came, unsurprisingly, from the Soviet Union. The USSR submitted a statement to the United Nations' (UN) newly established Committee on the Peaceful Uses of Outer Space. The Soviets referred to the US tests as 'an aggressive act' and accused the United States of 'extending the nuclear armaments race to outer space'. The Soviet statement also quoted from Lovell's very public objections to the tests.[49]

The nuclear test series started despite the protestations. A press release from the American Atomic Energy Commission (AEC) outlined the nature of the tests, although without indicating the intended purpose behind them. In an interesting turn of phrase which presented the tests as a form of exploratory scientific experiment, the press release referred to the bomb tests as spectacles which 'observers' could watch. In addition, apparently in response to scientific criticism of the tests, the press release argued that US President J. F. Kennedy had called on a number of American scientists to offer their assessment on the tests. These scientists, including James Van Allen (the discoverer of the Van Allen radiation belts), had agreed that the effects would not be too serious. As a further gesture the AEC press release also offered to provide precise details of the tests to world scientists in order that they could observe the effects and make 'measurements'.[50]

Then, as part of the series, on 9 July 1962 the Americans detonated a hydrogen bomb above Johnston Island in a test codenamed 'Starfish', also sometimes referred as the 'Rainbow' bomb. The blast was large and in the megaton range, subsequent reports placing it at 1.4 megatons. It took place some 200 miles up.[51] Newspaper reports stated that the explosion lit up the sky 750 miles away in Hawaii and could even be seen in New Zealand some 4,000 miles away.[52] The explosion showered large quantities of radiation into the atmosphere to an extent, it was later realised, far beyond that expected. By 18 July it was becoming clear in London that something was wrong with Ariel.

Reports had started to circulate that Ariel was no longer working. A telegram from the Foreign Office to the British embassy in Washington noted that there had been 'sporadic interruptions in transmissions' and sought permission from NASA and the US State Department to direct any enquiries received to them. It was noted that 'there may be suggestions that the interruptions are due to the recent high level nuclear tests', and that the United Kingdom would like to know the angle the United States intended to take.[53] NASA responded that they had not yet received any enquiries but if they did so would respond that 'Beginning last Friday, July 13, 1962, transmissions from the world's first international satellite, the United States/United Kingdom "Ariel", (S51), became intermittent.' A technical reason was given related to power supply and that the possible causes were under study. No mention was to be made of the nuclear test, but if forced to comment NASA would say that it was 'extremely unlikely' that this had caused the problem with Ariel.[54] One month elapsed before the British Government learned, from the press, that the Americans were now saying that the nuclear test had indeed been the cause of Ariel's malfunction. Furthermore, press reports suggested that the US view was that the satellite was, as a result, now coming to the end of its life.[55] This caused consternation in the Foreign Office: 'It is not merely the case that they did not consult us about the announcement; they had not even told us that they had come to this conclusion themselves.' Further,

> we think it was really rather remiss of them not to have told us of their conclusions before announcing them to the world. The news has been carried prominently in the press and on the BBC here and I shall be surprised if there is not a pretty sharp reaction in the course of the next few days.

The embassy was therefore directed to 'have a word with the Americans, more in sorrow than in anger, and seek some explanation of this surprising lapse on their part'.[56]

Much emphasis had been laid on the presentation of 'the world's first international satellite' by the British. From the UK perspective the American handling of the Ariel accident certainly seemed poor. The reason, it seems, was not down to NASA. The announcement that the US government had effectively 'nuked' the Ariel satellite was made by the Atomic Energy Commission and Department of Defence (AEC/DOD). NASA had asked that any announcement first be cleared with the United Kingdom, but the AEC/DOD ignored this, arguing that it was essential for an announcement to be made immediately and that there was not sufficient time to consult the British. In relaying this information the British embassy in Washington remarked to London that 'You may find this explanation as extraordinary as we do.'[57]

A PUZZLE

In the event, Ariel continued to transmit. NASA assessed its life span as being in the order of one year, although this turned out to be blighted by periods of non-transmission. When Ariel came back online more substantially in early September 1962, NASA wanted to make a press announcement of this fact undoubtedly hoping to rescue the co-operative civil nature of the project.[58] However, it was the military accident which up-staged the project, not least because Ariel was to become one of the main sources of information on the explosion.[59]

In reality what the Ariel incident highlights is a puzzle, as well as the unsurprising primacy of military and national interest in the Cold War context. As one Foreign Office official noted 'an ounce of defence outweighs a ton of science or international law in the American scales'.[60] Certainly, the US defence authorities had issued statements contrary to advice from NASA, and had shown an apparent disregard for British interests. This in itself is not necessarily controversial given the Cold War setting. However, there is something awkward about the sequence of events and the way in which the British were denied earlier confirmation of Ariel's demise. On the face of it, it looks as though the Starfish effects on Ariel (and in fact two other satellites) had not been anticipated. The fact that Ariel was affected presumably highlights the previously unrealised potential for the destructive effects of the electromagnetic pulse. This energy emitted by a nuclear explosion is now well known to disrupt electrical equipment. News reports from the time of the nuclear test show that its aim was to assess the effects of a nuclear explosion on telecommunications. This is borne out by official documents, which record that Starfish 'was not the testing of a weapon; the weapon was already tested and proven; it was rather a test of the effects of a nuclear explosion on telecommunications'.[61]

The fact that Ariel continued to operate after the explosion, albeit intermittently, suggests that the data from the experiments on board would have significant defence value. In effect Ariel was the only satellite then in orbit which was specifically carrying scientific experiments, many of which were intended for monitoring the physics of the atmosphere. Ariel would therefore have been in a unique position to record details of the explosion and its effects. Indeed, Ariel was also carrying equipment that monitored the physical nature of the satellite itself, such as its rate of spin and payload temperature.[62] Such was the interest in the scientific aspects of the explosion that the United States decided after the explosion to put together, somewhat hurriedly, a special satellite called 'Starad'. The plan was that this satellite would contain specialist instruments for recording the effects of Starfish.[63] This fact suggests there was a definite premium on scientific data. In the time after the explosion it must have been clear to the US defence authorities that the explosion was having wider effects than predicted. However, confirmation of the reason for the damage to Ariel did not reach the British government until a month after the explosion and in fact was initially denied by the US authorities. This was despite the fact that the possibility of nuclear test damage had been raised in the Foreign Office about 10 days after the Starfish test. This raises a number of possible explanations. It is possible that the US defence authorities were simply embarrassed by the incident and took their time to work through what happened. However, as outlined above, it is clear that Ariel must itself have recorded the reasons for its own expiration by virtue of the experiments it was carrying. Therefore, Ariel would have recorded how it came to be damaged. This being so, why was this not picked up by British scientists earlier, given that a month had elapsed before the news was confirmed by the US Department of Defence? Bearing in mind the importance of scientific data on the explosion, could it be that scientific information from Ariel did not reach British scientists earlier because the United States had intercepted it?

The British government provided tracking for Ariel by using its own tracking stations based in British territories, one in the Falklands and another at Tristan da Cunha (in fact on a Royal Navy ship anchored off Tristan as the island itself was experiencing a volcanic eruption).[64] However, given the significant American backing for the project, it would undoubtedly have been possible for the United States to have intercepted signals from Ariel if they so wished. It does seem a little unlikely that they would have done so, especially given that the British could presumably have been relied upon to pass over significant defence material. This is particularly so given the co-operative character of the Ariel project. That said, the scientists with experiments in Ariel were university academics, they were not government or military employees. Their co-operation would not have been guaranteed. As a result the US authorities could have decided that denying them the data in the first place was safer. This point is supported by the reaction of the British scientists with experiments in Ariel, who subsequently received an invitation to attend a meeting in the United States on Ariel and its nuclear destruction. The meeting was classified and so British scientists did not want to attend, fearing this would impose restrictions on their publications.[65] It is not clear what took place at this meeting, although it would appear that only the scientific aspects were discussed, and not the defence implications.[66] Two scientists from the University of London attended the event at American request, but reported back to the British government that they had been surprised at the 'very limited scope of the discussions with them'.[67]

So what precisely happened to Ariel is difficult to say. Undoubtedly it was accidentally damaged (it seems unlikely that the Americans would have sought to deliberately damage Ariel), but equally there are some questions to be answered about the exact sequence of events. One opinion piece in the *New Scientist* asked whether the United Kingdom would seek compensation for the experiments that had been disrupted. However, the author made clear this was unlikely to happen and indeed it did not.[68] The fact is that Ariel was in essence a very cheap gift from the United States. There is no way that Britain could then have launched its own satellite, given the infrastructure that such a feat entailed. Most of the cost of Ariel had been borne by NASA. Thus when Harold Macmillan who, despite his earlier misgivings about satellites, now came to take the matter extremely seriously and asked for a costing of Ariel, Hailsham wrote a carefully crafted minute outlining the degree to which the project had been subsidised and supported by the Americans. Hailsham noted that 'he cost us an identifiable £200,000 for equipment, tracking, etc. As he cost the Americans rather more than £2 million (they built the box, provided the solar batteries, gave us the rocket, and conducted the launch) we have not done so ill.' Further, Hailsham alludes to the possible military significance of the Ariel data: 'the actual explosion which damaged him did provide valuable scientific as well as military results, and Ariel played a gallant part in obtaining these'.[69]

'PLEASE LEAVE THIS SPACE AS YOU WOULD WISH TO FIND IT ...'[70]

The damage to Ariel was only one aspect of the Starfish explosion. As mentioned earlier, scientists such as Lovell had long pointed to the possible damage to the two Van Allen belts, natural belts of radiation encircling the earth. It was found that the natural belts had indeed suffered, but even more significant was the fact that an entirely new belt of radiation had been formed as a result of the Starfish test. It was the initial flux of particles forming this new belt which had damaged Ariel.[71] Hailsham received a number of letters from prominent astronomers complaining about the effects of the increased radiation from Starfish. In particular, many British radio-astronomers were far from impressed, seeing the new belt of radiation as an impediment to scientific research in space.[72] Hailsham therefore proposed to re-activate a committee which had previously examined another controversial US program, the West Ford project. West Ford, invariably presented publicly as a scientific 'experiment', was a radical plan for a new communications system. Based at the Lincoln Laboratory at the Massachussetts Institute of Technology (funded by the US Air Force), the project involved having a series of small copper needles circling the earth which would reflect back microwave signals to the ground. Originally called the 'Needles' project, the Lincoln Lab renamed the project West Ford after a nearby town, for fear that 'needles' might 'alarm the public by suggestion of dangerous things'. An initial feasibility study required three hundred million of the needles or 'dipoles' to be deployed 'into an orbiting belt about 35,000 miles in diameter, at a height of 2,000 to 3,000 miles above the earth'. Each needle was 0.5 inches long and 1/1,000 of an inch in diameter, and they would be separated from each other by a distance of 1,000 feet. Two belts would be required, one east – west over the equator, one north – south over the poles, which would provide almost world-wide coverage. The belts were expected to last at least a year before disintegrating.[73]

The rationale for the project was entirely military. At this point satellites were particularly complex devices and to put sufficient numbers into orbit for communications purposes would take a long time. The West Ford project, on the other hand, 'because complexity is all on the ground, will enable the military to take advantage of space as early as possible'. The system also had the advantage of being very difficult to attack, either in terms of jamming signals, or indeed of an airburst nuclear explosion, as this would simply create a hole in the orbiting belt that would quickly reduce over the course of subsequent belt rotations leading to only a slight reduction in signal strength.[74]

However, there was a serious disadvantage with this 'experiment'. As the briefing paper made clear, there was likely to be some interference with astronomical observations for both radio and optical astronomers. Whilst downplaying the significance of this, it was clear that many astronomers were deeply concerned over the effects of the Needles experiment.[75] The proposed first trial run of West Ford was generally considered not to have any grave effects, but if it was successful then the longer term installation of orbiting needles was deemed to be extremely detrimental to astronomy. One of the main critics was, again, Sir Bernard Lovell who was joined by other British scientists, including Professor Martin Ryle, and the then Astronomer-Royal, Richard Woolley. As Tanya Levin has documented, there were also domestic US scientists who were opposed to West Ford, but the British contingent was especially vocal.[76]

What is notable is that the Starfish incident has many similarities with the West Ford project in the way scientists reacted. Indeed, the two incidents were often considered together as they were contemporaneous examples of controversial American interventions into space.[77] Building on work by David DeVorkin, who identified two camps of scientists in his work on post-war atmospheric science, Levin has contended that with West Ford scientists chose their allegiances according to their particular scientific approaches.[78] There were those with an instrument-based approach who favoured West Ford and who were comfortable working within a military-backed setting, and then there were those (generally more traditional astronomers) who suspected West Ford would upset astronomical observations and did not rate the national security aspects as highly. The latter group also pointed to environmental concerns about damage to the atmosphere notably, as

Levin observes, several years before the popular environmental movement associated with the publication of Rachel Carson's *Silent Spring*.[79] This was also to be a feature of debate on Starfish and indeed on space activities more generally, with one contemporary article in the *New Scientist* arguing that the exhaust from rockets could damage the atmosphere and affect the weather.[80] Opposition to West Ford also turned on whether it was a specifically military project or was in fact a scientific experiment with military implications. Proponents argued for the latter, whereas opponents questioned its scientific basis. This approach can also be seen in the way Starfish was presented by proponents as an experiment or 'spectacle', almost as if it was not a military project at all. Hailsham's reactivation of the West Ford Working Party as the Working Party on High-Altitude Nuclear Tests serves to emphasise the similarities between the two issues.

The UK West Ford Working Party had come out against West Ford, although the eventual deployment of the needles turned out not to have the controversial consequences originally forecast.[81] However, West Ford was one early instance of very visible American unilateralism towards the uses of space, and it had caused a lot of bad feeling with scientists internationally. Bodies set up after the IGY, such as COSPAR and the UN Committee on the Peaceful Uses of Outer Space, were completely bypassed. When contrasted with the very slick way in which the US IGY arrangements had been made, West Ford showed up surprisingly poor diplomacy on the part of the Americans and, perhaps most of all, poor presentation, which had arguably been the most central part of the IGY policymaking.[82]

Hailsham's subsequent reactivation of the Working Party to examine Starfish had been intended to simply provide scientific advice on nuclear tests for the guidance of the government. However, chaired by JA Ratcliffe (a noted radio scientist), the membership of the Working Party, which included Lovell, was comprised mainly of academic scientists who saw their scientific work being potentially undermined by the US nuclear tests.[83] In this way, like with West Ford, they made an effective lobby group, and particularly so within the flimsy framework of the British science administration where the Minister (Hailsham) saw his main duty as simply being a conduit for the views of UK scientists. When the Working Party came to draft their report, Ratcliffe wanted to circulate it to COSPAR. It stated that the US tests would affect radio astronomy and concluded that any test above 1 kiloton was seriously harmful to the atmosphere. Ratcliffe argued that any defence tests should be scrutinised by an international body of scientists. Furthermore, the report pointedly quoted from a statement made to the UN General Assembly by the US Senator Albert Gore which stated:

> The United States believes that nations which conduct activities in outer space should take all reasonable steps to avoid experiments or other activities which seriously threaten to deny or to limit the use of outer space to other nations. This is consistent with well established principles of international law. We encourage prior international discussion concerning experimental activities in space which may have undesirable effects, and we are prepared in the future, as in the past, to consult with scientists of other countries as well as United States scientists wherever practicable and consistent with our national security.[84]

The Ratcliffe conclusions rattled Whitehall, which had intended the results not to be published and instead to be available only to 'embody in representations to the United States'.[85] However, such was the widespread condemnation of the United States over the Starfish test that Harold Macmillan decided to publish the Ratcliffe report in its entirety.[86] In practice it did not say anything that breached security, and in fact the scientific adviser to the Ministry of Defence, Solly Zuckerman, advised publication on the grounds that this would highlight that British scientists were fully aware of the issues involved.[87] It is also important to note that at the time a new attempt at a nuclear test ban was being urged in the House of Commons, a cause undoubtedly aided by the criticism in the report.[88] In any case, an only recently released official document also shows that Downing Street thought that the scientific members of the Working Party, in particular Lovell, were in any case likely to leak the report conclusions.[89] It is interesting to note that Lovell's continuing condemnation of Starfish and the other tests in the series had been taken in America 'as indicative that he was politically sympathetic to the Russians'. However, it seems that Lovell received an apology from some American scientists over this once it became clear that he had been right that Starfish would damage the atmosphere.[90]

The publication of the report awkwardly coincided with a meeting of the technical and legal section of the UN Committee on the

Peaceful Uses of Outer Space. One of the problematic elements for the Americans throughout the controversy over the Starfish test was the fact that it coincided with attempts at the United Nations to legislate for the control of space. As a result, the United States came in for continued and sustained attack from the Soviet Union. Much of this also took place during the tense period of the Cuban missile crisis when the United Nations had already been the stage for confrontation between America and Russia (although the issue of Cuba and Starfish were not mentioned together in official documents).[91]

Clearly irritated by the publication of the Ratcliffe report, despite the fact it had been passed to the US government well in advance, some American scientists criticised it for failing to give weight to the fact they had given advance warning of the Starfish test and had published scientific reports on it afterwards. This was however contested by the British, and indeed it looks like the United States had not given the kind of information they had purported to in advance. One issue that the Americans also raised was that the world was focusing on their tests when in fact the Russians had conducted similar high-altitude explosions. Again, however, this was contested on the grounds that, although the Soviets had not published data on the tests, the effects of the tests were not in the order of the US Starfish test. Clearly ruffled, M. Hodges at the Office of the Minister for Science commented: 'One gets rather weary of American complaints that the world applies different standards to US conduct from those it applies to the Russians. Would the Americans really have it otherwise? They should be gratified that the civilised world puts them in a different class.'[92]

The controversy over the Starfish nuclear test and the scientific concerns over the damage being done to the atmosphere, as well as the deliberations at the United Nations on the peaceful uses of outer space, all dovetailed into a renewed interest in a test ban of atmospheric nuclear weapons. So Starfish can be seen to some extent as the beginning of the end for atmospheric testing. The battered body of Ariel died within a year of being launched, although it did go on to experience some short bursts of life. However, several more Ariels were launched in a programme which finished with Ariel 6, launched in June 1979. It is unquestionable that the Ariel series was of great importance for the development of British space science and also of British industrial capacity in space technology.

CONCLUSION

What is clear from the Ariel story is that space in the Cold War context, like much Cold War science, turned on a central dichotomy between exploration in scientific terms and military utility. During the preparations for the IGY the Americans, carried along by the technocratic zeal of Lloyd V Berkner, carefully planned the launch of the world's first artificial satellite. Berkner was able to skilfully conflate the various interests of intelligence, military, geopolitics and scientific exploration into this one project. Despite the stage being carefully set, the Americans were of course beaten by the Soviets whom, it seems, the United States greatly underestimated. In Europe, however, the reaction to Sputnik was more restrained than in the United States. Britain in particular was careful not to advertise its interest, which in fact at that time was in any case minimal. British scientists too were at first uncommitted on a satellite, although soon they began to consider the possibilities. Following an ambivalent attitude from the British government, the American offer of satellite facilities was seized upon with enthusiasm by UK scientists.

This offer of satellite space to British scientists, and in fact to scientists of all countries, was undoubtedly a calculated move on the part of the Americans following on from their IGY experiences in space policy. NASA, a purposefully civilian organisation, had been formed with a particular emphasis on international co-operation. For the country now facing a space race with the Soviet Union, it was clearly sensible to share the burden with other friendly countries. This mirrors the idea behind the Marshall plan and of American interest in European scientific capability as a means of shoring up Europe economically against the Soviet Union.[93] Britain was the first of several countries to co-operate with the United States in space affairs. Canada and particularly Italy also benefited from close collaboration with NASA, and similar offers were made to the new European space organisations in the 1960s.

However, what NASA gave to the United Kingdom with one hand, the US Atomic Energy Commission/Department of Defence took with the other. The accidental destruction of Ariel shortly after its launch is to some extent still a source of mystery, as there are several questions over the timing of the announcement and the reaction of the British government. But the destruction of Ariel was only one facet of the controversy, the main issue in many ways being the potential damage to the Earth's atmosphere by the Starfish nuclear test. This test demonstrated a level of unilateralism in space which highlights the primacy of national interest, particularly military interest, in the Cold War context. During the period from 1957–63, space was a contested area. There was no comprehensive legal framework, or indeed even an accepted definition of where space began. In this environment activities in space were literally testing the boundaries.

With the case of Starfish the boundaries were clearly overstepped. The creation of a new belt of radiation was a source of great contention for radio astronomers and other scientists. It also handed a propaganda device to the Soviets who used it regularly at the United Nations, and who were always sure to also use the very public condemnations from British scientists, particularly Sir Bernard Lovell. However, the outspokenness of British scientists, although sometimes embarrassing for the British government, was vindicated.

The US/UK Ariel programme continued until the late 1970s. The British therefore owed a considerable debt of gratitude to the Americans for this co-operative programme. Nonetheless, the early unilateralism of the United States in space affairs which the Ariel incident highlights was, as Van Allen himself admitted, a 'shabby' affair; an affair which serves to demonstrate the differing Cold War conceptions of space as a territory for scientific exploration and investigation as well as military utility.[94]

9 High empire: Rocketry and the popular geopolitics of space exploration, 1944–62

Fraser MacDonald

> *Let it not be forgotten ... that the somewhat rude, rough, uncouth pioneer CORPORAL blazed the trail through a wilderness of dynamics, aerodynamics, and electronics, as applied to guided missiles, pointing out the path for manufacturers and military personnel to follow with the designing, fabrication, and operation of more refined, sophisticated second and third generations of such missile weapon systems.*[1]

It is often said that geopolitics, perhaps even geography itself, is a horizontal discourse.[2] Both deal with territory. The history of exploration has, for the most part, been conducted on this same plane. There are of course some important ups (mountaineering) and downs (oceanography) but at least until the end of the eighteenth century – and in practice until the middle of the nineteenth century – exploration was largely a surface matter. Exploration and the science of geography were both tied to Terra. All of this makes exploration's turn to the vertical axis, cutting adrift the solidity of Earth, such a remarkable development. Contrary to popular belief, this change in direction was not a rapid transition nor is it a recent phenomenon. There has long been an interest in acquiring high ground for the purposes of military survey. 'War is waged from high points', as Paul Virilio once observed. 'The logistics of perception was from the start the geographic logistics of domination from an elevated site.'[3] Elevation, however, need not imply land. After the first successful manned balloon flights in pre-revolutionary France, it took just 10 years for this technology to be put to work for military reconnaissance, later finding its niche in the Napoleonic wars and ultimately in the First World War. As early as the mid-nineteenth century, the bird's eye perspective afforded by the balloon was being used for remote sensing; that is to say, for cartography and aerial photography. In this important sense, ballooning foreshadowed many of the later functions of rocketry and satellites.

But none of this prior history of transcendence comes close to the revolution inaugurated by rocket propulsion in the twentieth century. Rocketry gave serious uplift to all manner of modernist exploration fantasies, from walking on the moon to interplanetary travel. None of these were exactly new. To be untethered to the Earth had been one of the most longstanding human ambitions. The ancient Greek Lucian of Samosata (AD 120–180) anticipated a voyage to the moon some time before the more celebrated pioneer of science fiction Jules Verne (1828–1905) wrote his famous novel *From the Earth to the Moon* (1865). The desire to leave Earth only became more pressing when Copernican heliocentrism took hold. Sigmund Freud describes Copernicus as providing the unwelcome cure to the 'narcissistic illness' of geocentrism, the idea that humans lay at the centre of the universe. But with the development of rocketry, the cold realisation of our cosmic peripherality could be offset by the plausible dream of a new mobility. While we may not be at the centre, we did not at least have to be stuck on the margins for ever. It was now possible to leave home and view our planet from the distanced perspective that had been the stuff of dreams since the age of Cicero.[4] Such an 'Apollonian gaze' – one that could hold the entirety of Earth within its field of vision – was first realised by the American astronauts of Project Apollo, whose photographs *The Whole Earth, Earthrise* and *22727* are perhaps the most famous exploration documents of all time.[5] The advent of rocketry not only unleashed a new geographical imagination but it also gave fresh momentum to older ideas about exploration and the discovery of new worlds. As Peter Redfield elegantly put it:

Although the airplane opened up the sky, and the radio tower filled the air with waves ... neither made the limits of the Earth entirely visible or transparent. Space technology closed the sky again, bounded it from above and sealed it whole. Only then could the sky become fully modern in an active, technological sense, and only then could what lay beyond it become meaningful as space, a vast sea of darkness surrounding a blue and green point of human place. At last the world was one.[6]

Having argued that the ship was *the* scientific instrument of exploration in the eighteenth century, Richard Sorrenson goes on to make a connection between the ship and its twentieth-century equivalent, the rocketship.[7] In Sorrenson's wake, other scholars have considered the sea as an enabling medium for discovery, adding significantly to the long-standing geographical literature on the culture and politics of exploration.[8] But geographers in particular have been reluctant to move their 'graphy' beyond the limits of the 'geo'. A geography of outer space might sound like a quixotic enterprise but it is towards this over-ambitious end that the essay is directed. In what follows, I step back from what is conventionally regarded as the inception of the Space Age: the dramatic launch of the Russian satellite *Sputnik* into a stable orbit on 4 October 1957. There is no question that *Sputnik* is the pre-eminent milestone in the history of the space race.[9] It is significant for all sorts of reasons, not least as the first in a technological lineage that would subsequently bequeath profound consequences for the nature of social life on Earth, from weather forecasting to telephony to surveillance to navigation to missile guidance and so on. *Sputnik* will doubtless remain an iconic marker of Cold War rivalry in the geopolitical contest for the heavens and the Earth. But even before a payload could be placed in orbit, the rival powers faced the earlier challenge – which interests me here – of leaving Earth's atmosphere in the first place.

*****

This essay is concerned with the evolving rocket programme of the American military from the end of the Second World War to the early 1960s. While this study includes a number of different rockets, intended for a variety of strategic, military and research purposes, I concentrate in particular on the development of the 'Corporal' (Figure 9.1),

FIGURE 9.1 Corporal Launch, White Sands Missile Range, date unknown. Declassified image from the archive of Firestone Tire and Rubber Company.

an overlooked part of a wider programme which includes its technical variants (such as the WAC Corporal) and immediate predecessors (such as the V-2 and the Bumper WAC). If I use the word 'rocket' in this context with some hesitation, it is because the word most frequently appended to the name Corporal is 'missile'.[10] The distinction seems a fine one, but in a sense the entire history of space exploration lies in this slippage between rocket and missile; between a peacetime research vehicle and a Cold War weapon of mass destruction. There is little, technically speaking, to differentiate rocket from missile. The terms are often used interchangeably, even if they each carry quite different semiotic freight. Rocket is a fairly benign descriptor that simply refers to a vehicle which obtains thrust by the ejection of a fast moving propellant. This is the term most obviously associated with exploration. Missile, by contrast, implies impact and annihilation – an intent to destroy. While this different discursive construction of the technology is worth noting, the vehicle itself is exactly the same: space exploration and perpetual readiness for nuclear war are simply two parts of one story. The Corporal programme is therefore the classic embodiment of these seemingly irreconcilable objectives, for it has the acclaim of being the first man-made object to reach outer space as well as being America's (and Britain's) first nuclear missile. It was, as David de Vorkin has described the V-2, a tool of science that would prepare the nation for the next war, with both 'warhead' and 'peacehead' applications.[11]

The Corporal missile has curiously escaped any detailed consideration either by historians of the Space Age or those of nuclearism.[12] To be sure, it was not the first significant rocket (that notoriety must go to its direct predecessor, the German V-2), nor was it the first nuclear weapon (the free-fall bomb 'Little Boy' whose accomplishment was the mass killing of 140,000 civilians in Hiroshima). The Corporal, being a 'tactical missile' with a modest range of 75 nautical miles, was also of limited strategic significance compared to subsequent Intercontinental Ballistic Missiles (ICBMs), like the more versatile 'Atlas', which could usefully dispatch death to remote peoples as well as place satellites into orbit. While the Corporal was briefly on the front line of nuclear defence, it was never used in conflict. This is perhaps just as well; in the early years, the Corporal had such a terrible record of target accuracy that its most likely casualties would have been its own troop battalions. It was, if anything, a bit of a dud. But an early version was still the first man-made object to leave the Earth's atmosphere.[13] And as the first guided missile authorised to carry a nuclear warhead, it arguably has particular significance as the progenitor of contemporary weapons of mass destruction. Moreover, at the time of its development it carried, however fleetingly, a raft of hopes and fears both about the Space Age and about nuclear war.

What interests me here is what we might call the 'cultural success' of the Corporal, an object that sat astride the categories of 'rocket' and 'missile', drawing on the popular enthusiasm for space to legitimate its underlying military purpose. In this essay then, I discuss the place of the Corporal within the popular and political cultures of the era. And in so doing I pay most attention to the ways in which the missile was figured across a diverse suite of cultural forms. I situate my argument within a wider literature on 'popular geopolitics', a recent emphasis within critical geopolitics that attends to the circulation of geopolitical power through popular culture rather than through familiar networks of statesmen, generals and ruling elites. To talk, therefore, of the 'popular geopolitics' of rocketry is to examine how the technologies of Cold War strategic advantage were activated and sustained through popular media and everyday experience. The essay argues that the power of the Corporal lay less in its technical ability to propel a 20 kiloton nuclear fission warhead 40 km high than in its presence as a flexible narrative prop, able to support popular enthusiasms about space while coyly doubling as a weapon of mass destruction. That the Corporal was 'domesticated' as a die-cast children's toy is, I argue, indicative of how the widespread enthusiasm for rocketry and space exploration in the 1950s eased nuclear weapons into the political mainstream.

In the first instance, I try to open up space and its exploration as a research theme which could usefully be considered within the orbit of geography. Drawing on earlier precedents for thinking of space as a sphere of the social, I emphasise the strategic, scientific and geopolitical continuities between space exploration and earlier episodes of imperial endeavour. The history of the Corporal programme is then understood in this light, as a technology variously configured as vehicle, instrument and projectile, which emerged from the aftermath of the Second World War to become a key weapon in NATO's Cold War arsenal. Lastly, I want to think more closely about the popular geopolitics of the Corporal programme, examining the by no means untroubled passage of the missile through domestic as well as state contexts.

TOWARDS AN HISTORICAL GEOGRAPHY OF SPACE EXPLORATION

An historical geography of space exploration has yet to be written. And such a task might only be one part of a broader geographical engagement with outer space which has, to date, been strangely limited. Strange, because it is now over 50 years since humans first cast their instruments into orbit. Our species has lived in space for more or less the last 20 years and is currently represented by the crew of the International Space Station. The journey through the Earth's atmosphere, once a major obstacle, is now made on an almost weekly basis. There are over 700 operational spacecraft in orbit and over 35 nations now have payloads in space. In short, the last 50 years has seen the outer-Earth become an ordinary and accessible sphere of human endeavour, with our presence in (and reliance on) space making it one of the enabling conditions for our current mode of everyday life. It would be easy to draw a rather superficial connection here, trading on the commodious meaning of the word 'space' as both the primary analytic for contemporary human geography and as the popular term for the expanse in which solar and stellar systems are located. But I want, in passing, to make the more ambitious argument that geography is the obvious disciplinary home for the study of the historical, cultural, political, economic and strategic contest over the outer-Earth. Such a project is not a search for the new, but rather going *back* boldly to some of geography's earlier origins – for if outer space is a scale that for the most part feels unfamiliar to human geographers, such limited disciplinary horizons are, paradoxically, a late modern tendency. David Livingstone has shown how, in figures like the sixteenth-century scholar-mathematician John Dee (1527–1608), astronomical enquiry and the study of cosmography aimed to connect the workings of heaven and earth.[14] It was the planetary scale which formed the background to much geographical teaching in the early modern period, the movements of the stars being afforded significance in the outcome of worldly affairs. There are, therefore, a number of geographical precedents for thinking about outer space.

A related argument here is that a geography of outer space is simply a logical extension of earlier geographies of imperial exploration.[15] Space exploration has used exactly the same discourses, the same rationales and even the same institutional frameworks (such as the International Geophysical Year, 1957–8) as terrestrial exploration. And like its terrestrial counterpart, the move into space has its origins in older imperial enterprises. Marina Benjamin argues that for the US outer space was 'always a metaphorical extension of the American West'.[16] When Frederick Jackson Turner argued in 1893 that the frontier was central to American identity and nationhood, his thesis could equally be applied to the US space programme's encounter with the 'final frontier' in the twentieth century.[17] Peter Redfield makes a similar point in relation to the French Arianne space programme which relied on its earlier colonial ties to take advantage of the fuel economies associated with an equatorial launch, rather than sites at lower latitudes. Looking at the imbricated narratives of colonialism and rocketry in French Guiana, he makes the case that 'outer space reflects a practical shadow of empire'.[18]

The history of the Corporal missile also stands in this shadow. Not only was the Corporal (configured as sounding rocket) part of a bid to open up the new empire of space on the part of the United States, but the Corporal (configured as missile) was also a means of shoring up imperial power back on Earth. When the British government bought the programme from the United States in 1954, it was purchased as a means of re-asserting Britain's geopolitical significance in the context of its own imperial anxieties.[19] Even before the ignominies of Suez, Britain had 'lost' India and Pakistan to independence movements; surrendered the Palestine mandate to the United Nations; and passed responsibility over Greece and Turkey to the United States. Possessing a nuclear missile was then seen by Winston Churchill as a shortcut back to the international stage at a time when Britain's own home-grown missile programme was in its infancy.[20] In this way did the imperative of space exploration go hand in hand with terrestrial geostrategic considerations, both of which were extensions of earlier regimes of imperial power. Even if the political geography literature has scarcely engaged with outer space, we can conceive the advent of rocketry as one expression of Cold War (imperial) geopolitics. All of this is to say, then, that a geography of space and its exploration, both in terms of its historical development and its contemporary politics, is not some far-fetched or indulgent distraction from the 'real world'; rather, it is constitutive of numerous familiar operations, from international relations and the conduct of war to the basic infrastructure maintenance of the state and to the lives of its citizenry.[21] Space, and how we got there, matters. And this is true not least because thinking about space and its exploration presents a series of challenges to the terrestrial character of geography as a discipline, as well as testing some of the basic tenets of social theory.[22] Moreover, the ability to leave the atmosphere has profoundly refocused attention on the geographical knowledge of Earth itself; in all sorts of ways, then, attaining orbit has helped remake Earthly geographies.[23] I consider the Corporal programme to be a useful starting point for considering many of these themes. And yet what is ultimately most interesting for our purposes here is to think about how this early unmanned space exploration engaged the popular imagination in ways that legitimated and sustained particular geopolitical logics here on Earth.

'AS EXPLORERS INTO THE UNKNOWN': PIONEERING WITH THE VEHICLE-INSTRUMENT-PROJECTILE

> The story of CORPORAL's birth, growth and development into a full-fledged guided missile system is one of trial and error, a pattern of devoted human endeavour studded with many failures and fewer heartening successes, acknowledging each failure and profiting from it, and striving towards the goal of providing the Army Field Forces with an efficient deterrent to aggression. The story is one of improvisations, of making do with what was available in materials and components, of feeling the way as explorers into the unknown, uncharted realm of rocketry.[24]

In recounting the history of the Corporal, one must first deal with its name. Why 'Corporal'? It was a question of rank. In 1944, the US Army had commissioned a new missile programme from a rocketry team at what became the Jet Propulsion Laboratory (JPL) at the California Institute of Technology.[25] Their first attempt was a primitive test vehicle called 'Private', a simple unguided ballistic missile which was launched in December 1944. As JPL engineer William H. Pickering recalled in an interview, 'when we started out, we said first of all we'd do Private, then we'd do the Corporal, and then we'd do Sergeant, and maybe get up to the General'. Laughing, at this point he added, 'we had the WAC Corporal too – Woman's Army Corps ... it was a little one [more laughter]'.[26] This was a regular little gag among rocket scientists. More accurately, WAC stood for 'Without Attitude Control', a reference to the fact that this simple prototype of a research-based sounding rocket had no stabilisation and guidance system.[27] But 'Women's Army Corps' fitted rather well with the unmistakably gendered assumptions about the (low ranking) place of women in the military and, indeed, about the perceived 'modesty' of this particular rocket. In due course, it was succeeded by the apparently more mature 'Corporal' proper and eventually by the 'Sergeant', both of which were authorised to carry nuclear warheads. But for all these deprecating remarks, the WAC Corporal was a crucial interim stage in the history of rocketry, for many years holding the record, when combined with the V-2, for the highest altitude ever attained by human technology. This combined 'BUMPER WAC Corporal' – so called because the V-2 would give a 'bump' to the WAC Corporal allowing it *start* its journey from a high-altitude platform – was the world's first two-stage liquid propellant rocket, and became after several attempts in 1948 and 1949, the first man-made object to penetrate space.

This 'mating' with the V-2 was essential in establishing rocket 'staging' as a viable means of high-altitude ascent. But to see the homegrown Corporal atop the V-2 provides an appropriate metaphor for the subsequent development of the US space programme: American strategic initiatives given a 'bump' by German engineering. For it was German rocket engineers, led by the inimitable Wernher von Braun, who developed Nazi Germany's V-2 ('Vergeltungswaffe 2' or 'Reprisal Weapon 2', as Goebbel's called it). As the world's first ballistic missile, it rained terror on London in the last desperate phase of the Second World War. Although 2700 civilians were killed and thousands more were injured, it was the morale-sapping psychological effects of the missile that stand out. Unlike other weapons, its arrival went unheralded by engine noise or sirens. It accomplished terror by travelling in complete silence and at supersonic speed. There was no warning, just instant destruction. Nor was there any defence against the V-2 attack. Unsurprisingly, when the end of the war came, rival military commanders were desperate to get hold of the weapon, leading to a scramble among the Allies for access to V-2 equipment and personnel. Only then did the full scale of the V-2 production and its reliance upon slavery become clear: a concentration camp at Mittelbau-Dora had been established – effectively an extension of the infamous Buchenwald – in order to provide labour for the construction of the V-2. In the 18 months of production, an estimated 20,000 people died: mass destruction was therefore the ancillary outcome of rocketry even from its inception, quite aside from its intended military impact.

The American success in acquiring the V-2 was principally achieved through the auspices of Operation Paperclip, an audacious programme which, under the leadership of Col Holger N. Toftoy, brought over 100 German scientists and engineers over to the United States, many of whom were put to work initially at the White Sands Proving Ground in New Mexico and then at the Redstone Arsenal at Hunstville, Alabama. Foremost among these was von Braun who eventually recruited his old mentor on the V-2, Hermann Oberth, whose book *By Rocket to Planetary Space*, published in 1923, is regarded as one of the founding documents of the Space Age (see Figure 9.2). In securing von Braun, the Americans had not just acquired an uncommon technical expertise and his undoubted skills as an engineering manager; unbeknownst to them, they had also enlisted the greatest popular advocate for space exploration as well as a doughty champion of maintaining nuclear weapons in space. Von Braun as celebrity boffin went on to bring both the promise and the reality of space exploration into every household in America via his regular TV shows, popular magazine articles and a close partnership with Walt Disney. While he was not the only 'Paperclip' émigré to popularise Cold War hardware – Heinz Haber was also influential in this respect, starring in Walt Disney's nuclear propagandist cartoon *Our Friend the Atom* – von Braun was unusual in combining high-profile advocacy with hands-on engineering.

Von Braun's V-2 was a gift to the nascent American space programme. Although not an especially versatile weapon of war, the enormous German investment necessary to develop the science of viable propulsion suddenly became available for a new era of space technology. In the vapour trails of Operation Paperclip,[28] the homegrown WAC Corporal was quickly overtaken by the success of the V-2 for high-altitude flights. With over 100 V-2s available for research purposes,[29] it soon established itself as indispensable for the study of near-Earth space phenomena. In one sense, it was the perfect research vehicle as the weight lost by the removal of the German warhead could be usefully replaced with scientific instrumentation, or, as happened in 1946, with camera equipment. And on 24 October 1946, launch number 13 produced the first pictures of the Earth from space. Writing in the *National Geographic*, the camera's engineer, Clyde Holliday, claimed that these were the first pictures to show the curvature of the Earth 'from the border of outer space', with 'single views cover[ing] 100,000 square miles'.[30] Holliday identifies the profound implications of this episode:

FIGURE 9.2 Officials of the Army Ballistic Missile Agency with model US rockets, Alabama, 1956. Pictured from left to right, Ernst Stuhlinger, Major General Holger Toftoy, Hermann Oberth, Wernher von Braun, and Robert Lusser. The Corporal missile is the second model from the right.

Results are now pointing to a time when cameras may be mounted on guided missiles for scouting enemy territory in war, mapping inaccessible regions of the earth in peacetime, and even photographing cloud formations, storm fronts, and overcast areas over an entire continent in a few hours, which would be of great benefit to weather forecasters.[31]

It could, he thought, even 'detect troop movements': 'camouflage would hide little from such an all seeing eye'.[32] Reaching the heights of the upper atmosphere with his camera allowed Holliday to anticipate the new horizons that would ultimately be opened up by satellite technology. Two and a half years after Holliday's film, on 24 February 1949, the BUMPER WAC broke all records attaining a speed of 5,150 miles per hour and an altitude of about 244 miles (Figure 9.3). The excitement of this event was not confined to von Braun, its principal engineer. Footage from these BUMPER flights inevitably generated a modest degree of public interest. To see the Earth receding at high speed gave

FIGURE 9.3 A Bumper WAC launch from Cape Canaveral, Florida on 24 July 1950. The Bumper WAC, a V-2 with a WAC Corporal second stage, became the first man-made object to penetrate outer space.

an altogether more tangible sense of the possibility of space travel. In 1956, Michael Todd's film version of Jules Verne's *Around the World in Eighty Days* opened with a Corporal being launched at the White Sands Missile range, followed by footage from the rocket. It was an early taste of rocketry's accelerated sublime.

Rocketry, however, was not straightforwardly about space exploration. The refinement of guidance systems – initially through the Corporal 'E' test vehicle – had very obvious applications for warfare. John E. Dahlquist, Commanding General of the US Army in the 1950s, argued that 'guided missiles, especially when atomic armed, represent the most radical change in weapons systems since the invention of gunpowder'.[33] They were, he said, 'bullets with brains'. The Corporal was the first that could warrant this description, being the first tactical surface-to-surface missile authorised to carry an atomic warhead. The Corporal in effect became the earliest nuclear missile, shifting from an experimental vehicle to a practical field weapon. The context for this transition was a wider set of geopolitical manoeuvres that had seen America's troop commitment scaled down from their expensive wartime heights while at the same time anticipating a new era of Cold War conflicts. The first successful Soviet nuclear test in 1949 prompted the Army Ordinance to ask the JPL to 'weaponise' their WAC Corporal research rocket as a tactical surface-to-surface guided missile.[34] The outbreak of the Korean War gave further impetus to the production process, though they would not be combat ready in time for deployment there. By the mid-1950s, President Eisenhower's 'New Look' policy had replaced conventional defence doctrine with an approach that simultaneously promised 'massive nuclear retaliation' while making peace with the Soviet Union and protecting America's economy. For the United States, like the United Kingdom, a compromise had to be found between a policy of massive nuclear retaliation and the doctrine of a 'flexible response', which might include the deployment of conventional forces as well as small-scale 'tactical' nuclear weapons. The changing security environment in Eastern Europe meant that the American policy, and that of NATO more broadly, was geared to the possibility of fighting a 'limited' nuclear war using lower-yield tactical weapons such as the Corporal. To the extent that the Corporal had escaped widespread public acclaim in relation to the Bumper WAC high-altitude flights, it had, by the late 1950s, acquired an entirely new public profile as the front line of missile defence.

Although reconfigured as a field weapon, the Corporal always retained the cumbersome handling of a research vehicle, rather than the versatility required by the Army at war. A single test firing required a battalion of 250 men equipped with 35 vehicles working 7–9 hours to complete preparation for launch in a process that involved handling liquid fuel and an extremely hazardous oxidant, red fuming nitrous oxide (RFNA). Until 1955, its in-flight reliability and accuracy was less than 50 per cent, with only modest improvements in this record thereafter.[35] So the power of the missile – which was never fired in combat – lay less in its potential for destruction (though this was still considerable – the warhead was significantly more powerful than what was dropped on Hiroshima) but rather in its status as a monument: as a symbol of power to be seen alike by American citizens and rival sovereign states. The Corporal had a monumental presence in a whole range of public contexts, from a life-size model for use as an Army recruiting prop[36] to being pictured, as we shall see, in collectors' cards in breakfast cereals. The US Army even used a couple of unarmed Corporals to augment the red carpet at the Munich premiere of Wernher von Braun's pompous biopic flop *I Aim At the Stars* (which the Jewish comedian Mort Sahl acerbically subtitled *But Sometimes I Hit London*).[37] It is in this context, then, that it seems appropriate to examine the popular geopolitics of the Corporal.

THE POPULAR GEOPOLITICS OF SPACE EXPLORATION

Geopolitics is not what it used to be. The critical geopolitics agenda, so formatively inaugurated by John Agnew, Simon Dalby and Gearóid Ó Tuathail in the 1990s,[38] has since broadened the terms of its enquiry, responding to criticism that it had reproduced the narrow focus of classical geopolitics on the state and its governing and intellectual elites of ministers, generals and tacticians.[39] New work on popular geopolitics has sought to redress this balance by looking at how geopolitical power is circulated in and through popular culture, 'ordinary experience' and everyday life.[40] In particular, a few researchers are taking up Nigel Thrift's injunction to attend to how 'the little things' – like the object world, the human body and even words as ordinary as the definite article – matter in the operation of statecraft.[41] This sort of approach is particularly instructive for thinking about Cold War militarism and space exploration, for in both cases these were sustained by popular movements and expressed through such mundane activities like child's play. Moreover, it is also a useful corrective not only to the state-dominated field of geopolitics but also to the no less state-dominated histories of nuclearism.[42] Much attention has already been directed at the impact of nuclearism on popular literary cultures.[43] John Canaday, for instance, has persuasively argued that 'nuclear weapons have exercised their power in the purely literary form of their fictional use in the future'.[44] But it is worth reiterating an important distinction here, that this is not merely a matter of *representing* the geopolitical power of nuclear weapons through fiction, but that this *is* the power of nuclear weapons: we are dealing with the effect (rather than the referent) of representation.[45] A similar point might be made in relation to space exploration which has its earliest origins in literary flights of fancy. Popular culture cannot be understood as responding to space exploration as much as being constitutive of it.[46]

All of this supports my argument that popular geopolitics is a suitable perspective from which to think about Cold War rocketry. At the same time, however, I do not want to rehearse some of the more obvious cultural arenas – television, film and literature – in which rocketry has been popularly figured. The Corporal has certainly featured as a narrative prop in all manner of screen and literary contexts, perhaps most famously in Ian Fleming's *Goldfinger*, in which the villain's plan to contaminate the gold reserves of Fort Knox with a stolen Corporal warhead is foiled by the deft (though decidedly straight) maneuvers of 007 and Pussy Galore.[47] I am a little wary, however, that much of the popular geopolitics literature has settled on film[48] which, while resolutely popular, is hardly in the spirit of the 'little thing' (quite aside, of course, from the embeddedness of Hollywood within wider state – corporate – military networks). Instead, I want to concentrate on the more ephemeral cultural presences of the Corporal, in order to think about how the geopolitics of militarism and space exploration were enacted in everyday contexts. And in a further departure from the mainstream of popular geopolitics I want to foreground, as far as I am able, the role of mundane social practices above artefacts or representations. I am interested in the geopolitics of two practices in particular, play and collecting, which are in turn examined through the representational forms of toys and cards.

Rocketry as child's play

It has never been clear to me why the perennially stupid question 'what do you want to be when you grow up?' often anticipates an answer like 'astronaut'. Arguably, the astronaut is the postwar version of the polar explorer, embodying certain qualities and virtues that adults would like to instill in their children. And yet for children too, space and its exploration have been fertile imaginative resources, even before the advent of rocketry. This last point is important. Play is the *precursor* to space exploration: it would be impossible to separate the serious business of rocketry from various forms of tinkering and toying with the (im)practicalities of propulsion. Hermann Oberth, one of the founders of rocket science, pictured in Figure 9.1, was known to have developed his expertise out of childhood play, having been fascinated with Jules Verne from the age of eleven. The same also applies to war games – playing at or with war is a constituent part of warfare itself.[49] So it should not be surprising that a technology like rocketry – doubling as vehicle of space exploration and weapon of mass destruction – would be such a prominent narrative prop in children's play in the 1950s. While there were doubtless many instances of rocketry featuring in play without any bespoke toy to facilitate the imagination, I want to think here about some specific forms of toy missile and the games they might have evoked. It is striking that there were very deliberate attempts to reproduce missile technology for the playroom and thus to translate the hardware of nuclear destruction and its wider geopolitical narrative into a domestic setting. My approach, then, is to take seriously the ludic activities of both children and adults as a suitable subject for geopolitical enquiry. While this project follows some recent attempts to re-think the status of children in political geography,[50] it is less aligned with the 'children's geographies' literature[51] than with a distinct concern with play and its cultural significance.[52]

In a recent paper, Nigel Thrift has examined the rise of the 'supertoy', a term borrowed from a short story by Brian Aldiss, by which he refers to a new generation of plaything, such as the *Tamagotchi*, which, as an assemblage of hardware and software, can 'intelligently' interact with its environment and users.[53] Thrift is interested in the toy as a form whose character is changing in ways that might reconfigure the sociality of its users. When talking about 'supertoys', it seems unlikely, however, that Thrift could have been aware of Dinky's series of 1950s die-cast models with exactly the same name. But his claim that 'the course of interactivity has nearly always been prefigured by the history of toys' seems to me an important one which would bear consideration in relation to the Dinky Supertoy.[54] The idea of 'interactivity' in my example is rather different from Thrift's, but there are some interesting points of connection nonetheless.

* * * * *

The Dinky Supertoy no. 666 – a Missile erector vehicle with Corporal missile and launching platform – was first advertised on the back page of *Meccano Magazine* in November 1959 (Figure 9.4). Inside the magazine, in an article called 'Dinky Toy News' by 'The Toyman', the reader is told that 'this fine new item is going to be one of the most sought for [sic] and popular of all the many fine Dinky Supertoys already available'.[55] It was, explained The Toyman, 'an accurately modeled miniature of Britain's famous guided weapon' and 'a working model that has lots of play value, for the rocket itself can be loaded on to its launching platform and fired in a realistic manner'. 'Britain's famous guided weapon' was a truth of sorts. Britain had bought the Corporal programme from the United States in 1954, and after building a firing range on the islands of South Uist and Benbecula in Scotland's Outer Hebrides, it had tested the first of their 113 missiles in June 1959.[56] The launch of the toy missile therefore coincided, as the advert itself implies, with the public interest in the Hebridean debut of the Corporal. It was, in other words, a momento of a notable event in household and nation alike. While there is no evidence that the British Army authorised this particular toy, in subsequent instances – Corgi's 'Corporal' model, for instance – the Army allowed the toy company's draughtsmen access to the real thing for the sake of accuracy.[57] In this way, then, the toys are licensed correlates that encourage an interest in and support for the original hardware in its strategic context. The awkwardness of this being an American missile is glossed over, the advert proudly claiming that the toy is 'Made in England'.

FIGURE 9.4 Advert for Dinky Supertoy no. 666, Missile erector vehicle with Corporal missile and launching platform, as it appeared in *Meccano Magazine*, November 1959.

The advert goes on to emphasise agency and control: this is 'the Corporal missile ... a rocket *you* can launch'; 'a realistic model that actually WORKS; 'it's new, it fires'. The toy could be finely manipulated by its child operative, even to the extent of gearing that enabled 'the boom to pick up the missile and swing it to the horizontal traveling position'. In this way, the work of 250 men, 35 vehicles and 9 hours could be accomplished by a child in a few seconds. It is the event of launch in miniature form. The launch event is integral to the toy; it is part, but by no means all, of its purpose. It achieves a particular experience of time and space, a series of anticipatory preparations followed by a countdown and the moment of launch in which the exact timing and target are established by the player through the symbolic manipulation of the object. The launch works as play in part because it successfully addresses what child psychiatrists John and Elizabeth Newson have called its 'happening-hunger'.[58] As Dan Fleming notes:

> children need things to happen and are impatient with the adult temper which, from time to time, simply wants things to stop happening. Many things can count as happenings, and in fact playing becomes a way of generating happenings when none are forthcoming from other sources.[59]

Children thus become geopolitical agents through their mastery of the missile event. And, characteristically, it must be repeated over and over again. Walter Benjamin recognised that 'repetition is the soul of play, that nothing gives ... [the child] greater pleasure than to "Do it again!"'.[60] For Benjamin, it is a way of overcoming frightening fundamental experiences. But what exactly is being repeated? Is this a rocket or a missile, a weapon or a vehicle? Is this about war or peace, space exploration or the Cold War defence of capitalism? Or something else altogether? It is all of these things, of course; the toy is propelled by the ambiguity. Toy theorists such as Brian Sutton-Smith have constantly emphasised that toys do not come with overdetermined meanings: they don't dictate play but rather 'the plans of the playful imagination dominate ... the toys, not the other way round'.[61] However, as Dan Fleming argues, this endless liminality of the toy is perhaps 'more in the eye of the critic-analyst than in the reality and materiality of a culture which appears rather more ruthless than this at deciding how things are'.[62]

When first introduced, both the Dinky missile and its Corgi rival were relatively 'open' to being either a weapon or space vehicle. The Corgi model in particular was marketed as part of its 'Rocket Age' series. But by 1961, it had tilted the meaning of the Corporal by introducing a 'percussion warhead' (model no. 1480) to be bought separately and 'easily and quickly fitted to your missile ... loaded with standard caps to give a really authentic explosion on impact'. The centrality of the launch had thus shifted to that of impact. This change in emphasis raises the question of the extent to which the geographies of Cold War missile pointing were part of the cultural meaning that the toy embodied. Between launch and impact, there is, of course, a vector of direction. But there is little to suggest a specific eastward orientation to these lines of flight, though one might argue that this is assumed by the Cold War context. It is safer only to suggest that the missile is pointed 'away' from 'us'.

In Dinky's advert, details of the toy (with 'a harmless soft hollow rubber nose cone to ensure safety') are placed alongside details of the 'real' missile, though the advert is shy of noting its nuclear capability. In other respects, absolute fidelity to the original is important. It is a scale model and the detail included in the miniature was considered to be essential. It was, after all, a competitive marketplace. The early Dinky versions of the 666 vehicle had neither windows nor driver, but both had to be introduced to respond to the rival Corgi's toy, advertised with the slogan 'Corgi – the one with windows'.[63] This sluggish attention to detail across Dinky's range was fatal for its market share and by the time the Corporal was withdrawn, it was in serious financial difficulties. But what does this level of detail mean? Fleming refers to the toy's degree of representational accuracy and realism as its 'modality' which runs alongside (sometimes in competition with) its mechanical activity.[64] The basic 'toyness' of the Corporal is achieved through miniaturisation, which in turn allows the operative a sense of control and superiority. But detail must still be preserved; it must be 'real enough', not least because the toymaker must satisfy some degree of technical knowledge on the part of the player. Toys like these both assume and impart serious technical skill, not only in terms of fine motor skills but also as an analogue of 'real' military field knowledge. Indeed, the full slippage between the worlds of play and of war are nowhere more apparent than elsewhere in the same issue of *Meccano Magazine*, where other adverts by the Army and the Royal Navy encourage boys of 14 to leave school and join up as a trade apprentice. The child-consumer which purchases a toy on one day might, on the next day, decide to enlist. There is no doubt other than that these toys assume the meta-context of the Cold War. In Thrift's description of the highly 'mediatized' contemporary supertoy, he notes that 'from *My Little Pony* to *Barbie*, the worlds on offer are a series of micro-ontologies which children can link into'.[65] But in the case of the 1950s Supertoy, the context was quite different: while the child might use the missile as part of a wider set of military toys, it was still within the narrative parameters of Cold War conflict. All of this might seem to be a long way from space exploration, but what I am arguing here is that this 'doubling' of the Corporal in 'real life', as weapon and as exploration vehicle, is opened up through play, and moreover such a mundane practice actually helps sustain these dual geopolitical logics of rocketry in the first place.

Stockpiling and Assembling

I mentioned that the Corporal could be one part of a wider military toy set. Corgi toys marketed its 'Rocket Age Sensations' *en masse*, encouraging the consumer to build up a complete set of the equipment necessary for launching a missile. This included everything from the Erector Vehicle (no. 1113), the International Army Truck (no. 1118), the R.A.F. Vanguard Staff Car (no. 352), the Decca Airfield Radar 424 Scanner (no. 353), the Decca Airfield Radar Van (no. 1106) and the R.A.F. Land Rover (no. 351). The missile was thus part of a wider repertoire of toys that would support the military endeavour of launch. At the same time however, the child collector might want to augment the Corporal with other model missiles produced by Corgi, such as the RAF's 'Bloodhound' – a home-grown British surface-to-air missile in service throughout the Cold War. The Corporal is thus not necessarily a stand-alone object, but rather it works as part of a collection, either of other ancillary equipment or of other comparable weapons.

In this latter case, there is an echo of the strategic state-military practice of stockpiling: the act of creating assemblages of weapons to be seen and thus to be entered into the calculus of geopolitical negotiation. A parallel collection can be seen in the US National Biscuit Company (Nabisco) drive to circulate trading cards published in 1959 in a series of

24 entitled 'Defenders of America', one of which featured the Corporal missile and another which featured the 'FIRST FAMILY of the Nation's big Missiles' (Corporal, Honest John and Nike-Ajax). On the reverse side, it explained how 'each of these cards is a full detailed reproduction of an official United States Army, Navy and Air Force or Marine photograph' (Figure 9.5). It went on to encourage the child-consumer to 'get the entire set by eating Nabisco Shredded Wheat regularly and trading with your friends'. Similar rewards were to be obtained from other forms of breakfast. Cheerios offered small collectible 'US Army Guided Missiles each with its own launcher', with brightly coloured versions of Redstone, Nike, Corporal and Honest John missiles. A quick trawl through eBay will illustrate a ready market in such artefacts; if the scholarly interest in the Corporal has been somewhat slow to take off, a popular enthusiasm among collectors is apparent in the high prices that such toys fetch at auctions.[66] Indeed, it is largely through these networks that I have become aware of these domestic Corporals in the first place. Such toys – even ephemeral ones – are significant; they are by no means innocent signifiers of the space race. A Bowman trading card series called 'Power for Peace' also featured the Corporal under the title 'the Corporal stands tough', going on to detail how it

DEFENDERS OF AMERICA*
U. S. ARMY MISSILES

"FIRST FAMILY" of the Nation's big Missiles, each one the first of its type to be made combat ready. The illustrations show the Army's HONEST JOHN the NIKE-AJAX and the CORPORAL. They were developed and produced by the Army Ordnance. The HONEST JOHN is a medium to long range rocket. The NIKE-AJAX is a high speed, long range guided missile designed to destroy the fastest military planes. The CORPORAL is a long range guided missile used against surface targets. Each is on its own launcher, except the HONEST JOHN being also a transporter.

This is No. 22 of a series of twenty-four cards, each illustrating and describing a different weapon or piece of equipment in the NABISCO Shredded Wheat "Defenders of America" series. Each of these cards is a full detailed reproduction of an official United States Army, Navy and Air Force or Marine photograph. One of these official photograph reproductions is packed in each package of Nabisco Shredded Wheat. Get the entire set by eating Nabisco Shredded Wheat regularly and trading with your friends.

NATIONAL BISCUIT COMPANY
NEW YORK 22, N.Y.

*TRADE MARK   U.S. ARMY PHOTOGRAPH

FIGURE 9.5   Reverse side of the Defenders of America Nabisco trading card, 1959.

could be 'equipped with an atomic or conventional type warhead'. Brian Sutton-Smith talks about collections as 'mixtures of imagination and mastery'.[67] In this case, they serve to make stockpiles of military hardware intelligible in, and transposable to, a domestic context.

Most of these versions of the Corporal – in die-cast miniature or on trading card – came already complete for use by the child. But in certain instances, the child was cast as the rocket engineer and was entered into the labour of building the Corporal in the first place. A variety of mostly American toy manufacturers including Revell, Hawk and Monogram also produced Corporal missiles, pre-assembled in a series of detachable moving plastic parts complete with appropriate stickers from which to build a precise scale model. In this case, the event of play was less concerned with launch or impact than with construction. But this too is an act of participation in a much wider sphere. Ruth Oldenziel has shown how model construction in mid-twentieth century America was a serious means of developing the technical skill, stamina, patience and initiative of adolescent boys.[68] In one sense, to describe this as 'play' is to risk trivialising an important if informal apprenticeship in the development of space technology. But this is surely a further reminder about the extent to which play and work, toy box and silo, are co-constitutive. It is through such unremarkable means that the space race and the Cold War were enacted.

CONCLUSION: THE TWO MOST EXCITING PROMISES OF MODERN SCIENCE

> Space and the atom are the two most exciting promises of modern science. Under the pressures of a world at war, the Atomic Age had an unfortunate start. As yet, fear casts a dark shadow that obscures the untold benefits that the atom has in store for us. Space flight, fortunately, will be different. It begins under the auspices of a noble international effort to be carried out in a spirit of peaceful cooperation among scientists of all civilized nations.[69]

Aside from notable advances in molecular biology, the 1950s saw two unprecedented scientific investigations into the fabric of Earth and outer-Earth alike. The development of space technologies like the BUMPER WAC Corporal and subsequent sounding rockets provided a much more detailed picture of Earth's atmosphere, as well as producing iconic images of the Earth from space. At the same time, however, exploration turned in on itself – an involution – to examine sub-atomic 'spaces' which, through nuclear testing, produced its own peculiar geographies in laboratory and field, and across subterranean and terrestrial realms.[70] These developments are linked by a common geopolitical rationale that aimed to cultivate weapons of mass destruction and the means by which they could be urgently delivered to the other side of the globe. In this way, both the Space Age and the Atomic Age are folded into the geopolitical strategies of the Cold War, the ascent into space being, in one sense, merely charismatic evidence of a more sinister capability. And yet the inseparable character of the nuclearism and rocketry is sometimes obsessively denied by the champions of space. 'Space flight, fortunately, will be different' wrote Heinz Haber in 1956, as it 'begins under the auspices of a noble international effort to be carried out in a spirit of peaceful cooperation'. But the ultimate extent of international co-operation manifest in the 1967 UN Outer Space Treaty conception of space as *res communis* ('a thing for all') rather than *res nullius* ('a thing for no-one') was always more of a Cold War fudge designed to check the territorial and astropolitical ambitions of the superpower adversary. Despite the existence of the International Space Station (at $100 billion, the most expensive piece of technology ever built), space exploration has proved to be little different from the technologies of the atom: it remains a matter of competition rather than cooperation, and of weaponisation as much as civilian infrastructure.[71] And the current push towards dual use (civilian and military) space hardware[72] is itself indicative of the abiding indistinction between vehicle and weapon that was apparent 50 years ago with the launch of the Corporal. The story of the Corporal can thus be seen as an early intimation of the fact that space exploration would primarily be a matter of projecting terrestrial geopolitical power. The aim of this essay, at least in part, has been to bring the history of rocketry down to Earth.

Seen in the light of terrestrial geopolitics, the development of Cold War rocketry and the wider endeavour of space exploration become more obviously linked. In the annals of exploration, this is plainly not a new story: earlier precedents of exploring the sea and polar ice would likely offer some interesting parallels with the account I have described here. So it is worth emphasising that the exploration and colonisation of space does not represent a radical departure from the past but should be considered as an extension of entrenched regimes of power. As Peter Redfield succinctly observed, to move into space is 'a form of return': it represents 'a passage forward through the very pasts we might think we are leaving behind'.[73] Some recent work on the historical geographies of extra-terrestrial spaces, for instance, has persuasively shown how long-standing geographical practices of naming, mapping and topographical description were instrumental in the construction of planetary bodies such as Mars.[74] All of this supports the idea that space has long been part and parcel of Earth's geography,[75] and that this earthly-celestial tradition should itself be an inducement for geographers to think more closely about the space of space in its many cultural, historical and (geo)political expressions.

In this essay, I have unapologetically concentrated on the popular place of rocketry within the Cold War, rather than forging some technical or strategic account. I have done so because it seems to me that this is where the rocket/missile derives much of its geopolitical power. The version of the popular in operation here is of course quite different from much of the work on popular geopolitics. Rather than reproduce the well-worn critique of, say, Hollywood film, I have chosen to focus on more mundane activities such as play and on such seemingly unlikely geopolitical agents as children. It is through these means, I have argued, that space exploration and the Cold War are enacted and made meaningful in domestic contexts. That is to say, through the ordinary rehearsal of defending 'us' (Western, free, capitalist) from 'them', using technologies that also offer a transcendent future, the child-consumer-player is inducted into a much wider frame. Not only do toys and play have extraordinary propagandist value, but more importantly, they also bring about an informal apprenticeship in domains that slip very readily into 'real world' technics and activities. Moreover, the play of rocketry naturalises the anxieties of the Cold War and arguably helps make sense of otherwise difficult concepts of loss (leaving our earthly home) and death (via nuclear destruction). Most important of all, such toys bestow in their child operative a proprietary sense of the future: that the realm of space and the technical development of its exploration is something that belongs to them in their impending adult lives.

10 Walking in your footsteps: 'Footsteps of the explorers' expeditions and the contest for Australian desert space

Christy Collis

The horse and camel days are over
Good old times are nearly done
Exploration jobs still linger
Through the sand and in the sun.
Modern Man with 4WD
Can do with soakage small
Where the poor old horse and camel
Couldn't get a drink at all.
Oh horse and camel days are gone now
Mechanised we break the way
For the others soon to follow
On the tracks we made today.
But we have the satisfaction
Know our motor is the first
To push along this virgin portion
Through this land of heat and thirst.[1]

This chapter begins with a generically classic narrative of Australian desert exploration. As this account opens, the men are tiring in the heat and the dust of what the exploration narrative constructs as a 'middle of nowhere',[2] 'hell'[3] of desert space. 'God, we're getting tired', the narrative begins, 'Tired of washing every three days in a bucket with just two inches of water in it, and feeling dirty after it. Tired of having to make impossible kilometres every day. Just tired.'[4] The flagging men continue their struggle as the expedition's water supply dwindles alarmingly; a party is sent out over a set of dunes to locate a rumoured well. The men consider, briefly, turning back to where they know they can find water. But then the well is found, and the forwards trajectory that impels both the journey and the narrative is maintained. 'We'd go on', the leaders write with gritty determination, squinting at the horizon, and 'not head back'.[5]

Then, through 'bulldust traps'[6] and the monotonous homogeneity of the 'sea of sand and spinifex',[7] the expedition's 'strike force'[8] sets out on the most perilous and significant leg of the trip. Four selected men disappear over the horizon, into the desert beyond. At the narrative and the epistemological heart of this exploration narrative, the four men reach their destination: a plaque hammered into the ground to mark the passage of their predecessors, the Royal Geographical Society's 1896 Calvert Expedition. The explorers erect their own plaque and record its coordinates, indelibly inscribing their presence on the land. In standard imperial exploration style, one of the men conducts a brief Christian ceremony at the sanctified site. Finally, and only after several anxious incidents in which the expedition's equipment appears to be failing, the mission emerges from the interior and arrives back at a coastal town. The men are tired and thirsty and triumphant as well as ready, as the narrative has it, for the 'promise ... of warm women'.[9]

The essential elements are all there: thirst, frustration, courage, empty desert, and men who will not quit. But this is not a nineteenth-century exploration narrative. This major expedition explicitly aligns itself with the 'heroic age' of imperial spatial conquest and production: in its generic textualization; its filial inclusion of the great-grandson of the desert explorer Lawrence Wells (the leader of the Calvert expedition); and, as I will argue, in its mission of spatial production. The expedition took place in 1996: the journey here is

Land Rover's Calvert Centenary Expedition. This expedition is not only aligned with imperial spatial production by dint of its Footsteps retracing of Calvert's expedition, but its relationship to imperial spatiality is further cemented by its participation in the contemporary Australian 'Footsteps[10] of the imperial explorers' expedition phenomenon.

This chapter attends to a phenomenally pervasive example of contemporary exploration spatiality: 'Footsteps of the imperial explorers' expeditions. It is an examination of a specific genre of travel and travel narrative. It asks, as does Tim Cresswell, 'who travels and why?'[11] But it asks more than who and why; a central concern here is what sorts of spatiality are produced and maintained by this travelling. Spatiality here is seen as a composite of physical, perceived, and practiced spaces.[12] This is a study of a special form of travel and traveller, of contemporary (from 1970 to the present) Australian exploration narratives – both textual and physical – which take place, as well as make place, in the 10 Australian central deserts. Footsteps narratives demonstrate that contemporary Australian exploration spatiality is not simply a reprisal of a nineteenth-century British model; Footsteps expeditions and expedition narratives offer a clear model of what contemporary Australian exploration spatiality looks like, how it works, and how it functions within the broader dynamic of postcolonial spatial production and the contest for desert possession.

To speak of exploration, and particularly of the exploration of 'final frontiers', is to conjure up visions of stiff nineteenth-century men bristling with beards and all manner of Victorian impedimenta. Similarly, 'exploration narrative' generally suggests great bricks of nineteenth-century prose, complete with interminable appendices and manly scenarios of grim determination. To be an exploration scholar, it is commonly assumed, is to spend one's time in dusty special collections rooms. Exploration as an organized practice, as the increasing body of exploration criticism seems to indicate, is an historical activity, to be reviled or respected, but ultimately to be relegated to Empire's past. Australian exploration studies such as Simon Ryan's *The Cartographic Eye*, Robert Dixon's *The Course of Empire*, Paul Carter's *The Road to Botany Bay*, Ross Gibson's *The Diminishing Paradise* and Roslyn Haynes's *Seeking the Centre*, among others, have productively opened up Empire's imperial exploration to analysis, attending in detail to the ways in which Empire's explorers produced and practised Australian spatiality. Yet none extends its exploration analysis beyond the turn of the century; none attends to imperial exploration as an ongoing Australian practice of spatial production and possession. This is not to argue that exploration critics deny the continuing potency of certain tropes and practices derived from Empire's exploration: Ryan, for instance, examines nineteenth-century exploration journals, but insists that his is not 'simply an autopsy of a dead genre',[13] and Haynes acknowledges that 'we cannot see the landscape without [Empire's explorers'] influence'.[14] Yet when it comes to imperial exploration as an ongoing Australian practice, rather than as a set of inherited spatial tropes, there is a curious critical silence.

While numerous reasons contribute to this lack of attendance to Australian imperial exploration, one in particular requires attention here. Richard Dyer explains in his study of whiteness that it is a potentially dangerous manoeuvre to insist on attendance to white, masculine, imperial cultural formations. There is the danger of foregrounding dominant spatiality at the expense of competing spatial practices and productions, thus replicating academically the very state that one wishes to undermine.[15] There is undeniable validity to this argument, but there is also a problem, a problem which manifests in the lack of critical attention to the recent upsurge in Australian imperial exploration in the deserts. Attending to non-dominant spatialities, and elucidating logical inconsistencies and weak spots within dominant cultural formations, is crucial work. But assuming that the dominant formations against which they are pitched are either moribund or so archaic as to require no further discussion ultimately cripples resistance work: in order to comprehend resistance fully, it remains necessary to attend to the adaptable tactics of dominance.

Contemporary Australian exploration spatiality articulates to, and historically derives from, Empire's, but is not synonymous with it. Generically, imperial spatiality is a mobile process of spatial acquisition which arrogates to itself the power of originary spatial production, a performance of possession which is generally referred to as 'discovery'. In order to differentiate between imperial exploration spatiality as practised and produced by Empire, and imperial exploration spatiality as it manifests in contemporary Australia, this study uses the term

'Empire's imperialism' in reference to the former. This phrase signals a cultural dynamic which is not always acknowledged; that is, that imperial exploration spatiality is not restricted to the British Empire and that it is a significant constituent of the complex matrix of contemporary Australian spatiality.

FOOTSTEPS

Since the mid-1970s, white[16] Australian culture has driven a major upsurge and reinvestment in imperial exploration spatiality. A key aspect of this reinvestment involves not just remembering – through reading Empire's explorers' narratives – historical imperial spatiality, but also activating and confirming its ongoing power in the present tense. This activation takes diverse forms; one of the most interesting – Footsteps expeditions – has become particularly popular and pervasive in Australia. There are any number of itineraries which could structure a desert trip: one could travel in search of a certain bird, follow a creek, drive seismological shot lines, or zigzag from one Aboriginal[17] settlement to the next. However, while these agendas may well underpin some desert travel routes, Footsteps itineraries stand out with remarkable consistency in contemporary Australian desert travel culture. It is narratives of this motivating itinerary which fill magazines, videos, guidebooks, and books; it is this spatial performance that repeatedly achieves public consumption. This spatializing practice is the following: again and again since the early 1970s, Australian travellers, most often in four-wheel drive vehicles (4WD), motor through the deserts in Footsteps retracings of Empire's explorers' routes.

Footsteps expeditions involve white Australians (often male) travelling along what they imagine to be the tracks of Empire's explorers; their own exploration narratives indicate that a central part of the trip is reading Empire's documents as they go and confirming their continued accuracy and currency. The desert is 'exactly how Giles described it',[18] confirms Footstepper Alec Mathieson in 1977 as he drives through the Gibson Desert with one hand on the wheel of his 4WD and the other on Empire's explorer Giles's 1889 narrative, *Australia Twice Traversed: the Romance of Exploration. Being a Narrative Compiled from the Journals of Five Exploring Expeditions into and Through Central South*

Australia and Western Australia from 1872–1876. Or as Eriksen states on his 1971 Footsteps of Giles expedition, 'all of [the desert] was Giles's country, as untouched as when he found it'.[19] Another motivation is to ensure that Empire's explorers remain canonized among national desert narratives: as Rothwell writes of Kelly's 2000 Footsteps of Augustus Gregory expedition, 'Kelly had set off on a simple journey of homage, intending to enshrine Gregory as a fit subject for the national education syllabus.'[20] Footstepper Carrie Williamson, who followed the footsteps of her great-great-great-uncle, Empire's explorer Ludwig Leichhardt, avers of her expedition that 'it was meant to be, and that's all there is'.[21] The deserts have become busy with white Footsteppers retracing Empire's explorers' routes and then emerging to publish their own exploration narratives including *Conquering the Continent*,[22] *Across the Gibson*,[23] *Hard Country Hard Men: In the Footsteps of Gregory*[24] and *West of Centre*.[25]

What is crucial to Footsteps expeditions is that they are not, and never figure themselves as, theatrical citations of an absent past. Unlike, for instance, the consciously spectacular costume performance of explorer Douglas Mawson's 1912 Antarctic walk filmed by David Parer and Elizabeth Parer-Cook (*Douglas Mawson: The Survivor*), the artificiality of which is signalled by its staging, as well as by the inevitable sight of 'nineteenth-century explorers' in digital watches, in Footsteps expeditions there are no costumes, no role-playing, and no anachronistic dialogue. Contemporary Footsteps exploration plays a vital role in negotiating Australia's relation to its Empire origins, but it is not an attempt to return to the past. What is at stake in Footsteps expeditions is less the superficial resemblance of the teams than it is the reinstatement and reactivation of imperial exploration spatiality.

A significant, and particularly Australian, phenomenon emerges in Footsteps expeditions. In her discussion of the family in nineteenth-century Empire's culture, Anne McClintock argues that as the great patriarchal family with its rituals of inheritance and gendered subordination began to crumble as an institution, it found new vigour as an organizing metaphor.[26] In particular, McClintock notes, the trope of the patriarchal family was affixed to Empire's imperialism: 'the image of the evolutionary family was projected onto the imperial nation and colonial bureaucracies as their natural, legitimizing shape'.[27] The role of the patrilineal family narrative – complete with its notions of inheritance, perpetuation, and dominant masculinity – clearly functions as one of the key organizing tropes in Australian exploration spatiality. It allows for a filial Australian connection to Empire origins, and at the same time incorporates the idea of progressive evolution from the paternal source. As Meaghan Morris argues, 'the family romance is a way of "inventing history" that allows us not only to change but to improve upon the received and socially sanctioned versions of our beginnings'.[28]

In late twentieth-century Australian exploration, however, a curious and significant shift takes place with this filial trope: it moves back into genetic reality. Suddenly, the deserts have become busy with sons and grandsons of Empire's explorers following the 'footsteps' of their forefathers; their genealogical filiation is a primary part of their self-construction and their exploratory motivation, as well as of their exploration narratives. Empire's explorer Lawrence Wells's great-grandson pounds through the deserts as the figurehead of a Footsteps expedition in order to bless a marker of his progenitor's 1896 passage;[29] explorer Cecil Madigan's grandson travels by camel through the Simpson Desert to hammer a plaque into a tree upon which his grandfather inscribed his initials in 1939;[30] and, in a literal model of patrilineal descent, Madigan's son – Sir Russell Madigan – flies over the same expedition in order to drop supplies out of a light plane to his son below.

This section has outlined some of the key generic features of Australian Footsteps expeditions; in order to understand exactly what kind of spatiality they generate, and how they figure in the contest for possession of the Australian deserts, it is necessary to address the nature and the history of imperial exploration spatiality in Australia.

EMPIRE'S EXPLORATION SPATIALITY

The reasons underpinning the contemporary activation of Australian imperial exploration are complex, but not difficult to discern: Empire's imperial exploration accounts are *the* documents of white territorial possession; they are *how* white Australians came to possess an entire continent, and 42 per cent of Antarctica; and they are authorized constructors of *what* it is that they own. They are the primary texts which establish what Aileen Moreton-Robinson refers to as 'the possessive logic of patriarchal white sovereignty' in Australian space. The cultural power of Empire's exploration texts cannot be overstated. But what, exactly, is imperial exploration spatiality in the Australian context?

It is crucial to understand imperial exploration as a ritual practice of spatial productivity and possession, and not as a search for material things. There is no doubt that Empire's explorers were despatched in part to locate potential pasturage, possible watercourses, and mineral deposits, but to argue that these material items constitute the motivating energy of imperial exploration is to overlook imperial exploration as a spatializing practice. Tim Flannery avers that Empire's imperial exploration of Australia was a complete failure because the explorers returned with journals full of emptiness rather than maps green with potential pasturage.[31] Flannery's argument is naive: the raison d'etre of imperial exploration is hardly the location of grass. Explorers did find grasslands and minerals, but their task is the establishment of possession – and of the terms of possession – of these physical entities and not a simple recording of their cartographic locations.

One of the foundational premises of spatial studies is that the job of imperial explorers is not to locate landforms, but to produce a discursive space. 'The early travellers', as Carter notes of Australian explorers, 'invented places rather than found them';[32] as Certeau similarly observes, the primary achievement of imperial exploration is to 'make space into a language.'[33] Despite the undisputed power of textuality, exploratory discourse alone cannot, and does not, produce spatial possessions: the power of imperial exploration is more than simply discursive. At international law, space can be acquired by imperial claimants in one of three main ways: through conquest, cession (treaty), or through 'unilateral possession, on the basis of first discovery and effective occupation'[34] of *terra nullius*, or land owned by no one. It was on the basis of the 'first discovery' of *terra nullius* that Australia was stitched into Empire's dominion. In the international law of discovery, explorers are not just symbolic representatives, but vessels of enormous legal force. According to international territorial law, sovereign title to 'new' territory – land defined (by Europeans) as *terra nullius*, or land belonging to no one – can be established through the eyes, feet, codified ritual performances, and documents of explorers. That is, once an authorized explorer saw land, put his foot on it, planted a flag, read a proclamation, then documented these acts in words and maps, that land became a possession.[35] In Australia, Empire's explorers' texts, ritual actions, and passage created the continent – including the deserts – as *terra nullius*, and thus, as a white possession.

Two aspects of *terra nullius* are central to an understanding of imperial spatiality in Australia: first, *terra nullius* is not a denial of Indigenous occupation, rather it is a means of suborning Indigenous spatialities within a dominant European system; because Indigenous Australians did not construct buildings or farms that Europeans would recognize as valid, the Eurocentric law of *terra nullius* judged that they therefore did not have sovereignty over the land. Indigenous spatialities were thus relegated to the realm of fauna by the explorers' *terra nullius*: occupying, but not owning the ground.

The second aspect of *terra nullius* of relevance here is that it is based on spatial practices or rituals of possession. These rituals comprise the cultural practice called 'imperial exploration and discovery': they include building cairns, inscribing trees, reading and writing formal proclamations of sovereignty, raising the flag, firing salutes, and walking – 'sen[ding] representatives on regular patrols about the whole'.[36] Imperial exploration, under *terra nullius*, becomes the suite of spatial practices by which white possession is performed and produced, and Indigenous spatial possession is erased. And in Australia, this imperial spatiality, installed by Empire's explorers, is the means through which the entire continent was transformed into a white possession.

CRISES

The foundational power of Empire's exploration narratives does not in itself account for the sudden resurgence of imperial exploration spatiality in Australia in the 1970s; in order to discern what triggered the need to re-explore, re-claim and re-produce the deserts, it is necessary to attend briefly to the crises which beset non-Indigenous Australian culture – and particularly its right to desert possession – in the 1970s.

In 1976, a turning point in Australian spatial history occurred: the *Aboriginal Land Rights (NT) Act* developed by the Whitlam government came into force. Under the *Act*, Indigenous Australians could assert legal title ('Native Title') on Aboriginal reserves and on officially empty Crown Land; they could also claim royalties from mining practiced on their lands. The impact of the *Act*, and similar Acts that followed it in other states,[37] was profound: suddenly, non-Indigenous possession of the continent was under not only moral, but also legal challenge. As Land Claims worked their way through imaginary and juridical spatialities, Sydneysiders regarded their suburban backyards with anxiety.[38] Indigenous territoriality has not been restricted to discrete Land Claims: in a highly visible performance of spatial invasion and settlement, the 1972 Aboriginal Tent Embassy was erected on the grounds of Parliament in Canberra, and in 1979 Paul Coe insisted that non-Indigenous title to the entire continent was entirely invalid and called for immediate Indigenous sovereignty over Australian land.[39] In 1985, the Anangu people won back Uluru: one of white Australia's mythologized sites of national spatial identity and desert possession was returned to its Aboriginal owners.

This brief summary is not intended as a comprehensive report on Indigenous spatiality since the 1970s: works such as Tim Rowse's *After Mabo: Interpreting Indigenous Traditions*, Kenneth Maddock's *Anthropology, Law, and the Definition of Australian Aboriginal Rights to Land*, Nicholas Peterson and Marcia Langton's *Aborigines, Land, and Land Rights*,[40] among numerous others, attend to the moral and legal politics of Indigenous territoriality. The point here is that for the first time in Australia's history, the very grounds of non-Indigenous spatial production and possession – specifically the principle of *terra nullius* installed by Empire's explorers – came into formal, and very public, question.

A significant point arising from Indigenous spatial politics which is of primary relevance here relates to the grounds upon which Native Title is legally based. In Native Title claims, the Australian courts for the first time recognized Indigenous genealogy as a legal basis for a land claim: Indigenous 'traditional attachment' to land was granted legal power.[41] Second, Indigenous spiritual attachment to specific sites was legally mobilized as grounds for spatial possession, this spiritual attachment often demonstrated through narratives of the sites' discovery, creation, and occupation by ancestors. The logic and the laws of Australian spatial possession suddenly took on added dimensions: claims of Empire's explorers, it seemed, were no longer enough to comprise the entire spatiality and possession of the continent.

A reactive rationale thus underpins the return of explorers' sons and grandsons to the Footsteps of their fathers. In the 1970s, Aboriginal Land Rights claims began moving through the courts, and through the nation's spatial imaginary, substantially fuelled by the argument of familial inheritance. 'That is my father's country', Yungngora elder Dicky Skinner asserts in a representative citation of Aboriginal genealogical territoriality,[42] or as Eddie Mabo's representatives stated on his behalf at his landmark case, 'My father told me that this land would belong to me when he died.'[43] While non-Indigenous Australians had been able to pretend that Indigenous claims were invalid because Indigenous spatial practices differ from European ones – this is the logic of *terra nullius* – the logic of familial inheritance was too recognizable to be dismissed. And the logic of Indigenous familial inheritance began to transform Australian legal and conceptual space.

For a relatively recent settler/invader culture, Aboriginal genealogical claims are profoundly threatening, particularly when it comes to deserts. Scattered non-Indigenous desert cattle and sheep stations may have been 'in the family' for several generations, but how could non-Indigenous Australians counter the depth of familial Aboriginal claims to the deserts? Suddenly, the deserts erupted with the sons and grandsons of Empire's explorers on Footsteps expeditions. The anxiety provoked by Aboriginal claims based on familial inheritance is thus met with a counter-claim of a white, imperial genealogy of explorers. This, the imperial sons assert as they tread their fathers' tracks, is the land of our fathers, and it is ancestrally ours. When the sons of the fathers in *The Madigan Line* Footsteps expedition[44] gather ceremonially around a tree inscribed by Madigan, they are not simply validating familial history – they are staking a counter-Aboriginal genealogical claim. 'My father', they tacitly assert, 'said this land would belong to me when he died'.

As with the sudden influx of Empire's explorers' offspring into contemporary Australian spatiality, Footsteps expeditions themselves relate to Aboriginal spatial practices, demonstrating that Australian imperial exploration spatiality is not simply an anachronistic monolith, but a dynamic and adaptive force. Footsteps expeditions have obvious European roots in the Christian pilgrimage and the Stations of the Cross, but in their contemporary Australian manifestation, their field of reference is far broader than the solely-European derived. To discern the relation of Footsteps expeditions to Aboriginal spatialities, it is useful to consider them anthropologically. Certain members of the tribe travel along invisible paths across the deserts, reciting ancestral narratives of those spaces' original production as they go.

They travel to specific sacralized sites, at which traces of the ancestors' passage are visible, usually in the form of rock carvings or inscribed trees. The group then retells the ancestral stories and appends its own: they are narrating the country into being; they are activating it through rituals of storytelling and motivated travel. The similarity of white Footsteps expeditions to non-Aboriginal conceptions of Aboriginal songlines spatiality is clear. Footsteps expeditions are thus imbued with the autochthonous authority and authenticity of Aboriginal songlines, yet at the same time as they adopt Aboriginal practices of possession, it is Aboriginal possession that they work to deny.

Attempting to compress the epistemological and political shifts of the 1970s into one section of course results in debatable generalities, but one indisputable fact emerges: in the 1970s, non-Indigenous Australian spatiality and spatial possession – specifically the desert spatiality installed by Empire's explorers – came under fundamental challenge.

FOOTSTEPS EXPEDITIONS

As this spatial crisis mounted in Australia, the Footsteps phenomenon emerged. At a moment of spatial crisis, the phenomenon promised to legitimate non-Indigenous – and specifically white – ownership, configurations, and uses of Australian desert space. But it needs to be noted that identifying Footsteps of the explorers expeditions as a component of Australian imperial spatiality does not entail a judgemental resort to cliches which condemn all Footsteppers as rapacious imperialists consciously bent on masculine conquest of the deserts. Similarly, pointing up the racial anxieties articulated in Footsteps discourse and practice does not translate to damning Footsteppers as racists. The intention here is to investigate the ways in which imperial exploration spatiality is produced, practiced, and maintained by Footsteps of the explorers' expeditions, and not to indict individuals. Footsteppers frequently assert love of the deserts as their motivation for travel, and there is no question that this love is genuine and sincerely felt. The question here, however, is what kind of spatiality is the object of this deep emotional engagement. To answer this question, this section attends closely to two representative Australian Footsteps expeditions.

Assessing the relationship of the following Footsteps desert exploration narrative to imperial exploration spatiality does not require much searching for recondite inferences. *Conquering the Continent*, a video[45] distributed by Outback Explorer Productions in 1990, narrates a private Footsteps expedition as it travels from Adelaide to Darwin. If the title leaves any doubt as to the epistemological motivation driving the trip and its spatializing narrative, the subtitle erases it: the expedition will conquer the continent by *Retracing ... John McDougall Stuart's Transcontinental Expedition of 1862*. The title's ambiguous attribution of conquest strategically performs the narrative's central function: the elision of the Empire's explorer Stuart's expedition and spatiality, and that of Australian Kelvin Hogarth, the leader of the 1990 *Conquering* expedition. Stuart conquered the continent by walking (and at times being carried) across it from south to north; Hogarth will conquer it by retracing Stuart's route in a 4WD with his three children. The two expeditions are collapsed from the outset: Hogarth and Stuart, as the title's singular conquest indicates, are parts of the same, unbroken narrative of imperial desert production and possession.

Graham McInerney and Alec Mathieson's 1978 book, *Across the Gibson*, similarly relies on the Footsteps of one of Empire's explorers – Ernest Giles – as its motivating context. Unlike Hogarth's, Mathieson and McInerney's expedition was not a private one: Daihatsu Australia, the *Adelaide Advertiser* newspaper, and BP petrol sponsored their Footsteps mission.[46] *Across the Gibson* not only sutures the contemporary explorers to Giles by positioning the two expeditions as constituents of the same, ongoing imperial narrative of desert production and possession; it also activates Giles's 'spirit'. 'Whether lying by the campfire on a clear night after reading a section of his journal, or bounding uncomfortably over spinifex in our vehicles seeing the country he so vividly described, Giles definitely rode with us – resurrected through his writings' the men aver.[47] In McInerney and Mathieson's expedition narrative, the deserts become a site in which Giles – and his imperial exploration spatiality – remain present and relevant.

The central focus of McInerney and Mathieson's narrative is the 'discover[y]'[48] of 'blaze trees', that is of trees inscribed by Giles in 1876. For four months before they depart, the explorers pore over Giles's journals and maps, tracing his route onto their newer maps and trying to pinpoint the location of his inscribed trees. As the men's mission is not only to visit the sacralized traces of Giles's passage, but also to confirm the accuracy and continuing legitimacy of his spatializing text, they are somewhat disconcerted when they detect errors in his cartography. 'Although generally Giles was accurate', they write, 'we found these errors confusing and they almost broke the bond we felt with him.'[49] However, the Australian explorers manage to salvage the filial 'bond' by admiring Giles's valiant efforts, and then correcting his coordinates: true to the logic of filial evolution, McInerney and Mathieson 'improve' on Giles's spatial accuracy.

The term 'blaze' used for inscribed trees metaphorically signals the spatial work which these marked trees are made to perform in exploration discourse. Carter observes that blaze trees are not only markers of passage – travellers' graffiti – but beacons of 'blazing' legibility in otherwise meaningless space: 'the white blaze marks were like lanterns along a street', he writes.[50] In this way, blaze trees articulate an imperial semiotic of presence, giving what Howard McNaughton refers to as 'an edge and a syntax to Empire'.[51] As Footsteppers Jim and Cheryl Foster indicate, blazes are also repositories of the imperial 'spirit', sacred sites at which the foundation narratives of white possession can be activated and imbibed: 'running your fingers over those rough characters carved into the living wood ... is an eerie feeling. You are making direct contact with living history, a history of hardship and exploration that stretches back 154 years to when our nation was very young.'[52] As Michael Gebicki writes of Footstepper Carrie Willamson's expedition in the footsteps of her great-great-great uncle, Empire's explorer Ludwig Leichhardt, finding an inscription which might have been generated by Leichhardt's expedition is 'a revelation, a gift from the heavens'.[53]

A recurring assertion in Footsteps expedition narratives is the essential sameness of the land today to the land travelled by Empire's explorers. Or rather, it is the continuing accuracy of the original explorers' spatial production which is repeatedly asserted. McInerney and Mathieson's Gibson Desert expedition opens as the men come across large anthills 'swimming in a November haze'.[54] Their first response to the anthills is to pull out Giles's 1876 journal and map and to spread them out on the 4WD's bonnet. 'There, sure enough, is the notation "anthills up to eight feet high"' in Giles's journal.[55] McInerney and Mathieson are thrilled: 'Giles's latitude is spot on. These must be the ones he saw';[56] the accompanying photo depicts one of the expedition members holding and staring at 'one of the anthills that Giles wrote about in his diary'.[57] The Australian Footsteppers express admiration for Giles's cartographic exactitude, but the sense of satisfaction they derive from the anthills stems also from their ability to confirm his imperial spatiality: nothing has changed, their narrative asserts.

The second effect of Footsteps expeditions' discoveries of sameness is to reinforce the imperial fantasy of desert stasis, the notion that other than imperial exploration, nothing has or does happen in Australia's arid regions. Insisting on the deserts' continuing virginity also conceals the physical effects of over 100 years of colonization: roads, seismic exploration sites, extinct species, ruined water sources, feral vegetation, and numerous communities all disappear under the production of spatial sameness. 'The country,' as Ray Eriksen writes in his Footsteps of Giles narrative, 'is nearly as virgin now as it was when Giles became the first white man to see it ... the greater part is still virtually trackless desert – a blank space on the map',[58] in other words, it is *terra nullius*. As a video, Conquering sutures Stuart's imperial spatiality to Hogarth's in a way that print texts cannot. The video's key editing technique is superimposition: over and over, shots from Hogarth's expedition fade into Stuart's sketches of the same spot. The superimposition strategy collapses Stuart's and Hogarth's exploratory gazes, and more importantly, the spaces they produce. But it is not just the edit that visually confirms the sameness of Stuart's and Hogarth's deserts: the video solicits the viewer, who is granted the power of the exploratory gaze[59] through the ostensibly neutral lens of the documentary camera, to become the confirmational nexus between the two images. The visual message is clear: the only difference between the desert spatiality produced by Stuart and that generated by Footstepper Hogarth is colour film, otherwise, the two are exactly the same. The superimpositions set up a closed circuit of legitimation in which Stuart's authority is confirmed by Hogarth, and Hogarth's spatiality is in turn legitimated by its filiation to Stuart's.

Conquering the Continent opens with a cautionary note advising viewers that 'People die in the Outback every year. A journey such as you are about to see should only be done by the experienced.' This, the warning makes clear, is not simply a holiday; rather, it is a ritualized and heroic sortie into an inimical space. The film then cuts to its establishing shot: Hogarth stands alone on a rocky outcrop, silhouetted by the setting sun. The image inserts Hogarth into what Ryan refers to as the standardized imperial position of privileged 'elevation and surveillance'.[60] Hogarth stands at what appears to be the edge of the land, staring out at the invisible space beyond. In the shot, the land is visible only to Hogarth: the viewer is thus required to subscribe to his privileged vision in order to access what lies beyond. The shot also establishes the narrative's two protagonists: there is the man, his Australianness signalled by the silhouette of his iconic Akubra hat, and there is the land below, anonymous and dark and awaiting illumination. With his exploratory gaze established, the voiceover informs the viewer what it is that Hogarth sees. What he sees is a space defined solely by Stuart's passage: 'This remote area of South Australia was largely unexplored by Europeans as recently as 130 years ago, when it was finally opened up by a Scotsman named John McDougall Stuart.' *Across the Gibson* deploys the same manoeuvre: a large photo depicts expeditioner Dick Lang 'scan[ning] the horizon' with binoculars from a high vantage point;[61] the desert stretches away before him, its only meaning residing in the invisible line of Giles's footsteps.

Along with the superimposition technique, *Conquering*'s voiceovers work to tether the two exploration narratives into a single narrative of uninterrupted spatial similitude. *Conquering* is narrated by two voices: Hogarth's and of a Scottish man who reads from Stuart's journal. These two men's voices are the only ones heard in the film; their dialogue is a two-part harmony of mutual confirmation. At one point, the camera shows Hogarth sitting beside a campfire reading Stuart's journal to his children. Hogarth's voiceover fades into the Stuart voice: Hogarth becomes a medium through which Stuart speaks to the present. This moment invokes a patriarchal genealogy, with Stuart as the originary Father. At another point in the video, the children point to dried fish in a salted littoral as the Stuart voiceover describes his own discovery of dried fish around a salt lake. As Stuart continues to discuss the local clay, the children on screen pick up lumps of clay and present them to the camera. The Stuart voiceover narrates several shots of the 4WD churning through the sand, smoothing over the potential difference between the two expeditions that the modern vehicle might suggest.

In the scene which marks the narrative heart of the video, the expedition arrives at what the Stuart voiceover proclaims as the centre of the continent; the sudden appearance of writing from Stuart's journal on screen emphasizes Stuart's textual production of this centre, as well as the originary power of his text. As Hogarth's children approach the hill, the Stuart voiceover, echoed by the onscreen text, declares it Central Mount Stuart; it is as if the children's act of following Stuart's footsteps reactivates this fundamental moment of originary spatial production at the symbolic heart of the continent. As the Stuart voiceover describes the epic difficulties of climbing the hill, the children ascend it. In a climactic moment of simultaneity, the children reach the summit; the Stuart voiceover articulates one of Australian exploration's iconic speeches; and the camera merges Stuart's, Hogarth's, the children's, and the viewer's gazes in a 360 degree panorama shot. As we survey the land together, Stuart proclaims:

> We built a large cone of stones in the centre of which I placed a pole with the Union Jack nailed to it. We gave three hearty cheers for the flag, the emblem of civil and religious liberty. And may it be a sign to the natives that the dawn of liberties, civilization, and Christianity is about to break upon them.

The video's music swells throughout the speech, then climaxes as the children raise the Australian flag from a rock cairn atop the hill.

Footsteps accounts often manage Aboriginal desert spatialities and occupation through the familiar imperial strategies of evacuation and primitivism. That is, when forced to drop the pretence of Aboriginal non-existence (which *Conquering the Continent* never does), Footsteps narratives often opt for an archaeological register which situates Aborigines in an amorphous prehistory from where they can exert little other than an ornamental effect on desert spatiality. The Land Rover Calvert Centenary expedition admits to Aboriginal presence only in the form of 'ancient' rock art on an evolutionarily distant 'Neanderthal red ridge'.[62] In Glover and Whiting's neutralizing rhetoric, the 'graffitised' gorge in which they find the rock art features a meaningless agglomeration of seemingly random 'freshwater turtles, von Daniken extraterrestrials, emus, and kangaroos',[63] and has significance only insofar as it represents an archaeological 'discovery' by the expedition's scientists.

Glover and Whiting further counteract the spatializing potential of the Aboriginal inscriptions by positioning photos of them in an informational appendix titled 'the Scientists', headed by a photo of a man peering through a magnifying glass at a lizard.[64] Carter's identification of the epistemological emplacement of Aborigines in nineteenth-century exploration narratives remains salient: as in the Empire's explorers' accounts, in Glover and Whiting's Footsteps narrative, Aborigines 'find themselves, if at all, consigned to the category of miscellaneous information, sailing directions, prospects for trade, geological specimens and the climate. They inhabit the realm of the etc.'[65] Neatly segregated into the passive realm of scientific objectification, the Aboriginal inscriptions, along with dune behaviour and fossils, are reduced to yet another of the expedition's 'discoveries' and 'advancements in knowledge'.[66]

It is not only the present tense from which these Footsteps narratives evacuate Aboriginal presence: each narrative also performs a retroactive erasure, a removal of Aborigines from the nation's past. Glover and Whiting's Calvert Footsteps accounts are a case in point. Well's 1902 *A Journal of the Calvert Scientific Exploring Expedition* is undeniably an account of travel through occupied territory: although the logic of *terra nullius* allowed Wells to figure Aboriginal presence as inconsequential and ephemeral, his narrative is populated by Aboriginal campfire smoke, Aboriginal camps, Aboriginal wells, and Aborigines themselves. Wells's engagements with Aborigines were not simply sightings: he not only relied on Aboriginal directional assistance, but also regularly captured and tortured Aborigines for water, and for information. Wells manacled Aborigines' legs together; he chained them by their necks to trees; he had his assistant assault them with their own spears; and he refused his captives water until they would disclose their water sources. Wells's narrative is less a battle against the desert than it is a battle with its inhabitants for the desert.

There is no chance that members of the Calvert Footsteps expedition missed these instances of frightened savagery: like McInerney and Mathieson, the explorers spend months before their departure poring over Wells's journal, and they carry the journal along with them for daily readings, and for the necessary affirmations of similitude. Yet in Glover and Whiting's narrative, Wells's engagements with Aborigines – whether curious, frightened, begrudgingly grateful, or violent – simply disappear. McInerney and Mathieson euphemistically refer to David Carnegie's 1898 practice of capturing and torturing Aborigines as 'more practical, but less ethical'[67] than searching for water. 'Knowing there were no longer Aborigines in the area', they continue in the next sentence, 'we took our water with us.'[68]

McInerney and Mathieson emerge from the desert back into 'civilization'[69] triumphantly: they have reactivated Giles's spirit; they have reclaimed the desert as their own. In *Across the Gibson*, Giles is reinstated as the desert's sole source of meaning: 'we had no one and nothing to relate to on our trip except Giles's journals. There were no comparisons. Only he had been there before us. Only he knew what lay ahead.'[70] But at the conclusion of the narrative, Giles is no longer alone: with their own inscriptions on Giles's blaze trees dotting the desert behind them, and with their tyre tracks reinscribing Giles's route, McInerney and Mathieson have become a new instalment in the imperial narrative of Australian desert exploration, production, and possession. Similarly, *Conquering the Continent* concludes with another triumphant flag-raising – complete with Stuart superimposition showing Stuart's flag-flying on the same Carpentarian beach – but with one crucial difference. As *Conquering the Continent*'s musical score draws to its final crescendo, the three blonde children hoist the Australian – and not the British – flag from the bonnet of their 4WD.

CONCLUSION

In Footsteps of the explorers expeditions and expedition narratives, imperial exploration spatiality persists. To conceptualize dominant spatiality as Certeau does in 'Walking in the City', that is as the archaic ruins of a moribund culture through which transgressive guerrillas enact tactical sorties, is to deny imperialism's adaptability, and worse to assume its demise. The aim of this chapter, then, is to attend to the dynamics, the shapes, the narratives, the practices, and the ubiquitous power of Australian imperial spatiality in order to participate in the process of its denaturalization. This is not to argue that the multiple projects pointing up the business of desert spatialities – their heterogeneous natures and histories – are not worthwhile. It is, however, to intervene in the progressivist narrative which proclaims imperialism's demise. As Australian Footsteppers churn through the deserts, one point is made clear: Australian imperial exploration spatiality has not disappeared.

11 Modern explorers

Felix Driver

For well over a century now, pundits and philosophers have been announcing the end of the age of exploration. Once the true shape of the earth was known, in broad outline, the true business of science would begin; once contact had been established with virtually all peoples across the globe, the idea of the first encounter could only be a distant memory, or perhaps a sham; once the global village had become a reality, courtesy of all manner of technological innovations, what hope could there be for genuine travelling into the unknown? Whether in a spirit of celebration or mourning, the idea of exploration has so often been consigned to the past, its inevitable demise written into the very fabric of our histories of science, culture and travel, that it may at first appear perverse to suggest that it is anything but an anachronism in the modern age. Against this background, this book makes a signal contribution. By moving our focus into the twentieth century, and in particular by raising our eyes to the heavens as well as to the extremities of the earth, the authors demonstrate the modernity of exploration right up to our own time, even in – maybe especially in – an era of hyperglobalisation.

References to explorers and exploration in the literature of contemporary science, education or geopolitics are not simply manifestations of inertia or nostalgia: they indicate the transformative capacities of the discourse of exploration and highlight something of its imaginative appeal. As Kathryn Yusoff shows in her study of Antarctic expedition photography, the process of discovery is not so much about finding as taking and making: it transforms its objects, leaving the world a different place. And the rituals of possession enacted by explorers and navigators of previous 'golden ages' of exploration have their direct equivalents today: to cite just three examples from 2007–8, in the sending of a Russian flag to the bottom of the Arctic Sea, the waving of a Chinese flag in outer space and the dropping of an Indian flag onto the surface of the Moon. Instead of being witnessed by incredulous locals on far-flung shores, and transmitted to Europe via fragile documents sent across the world in rat-infested ships, these modern rites are instantly available to a much larger and genuinely cosmopolitan audience via television and the world wide web. They may have lost their strictly legal status (a moot point given the state of international law relating to the polar regions and outer space), but they have certainly not lost their cultural power or their geopolitical significance.

This trio of flags had a peculiar, shared destiny: blasted into outer space or onto the seabed, in locations as remote as one could possibly imagine, they were destined to be seen almost instantaneously by an enormous global audience following the events on television, on the web and in the newspapers. The first, encased within a rust-proof titanium capsule, was affixed to the Arctic seabed, 14,000 feet beneath the surface at the North Pole, having been transported there on board a Russian mini-submarine attached to a nuclear-powered ice-breaker, in the summer of 2007. On hearing the news, the Canadian Foreign Minister disdainfully remarked that 'This isn't the fifteenth Century', dismissing the symbolism as archaic if not entirely redundant; but the much-publicised deed had already done its work, highlighting the Russian claim to a large expanse of territory said to contain extensive reserves of oil, gas and minerals. The second flag, representing the People's Republic of China, was clutched by astronaut Zhai Zhigang 213 miles above the earth as his capsule orbited the planet, on 28 September 2008. Pictures of his spacewalk, the first by a Chinese astronaut, were beamed live on prime-time television to an audience of millions – the same audience, no doubt, which weeks earlier had tuned in to the spectacle of the Beijing Olympics. The third flag – this one in the colours of India – was blasted off from an island in the Bay of Bengal a few weeks later in the unmanned Chandrayaan 1 spacecraft on a much-publicised mission to orbit the Moon and compile a three-dimensional atlas of its features. If all goes to plan, this flag will be fired into the lunar surface from a probe, becoming the fourth of its kind to be planted on the Moon (after those of the United States, Russia and Japan). There are after all many ways of colonising a planet.

The immense scale of the resources required to mount a space programme, or to support submarine expeditions to the North Pole, tells us something about the value placed on this form of exploration by powerful states in the modern world. For those key decision-makers who control the budgets of the state agencies concerned, the military and industrial applications of space science and technology ultimately provide the most important rationale for support of these expeditions. In addition, of course, space exploration offers powerful iconographic possibilities. The state-sponsored scientific mission, complete with guns and flags, has a long history, notably including the French, British and Spanish expeditions in the eighteenth-century Pacific, and the associations between science and military power are as close today, if not closer, as they were in the age of Captain Cook. Of course many of today's military adventures in space require international cooperation, but even this is not new, as any historian will tell you. The merry dance between international treaty-making and national self-interest which has characterised global geopolitics for centuries continues alive and well in the field of exploration and discovery. As Klaus Dodds and Matthew Godwin show here and elsewhere, a similar pattern of geopolitical manoeuvring is visible in the planning and outcome of the International Geophysical Year (IGY), 1957–8, and also in the wider context of space exploration during and after the Cold War. For all the lofty rhetoric which surrounded it, the IGY did not actually turn Antarctica into a multinational scientific laboratory, liberated from the claims of national self-interest; indeed, in some respects, especially given the connections between military interests, satellite technology and atmospheric physics, it reinforced those claims.[1] And the civilian and military components of space research remain closely and inevitably intertwined, as the budgets required for science escalate ever further, their interdependence nicely encapsulated in Fraser Macdonald's discussion of the constant slippage between the terms 'rocket' and 'missile'.

The story of the accelerating 'space race' during the 1950s and 1960s, several aspects of which are highlighted in this book, is often understood through the lens of Cold War geopolitics.[2] Here it is seen as a struggle for primacy in the scientific and cultural sphere, especially as reflected in international competition for a series of 'firsts', including the first unmanned space flight, the first animal in space and the first human in space, reaching its climax with the first moon landing on 20 July 1969. This account contains many echoes of earlier moments in the history of exploration in which geopolitics loomed large, including rivalries between European navigators in the Pacific during the eighteenth century, explorers of river and lake systems in East Africa during the nineteenth century, expeditions to the North and South poles during the early twentieth century and successive attempts to climb Mount Everest culminating in the successful 1953 ascent by Hillary and Tenzing.[3] While such events have often been celebrated as feats of individual heroism, that should not blind us to the necessarily collective sources of both their success and their appeal. The achievement of being first in itself meant nothing: what counted, of course, was the recognition that came with it.

The large-scale organisation and mega-politics of twentieth-century scientific exploration, whether terrestrial, marine or interplanetary, thus suggests a direct lineage with the larger, more organised expeditions of earlier eras: in this sense, Neil Armstrong is a worthy successor to Captain Cook. But what of the more idiosyncratic figures whose sensational explorations and adventures are so often in the public eye, who also accrue to themselves ever-expanding lists of 'firsts': the first solo walk to the North Pole, the first unaided crossing of the Antarctic, the first nonstop circumnavigation of the earth by balloon...; whatever the feat, it must always be represented as the original from which copies can (indeed must) be made. An obvious exemplar here is Sir Ranulph Fiennes, almost inevitably dubbed 'the world's greatest living explorer' by the Guinness Book of Records, who has skilfully exploited the public appetite for stories of questing adventure and astonishing endurance. Like the journalist-turned-explorer Henry Morton Stanley, Fiennes' celebrity in the field of exploration is closely tied up with his success as an author: they are, almost literally, two sides of the same coin. Stanley engaged in promotional lecture tours following his return from each of his African expeditions; Fiennes is a regular speaker on the global business circuit, offering motivational presentations under the title 'Nothing is beyond your reach', 'Living dangerously' and 'To the ends of the earth'. In the words of one promotional website:

> The elements vital to the success – indeed the survival – of Fiennes and his expedition colleagues include teamwork, leadership,

determination, patience, discipline, enthusiasm and creative thinking: all equally important in less hazardous occupations. Building a team with the right character and attitude is of paramount importance. Persistence; tolerance; understanding; planning skills; high organisational ability; fitness for the task in hand; flexibility to meet and beat unexpected obstacles; goalsetting and performing under extreme pressure are clearly all factors in Fiennes' remarkable endeavours.[4]

On this account, success in the field of exploration depends ultimately on qualities of character, especially risk-taking and leadership. Similar associations between daredevil adventure and business success are also evident in publicity surrounding the exploits of the late Steve Fossett, the American millionaire turned aviator and long-distance solo balloonist whose plane went missing over the Nevada desert in September 2007. During his lifetime, Fossett had at his disposal a highly effective publicity machine, courtesy of his friend Richard Branson; given the nature of his demise, his fame as an adventurer seems likely to have achieved legendary status. Like Sir John Franklin, who vanished in the course of an expedition to find the North-West passage in 1845, the mystery of Fossett's disappearance was the subject of much sensational press speculation; indeed, and quite predictably, it was even suggested that he had faked his own death. After repeated attempts to find clues in the desert, on 29 September 2008 a hiker in the Sierra Nevada range in California stumbled on personal items including identity papers, which were later confirmed as Fossett's. Over the following week, aerial searches located the wreckage, and the pitifully few human remains that are currently undergoing DNA analysis. The Fossett search is finally over.

The parallels between a Fiennes and a Stanley (or indeed a Fossett and a Franklin) are difficult to discern if one takes the view that the age of exploration came to an end around the beginning of the twentieth century; but they are difficult to ignore if you want to understand the continued imaginative appeal of exploration in the modern world. Exploration is dead, long live exploration! That at least is the cry of the market. From this scene, of sensationalism and adventure, scientists have sometimes stood aloof, as if the practice of science had nothing to do with the pursuit of fame or fortune. 'I hate the claptrap and flattery and flummery of the Royal Geographical [Society], with its utter want of Science and craving for popularity and excitement', grumbled Joseph Hooker, director of Kew Gardens, in the midst of a season of sensational reports concerning African exploration in 1864.[5] In the Victorian era, the more gentlemanly the amateur, the more disdainful he could afford to be of those who sought to make a living from either science or exploration: the true vocation of the man of science was, in this elite view, to be philosophical.[6] But such a lofty view obscured the large-scale social and economic shifts that were turning the vocation of science into a career: the era of specialism was at hand.

The increasing specialisation of science and its challenge to conventional models of 'the explorer' are themes considered by several contributors to this volume, notably Elizabeth Baigent's account of the gentlemanly amateur tradition in polar exploration. In this context, the explorer has often been treated as the representative of a dying race – necessary to the opening up of new worlds for science, but redundant once these worlds were surveyed and mapped. In broader terms, this view finds support in broad-brush interpretations of the historical evolution of scientific inquiry, in which a descriptive, place-based 'natural history' model is said to give way to systematic analysis, as the natural sciences moved from survey to experiment. Echoes of the same refrain can be heard across many fields during the twentieth century, from the polar regions to the deserts, from terrestrial worlds to those of outer space. It reflects the generalisation of a particular kind of understanding of the history of science as it is said to evolve towards mature, normal science. It also tends to go hand in hand with a model of 'professionalisation', through which the integrity and indeed moral authority of science is at last assured: once the pursuit of the dilettante and the flaneur, in this model scientific inquiry is now the domain of the disinterested and disciplined expert. The scientist in this account is supposed to stand for all that is modern.

It is against this model, of course, that modern explorers so often rail. They are precisely not specialists, at home in their own constricted worlds: their claims to authority do not rest on training or education within a well-bounded discipline, still less on the arcane language of the expert. If, as Baigent suggests, it is hard to date the transition from amateurism to professionalism in the field of polar exploration, might that be because in some respects it never actually took place? Or if it did, it remained a matter of some regret, especially as far as British explorers were concerned. The advent of more specialised forms of knowledge, including scientific and technological expertise, often provides a foil for their descriptions of the joy of adventurous exploration – which, almost by definition, knows no limits. Where nineteenth-century explorers lampooned the comfortable theorising of 'armchair geographers', the publicity surrounding their latter-day equivalents frequently highlights the need to reinvent a culture of risk-taking in a world dominated by the imperatives of routine and security. In both cases, it is surely significant that modernity is figured in feminine terms: in this perspective – as it is for much of this book – exploration is an inherently masculine space, the antithesis of domestic comfort. In this context, we might even say that the explorer stands for all that is *not* modern.

The truth is, as usual, much more complicated. For one thing, the notion of a confrontation between a 'natural history' model of science dominated by mapping, fieldwork and inventory and one characterised by analysis and experiment is highly partial. Historically, mapping and exploration have provided creative intellectual and imaginative resources, as well as vital information, within a variety of dynamic scientific fields, including for example astronomy and biogeography.[7] At various moments during the twentieth century, elements of the opposition between these models of science have certainly figured within many debates in the fields of ecology, biology, meteorology, glaciology, geomorphology and the wider earth sciences, as well as within geography itself, as recently suggested by Trevor Barnes and Matthew Farish.[8] Similar arguments and tensions are also evidenced in this book, notably in the chapters by Fae Korsmo, Nicola J. Thomas and Jude Hill. It is significant, however, that this contrast between paradigms has often been put to rhetorical use in the context of arguments over funding, in order to justify investment in certain kinds of science over others: it is surely less persuasive as a summary version of historical shifts in the nature of scientific investigation itself. Sverker Sörlin's recent work on the history of ideas of climate change indicates some of the complexities in the case of Swedish, British and American meteorology and glaciology during the middle decades of the twentieth century.[9] Moreover, the imperative of mapping and reconnaissance on which the 'natural history' model of science is said to depend remains important within many contemporary sciences, though its scale, focus and techniques have certainly changed dramatically. And fieldwork itself, as Simon Naylor shows here in the case of Griffith Taylor, can also be a source of authority. In this perspective, then, the practices of fieldwork and mapping – essential features of the business of exploration – remain central to the pursuit of modern science, and not simply its doomed ancestors.

Turning from the intellectual frameworks of modern science to its educational and institutional contexts, there is no doubt that the history of industrial capitalism during the twentieth century and the massive state-sponsored expansion of programmes for the specialist training and employment of scientists have created a very different world to that which shaped the production of science in the nineteenth century. This clearly had implications for the development of new models of expertise within the field of exploration, most notably in the context of space science. However, while the idea of 'professionalisation' was once regarded as an almost self-evident description of this process, the teleological aspects of the concept deserve to be re-examined.[10] Secreted within the term remains a number of questionable assumptions, notably about the embryonic modernity of nineteenth-century science, the relationships between expert and amateur knowledge and the 'disinterestedness' of the modern professional. As Jim Endersby has shown, for much of the nineteenth century, elite natural history remained dominated by a class-based model in which 'philosophical' inquiry was the antithesis of paid employment: Charles Darwin was, in this sense, anything but a professional scientist.[11] Today, universities and government research institutes certainly employ a very large number of research scientists, and there are a large number of 'professional' bodies representing their interests: but 'amateur' engagements with science and technology remain significant, especially in the context of field-based research, and few if anyone today would make the claim that professional science is essentially disinterested.

Meanwhile, the very same explorers who lament the passing of an age of adventurous travel rely necessarily on the latest technologies of modern communication, both in undertaking their technologically sophisticated expeditions across geographical space and in plying their trade as authors, publicists and pundits across the global media. Far from being a throwback to an earlier era of exploration, feats of modern exploration during the twentieth century can tell us much about what is distinctively modern about our own world and its intersecting circuits of science, culture and communication. As with the 'footsteps narratives' which Christy Collis takes as her subject, these ventures do not so much reprise earlier histories of exploration as to reactivate them. If the contents of the present volume are any guide, the history of exploration during the twentieth century is at last being re-discovered.

Notes

CHAPTER 1

1. Examples of successful popular works in the genre include Moorehead, Alan, *The White Nile* (New York, 1960) and Moorehead, Alan, *The Blue Nile* (New York, 1963).
2. There are of course some notable exceptions, including for example Rotberg, Robert I. (ed.), *Africa and its Explorers: Motives, Methods, and Impact* (Cambridge, MA, 1970).
3. Said, Edward W., *Orientalism* (New York, 1979).
4. Carter, Paul, *The Road to Botany Bay: An Essay in Spatial History* (London, 1987); Pratt, Mary Louise, *Imperial Eyes: Travel Writing and Transculturation* (London, 1992).
5. For an excellent review of the historiography of British nineteenth-century exploration, see Kennedy, Dane, 'British Exploration in the Nineteenth Century: A Historiographical Survey', *History Compass*, 5/6 (2007), pp. 1879–1900.
6. Kennedy, 'British Exploration', p. 1883.
7. See, for example, Brosse, J., *Great Voyages of Discovery: Circumnavigation and Scientists, 1764–1843*, translated by S. Hochman (New York, 1983); Frost, A., 'Science for Political Purposes: European Explorations of the Pacific Ocean, 1764–1806', in MacLeod, R. and Rehbock, P. E. (eds) *Nature in its Greatest Extent: Western Science in the Pacific* (Honolulu, 1988), pp. 27–44; Burnett, D. Graham, *Masters of All They Surveyed: Exploration, Geography, and a British El Dorado* (Chicago, 2000); Pang, Alex Soojung-Kim, *Empire and the Sun: Victorian Solar Eclipse Expeditions* (Stanford, 2002).
8. Mackay, David, *In the Wake of Cook: Exploration, Science and Empire, 1780–1801* (New York, 1985).
9. Edney, Matthew H., *Mapping an Empire: The Geographical Construction of British India, 1765–1843* (Chicago, 1997). See also Bravo, Michael, 'Precision and Curiosity in Scientific Travel: James Rennell and the Orientalist Geography of the New Imperial Age (1760–1830)', in Elsner, Jaâs, and Joan-Pau Rubiâes (eds), *Voyages and Visions: Towards a Cultural History of Travel* (London, 1999), pp. 162–83.
10. Burnett, *Masters of All They Surveyed*; Stoddart, David R., *On Geography: And its History* (Oxford, 1986); Livingstone, David N., *The Geographical Tradition: Episodes in the History of a Contested Enterprise* (Oxford, 1993); Clayton, Daniel W., *Islands of Truth: The Imperial Fashioning of Vancouver Island* (Vancouver, 2000).

11 Driver, Felix, *Geography Militant: Cultures of Exploration and Empire* (Oxford, 2001); Stafford, Robert A., *Scientist of Empire: Sir Roderick Murchison, Scientific Exploration and Victorian Imperialism* (Cambridge, 1989); Stafford, Robert A., 'Scientific Exploration and Empire', in Porter, Andrew (ed.), *The Oxford History of the British Empire, Vol. 3, The Nineteenth Century* (Oxford, 1999), pp. 294–319.
12 MacKenzie, John M., 'The Provincial Geographical Societies in Britain, 1884–1914', in Bell, Morag, Butlin, Robin, and Heffernan, Michael (eds), *Geography and Imperialism 1820–1940* (Manchester, 1995), pp. 93–124; Bayliss-Smith, T., 'Papuan Exploration, Colonial Expansion and the Royal Geographical Society: Questions of Power/Knowledge Relations', *Journal of Historical Geography* 18/3 (1992), pp. 319–29; Staum, M. S., 'The Paris Geographical Society Constructs the Other, 1821–1850', *Journal of Historical Geography* 26/2 (2000), pp. 222–38; Goren, H., 'Scientific Organizations as Agents of Change: The Palestine Exploration Fund, the Deutsche Verein Zur Erforschung Palastinas and Nineteenth-Century Palestine', *Journal of Historical Geography* 27/2 (2001), pp. 153–65.
13 Heffernan, Michael, '"A Dream as Frail as Those of Ancient Time": The In-Credible Geographies of Timbuctoo', *Environment and Planning D: Society and Space* 19/2 (2001), pp. 203–25; Withers, Charles W. J., 'Travelling and Credibility: Towards a Geography of Trust', *Geographie et Cultures* 33 (2000), pp. 3–17.
14 Brockway, Lucile, *Science and Colonial Expansion: The Role of the British Royal Botanic Gardens* (New York, 1979); Drayton, Richard H., *Nature's Government: Science, Imperial Britain, and the 'Improvement' of the World* (New Haven, 2000); Ritvo, Harriet, *The Animal Estate: The English and Other Creatures in the Victorian Age* (Cambridge, MA, 1989); Sheets-Pyenson, Susan, *Cathedrals of Science: The Development of Colonial Natural History Museums During the Late Nineteenth Century* (Kingston, Ont., 1988).
15 Driver, *Geography Militant*, Chapter 3.
16 Bourguet, Marie-Noèelle, Christian Licoppe, and Heinz Otto Sibum, *Instruments, Travel, and Science: Itineraries of Precision from the Seventeenth to the Twentieth Century* (London, 2002).
17 Driver, *Geography Militant*, p. 66.
18 Livingstone, David N., *Putting Science in its Place: Geographies of Scientific Knowledge* (Chicago, 2003).
19 Kucklick, Henrika and Robert Kohler (eds), *Science in the Field* (Chicago: University of Chicago Press, 1996); Hevly, Bruce, 'The Heroic Science of Glacier Motion', *Science in the Field* (Chicago, 1996), pp. 66–86; Collier, P. and Inkpen, R., 'The RGS, Exploration and Empire and the Contested Nature of Surveying', *Area* 34 (2002), pp. 273–83; Robert E. Kohler, *Landscapes and Labscapes: Exploring the Lab-Field Border in Biology* (Chicago, 2002).
20 See Driver, Felix, 'Henry Morton Stanley and His Critics: Geography, Exploration and Empire', *Past & Present* 133/1 (1991), pp. 134–66; Heffernan, Michael, 'The Limits of Utopia: Henri Duveyrier and the Exploration of the Sahara in the Nineteenth Century', *Geographical Journal* 155/3 (1989), pp. 342–52.
21 Pratt, Mary Louise, *Imperial Eyes: Travel Writing and Transculturation* (London, 1992).
22 Smith, Bernard, *European Vision and the South Pacific* (New Haven, 1985).
23 Lamb, Jonathan, *Preserving the Self in the South Seas, 1680–1840* (Chicago, 2001); Kucklick, Henrika, *The Savage Within: The Social History of British Anthropology, 1885–1945* (Cambridge, 1991); Thomas, Nicholas, *Colonialism's Culture: Anthropology, Travel, and Government* (Princeton, 1994).

24 One early account of the contribution of Africans to exploration in the nineteenth century is Simpson, Donald, *Dark Companions: The African Contribution to the European Exploration of East Africa* (London, 1975). A more recent study of the importance of Arab traders in East African exploration is Rockel, Stephen J., *Carriers of Culture: Labor on the Road in Nineteenth-Century East Africa* (Portsmouth, 2006). See also Waller, D. J., *The Pundits: British Exploration of Tibet and Central Asia* (Kentucky, 1990).

25 See, for example, Naylor, Simon, 'Discovering Nature, Rediscovering the Self: Natural Historians and the Landscapes of Argentina', *Environment and Planning D: Society and Space* 19/2 (2001), pp. 227–47.

26 Fabian, Johannes, *Out of Our Minds: Reason and Madness in the Exploration of Central Africa* (Berkeley, 2000); Wylie, John, 'Becoming-Icy: Scott and Amundsen's South Polar Voyages, 1910–1913', *Cultural Geographies* 9/3 (2002), pp. 249–65.

27 Smith, *European Vision*; Goetzmann, William H., *New Lands, New Men: America and the Second Great Age of Discovery* (New York, 1986); Carruthers, Jane and Marion I. Arnold, *The Life and Work of Thomas Baines* (Vlaeberg, South Africa, 1995); Quilley, Geoff and John Bonehill (eds), *William Hodges, 1744–1797: The Art of Exploration* (New Haven, 2004); Guest, Harriet, *Empire, Barbarism, and Civilisation: James Cook, William Hodges, and the Return to the Pacific* (Cambridge, 2007); Driver, Felix and Luciana Martins (eds) *Tropical Visions in an Age of Empire* (Chicago, 2005); Martins, Luciana, 'A Naturalist's Vision of the Tropics: Charles Darwin and the Brazilian Landscape', *Singapore Journal of Tropical Geography* 21/1 (2000), pp. 19–33.

28 Burnett, *Masters of All They Surveyed*; Edney, *Mapping an Empire*; Collier and Inkpen, 'The RGS, Exploration and Empire'; Ryan, Simon, *The Cartographic Eye: How Explorers Saw Australia* (Cambridge, 1996); Clayton, Daniel, 'The Creation of Imperial Space in the Pacific Northwest', *Journal of Historical Geography* 26/3 (2000), pp. 327–50. See also the collection of essays in Cosgrove, Denis E. (ed.), *Mappings* (London, 1999); Winlow, Heather, 'Anthropometric Cartography: Constructing Scottish Racial Identity in the Early Twentieth Century', *Journal of Historical Geography* 27/4 (2001), pp. 507–28; Withers, Charles W. J., 'Authorizing Landscape: "Authority", Naming and the Ordnance Survey's Mapping of the Scottish Highlands in the Nineteenth Century', *Journal of Historical Geography* 26/4 (2000), pp. 532–54.

29 Ryan, James, *Picturing Empire: Photography and the Visualisation of the British Empire* (London, 1997); Schwartz, Joan M. and James R. Ryan (eds), *Picturing Place: Photography and the Geographical Imagination* (London, 2003); Edwards, Elizabeth and Janice Hart, *Photographs Objects Histories: On the Materiality of Images* (London, 2004); Edwards, Elizabeth (ed.), *Anthropology and Photography, 1860–1920* (New Haven, 1992).

30 Tucker, Jennifer, *Nature Exposed: Photography as Eyewitness in Victorian Science* (Baltimore, 2005); Pang, *Empire and the Sun*. For an important study of the emergence of objectivity in mid-nineteenth-century science, see Daston, Lorraine and Peter Galison, *Objectivity* (Boston, 1997).

31 Driver, Felix, 'The Active Life: The Explorer as Biographical Subject', in Matthew, H. C. G., Brian Harrison, and Lawrence Goldman (eds), *Oxford Dictionary of National Biography (Oxford DNB)* (Oxford, 2004–), online edition.

32 Robinson, Michael F., *The Coldest Crucible: Arctic Exploration and American Culture* (Chicago, 2006).

33 See, for example, Fiennes, Ranulph, *Captain Scott* (London, 2003).

34 See, for example, French, Patrick, *Younghusband: The Last Great Imperial Adventurer* (London, 1994); Kennedy, Dane K., *The Highly Civilized Man: Richard Burton and the Victorian World* (Harvard, 2005); Jeal, Tim, *Stanley: The Impossible Life of Africa's Greatest Explorer* (New Haven, 2007).
35 Guelke, Jeanne Kay, and Karen M. Morin, 'Gender, Nature, Empire: Women Naturalists in Nineteenth Century British Travel Literature', *Transactions of the Institute of British Geographers* 26/3 (2001), pp. 306–26; McEwan, Cheryl, *Gender, Geography, and Empire: Victorian Women Travellers in West Africa* (Aldershot, 2000); Sparke, Matthew, 'Displacing the Field in Fieldwork: Masculinity, Metaphor and Space', in Duncan, Nancy (ed.), *Bodyspace: Destabilizing Geographies of Gender and Sexuality* (London, 1996), pp. 212–33; Rose, Gillian, *Feminism and Geography: The Limits of Geographical Knowledge* (Cambridge, 1993).
36 Jones, Max, *The Last Great Quest: Captain Scott's Antarctic Sacrifice* (Oxford, 2003).
37 Burnett, *Masters of All They Surveyed*; see also Naylor, Simon, '"That Very Garden of South America": European Surveyors in Paraguay', *Singapore Journal of Tropical Geography* 21/1 (2000), pp. 48–62.
38 See, for example, *Royal Geographical Society Illustrated: A Unique Record of Exploration and Photography* (RGS London, 1997) which, as a celebratory picture book of famous exploration functions, as Driver puts it, as 'more fetish than relic'. Driver, *Geography Militant*, p. 219. The US-based *National Geographic* chose to commemorate its 100th anniversary in 1988 in a National Geographic centennial issue (September 1988) and video titled 'The Explorers: A Century of Discovery'. For a useful critique, see Bloom, Lisa, *Gender on Ice: American Ideologies of Polar Expedition* (Minnesota, 1993), p. 84.
39 Our discussion of Conrad is taken from Driver, *Geography Militant*, p. 3, and Driver, Felix, 'Geography's Empire: Histories of Geographical Knowledge', *Environment and Planning D: Society and Space*, 10 (1992), pp. 23–49, 23–4.
40 Goetzmann, William H., *Army Exploration in the American West, 1803–1863* (New Haven, 1959); *Exploration and Empire: The Explorer and the Scientist in the Winning of the American West* (New York, 1966); *New Lands, New Men: America and the Second Great Age of Discovery* (New York, 1986).
41 Rice, Tony, *Voyages of Discovery: Three Centuries of Natural History Exploration* (London, 2000).
42 Deacon, Margaret, *Scientists and the Sea, 1650–1900: A Study of Marine Science* (London, 1971), p. xii.
43 Robinson, Michael F., *The Coldest Crucible: Arctic Exploration and American Culture* (Chicago, 2006).
44 French, *Younghusband*, p. 258.
45 See also Dodds, Klaus J., *Geopolitics in Antarctica: Views from the Southern Ocean Rim* (Chichester, 1997); Dodds, Klaus J., 'The Great Game in Antarctica: Britain and the 1959 Antarctic Treaty', *Contemporary British History* 22/1 (2007), pp. 43–66; Dodds, Klaus J., *Pink Ice: Britain and the South Atlantic Empire* (London, 2002); Dodds, Klaus, J., 'Post-Colonial Antarctica: An Emerging Engagement', *Polar Record* 42/1 (2006), pp. 59–70.
46 Dodds, Klaus J., 'Putting Maps in Their Place: The Demise of the Falkland Islands Dependency Survey and the Mapping of Antarctica, 1945–1962', *Ecumene* 7 (2000), pp. 176–210.
47 Hamblin, Jacob, *Oceanographers and the Cold War* (Seattle, 2005), p. xix.
48 Dean, J. R., 'The International Hydrographic Bureau', *The Geographical Journal* 129/4 (1963), p. 503.

49 Deacon, *Scientists and the Sea*.
50 Fogg, G. E., 'The Royal Society and the South Seas', *Notes and Records of the Royal Society of London* 55/1 (2001), pp. 81–103.
51 Ibid.; Helen Rozwadowski, *Fathoming the Ocean: The Discovery and Exploration of the Deep Sea* (London, 2005).
52 Hamblin, *Oceanographers*, p. xix.
53 Ibid.; Helen Rozwadowski, 'Science, the Sea, and Marine Resource Management: Researching the International Council for the Exploration of the Sea', *The Public Historian* 26/1 (2004), pp. 41–64.
54 Kai-Henrik Barth, 'The Politics of Seismology: Nuclear Testing, Arms Control, and the Transformation of a Discipline', *Social Studies of Science* 33/5 (2003), pp. 743–81.
55 Hamblin, Jacob Darwin, 'The Navy's "Sophisticated" Pursuit of Science: Undersea Warfare, the Limits of Internationalism, and the Utility of Basic Research, 1945–1956', *Isis* 93/1 (2002), pp. 1–27.
56 Weir, Gary E., 'Review of *The Silent War*', *The Journal of Military History*, 66/4 (2002), pp. 1251–2.
57 National Academy of Sciences, *"Planet Earth": A Mystery with 100,100 Clues* (Washington, DC, 1958), p. 11.
58 Sullivan, Walter, *Assault on the Unknown: The International Geophysical Year* (London, 1962).
59 Black, Jeremy, *Visions of the World: A History of Maps* (London, 2003), p. 140.
60 Chapman, Walker, *The Loneliest Continent: The Story of Antarctic Discovery* (Connecticut, 1964).
61 See Dean, Katrina, Simon Naylor, Simone Turchetti and Martin Siegert, 'Data in Antarctic Science and Politics', *Social Studies of Science* 38 (2008), pp. 571–604.
62 See Naylor, Simon, Katrina Dean and Martin Siegert, 'The IGY and the Icesheet: Surveying Antarctica', *Journal of Historical Geography* 34/4 (2008), pp. 574–95; Turchetti, Simone, Katrina Dean, Simon Naylor and Martin Siegert J., 'Accidents and Opportunities: A History of Radio Echo Sounding in Antarctica, 1958–1979', *British Journal for the History of Science* 41/3 (2008), pp. 417–44.
63 Quoted in Kitty Hauser, *Shadow Sites: Photography, Archaeology, & the British Landscape 1927–1955* (Oxford, 2007), p. 155.
64 Ibid., p. 157.
65 Black, *Visions of the World*, p. 151; Cosgrove, Denis, *Apollo's Eye: A Cartographic Genealogy of the Earth in the Western Imagination* (Baltimore, 2001).
66 Fernândez-Armesto, Felipe, *Pathfinders: A Global History of Exploration* (New York, 2006), p. 350.
67 Ibid.
68 On the latter, see Driver's discussion of the contemporary reworkings of 'fantasies of a more adventurous kind of exploration'. Driver, *Geography Militant*, p. 212.
69 Miller, John W., 'Why Miners Look for Buried Treasure in Belgian Museum', *Wall Street Journal* (Eastern edition), 20 March 2007, p. A.1. We are grateful to Federico Caprotti for this reference.
70 See Naylor, Simon, Martin Siegert, Katrina Dean and Simone Turchetti, 'Science, Geopolitics and the Governance of Antarctica', *Nature Geoscience* 1/3 (2008), pp. 143–5.
71 Dodds, Klaus J., 'Icy Geopolitics', *Environment and Planning D: Society and Space* 26/1 (2008), pp. 1–6.

CHAPTER 2

This essay was originated in a paper given in an *Oxford Dictionary of National Biography* seminar series in 2005, at the invitation of Brian Harrison, the session being chaired by Lawrence Goldman. I should like to thank them, participants in that seminar particularly Jack Langton, and *DNB* colleagues for good companionship in the period 1993–2003 when I was engaged in the preparation of the dictionary and first came into sustained contact with polar explorers. Anita McConnell, the late Godfrey Jones, Ann Savours, and Mark Pottle were of particular help with polar matters.

1 Cherry-Garrard, Apsley George Benet, 'Introduction', *The Worst Journey in the World* (London, 1922).
2 Wilson, D. M. and D. B. Elder, *Cheltenham in Antarctica: The Life of Edward Wilson* (Cheltenham, 2000), title page.
3 Cherry-Garrard, *Worst Journey*, 'Introduction'; Wheeler, Sara, *Cherry: A Life of Apsley Cherry-Garrard* (London, 2002).
4 Driver, Felix, 'The Active Life: The Explorer as Biographical Subject', in Matthew, H. C. G., Brian Harrison, and Lawrence Goldman (eds), *Oxford Dictionary of National Biography* (*Oxford DNB*) (Oxford, 2004–), online edition.
5 Lowerson, John, *Sport and the Middle Classes* (Manchester, 1993), p. 70.
6 Desmond, Adrian, 'Redefining the X Axis: "Professionals", "Amateurs" and the Making of Mid-Victorian Biology – A Progress Report', *Journal of the History of Biology* 34 (2001), pp. 3–50, 22–4; Addison, Paul, 'The Few', *Oxford DNB*.
7 Holt, Richard, J. A. Mangan and Pierre Lafranchi (eds), *European Heroes: Myth, Identity, Sport* (London, 1996); Holt, Richard, 'Sport and the English Hero', *Oxford DNB* lecture, Oxford, February 2004; Wormald, Patrick, 'Alfred', *Oxford DNB*.
8 Withers, Charles and Chris Philo, 'Student Geographical Magazines and Geographical Knowledge', *Newsletter of the History and Philosophy of Geography Study Group* (1996), pp. 9–16, 9–10.
9 Mackenzie, John (ed.), *Imperialism and Popular Culture* (Manchester, 1986).
10 Geographical examples include Pedley, Mary Sponberg, *The Map Trade in the Late Eighteenth Century: Letters to the London Map Sellers Faden and Jefferys* (Oxford, 2000); *The Commerce of Cartography: Making and Marketing Maps in Eighteenth-century France and England* (Chicago, 2005); Herbert, Francis, 'The Royal Geographical Society's Membership, the Map Trade, and Geographical Publishing in Britain 1830 to ca 1930: An Introductory Essay with Listing of Some 250 Fellows in Related Professions', *Imago Mundi* 35 (1983), pp. 67–95; Bederman, Sanford H., 'The Royal Geographical Society, E. G. Ravenstein, and "A Map of Eastern Equatorial Africa": 1877–1883', *Imago Mundi* 44 (1992), pp. 106–19.
11 Baigent, Elizabeth, 'The Geography of Biography, the Biography of Geography: Rewriting the *Dictionary of National Biography*', *Journal of Historical Geography* 30 (2004), pp. 531–51; Driver, Felix and Elizabeth Baigent, 'Biography and the History of Geography: A Response to Ron Johnston', *Progress in Human Geography* 31 (2007), pp. 101–6; Langton, John, review of Johnston, Ron J. *Geography and Geographers: Anglo-American Human Geography since 1945* (London, 1979), *Journal of Historical Geography* 8 (1982), pp. 102–4.
12 Anon, 'Prospectus of the Royal Geographical Society', *Journal of the Royal Geographical Society of London* (hereafter *Journal RGS*) 1 (1831), pp. vii–xii, vii.
13 Cameron, Ian, *To the Farthest Ends of the Earth: The History of the Royal Geographical Society, 1830–1980* (London, 1980); Markham, Clements R., *The Fifty*

NOTES

     Years Work of the Royal Geographical Society (London, 1881); Mill, Hugh R., *The Record of the Royal Geographical Society, 1830–1930* (London, 1930).
14   *Journal RGS* 1 (1831), p. xi; Driver, Felix, *Geography Militant: Cultures of Exploration and Empire* (Oxford, 2001).
15   Riffenburgh, *Myth of the Explorer*, p. 1 and Chapter 9; Adams, Percy, *Travelers and Travel Liars 1660–1800* (Berkeley, 1962).
16   Amundsen, Roald, *The South Pole: An Account of the Norwegian Antarctic Expedition in the 'Fram' 1910–1912*, trans. A. G. Chater, 2 vols. (London, 1912), chapter 12, online edition via Project Gutenberg, no pagination; Riffenburgh, *Myth of the Explorer*, pp. 43–4.
17   Riffenburgh, *Myth of the Explorer*.
18   Zachs, William, Peter Isaac, Angus Fraser, and William Lister, 'Murray Family', *Oxford DNB*. Leach, Hugh with Susan Maria Farrington, *Strolling about on the Roof of the World: The First Hundred Years of the Royal Society for Asian Affairs (formerly Royal Central Asian Society)* (New York, 2002).
19   Crone, G. R., Charles F. Arden Close, and Kenneth Mason, 'Arthur Robert. Hinks, CBE, FRS, Secretary 1915–1945', *Geographical Journal* 105/3–4 (1945), pp. 146–51.
20   Strachey, Richard, 'Annual Address on the Progress of Geography', *Proceedings of the Royal Geographical Society* 10 (1888), pp. 408–9, cited in Jones, Max, *The Last Great Quest* (Oxford, 2003), p. 37.
21   Markham, Clements, 'Field of Geography', *Geographical Journal* 11 (1898), pp. 4–5, my italics.
22   Jones, *Last Great Quest*, pp. 26–7.
23   Amundsen's science was defended by Nansen who claimed that it would prove complementary to Scott's: Nansen, Fritjof, 'Introduction' to Amundsen, Roald, *Sydpolen: den norske sydpolsfaerd med Fram 1910–1912*, 2 vols. (Kristiana, 1912). Young later pointed out that his observations had been used by scientists: Young, Wayland, 'On the Debunking of Captain Scott', *Encounter* 54/5 (May 1980), pp. 8–19, 16.
24   Stoddart, David R., *On Geography: And its History* (Oxford, 1986), p. 151, note 34; Robin, G. le Q., 'Priestley, Sir Raymond Edward', *Oxford DNB*; Steers, J. A. and Elizabeth Baigent, 'Debenham, Frank', *Oxford DNB*.
25   Stoddart, *On Geography*, chapters 4 and 5.
26   Desmond, 'X Axis'; Brian Harrison, personal communication.
27   Steel, Robert W., *The Institute of British Geographers: The First Fifty Years* (London, 1984); Stoddart, David R. (ed.), 'The Institute of British Geographers 1933–1983', *Transactions of the IBG* 9 (1983) pp. 1–124; Wise, Michael J., 'Three Founder Members of the IBG: R. Ogilvie Buchanaan, Sir Dudley Stamp, S. W. Wooldridge. A Personal Tribute', *Transactions of the IBG* 8 (1983), pp. 41–54; Stoddart, *On Geography*, p. 49.
28   Obituaries of academic geographers are the only biographical remnant.
29   Annual report of Council, King's College, Cambridge, November 1951, pp. 23–4, cited in Stoddart, *On Geography*, p. 103.
30   http://www.spri.cam.ac.uk/library/archives/shackleton/articles/1537,4,6,1.html
31   Wråkberg, Urban, 'The Politics of Naming: Contested Observations and the Shaping of Geographical Knowledge', pp. 155–97 in Bravo, Michael and Sverker Sörlin (eds), *Narrating the Arctic: A Cultural History of Nordic Scientific Practices* (Cambridge, Mass., 2002); Debenham, Frank, 'Polar Place-Names', *Polar Record*, 3/24 (1942), pp. 541–52.
32   *Manchester Guardian*, 30 December 1913, cited in Tyler-Lewis, Kelly, *The Lost Men: The Harrowing Story of Shackleton's Ross Sea Party* (London, 2006), p. 19.

33 Debenham, 'Polar Place-Names', p. 549; Spufford, Francis, *I May be Some Time: Ice and the English Imagination* (London, 1996), p. 156.
34 Campbell, Victor L. A., *The Wicked Mate: The Antarctic Diary of Victor Campbell* (ed. Harold G. R. King) (Bluntisham, 1988), p. 185; King, Harold G. R., 'Campbell, Victor Lindsey Arbuthnot', *Oxford DNB*.
35 Scott, Robert F., *The Voyage of the 'Discovery'* (London, 1905); King, Harold G. R., 'Scott, Robert Falcon', *Oxford DNB*. Debenham, 'Polar Place-Names', pp. 545–6.
36 Savours, Ann, 'Shackleton, Sir Ernest Henry', *Oxford DNB*.
37 Moss, Michael S., 'Beardmore, William', *Oxford DNB*; King, Graham, 'Caird, James Key', *Oxford DNB*; Speak, Peter, 'Bruce, William Speirs', *Oxford DNB*.
38 Campbell, *Wicked Mate*.
39 Savours, 'Shackleton'.
40 Campbell, *Wicked Mate*, pp. 183–4, 190; Priestley, Raymond E., *Antarctic Adventure: Scott's Northern Party* (London, 1914, repr. London, 1974); Priestley, Raymond E., 'Captain V. L. A. Campbell, DSO, RN', *Geographical Journal*, 123 (1957), pp. 131–2; King, 'Campbell', *Oxford DNB*.
41 Conrad, Joseph, 'Geography and Some Explorers', in *Last Essays*, ed. R. Curle (London, 1926), cited in Jones, *Last Great Quest*, pp. 27–8.
42 Cited in Huntford, Roland, *The Shackleton Voyages* (London, 2002), pp. 242–3.
43 Bickel, *Shackleton's Forgotten Men*, p. 128; Richards, *Ross Sea Shore Party*, p. 24.
44 Savours, 'Shackleton'.
45 Macklin, A. H., letter to Alfred Lansing, c. 1957, cited in Savours, 'Shackleton'.
46 Spufford, *Ice*; Jones, *Last Great Quest*; Young, 'Debunking'; Barczewski, Stephanie, *Antarctic Destinies: Scott, Shackleton, and the Changing Face of Heroism* (London, 2007); Huntford, Roland, *Scott and Amundsen* (London, 1979); Huntford, Roland, *Shackleton* (London, 1985); Baigent, Elizabeth, Review of Barczewski, Stephanie, *Antarctic Destinies: Scott, Shackleton, and the Changing Face of Heroism* (London, 2007) in *Journal of Historical Geography* 34/4 (2008), pp. 685–7.
47 Berman, Morris, '"Hegemony" and the Amateur Tradition in British Science', *Journal of Social History* 8 (1974–5), pp. 30–50, 39–40.
48 Desmond, 'X Axis', p. 15, for amateurism and public calling in science.
49 Holt, Richard and J. A. Mangan, 'Prologue: Heroes of a European Past', pp. 1–13 in Holt, Mangan and Lafranchi, *European Heroes*, p. 8; Holt, Richard, 'Amateur Athletics Association', *Oxford DNB*. Holt, Richard, 'Cricket and Englishness: The Batsman as Hero', pp. 48–70, in Holt, Mangan and Lanfranchi, *European Heroes*; Holt, 'Sport and the English Hero'; Holt, 'Amateur Athletics Association'; Desmond, 'X Axis'.
50 Richards, Denis, 'Hillary, Richard Hope', *Oxford DNB*; Ray, John, 'Lacey, James Harry [Ginger]', *Oxford DNB*; Addison, 'The Few'.
51 Stafford, Robert, 'Exploration and Empire', pp. 290–301, in Winks, Robin W. (ed.), *Historiography*, vol. 5 of *The Oxford History of the British Empire*, series editor Wm. Roger Louis (Oxford, 1999), p. 295; Spufford, *Ice*, p. 5.
52 Stoddart, *On Geography*, pp. 59–63.
53 Brown, R. N. R., 'Scott, Robert Falcon', *DNB* accessed via *Oxford DNB* online; Brown, R. N. R., 'Oates, Lawrence Edward Grace', *DNB*, accessed via *Oxford DNB* online.
54 Mackenzie, Compton, *Sinister Street*, 2 vols. (London, 1913), p. 542, cited in Wheeler, *Cherry*, p. 34.
55 Letter, 17 August 1914, cited in Tyler-Lewis, *Lost Men*, p. 31.
56 See also Brown, R. N. R., 'Wilson, Edward Adrian', *DNB*, accessed via *Oxford DNB* online.

NOTES

57 James Paton's diary, cited in Tyler-Lewis, *Lost Men*, p. 55.
58 Jones, *Last Great Quest*, p. 141; Jones, Max, 'Introduction', in Scott, Robert F., *Journals: Scott's Last Expedition* (Oxford, 2005), p. xxxvi.
59 Jones, *Last Great Quest*, p. 201.
60 Campbell, *Wicked Mate*, p. 62.
61 Wilson and Elder, *Cheltenham in Antarctica*, p. 113. Seaver published *The Faith of Edward Wilson* (London, 1948), apparently in response to public requests (p. 1), which also occasioned a 1950 reprint. This is the only example I know of the public appeal of overtly religious works about polar explorers.
62 E.g. Roberts, Brian, *Edward Wilson's Birds of the Antarctic* (London, 1967), though Wilson and Elder, *Cheltenham in Antarctica* includes religious epigraphs by Wilson.
63 Ensor, Robert C. K., *England, 1870–1914* (Oxford, 1936), p. 553 fn 1; Seaver, *Faith of Wilson*, p. 4; Cherry-Garrard, Apsley, 'Introduction' to Seaver, George, *'Birdie' Bowers of the Antarctic* (London, 1938), p. xii.
64 Wilson and Elder, *Cheltenham in Antarctica*, p. 108; Caesar [Hodder, J. E.], *Like English Gentlemen* (London, 1913).
65 Jones, *Last Great Quest*, pp. 11, 121–6.
66 Wheeler, *Cherry*, p. 221.
67 Young, 'Debunking', pp. 9–10.
68 *Polar Record* 17 (1939), pp. 2–3; *Geographical Journal* 93 (1939), pp. 183–4; Addison, 'The Few'.
69 Cherry-Garrard, Apsley, 'Introduction' to Seaver, George, *'Birdie' Bowers of the Antarctic* (London, 1938), p. xii.
70 Seaver, *Bowers*, p. 250.
71 Seaver, *Bowers*. See also Lagerbom, Charles, *The Fifth Man: Henry R. Bowers* (Whitby, 1999) and Pottle, Mark, 'Bowers, Henry Robertson', *Oxford DNB*.
72 Letter, Bowers to Kathleen Scott, cited in Lashly, William, *Under Scott's Command: Lashly's Antarctic Diaries*, ed. Ellis, Anthony R. (London, 1969), p. 129.
73 Seaver, *Bowers*, p. 262.
74 Caesar [Hodder], *Like English Gentlemen*, cited in Jones, *Last Great Quest*, pp. 109–12.
75 Jones, *Last Great Quest*, pp. 295–6.
76 Heren, Louis, *Growing up Poor in London* (London, 2002), p. 117, cited in Barczewski, *Antarctic Destinies*, p. 138.
77 Rogers, A. F., 'The Death of Chief Petty Officer Evans', *The Practitioner* 212 (1974), pp. 570–80; Falckh, R. C. F., 'The Death of Petty Officer Evans', *Polar Record* 23/145 (1987) pp. 397–403.
78 Gregor, Gary C., *Swansea's Antarctic Explorer: Edgar Evans, 1876–1912* (Swansea, 1995); Mason, Tony, 'Our Stephen and Our Harold: Edwardian Footballers as Local Heroes', pp. 71–85, in Holt, Mangan and Lanfranchi, *European Heroes*. Gentleman can occupy local and wider stages simultaneously: Wilson and Elder, *Cheltenham in Antarctica*; Johnson, Anthony M., *Scott of the Antarctic and Cardiff* (Cardiff, 1984).
79 Smith, Michael, *I am Just Going Outside: Captain Oates – Antarctic Tragedy* (Staplehurst, 2002), pp. 191, 212, 215.
80 Hallock, Judith Lee, 'Profile: Thomas Crean', *Polar Record* 22/141 (1985), pp. 665–78, 670. 'Bluejacket' has since 1830 denoted a non-commissioned sailor, from the colour of the men's jackets and in contradistinction to the (red coated) marines. *Oxford English Dictionary* online edition.
81 Smith, Michael, *An Unsung Hero: Tom Crean, Antarctic Survivor* (London, 2000); Hallock, 'Thomas Crean'; Pottle, Mark, 'Crean, Thomas [Tom]', *Oxford DNB*.

82 *Irish Independent*, cited on dustjacket of Smith, *Going Outside*.
83 *Oxford Times*, 4 May 2007.
84 Lashly, *Under Scott's Command*, pp. 57, 83, 144.
85 Lashly, *Under Scott's Command*; J. M. W and R. E. P., Obituary, *Geographical Journal* (1940), pp. 303–4; Hughes, M. M. T., Review, *Geographical Journal*, 135/3 (1969), pp. 449–50. The privately published version is virtually untraceable save for mention in the above works and at http://66.102.9.104/search?q=cache:NRiJ0aPXFr0J:www.reading.ac.uk/library/colls/special/exhibitions/gibbings1989.html+lashly+diary&hl=en&ct=clnk&cd=12&gl=uk
86 Fuchs, Vivian, 'Introduction', pp. 9–10 in Lashly, *Under Scott's Command*, p. 10.
87 Hughes, Review, p. 450.
88 Jacka, F. J., 'Mawson, Douglas', *Australian Dictionary of Biography Online* (Canberra, 2006).
89 E.g. Jones, *Last Great Quest*, p. 7.
90 Shackleton, Ernest, *South*, ed. King, Peter (London, 1999), marginal note to p. 167.
91 Joyce, *South Polar Trail*; Richards, Richard, *The Ross Sea Shore Party 1914–1917* (Cambridge, 1962, repr. Banham and Bluntisham, 2003); Bickel, Lennard, *Shackleton's Forgotten Men: The Untold Tragedy of the Endurance Epic* (London, 2001). See also McElrea, Richard and David Harrowfield, *Polar Castaways: The Ross Sea Party of Sir Ernest Shackleton, 1914–17* (Christchurch, New Zealand, 2004).
92 Richards, *Ross Sea Shore Party*, p. 14 and e.g. p. 11 for criticism of Mackintosh.
93 Bickel, *Forgotten Men*, blurb and p. 16.
94 Bickel, *Forgotten Men*, p. 201; Richards, *Ross Sea Shore Party*, p. 25.
95 Mill, Hugh Robert, 'Introduction', pp. 11–26, in Joyce, Ernest Edward Mills, *The South Polar Trail: The Log of the Imperial Trans-Antarctic Expedition* (London, 1929), pp. 12, 25.
96 Joyce, *South Polar Trail*, p. 187; Richards, *Ross Sea Shore Party*, p. 38; Bickel, *Forgotten Men*, p. 213.
97 Bickel, *Forgotten Men*, pp. 170–1.
98 Ibid., p. 107.
99 Bickel, *Forgotten Men*, pp. 171–2, 230; Joyce, *South Polar Trail*, p. 162; Tyler-Lewis, *Lost Men*, p. 191. Similarly Birdie Bowers, after Christmas dinner in the tent, suggested 'if all is well next Christmas we will get hold of all the poor children we can and just stuff them full of nice things', Evans, E. G. R. G., *South with Scott* (London, 1921), cited in Seaver, *Bowers*, p. 246.
100 Tyler-Lewis, *Lost Men*, examples throughout, but especially p. 109. Quotation from letter of Davis to Howard Ninnis, 12 October 1919, cited in Tyler-Lewis, *Lost Men*, p. 248.
101 E.g. Tyler-Lewis, *Lost Men*, p. 106.
102 Jones, A. G. E., *Polar Portraits: Collected Papers* (Whitby, 1992); Stafford, 'Exploration and Empire', p. 297.
103 Baughman, T. H., *Before the Heroes Came: Antarctica in the 1890s* (Lincoln, Nebraska, 1994), pp. 46–7.
104 Correspondence, *DNB* archive, Oxford University Press; Lambert, Andrew D., *The Foundations of Naval History: John Knox Laughton, the Royal Navy, and the Historical Profession* (London, 1998); Lambert, Andrew D., '"Our Naval Plutarch": Sir John Knox Laughton and the Dictionary of National Biography', *Mariner's Mirror* 84/3 (1998), pp. 308–15.
105 Barczewski, *Antarctic Destinies*, pp. 30, 42.
106 Macleod, Margaret Arnett and Richard Glover, 'Franklin's First Expedition as Seen by the Fur Traders', *Polar Record* 15/98 (1971), pp. 669–82.

This paper has proved controversial in its treatment of Arctic explorer John Richardson, but nonetheless is a useful illustration of polar professionals taking naval explorers with a pinch of salt. See also Cavell, Janice, 'The Hidden Crime of Dr Richardson', *Polar Record* 43/225 (2007), pp. 155–64.
107 Wråkberg, 'Politics of Naming', pp. 170–73.
108 Jones, A. G. E., 'Sportseileren i Arktis: Sir James Lamont', *Polarboken* (1979), pp. 50–57; Jones, A. G. E., 'Benjamin Leigh Smith: Arctic Yachtsman', *The Musk Ox* 16 (1975), pp. 24–31; Credland, A. G., 'Benjamin Leigh Smith: A Forgotten Pioneer', *Polar Record* 20 (1980–81), pp. 127–45; Jones, A. G. E. and Elizabeth Baigent, 'Smith, Benjamin Leigh', *Oxford DNB*; Davenport-Hines, Richard, 'Blackwood, Frederick Temple Hamilton-Temple-, first marquess of Dufferin', *Oxford DNB*.
109 Wheeler, *Cherry*. He is remembered to have suffered later from depression, though Wheeler praises his doggedness, p. 3.
110 Faure, Jean-Michel, 'National Identity and the Sporting Champion: Jean Borota and French History', pp. 86–100, in Holt, Mangan, and Lanfranchi, *European Heroes*, p. 86, my italics.
111 Mangan, J. A. and Richard Holt, 'Epilogue: Heroes for a European Future', pp. 169–75 in Holt, Mangan, and Lanfranchi, *European Heroes*, p. 174.
112 Seaver, *Bowers*, p. 237; Baughman, *Before the Heroes Came*, pp. 46–7, 117; Joyce, *South Polar Trail*, p. 142.
113 Swan, R. A., 'Borchgrevink, Carsten Egeberg', *Australian Dictionary of Biography*, vol. 7 (Melbourne, 1979), p. 348; Swan, R. A., *Australia in the Antarctic* (Melbourne, 1961); Baughman, *Before the Heroes Came*; Evans, H. B. and A. G. E. Jones, 'A Forgotten Explorer: Carsten Egeberg Borchgrevik', *Polar Record* 108 (1975), pp. 221–35.
114 Gran, Jens Tryggve Herman, *Hvor Sydlyset Flammer: Leir-og Expeditionsliv paa Antarktis: Dagsboksoptegnelser fra Scotts Ekspedition* (Kristiania and Copenhagen, 1915).
115 Speak, 'Bruce'.
116 Speak, 'Bruce'; Baughman, *Before the Heroes Came*.
117 Wråkberg, Urban, *The Centennial of S. A. Andrée's North Pole Expedition: Proceedings of a Conference on S. A. Andrée and the Agenda for Social Science Research of the Polar Regions* (Stockholm, 1999); Hestmark, Geir, 'Review of *The Centennial of S. A. Andrée's North Pole Expedition*', *Isis* 91/4 (2000), pp. 805–6.
118 Spufford, *Ice*, p. 129.
119 Wråkberg, Urban, *Vetenskapens vikingatåg: Perspektiv på svensk polarforskning 1860–1930* (Uppsala, 1999); Spufford, *Ice*, p. 5.
120 *Daily Telegraph*, 27 October 2007. I am grateful to my mother for this reference.
121 Stefánsson, Vilhjálmur, *My Life with the Eskimo* (London, 1913), p. 164.
122 Riffenburgh, *Myth of the Explorer*, p. 161.
123 Amundsen, *South Pole*; Amundsen, *Sydpolen*.
124 Jones, *Last Great Quest*, p. 169; Simpson, Donald, *Dark Companions: The African Contribution to the European Exploration of East Africa* (London, 1975); Vetch, R. H. and Elizabeth Baigent, 'Montgomerie, Thomas George', *Oxford DNB*.
125 Young, 'Denbunking', p. 9; Gran, Tryggve, *The Norwegian with Scott: Tryggve Gran's Antarctic Diary 1910–1913* (London, 1984); Huntford, *Scott and Amundsen*.
126 Simpson, *Dark Companions*; but see Bravo and Sörlin, *Narrating the Arctic*; Wråkberg, *Vetenskapens vikingatåg*.

127 Riffenburgh, *Myth of the Explorer*, pp. 170, 182, 185–90.
128 Morrissey, Katherine G., 'Henson, Matthew Alexander', *American National Biography (ANB)* online edition (2005); Robinson, Bradley, *Dark Companion* (London, 1948).
129 Baughman, *Before the Heroes Came*, pp. 93, 99, 100. The British did adopt reindeer sleeping bags and *finnesko* ('Finnish shoes').
130 Bertram, G. Colin L., *Arctic and Antarctic: A Prospect of the Polar Regions* (Cambridge, 1957), p. 45.
131 Scott, Robert F., *Voyage of the Discovery*, vol.1, p. 417. The class element is evident in that Petty Officer Evans was judged to have proved unequal to the challenge.
132 Jones, *Last Great Quest*, p. 134.
133 Joyce, *South Polar Trail*, pp. 171, 182.
134 Bickel, *Forgotten Men*, p. 49; Joyce, *South Polar Trail*, p. 171; Barczewski, *Antarctic Destinies*, p. 35; Seaver, *Bowers*, p. 164.
135 I am grateful to Brian Harrison for this point; Desmond, 'X Axis', p. 17.
136 Jones, *Last Great Quest*, p. 51.
137 Heckathorn, Ted, 'Peary, Josephine Diebitsch', *ANB*.
138 Wheeler, *Cherry*, p. 70; Wilson and Elder, *Cheltenham in Antarctica*, p. 85; Smith, *Going Outside*, p. 119.
139 Cited in Lashly, *Under Scott's Command*, p. 90.
140 Tyler-Lewis, *Lost Men*, p. 21.
141 Aubrey Howard Ninnis, cited in Tyler-Lewis, *Lost Men*, p. 42.
142 For nicknames, see Wheeler, *Cherry*, p. 67. Cherry had a photo of Marie Lohr by his bed, p. 106.
143 Smith, *Going Outside*, p. 211.
144 Morrell, Margot and Stephanie Capparell, *Shackleton's Way: Leadership Lessons from the Great Antarctic Explorer* (London, 2001), p. 36.
145 Wilson and Elder, *Cheltenham in Antarctica*; Limb, Sue and Patrick Cordingley, *Captain Oates: Soldier and Explorer* (London, 1995); Seaver, *Bowers*; Debenham, 'Polar Place-Names', p. 546.
146 Limb and Cordingley, *Oates*; Smith, *Going Outside*.
147 Desmond, 'X Axis', p. 19.
148 McConnell, Anita, 'Dunsheath, Cissie Providence [Joyce]', *Oxford DNB*; *The Times*, 27 March 1974.
149 Solomon, Susan, *The Coldest March: Scott's Fatal Antarctic Expedition* (New Haven, 2001).
150 Chipman, Elizabeth, *Women on the Ice: A History of Women in the Far South* (Carlton, Vic., 1986).
151 *Photographic News*, 5 June 1885, p. 360. I am grateful to Brian Harrison for this reference.
152 Arnold, Harry J. P., *Photographer of the World: The Biography of Herbert Ponting* (London, 1969); Savours, Ann (ed.), *Scott's Last Voyage: Through the Antarctic Camera of Herbert Ponting* (London, 1974); Christian, M., 'Ponting, Herbert (George)', *New Grove*, online edition; Boddington, Jennie and Vivian Fuchs, *Antarctic Photographs, 1910–1916: Herbert Ponting and Frank Hurley* (London, 1979); Christie, Ian, 'Ponting, Herbert George', *Oxford DNB*; Legg, Frank and Toni Hurley, *Once More on My Adventure* (Sydney, 1966); Bickel, Lennard, *In Search of Frank Hurley* (Melbourne, 1980); Baker, Anne Pimlott, 'Hurley, James Francis [Frank]', *Oxford DNB*; Jones, *Last Great Quest*, pp. 76, 80.
153 Holt, 'Batsman as Hero', p. 62.
154 Wilson and Elder, *Cheltenham in Antarctica*, p. 80.

155 Savours, 'Shackleton'; *The Times*, 31 August 1909, 1 September 1909, 27 September 1909, 30 September 1909, 5 October 1909, 25 October 1909, 17 November 1910.
156 Brown, R. N. Rudmose, 'Shackleton, Ernest Henry', *DNB*, accessed via *Oxford DNB* online.
157 Huntford, *Scott and Amundsen*.
158 Bickel, *Forgotten Men*, pp. 17, 38–40, 49, 50, 128, 206, x.
159 Elzinga, Aant, 'Review of Wråkberg: *Vetenskapens vikingatåg*', *Isis* 92 (2002), pp. 185–6.
160 Limb and Cordingley, *Oates*, p. 7.
161 Ibid.
162 Ibid., p. 115.
163 Scott, *Journals*, p. 410.
164 Bernacchi, Louis C., *A Very Gallant Gentleman* (no place, 1933).
165 Huntford, *Scott and Amundsen*, pp. 542–3; Smith, *Going Outside*, Ch. 26.
166 Smith, *Going Outside*, p. 145.
167 Limb and Cordingley, *Oates*, pp. 168–9, 196.
168 Ibid., pp. 43, 123.
169 Ibid.
170 Limb and Cordingley, *Oates*, p. 114; Evans, E. R. G. R., 'Captain Oates: My Recollections of a Gallant Comrade', *Strand Magazine* (Dec 1913), pp. 615–26; Solomon, Susan, *The Coldest March: Scott's Fatal Antarctic Expedition* (London, 2001); Smith, Michael, *I am Just Going Outside: Captain Oates – Antarctic Tragedy* (Staplehurst, 2002); Spufford, *Ice*; Pottle, Mark, 'Oates, Lawrence Edward Grace', *Oxford DNB*. Quotation from Gregor, *Swansea's Antarctic Explorer*, p. 34.
171 Limb and Cordingley, *Oates*, p. 117.
172 Ibid., p. 120.
173 Ibid. *Oates*, 115–120; Smith, *Going Outside*, pp. 54, 112.
174 Limb and Cordingley, *Oates*, p. 218.
175 Ibid., p. 120.
176 Ibid., pp. 114, 120.
177 Ibid., *Oates*, pp. 45, 63, 132, 217; Seaver, *Bowers*, p. 194 (original punctuation).
178 Heren, *Growing up Poor*, p. 117.
179 Seaver, *Bowers*, p. 211; Wilson and Elder, *Cheltenham in Antarctica*.
180 Holt, Richard and J. A. Mangan, 'Prologue: Heroes of a European Past', pp. 1–13, in Holt, Mangan, and Lanfranchi, *European Heroes*, p. 10. Barczewski, *Antarctic Destinies*, p. 237, disagrees with this fundamental need for accomplishments.
181 Wheeler, *Cherry*, fns to p. 110 and see fns to pp. 67, 89, 113, 149, 211, 228 for more commentary based on first-hand knowledge.
182 Joyce to Charles Royds, 7 April 1930, cited in Tyler-Lewis, *Lost Men*, p. 5; Cherry-Garrard, 'Introduction', p. xix.
183 Fiennnes, Ranulph, *Captain Scott* (London, 2003); Young, 'Debunking'. 'Owner' was a more general naval term but is known widely particularly in connection with Scott. Wheeler, *Cherry*, p. 67.
184 Morrell and Capparell, *Shackleton's Way*, pp. 11, 49.
185 Faure, Jean-Michel, 'National Identity and the Sporting Champion: Jean Borota and French History', pp. 86–100, in Holt, Mangan and Lanfranchi, *European Heroes*, p. 86, my italics.
186 *Blizzard: The Race to the Pole* (BBC, 2006); 'Scott v Amundsen – the Deadliest Rematch on Earth', *The Sunday Times*, 26 December 2008.

187 Morrell and Capparell, *Shackleton's Way*, p. 53. Quotation from Tyler-Lewis, *Lost Men*, p. 13.
188 Hattersley-Smith, G., 'Carse (Verner) Duncan', *Oxford DNB*; Winser, N. and S. Winser, 'Fiennes, Virginia Frances [Ginny] Twisleton-Wykeham', *Oxford DNB*; Cosgrove, Dennis, 'Woodward, David', *Oxford DNB*.
189 Cameron, *Farthest Ends*.
190 Baigent, Elizabeth, 'Founders of the Royal Geographical Society of London', *Oxford DNB*.
191 Stoddart, *On Geography*; Driver, Felix, 'Sub-Merged Identities: Familiar and Unfamiliar Histories', *Transactions of the Institute of British Geographers* 20/4 (1995), pp. 410–13.
192 Jack Langton, personal communication; Withers, Charles W. J., *Geography, Science, and National Identity: Scotland since 1520* (Cambridge, 2001); Driver, 'Sub-Merged Identities', p. 413.
193 Although tangential to her main thesis, this point is one of the most interesting made by Barczewski, *Antarctic Destinies*. See also Baigent, Elizabeth, 'Crozier, Francis Rawdon Moira', *Oxford DNB*; Smith, Michael, *Captain Crozier – Last Man Standing?* (Cork, 2006).
194 Driver, 'Sub-Merged Identities', p. 413.

CHAPTER 3

1 Nietzsche, Friedrich, *Beyond Good and Evil: Prelude to a Philosophy of the Future*, Trans. Kaufmann, Walter (New York, 1966), p. 105.
2 Benjamin, Walter, *Reflections* (London, 1979), p. 11.
3 The hidden icebergs painting was discovered by x-ray during the London Maritime Museum's preparation for the 2004 exhibition, *William Hodges, 1744–1797: The Art of Exploration*. Pieter Van der Merwe comments that 'There is a longstanding consensus, though one lacking documentary proof, that A View in Pickersgill Harbour (ill. 1.1) was painted on the spot in April 1773. Under X-radiography its lush rainforest has now been shown to conceal a startlingly different and unfinished view of Antarctic icebergs in a rough sea (ill. 1.2). This is a significant discovery, since Hodges was not previously known to have attempted painting the Antarctic in oil. It is probably the first-ever Antarctic painting in that medium by an eyewitness and its presence under Pickersgill Harbour tends to strengthen the probability that the latter was painted over it on the voyage ... The absence of Antarctic oil paintings by Hodges has long been a puzzle and discovery of the "Icebergs" in turn raises the question of why it was obliterated. The answer is probably that such icy themes – even Alpine scenery – had not yet become part of the conventional European landscape repertoire.' See van der Merwe, Pieter, "Icebergs" and other recent discoveries in paintings from Cook's second voyage by William Hodges' in *Journal for Maritime Research* (March 2006). Available at http://www.jmr.nmm.ac.uk/server/show/ConJmrArticle.212/setPaginate/No (accessed 21 November 2007).
4 Borchgrevink's *Southern Cross* expedition (1898–1900) established the first base on the continent at Cape Adare and the first darkroom (see album 1396, National Maritime Museum).
5 An album captioned by Shackleton also records this aerial photograph (National Maritime Museum, Historic Photographs Collection, Album ALB0346, National Antarctic Expedition, 1901–3). All information about the National Maritime Museum's polar photographic holdings was kindly supplied by Jeremy Mitchell, Manager, Historic Photographs and Ship Plans.

NOTES

6 A brief Antarctic photographic chronology is as follows: 1903–5, Jean-Baptise Charcot took the photographer Paul Pleneau with his expedition; 1907–9 Ernest Shackleton took a cinematograph machine and made 4,000 feet of film; 1910 Herbert Ponting was the first professional photographer hired by an Antarctic expedition (first colour photos, autochromes and first Antarctic film); 1911 professional photographer Frank Hurley accompanied Mawson; 1928 Admiral Byrd made the first flights over the south pole and conducted aerial surveys; 1939 the first photogrammetry was conducted by the German Alfred Ritscher. His expedition dropped aluminium javelins with swastikas along flight paths to give ground references; 1946–7, over 70,000 aerial trimetrogon photographs were taken by the United States during *Operation High Jump*.

7 Photography was used in the Arctic from 1852. The Maritime Museum holds four calotypes (a silver iodine process patented by Henry Fox Talbot) of the Belcher Expedition, most likely to be of Disko Bay, Greenland, taken by Dr. William Domville using apparatus supplied to him by the Admiralty. These photographs complement the glass plate negatives of Captain A. E. Inglefield whose supply expedition in 1854 recorded the indigenous and Danish population and ships in Disko Bay (NMM, Historic Photographs Collection, Album ALB1396, Colbeck Album). Arctic photography continued in 1864 with William H. Pierce, a photographer with James Wallace Black in Labrador, then John L. Dunmore and George Critcherson who accompanied William Bradford and produced the first photographic book, *The Arctic Regions* (1869). In the Antarctic, the first photograph of a tabular berg was taken in 1874 on the *Challenger Expedition* under the leadership of Charles Wyville Thomson. See www.antarctic-circle.org/foc.htm (accessed 1 February 2007) for details. For a discussion of polar film, see McKernan, Luke, 'The Great White Silence: Antarctic Exploration and Film' in *South: The Race to the Pole* (London, 2000), pp. 91–103.

8 Driver, Felix, 'Editorial: Fieldwork in Geography' *Transactions of the Institute of British Geographers* 25 (2000), pp. 267–8. Also see Driver, Felix, *Geography Militant: Cultures of Exploration and Empire* (Oxford, 2001) and Driver, Felix, 'Making Space' *Ecumene* 1 (1994), pp. 386–90.

9 Crary, Jonathan, *Techniques of the Observer: On Vision and Modernity in the Nineteenth Century* (Massachusetts, 1992), p. 20.

10 Snyder, Joel and Neil Walsh Allen, 'Photography, Vision, and Representation' *Critical Inquiry* 2 /1 (1975), pp. 143–69.

11 Crary, *Techniques of the Observer*, p. 5.

12 Ibid., p. 3.

13 Grosz, Elizabeth, *Time Travels: Feminism, Nature, Power* (London, 2005), p. 141.

14 See Carter, Paul, *The Road to Botany Bay* (London, 1987).

15 See McKernan, 'The Great White Silence', p. 91.

16 Crary, *Techniques of the Observer*, pp. 6–9.

17 Synder, Joel, 'Territorial Photography' in W. J. T. Mitchell (ed.), *Landscape and Power* (Chicago, 1994), pp. 175–202.

18 For a detailed discussion on Walter Benjamin's concept of history and photography, see Yusoff, Kathryn, 'Antarctic Exposure: Archives of the Feeling Body' in *Cultural Geographies* 14/2 (2007), pp. 211–33 and Cadava, Eduardo, 'Words of Light: Theses on the Photography of History' in P. Petro (ed.), *Fugitive Images* (Indianapolis, 1995), pp. 228–44.

19 It is important to note that the histories of modernity and the globalism of its 'vision' were configured by the density of life in the peripheries of empire as much as it was through urban visualities.

20 Benjamin, Walter, 'The Work of Art in the Age of Mechanical Reproduction' in H. Arendt (ed.), *Illuminations* (London, 1999), pp. 219–53, 242.

21 Grosz, *Time Travels*, p. 139.
22 For a discussion of the different climate-induced modalities of sight, see Kathryn Yusoff, '"Climates of Sight": Mistaken Visibilities, Mirages and "Seeing Beyond" in Antarctica' in Denis Cosgrove & Veronica della Dora (eds), *High Places: Cultural Geographies of Mountains and Ice* (London, 2008), pp. 53–72.
23 For a cultural history of exploration and perceptions of polar explorers, see Spufford, Francis, *I May be Some Time* (London, 1996).
24 For a discussion of the performative dimension of photography, see Edwards, Elizabeth, *Raw Histories: Photographs, Anthropology and Museums* (Oxford, 2001), pp. 16–17.
25 Orsman, Chris, 'Behind the Lines, 1915' *Black South* (Wellington, New Zealand, 1997).
26 Ponting, Herbert, *The Great White South* (London, 1921).
27 Letters received from the Rev. F. I. Anderson, Senior Chaplain to the forces, extract printed on sleeve of Ponting, *The Great White South*, 1921.
28 Christie, Ian, *90° South*, Academy Video release from Argos Films and the British Film Institute, 1933.
29 Christie, *90° South*.
30 Ponting, Herbert, *Another World* (London, 1975), p. 33.
31 See Pearson, Mike, 'No Joke in Petticoats', *The Drama Review* 48/1 (2004), pp. 44–59.
32 Anderson in Ponting, *The Great White South*, 1921.
33 Promotional postcard for Philharmonic Hall film showings, 1911.
34 Quoted in Riffenburgh, Beau and Liz Cruwys, *The Photographs of H G Ponting* (London, 1998), p. 107.
35 Quoted in Katz, Cindy and Andrew Kirby, 'In the Nature of Things: The Environment and Everyday Life', *Transactions of the Institute of British Geographers* 16 (1991), pp. 259–71, 260.
36 Cited in Katz and Kirby, 'In the Nature of Things', p. 265.
37 Ponting, *Another World*, p. 32.
38 Ibid., p. 33.
39 Solomon, Susan, *The Coldest March* (London, 2001), p. 325.
40 The *iconographie photographique de la Salpêtrière* was published between 1875, 1880, and between 1888 and 1918 and depicted chronophotographs of 'Hysterical' women. Photography and his performances in the *Salpêtrière* were the main diagnostic tool that Charcot used for his analytical method to determine the medical condition of hysteria.
41 Christie's, *The Polar Sale, Including the Shackleton Collection*, Tuesday, 25 September 2001 (London, 2001).
42 Serra, Richard, *Writing Interviews* (Chicago, 1994), p. 100.
43 Osborn, Ed, 'Southern Exposure', *Cabinet* 10 (2003), p. 41.
44 Osborn, 'Southern Exposure', p. 41.
45 Frank Hurley followed the same montage practice on the Western Front, much to the distain of his commanding officers, who perceived his work as a form of propaganda rather than an accurate record of the war effort.
46 Larsgaard, Mary Lynette, 'Part VII: Planimetric Mapping of World Continential Land Surfaces'. See http://www.library.ucsb.edu/people/larsgaard/antarev.html (accessed 13 October 2007).
47 Air-photo analysis as a geographic research technique was called photogeography. See J. Roscoe, 'Antarctic Photogeography', in A. P. Crary, L. M. Gould, E. O. Hulbert, H. Odishaw, W. E. Smith (eds), *Antarctica in the International Geophysical Year* (Washington, DC, 1956), pp. 18–21.

NOTES

CHAPTER 4

Research for this paper was funded by the British Academy (SG-43020). Archival material was consulted at the Special Collections of the University of Exeter, the Royal Geographical Society and the Honourable Society of Middle Temple, and our thanks are extended to the archivists who assisted us. Thanks also to James R. Ryan, Simon Naylor, Robert Mayhew, David C. Harvey, Harriet Hawkins, Helen Jones and Sue Rouillard of the Department of Geography, University of Exeter Drawing Office and members of the Postcolonial Research Seminar at Leicester University for their support during this research.

1. Hogarth, D. G., 'Problems in Exploration: I. Western Asia', *The Geographical Journal* 32 (1908), p. 549.
2. Ibid., pp. 549–63; Carles, W. R., 'Problems in Exploration: II. Ordos', *The Geographical Journal* 33 (1909), pp. 668–79; Huntington, Ellsworth, 'Problems in Exploration: Central Asia', *The Geographical Journal* 35 (1910), pp. 395–419; Cana, Frank R., 'Problems in Exploration: Africa', *The Geographical Journal* 38 (1911), pp. 457–69.
3. Hogarth, 'Problems in Exploration', p. 549.
4. Ibid.
5. For further discussion of the role of the Royal Geographical Society in nineteenth-century exploration, see Driver, Felix, *Geography Militant: Cultures of Exploration and Empire* (Oxford, 2001).
6. Hogarth, 'Problems in Exploration', p. 549.
7. Harding King, Letter from Harding King to Keltie, 4 June 1907, RGS/CB7/51 KING 1881–1910 Royal Geographical Society (hereafter RGS).
8. Keltie, Letter from Keltie to Harding King, 6 June 1907, RGS/CB7/51 KING 1881–1910, RGS.
9. Ibid.
10. Ibid.
11. Harding King was admitted to the Honourable Society of Middle Temple on 15 June 1893. He was not called to the bar though he appears to have worked in the law until 1907.
12. Harding King, W. J., 'A Visit to the Hoggar Twaregs', *The Geographical Journal* 20 (1902), pp. 507–17; Harding King, W. J., 'Myths Current in the Sahara Desert', *Folklore* 13 (1902), pp. 284–8; Harding King, W. J., *A Search for the Masked Tawareks* (London, 1903).
13. Harding King, Letter from Harding King to Keltie, 4 June 1907, RGS/CB7/51 KING 1881–1910 RGS. Harding King's father's death was registered at Stourbridge in the 2nd quarter of registration, 1903. It must be noted that Harding King frequently referred to his 'limited' financial resources in planning expeditions.
14. Driver, *Geographical Militant*, pp. 50–6.
15. By the time Harding King undertook his expeditions, *Hints to Travellers*, the manual published by the RGS to instruct travellers in the arts of scientific field observation, measurement and appropriate use of instruments, was into its ninth edition, and the type of observations that Harding King made can be identified clearly within this text. For further discussion on *Hints to Travellers*, see Driver, *Geography Militant*, pp. 49–67.
16. For further discussion of the entwined cultures of geography, exploration and empire, see Livingstone, David N., *The Geographical Tradition: Episodes in the History of a Contested Enterprise* (Oxford, 1992).
17. Collier, P. and R. Inkpen, 'The Royal Geographical Society and the Development of Surveying 1870–1914', *Journal of Historical Geography* 29 (2003),

pp. 93–108; Collier, P. and R. Inkpen, 'The RGS, Exploration and Empire and the Contested Nature of Surveying', *Area* 34 (2002), pp. 273–83. See also Edney, Matthew H., *Mapping an Empire: The Geographical Construction of British India, 1765–1843* (Chicago, 1997).

18   This echoes a familiar theme in the history of science regarding the contested negotiation of the right to undertake scientific activity, the behaviour of actors in the production of knowledge and the control of the sort of knowledge that is produced. See Dewsbury, J. D. and S. Naylor, 'Practising Geographical Knowledge: Fields, Bodies and Dissemination', *Area* 34/3 (2002), pp. 253–60; Livingstone, David N., *Putting Science in its Place: Geographies of Scientific Knowledge* (Chicago, 2003).

19   Livingstone, *Putting Science in its Place*, p. 183.

20   Driver, Felix, 'Sub-Merged Identities: Familiar and Unfamiliar Histories', *Transactions of the Institute of British Geographers* 20 (1995), pp. 410–13. For further discussion on the utility of a critical, contextual, biographical approach, see Thomas, Nicola. J., 'Broadening the Boundaries of Biography and Geography: Lady Curzon, Vicereine of India 1898–1905', *Journal of Historical Geography* 30 (2004), pp. 496–519.

21   For discussion on the culture of the RGS, see Driver, *Geography Militant*, and Livingstone, *Geographical Tradition*.

22   For discussion of the development of geography as an academic discipline, see Livingstone, *Geographical Tradition*, pp. 177–215.

23   Harding King published a series of papers on arid zone geomorphology and entered into heated debate with figures such as Vaughan Cornish on theories of sand movement. Harding King, W. J., 'The Nature and Formation of Sand Ripples and Dunes', *The Geographical Journal* 47 (1916), pp. 189–207; Harding King, W. J., 'Study of a Dune Belt', *The Geographical Journal* 51 (1918), pp. 16–33. This paper went through a lengthy review process with discussion between Vaughan Cornish and Harding King.

24   See Livingstone, *Geographical Tradition*, pp. 216–59.

25   Edney, *Mapping an Empire*.

26   Harding King, Letter from Harding King to Keltie, dated 8 June 1907, RGS/CB7/51 KING 1881–1910 RGS.

27   See Floyer, Earnest A., 'Further Routes in the Eastern Desert of Egypt', *The Geographical Journal* 1 (1893), pp. 408–31, 411; Harding King, W. J., 'Travels in the Libyan Desert', *The Geographical Journal* 39 (1912), pp. 133–7, 135; Harding King, W. J. 'The Libyan Desert from Native Information', *The Geographical Journal* 42 (1913), pp. 277–83, 282; Ball, John, 'Problems of the Libyan Desert' *The Geographical Journal* 70 (1927), pp. 21–38; continued pp. 105–28; continued pp. 209–24; citations on p. 22 and pp. 209–10.

28   Both Harding King and Ball mentioned Rohlfs' references to the Zerzura oasis; Harding King, 'The Libyan Desert from Native Information', pp. 279, 283; Ball, 'Problems of the Libyan Desert', p. 121. King also noted the German explorer's 'limitless sea of impassable sand' whilst Ball outlined the output of Rohlfs' 1874 expedition; Harding King, 'Travels in the Libyan Desert', p. 136; Ball, 'Problems of the Libyan Desert', p. 29.

29   Harding King, Letter from Harding King to Hinks, 15 October 1929, RGS/CB9/93/Harding King RGS. Harding King apparently read this book in French translation prior to his first season. From his letters it would appear that this manuscript was the same source as an Arabic manuscript owned by the orientalist scholar E. A. Johnson Pasha which was later translated into English. This manuscript is discussed in Johnson Pasha, E. A., 'Zerzura', *The Geographical Journal* 75 (1930), pp. 59–61.

30 Johnson Pasha, 'Zerzura'.
31 Lyons, H. G., *The Cadestral Survey of Egypt, 1892–1907* (Cairo, 1909), reviewed in *The Geographical Journal* 34 (1909), pp. 564–5.
32 C. A. G. M., 'Apologia', *Survey Notes*, 1 (1906) p. 3. *Survey Notes* was re-launched to a wider audience as *The Cairo Scientific Journal* in 1908.
33 C. A. G. M., 'Apologia', p. 4.
34 Collier and Inkpen, 'The RGS and the Development of Surveying', p. 299.
35 Ibid.
36 Harding King drew attention to the shortage of resources for surveying the areas he travelled in, noting that for his final season's work he aimed to complete an unfinished Egyptian Government survey of the Farafra Depression. Harding King, W. J., 'The Farafra Depression and Bu Mungar Hattia', *The Geographical Journal* 42 (1913), pp. 455–61.
37 Harding King, Letter from Harding King to Keltie, 3 August 1909, RGS/CB7/51 KING 1881–1910 RGS. This work was published in Harding King, W. J.,'Ethnographic Notes on Dakhla Oasis', *The Cairo Scientific Journal* 7/83 (1913), pp. 231–46.
38 Camerini, Jane, 'Remains of the Day: Early Victorians in the Field', in Lightman, Bernard (ed.),*Victorian Science in Context* (Chicago 1997), pp. 354–77; Camerini, Jane, 'Wallace in the Field', in Kuklick, H. and R. Kohler (eds), *Science in the Field* (Chicago, 1996), pp. 44–65.
39 Harding King, Letter from Harding King to Keltie, 22 January 1908, RGS/CB7/51 KING 1881–1910 RGS.
40 Ibid., 8 December 1908, RGS/CB7/51 KING 1881–1910 RGS.
41 Ibid., 3 August 1909, RGS/CB7/51 KING 1881–1910 RGS.
42 Ibid.
43 Ibid.
44 Harding King, W. J., *Mysteries of the Libyan Desert* (London 1925), p. 120.
45 Ibid., p. 131.
46 Ibid., p. 198.
47 Ibid.
48 Ibid., p. 199.
49 Ibid., pp. 200, 209.
50 Ibid., p. 233.
51 Ibid., p. 244.
52 Livingstone, *Putting Science in its Place*, p. 153, original emphasis.
53 Ibid., p. 19.
54 See, for example, Balfour, H. et al., 'The Influence of Its Geography on the People of the Aures Massif, Algeria: Discussion', *The Geographical Journal* 59 (1922), pp. 34–6; Clayton, Gilbert et al., 'Across the Libyan Desert to Kufara: Discussion', *The Geographical Journal* 58 (1921), pp. 174–8; Bey, Ahmed Hassanein et al., 'Through Kufra to Darfur: Discussion', *The Geographical Journal* 64 (1924), pp. 363–6.
55 Harding King, W. J., 'Pioneer Desert Information', *The Geographical Journal* 77 (1931), pp. 541–7. Sections of this article were later published in the final edition of the RGS's *Hints to Travellers* (London, 1934).
56 Harding King, 'Travels in the Libyan Desert'.
57 Lyons, Letter from Lyons to Keltie, 9 November 1911, RGS/CB8/S2/King RGS.
58 Ibid.
59 Unfortunately no copy of this letter survives in the RGS archives but it is referred to in letters from Keltie to Harding King, 21 November 1911, RGS/CB8/S2/King RGS.

60 Harding King, Letter from Harding King to Keltie, 22 November 1911, RGS/CB8/S2/King RGS.
61 Keltie, Letter from Keltie to Harding King, 22 and 24 November 1911, RGS/CB8/S2/King RGS.
62 Harding King, Letter from Harding King to Keltie, 14 December 1911, RGS/CB8/S2/King RGS.
63 Lyons, Letter from Lyons to Keltie, 15 December 1911, RGS/CB8/S2/King RGS.
64 Keltie, Letter from Keltie to Harding King, 18 December 1911, RGS/CB8/S2/King RGS.
65 Harding King, Letter from Harding King to Keltie, 29 December 1911, RGS/CB8/S2/King RGS.
66 Ibid., 23 May 1913, RGS/CB8/S2/King RGS.
67 Harding King, Letter from Harding King to Hinks, 26 March 1919, Annual Awards CB8, RGS.
68 Hinks, Letter from Hinks to Harding King, 24 March 1919, Annual Awards CB8, RGS.
69 Secretary's copy of the medals and awards committee notes, 10 March 1919, Annual Awards CB8, 1919 RGS.
70 Hinks, Letter from Hinks to Harding King, 14 March 1921, RGS/CB9/93/Harding King Correspondence 1921–1930 RGS.
71 See Domosh, Mona, 'Toward a Feminist Historiography of Geography', *Transactions of the Institute of British Geographers* 16 (1991), pp. 95–101; Blunt, Alison, *Travel, Gender and Imperialism. Mary Kingsley and West Africa* (London, 1994).
72 For detailed discussion of exploration of the desert by car, see Goudie, Andrew, *Immensity: Exploration of the Western Desert by Motorcar* (Oxford, 2006).
73 Sarsfield Hall, E. G., 'Note on Map of Northern Darfur Compiled from Native Information', *The Geographical Journal* 56 (1920), pp. 401–3; Letter from Harding King to Hinks, 6 December 1920, and return letter from Hinks to Harding King, December 1920, RGS/CB9/93/Harding King Correspondence 1921–1930 RGS.
74 Harding King, Letter from Harding King to Hinks, 10 December 1920, RGS/CB9/93/Harding King Correspondence 1921–1930 RGS.
75 See Goudie, *Immensity* and Kelly, Saul, *The Hunt for Zerzura: The Lost Oasis and the Desert War* (London, 2002).
76 Harding King, W. J., 'The Dakhla–Owenat Road', *The Geographical Journal* 65 (1925), pp. 153–6.
77 Harding King, Letter from Harding King to Hinks, 19 December 1924, RGS/CB9/93/Harding King Correspondence 1921–1930 RGS.
78 Hinks, Letter from Hinks to Harding King, 24 December 1924, RGS/CB9/93/Harding King Correspondence 1921–1930 RGS. The 'Egyptian Prince' Hinks refers to was Prince Kemal el Din Hussein whom John Ball accompanied on several expeditions. See Ball, 'Problems of the Libyan Desert', p. 23.
79 Harding King, *Mysteries of the Libyan Desert*.
80 Newbold, Letter from Newbold to Rodd, 25 April 1926, Rodd's Scrapbook, RGS. Douglas Newbold was a member of the Sudan Political Service in the 1920s and 1930s and explored the Libyan Desert during this time. Francis Rodd had a career in the army and diplomatic service, serving various times in North Africa. He was President of the RGS during 1945–8.
81 F. R.[Rodd, Francis], 'Review: Mysteries of the Libyan Desert by W. J. Harding King', *The Geographical Journal* 65 (1925), p. 538–9.
82 Rodd, Letter from Rodd to Hinks, 1 July 1925, RGS/CB9/93/Harding King Correspondence 1921–1930 RGS.

83 Harding King, Letter from Harding King to Hinks, Undated c. July 1925, RGS/CB9/93/Harding King Correspondence 1921–1930 RGS. This letter relates to the content on a letter from Rodd to Hinks, 1 July 1925, RGS/CB9/93/Harding King Correspondence 1921–1930 RGS.
84 Rodd, Letter from Rodd to Hinks, 3 July 1925, RGS/CB9/93/Harding King Correspondence 1921–1930 RGS.
85 Harding King, Letter from Harding King to Hinks, 19 June 1925, CB9/93/Harding King Correspondence 1921–1930 RGS.
86 Ball, 'Problems of the Libyan Desert', pp. 211–12.
87 Harding King, W. J., 'Lost Oases of the Libyan Desert', *The Geographical Journal* 72 (1928), pp. 244–9.
88 De Lancey Forth, N. B., 'More Journeys in Search of Zerzura', *The Geographical Journal* 75 (1930), pp. 48–59; Johnson Pasha, 'Zerzura'; Harding King, W. J., 'The Lost Oases', *The Geographical Journal* 75 (1930), pp. 61–4; Newbold, D. and W. B. K. Shaw, 'An Exploration in the South Libyan Desert: Review', *The Geographical Journal* 75 (1930), pp. 65–7.
89 Bagnold, R. A., *The Physics of Blown Sand and Desert Dunes* (London, 1941), p. xxii.
90 See Stoddart, D. R., 'The RGS and the "New Geography": Changing Aims and Changing Roles in Nineteenth Century Science', *The Geographical Journal* 146 (1980), pp. 190–202; Livingstone, *Geographical Tradition*, pp. 172–6.
91 Harding King, *Mysteries of the Libyan Desert*, p. 11.
92 Harding King, Letter from Harding King to the RGS, 14 August 1939, RGS/CB10/King 1931–40 RGS.

CHAPTER 5

Research for this chapter was conducted at the National Library of Australia, Canberra; the Royal Geographical Society archives, London, and the University of Sussex archives, Brighton, both in the UK; the Johns Hopkins University archives, Baltimore, and the American Geographical Society archives, New York, both in the USA; and the University of Toronto archives, in Canada. Funding for this research was in part provided by the University of Bristol. Much of this chapter was written during a sabbatical at the University of Melbourne – thanks in particular to Fraser Macdonald for hosting me during that visit.

1 Driver, Felix, *Geography Militant: Cultures of Exploration and Empire* (Oxford, 2001), p. 4.
2 Ibid., p. 201.
3 Heffernan, Michael, 'The Science of Empire: The French Geographical Movement and the Forms of French Imperialism, 1870–1920', in A. Godlewska and N. Smith (eds), *Geography and Empire* (Oxford, 1994), pp. 92–114; Livingstone, David, *The Geographical Tradition* (Oxford, 1992).
4 Kohler, Robert, *Landscapes and Labscapes: Exploring the Lab-Field Border in Biology* (Chicago, 2002).
5 Kohler, Robert, 'Place and Practice in Field Biology', *History of Science* 40 (2002), pp. 189–210.
6 Kuklick, Henrika and Robert Kohler (eds), *Science in the Field* (Chicago, 1996), p. 3. See also Driver, Felix, 'Editorial: Fieldwork in Geography', *Transactions of the Institute of British Geographers* 25 (2000), pp. 267–8.
7 McEwan, Cheryl, 'Gender, Science and Physical Geography in Nineteenth-century Britain', *Area* 30 (1998), pp. 215–23; Sparke, Matthew, 'Displacing

the Field in Fieldwork: Masculinity, Metaphor and Space', in N. Duncan (ed.) *Bodyspace* (London, 1996), pp. 212–33.
8   Hevly, Bruce, 'The Heroic Science of Glacier Motion' in H. Kuklick and R. Kohler (eds) *Science in the Field* (Chicago, 1996), pp. 66–86; Bowd, G. and D. Clayton, 'Fieldwork and Tropicality in French Indochina: Reflections on Pierre Gourou's Les Paysans Du Delta Tonkinois, 1936', *Singapore Journal of Tropical Geography* 24 (2003), pp. 147–68.
9   Outram, Dorinda, 'New Spaces in Natural History', in N. Jardine, J. Secord and E. Spary (eds) *Cultures of Natural History* (Cambridge, 1996), pp. 249–66; Dettelbach, Michael, 'The Face of Nature: Precise Measurement, Mapping, and Sensibility in the Work of Alexander von Humboldt', *Studies in the History and Philosophy of the Biological and Biomedical Sciences* 30 (1999), pp. 473–504.
10 Sorrenson, Richard, 'The Ship as a Scientific Instrument in the Eighteenth Century', in H. Kuklick and R. Kohler (eds) *Science in the Field* (Chicago, 1996), pp. 221–36; Turchetti, Simone, Katrina Dean, Simon Naylor and Martin Siegert 'Accidents and Opportunities: A History of the Radio Echo-sounding of Antarctica, 1958–79', *British Journal for the History of Science* 41 (2008), pp. 417–44.
11 Larsen, A., 'Equipment for the Field', in N. Jardine, J. Secord and E. Spary (eds) *Cultures of Natural History* (Cambridge, 1996), pp. 358–77; Tucker, Jennifer, *Nature Exposed: Photography as Eyewitness in Victorian Science* (Baltimore, 2005).
12 Details of Taylor's upbringing, education and career are taken from the writings of a number of historical geographers, including Powell, Sanderson, Spate and Taylor himself: Powell, J. M., 'The Cyclist on the Ice: Griffith Taylor as Explorer', *Proceedings of the Royal Geographical Society of Australasia* 80 (1979), pp. 1–28; Powell, J. M., *An Historical Geography of Modern Australia: The Restive Fringe* (Cambridge, 1988); Powell, J. M., 'Griffith Taylor and "Australia Unlimited"' *The John Murtagh Macrossan Memorial Lecture 1992* (Brisbane, 1992); Sanderson, M., *Griffith Taylor: Antarctic Scientist and Pioneer Geographer* (Carlton, 1988); Spate, O. H. K., 'Journeyman Taylor: Some Aspects of his Work', *The Australian Geographer* 12 (1972), pp.115–22; Taylor T. G., *Journeyman Taylor: The Education of a Scientist* (London, 1958).
13 It should be noted that this was not the first time Taylor had given lectures in geography. He had actually provided postgraduate teaching and demonstrating in the subject at Sydney as early as 1907. Then, in 1918, he gave a course of lectures at the University of Melbourne, to which he had been elected to the Faculty of Science in 1916. Spate, 'Journeyman Taylor'; Taylor, *Journeyman Taylor*, p. 167.
14 Powell, 'The Cyclist on the Ice'.
15 Ibid.
16 Ibid., p. 18.
17 Stamp, L. D., Letter to External Registrar, University of London, dated 7 June 1922, Sir L. Dudley Stamp Archive, University of Sussex, UK. Stamp published a number of studies based on his time in Burma, including Stamp, L. D., 'The Ecology of Part of the Riverine Tract of Burma', *Journal of Ecology* 11 (1923), pp. 129–59; Stamp, L. D., 'Notes on the Vegetation of Burma', *Geographical Journal* 64 (1924), pp. 231–7; Stamp, L. D., 'The Aerial Survey of the Irrawaddy Delta Forests (Burma)', *Journal of Ecology* 13 (1925), pp. 262–76.
18 Ogilvie, A. G., Letter to Arthur Hinks, Secretary of the Royal Geographical Society, dated 26 Jan 1921, Ogilvie Archive, Royal Geographical Society; Ogilvie, A. G., 'Impressions of the Vegetation in the United States of America', *Geographical Journal* (1913), pp. 342–57.
19 Smith, Neil, *American Empire: Roosevelt's Geographer and the Prelude to Globalization* (California, 2003).

NOTES

20 Taylor, *Journeyman Taylor*, p. 170.
21 Ibid.
22 On the 'narrativisation' of the field, see Lorimer, Hayden and Nick Spedding, 'Locating Field Science: A Geographical Family Expedition to Glen Roy, Scotland', *British Journal for the History of Science* 38 (2005), pp. 13–34.
23 Taylor T. G., Letter from Taylor to his wife, dated August 1924 MS1003/9/780 T. G. Taylor Archives, National Library of Australia.
24 Anderson, Warwick, *The Cultivation of Whiteness: Science, Health and Racial Destiny in Australia* (Melbourne, 2002).
25 Taylor, T. G., Letter from Taylor to his wife, dated August 1922 MS1003/4/414 T. G. Taylor Archives, National Library of Australia.
26 Matless, David, 'Regional Surveys and Local Knowledges: The Geographical Imagination in Britain, 1918–39', *Transactions of the Institute of British Geographers* 17 (1992), pp. 464–80.
27 Taylor, Letter to his wife, dated August 1922.
28 Ibid.
29 In a letter to Arthur Hinks, the Secretary of the Royal Geographical Society, Taylor complained about a lack of coverage of 'settlement problems' in the Society's in-house journal, the *Geographical Journal*: 'It is the leading Journal as regards exploration but (dare I say it?) possibly some other professional geographers may be like myself, and think that settlement is more important than exploration in geographical research'. Of course this comment may be read as more of a complaint about the lack of coverage of *Taylor's* work in the *Journal* than about work on settlement per se. Taylor, T. G., Letter from Taylor to Hinks, dated 14 July 1924, T. G. Taylor Archive, Royal Geographical Society.
30 Taylor, T. G., *Climatic Control of Australian Production: An Attempt to Gauge the Potential Weather of the Commonwealth Bulletin No. 11* (Melbourne, 1915); Taylor, T. G., *The Control of Settlement By Temperature and Humidity With Special Reference to Australia and the Empire: An Introduction to Comparative Climatology Bulletin No. 14* (Melbourne, 1916).
31 Taylor, T. G., 'Geographical Factors Controlling the Settlement of Tropical Australia', *Proceedings, Queensland Branch, Royal Geographical Society of Australasia* 32 (1917), pp. 1–67; Taylor, T. G., *The Australian Environment, Especially as Controlled by Rainfall – A Regional Study of the Topography, Drainage, Vegetation and Settlement and of the Character and Origin of the Rains* Memoir No. 1 (Melbourne, 1918).
32 Taylor, 'Geographical Factors', p. 63.
33 Ibid.
34 Taylor, *The Australian Environment*, p. 28.
35 Huntington, Ellsworth, Letter from Huntington to Taylor, dated 27 June 1921 *MS1003/9/651*, T. G. Taylor Archives, National Library of Australia. On the close connections between Taylor, Huntington and another influential American geographer, Isaiah Bowman, see Powell, J. M., 'The Bowman, Huntington and Taylor Correspondence, 1928', *The Australian Geographer* 14 (1978), pp. 123–5; for a biography of Huntington, see Martin, G., *Ellsworth Huntington: His Life and Thought* (Connecticut, 1973); and for Bowman, see Smith, *American Empire*.
36 Livingstone, *Geographical Tradition*, p. 225.
37 Powell, *An Historical Geography of Modern Australia*; Powell, 'Griffith Taylor and "Australia Unlimited"'.
38 Taylor, *Journeyman Taylor*, p. 139.
39 Lorimer and Spedding, 'Locating Field Science', p. 27.
40 Taylor, T. G., Letter from Taylor to his father, dated 31 August 1922 *MS1003/4/419* T. G. Taylor Archives, National Library of Australia.

41 Taylor, Letter to his wife, dated August 1922.
42 Taylor, T. G., Letter from Taylor to his wife, dated 31 August 1922 *MS1003/4/416* T. G. Taylor Archives, National Library of Australia.
43 Taylor, Letter to his wife, dated August 1922.
44 Taylor, *Journeyman Taylor*, p. 172.
45 Driver, *Geography Militant*.
46 Taylor, T. G., 'Scientific Travel in Australia', in J. Brouwer (ed.), *Practical Hints to Scientific Travellers* (The Hague, 1926), p. 85.
47 A letter to his son, Bill, whilst surveying the mountains west of Sydney in January 1926 recounted a camp site similar to the one detailed above, and probably formed the basis of the description in *Scientific Travel in Australia*.
48 Taylor, Letter to his wife, dated 31 August 1922.
49 Powell, 'Griffith Taylor and "Australia Unlimited"', p. 18.
50 Taylor, 'Scientific Travel in Australia', p. 83.
51 Taylor, T. G., Letter from Taylor to his wife, dated 26 August 1922 *MS1003/4/415* T. G. Taylor Archives, National Library of Australia.
52 See Hevly, 'Heroic Science of Glacier Motion'.
53 Taylor, T. G., Letter to his wife, dated 31 August 1922.
54 Ibid.
55 Ibid.
56 See for instance Stefansson, V. *The Friendly Arctic* (New York, 1921); Stefansson, V. *Central Australia Report* (Canberra, 1924). For a recent biography of Stefansson, see Gísli Pálsson, *Travelling Passions: The Hidden Life of Vilhjalmur Stefansson* (Manitoba, 2003).
57 Powell, J. M., 'Taylor, Stefansson and the Arid Centre: An Historic Encounter of "Environmentalism" and "Possibilism"', *Journal of the Royal Australian Historical Society* 66 (1980), p. 167.
58 Ibid. On Stefansson's notion of the 'friendly Arctic', see Pálsson, Gísli, 'Arcticality: Gender, Race, and Geography in the Writings of Vilhjalmur Stefansson', in M. Bravo and S. Sorlin (eds), *Narrating the Arctic: A Cultural History of Nordic Scientific Practices* (Sagamore Beach, 2002), pp. 275–310.
59 Bowman, Isaiah, Letter from Bowman to Taylor, dated 5 January 1924 MS1003/9/735 T. G. Taylor Archives, National Library of Australia. Taylor and Bowman maintained an extensive correspondence from the mid-1920s through to 1950. Many of these letters remain in the Isaiah Bowman archives, Johns Hopkins University, Baltimore. There are others in the Director's Correspondence files in the archives of the American Geographical Society, New York.
60 Ibid.
61 Powell, 'Taylor, Stefansson and the Arid Centre', p. 173.
62 Ibid.
63 Taylor, T. G., Letter from Taylor to Huntington, dated 19 December 1924 *MS1003/9/779* T. G. Taylor Archives, National Library of Australia.
64 Bowman, Isaiah, Letter from Bowman to Taylor, dated 23 June 1924 MS1003/9/742 T. G. Taylor Archives, National Library of Australia. Stefansson's high standing in the geographical and expeditionary communities, especially in North America, presumably dictated that Bowman be seen to publically endorse his visit to Australia and explains the very different tenor of the two letters Bowman wrote to Taylor – the first a very public statement of support; the second the expression of much more private misgivings.
65 Taylor, T. G. with Seivewright, D. J. and Lloyd, T., *Southern Lands* (Toronto, 1953), p. 180; Powell, 'Taylor, Stefansson and the Arid Centre', pp. 175, 180.
66 Taylor, *Southern Lands*, p. 180.

NOTES

67 Huntington, Ellsworth, Letter from Huntington to Taylor, dated 23 February 1925 MS1003/9/800 T. G. Taylor Archives, National Library of Australia.
68 Taylor quoted in Powell, 'The Bowman, Huntington and Taylor Correspondence', p. 175.
69 Bowman, Letter to Taylor, dated 23 June 1924.
70 Powell, 'Taylor, Stefansson and the Arid Centre', p. 173.
71 Taylor, T. G., 'Tropical Problems. The Gate of the Territory. I', *The Argus* 23 September MS1003/4/225 T. G. Taylor Archives, National Library of Australia.
72 Taylor, T. G., Letter to Huntington, dated 19 December 1924.
73 Taylor, T. G., Letter from Taylor to his wife, undated (but August 1924) MS1003/9/781 T. G. Taylor Archives, National Library of Australia. Results from this trip were published in Taylor, T. G. and F. Jardine, 'Kamilaroi and White: A Study of Racial Mixture in New South Wales', *Journal of the Royal Society of New South Wales* (1924), pp. 268–92.
74 'Racial geography' was the title of Taylor's own chapter in his edited book, *Geography in the Twentieth Century* (New York, 1952).
75 Taylor, T. G., *Topographic Structure along the International Boundary*, unpublished MS, Box 14, T. G. Taylor Archive, University of Toronto.

CHAPTER 6

This material was based on work supported by the National Science Foundation, granted to the author while working at the Foundation. Any opinion, findings, and conclusions or recommendations expressed in this material are those of the author and do not necessarily reflect the views of the National Science Foundation. The author would like to thank the archivists and their staff for the use of the following collections: (a) Library of Congress, Manuscripts Division, Collections of Alan T. Waterman and Nathaniel C. Gerson, Washington, DC; (b) National Academies of Science, Archive of the US National Committee on the International Geophysical Year, 1957–8, Washington, DC; (c) National Archives and Records Administration, US Department of Defense, Research and Development Board, Record Group 330, College Park, Maryland; and (d) University of Alaska Fairbanks, Rasmuson Library, William O. Field Papers, Fairbanks, Alaska.

1 See the description of SEARCH by the Arctic Research Consortium of the United States, available at http://www.arcus.org/SEARCH/index.php.
2 Korsmo, Fae L., 'The Early Cold War and US Arctic Research', in K. R. Benson and H. M. Rozwadowski (eds), *Extremes: Oceanography's Adventures at the Poles* (Sagamore Beach, 2007), pp. 173–99.
3 Sullivan, Walter, *Assault on the Unknown: The International Geophysical Year* (New York, 1961).
4 Barnes, Trevor J. and Matthew Farish, 'Between Regions: Science, Militarism, and American Geography from World War to Cold War', *Annals of the Association of American Geographers* 96/4 (2006), pp. 807–26.
5 Farish, Matthew, 'Frontier Engineering: From the Globe to the Body in the Cold War Arctic', *The Canadian Geographer* 50/2 (2006), pp. 177–96.
6 Doel, Ronald E., 'Constituting the Postwar Earth Sciences: The Military's Influence on the Environmental Sciences in the USA after 1945', *Social Studies of Science* 33/5 (2003), pp. 635–66.
7 National Archives and Records Administration, Finding Aid to Record Group 330, Entry 341, Office of the Secretary of Defense, Research and Development Board.

8   Siple, Paul A., Memorandum for Lt. Col. Robert B. Simpson, 14 April 1948, p. 4. Research and Development Board, Record Group 330, E341, Box 452, Folder 1, 'GAE, Stefansson, Dr. Vilhjalmur'.
9   Mathews, A. G., Colonel, Corps of Engineers and Chief, Military Intelligence Division, to Charles B. Hunt, Geologist in Charge, Military Geology Unit, US Geological Survey, 28 July 1945. Research and Development Board, Record Group 330, E341, Box 452, Folder 2, 'Snow, Ice and Permafrost'.
10 Rossby, Carl G., Chairman, Panel on Meteorology, Committee on Geophysical Sciences, Joint Research and Development Board, to Executive Secretary of the Board, 21 April 1947. RDB, RG 330, E341, Box 452, Folder 2, 'Snow, Ice and Permafrost'.
11 Siple, Paul, *90° South: The Story of the American South Pole Conquest* (New York, 1959), p. 76.
12 Ahlmann, Hans W., 'Glaciological Methods', *Polar Record* 4/31 (1946), pp. 315–19.
13 Bentley, Charles R., 'The Structure of Antarctica and Its Ice Cover', in H. Odishaw (ed.), *Research in Geophysics* (Cambridge, MA, 1964), pp. 335–89.
14 Siple, Paul A., Biogeographer, Research Group, Research and Development Division, War Department General Staff, to Director of Research and Development, 21 July 1947. RDB, RG 330, E341, Box 452, Folder 2, 'Snow, Ice and Permafrost'.
15 Siple, *90° South*.
16 Stefansson to Vannevar Bush, 3 March 1948. RDB, RG 330, E341, Box 452, Folder 1, 'GAE, Stefansson, Dr. Vilhjalmur'.
17 Ibid.
18 Baldwin, Hanson W., 'Arctic Repels Warfare – US Exercises Show Great Difficulties, Make Large-scale Operations Unlikely', *The New York Times*, 8 February 1948. RDB, RG 330, E341, Box 452, Folder 1, 'GAE, Stefansson, Dr. Vilhjalmur'.
19 Steffansson, Letter to Bush, 3 March 1948.
20 The discussion that follows is based on Siple's memorandum to Lt. Col. Robert B. Simpson, 14 April 1948, and attached report, 'Suggestions Regarding Integrated Plans from an Army point of view.' RDB, RG 330, E341, Box 452, Folder 1, 'GAE, Stefansson, Dr. Vilhjalmur'.
21 Siple, 'Suggestions Regarding Integrated plans', p. 2.
22 Ibid.
23 Ibid., p. 7.
24 See Diubaldo, Richard J., *Stefansson and the Canadian Arctic* (Montreal, 1978); Sfraga, Michael P., *Bradford Washburn: A Life of Exploration* (Corvallis, 2004), Chapter 3.
25 Siple, *90° South*, pp. 73–82.
26 For an account of expedition planning, see Welch, David F, *Operation Highjump II: An Exercise in Planning* (Washington, DC: 1970).
27 Siple, *90° South*, p. 81.
28 Siple, 'Statement by Dr. Paul A. Siple', to the Panel on Arctic Environments, Committee on Geophysics and Geography, RDB, 17 November 1949. RDB, RG 330, E341, Box 169, Folder 4, 'Panel on Arctic Environments'.
29 Fechteler, W. M., Acting Chief of Naval Operations, to Navy Secretary, RDB, 28 December 1948. RDB, E341, Box 169, Folder 2, 'Panel on Arctic Environments Agenda'. See also Welch 1970, pp. 2–10.
30 Siple, 'Statement' to the Panel on Arctic Environments.
31 Benson, Carl, Interview with Karen Brewster, 22 June 2001, p. 3 (Ohio State University Libraries, Byrd Polar Research Center, Polar Oral History Program).
32 Benson, interview; William O. Field Papers, Correspondence Files on Mint Julep (University of Alaska Fairbanks, Rasmuson Library).

33 Siple, 'Proposal for Consideration by the US National Committee: Climate Change Study', no date, in the US National Academy of Sciences (NAS) IGY Archive, Washington, DC. Drawer 1, Program Proposals for IGY (1952–3).
34 With 50-plus years of new knowledge, technology, and methodology, climate scientists are now more nuanced yet equally convinced that at the present rate of change, a summer ice-free Arctic Ocean within a century is a real possibility.
35 Ahlmann, Hans W., 'Glaciärer och klimat i Norden under de seneste tusentalen år', *Norsk geografisk tidsskrift* 13/3–8 (1954), pp. 56–75.
36 Siple, 'Proposal for Consideration by the US National Committee'.
37 See, for example, Lawrence, Donald B., 'Glacier Fluctuation in Northwestern North America within the Past Six Centuries', *Geographical Review* 40 (1950), pp. 191–223.
38 Donald B. Lawrence to Joseph Kaplan, Chairman, US National Committee for the IGY, 6 May 1953, in the National Academies of Sciences (NAS) IGY Archive, Washington, DC. Drawer 1, Program Proposals for IGY (1952–3).
39 Climate change theories were being debated in the late 1940s and early 1950s, and even the popular press latched on to the notion that the earth was warming up. See Fleming, James, *Historical Perspectives on Climate Change* (Oxford, 1998), Chapter 9.
40 See Mayewski, Paul A. and Frank White, *The Ice Chronicles: The Quest to Understand Global Climate Change* (Hanover, 2002), pp. 25–6.
41 Field, William O., Department of Exploration and Field Research, American Geographical Society, to Paul A. Siple, Director of Basic Research Sciences, Office of the Assistant Chief of Staff, Department of the Army, 12 January 1954. William O. Field Collection, University of Alaska Fairbanks, Rasmuson Library, Box 113, 'IGY – 1954'.
42 In August 1953, upon his return from an international IGY meeting in Brussels, Atwood wrote to the Arctic Institute's Linc Washburn, 'If it had not been for our strong belief [that of Atwood and British glaciologist James Mann Wordie] that Glaciological and Climate Change Studies should be included in the program of IGY, this whole subject would have been eliminated by those in attendance at the Brussels meeting. It behooves us to do what we can to encourage other committees to formulate programs in this field'. Atwood to Washburn, 3 August 1953. National Academies of Sciences (NAS) IGY Archive, Washington, DC. Drawer 1, 'Organization USNC 1953'.
43 Field, William O., *With a Camera in my Hands: A Life History as Told to C. Suzanne Brown* (Fairbanks, 2004), p. 88.
44 Field Papers, Correspondence on Mint Julep.
45 Needell, Alan, *Science, Cold War, and the American State* (Washington DC, 2000). Other accounts of the IGY include the classic volume by Sullivan, Walter, *Assault on the Unknown: The International Geophysical Year* (New York, 1961) and The Library of Congress, Congressional Research Service booklet (author Harold Bullis, Analyst in Science and Technology) prepared for the US House of Representatives, Committee on Foreign Affairs, Subcommittee on National Security Policy, *Science, Technology, and American Diplomacy: The Political Legacy of the International Geophysical Year* (Washington DC, 1973).
46 Van Allen, James A., 'Genesis of the International Geophysical Year', *The Polar Times* 21 (1998), p. 5.
47 Handwritten notes by N. C. Gerson, 1st USNC Meeting, 27 March 1953, Box 8 Folder 1, N. C. Gerson Papers, Library of Congress, Manuscripts Division. See also Needell, *Science, Cold War and the American State*, p. 308.

48 Outline of Proposed Glaciological Program for the United States National Committee, International Geophysical Year 1957–8, submitted by Reporter for Glaciology, W. O. Field, 7 May 1954, in NAS/NRC IGY Correspondence, 1954, Glaciology, Drawer 10/44; United States National Report Presented to the Rome Meeting of CSAGI by the US Committee for the International Geophysical Year. Washington, DC, June 1954. In NAS/NRC IGY CSAGI Assemblies, Second, Rome. USNC Report to CSAGI, 1954.
49 NAS IGY Archive, CSAGI Assemblies, Third: Brussels Correspondence, Aug–Oct, 1955, two-page questionnaire annotated by E. O. Hulbert, 2 May 1956.
50 Report of Brussels CSAGI Meeting, 7–14 September 1955, by W. O. Field, Representing Glaciology on the US Delegation, 21 September 1955. NAS IGY Archive, Folder CSAGI Assemblies, Third: Brussels Working Groups, General, 1955. Eventually, Siple's proposal did lead to a world glacial inventory. See National Snow and Ice Data Center, World Glacier Inventory, available at http://nsidc.org/data/docs/noaa/g01130_glacier_inventory/.
51 NAS IGY Archive, CSAGI Assemblies, Third: Brussels Working Groups, General, 1955, Report of Brussels CSAGI meeting 7–14 September 1955, by W. O. Field, Representing Glaciology on the US Delegation, 21 September 1955.
52 Field, Representing Glaciology on the US Delegation, pp. 20–1.
53 NAS IGY Archive, CSAGI Assemblies, Third: Brussels Working Groups, General, 1955, Memorandum from N. C. Gerson to Hugh Odishaw, 6 October 1955.
54 NAS IGY Archive, Drawer 32, Minutes, Arctic Committee, First Meeting of the Ad Hoc Arctic Committee, 1 December 1955.
55 NAS IGY Archive, Drawer 66, The United States IGY Arctic Program, by John C. Reed, Chairman, USNC-Arctic Committee, presented at a special meeting of the US National Committee for the IGY, 27–29 June 1957.
56 NAS IGY Archive, Drawer 30, IGY Arctic 1956, Excerpts from US Delegate Reports, CSAGI Arctic Conference, Stockholm, 22–25 May 1956.
57 Hall, R. Cargill, 'The Truth about Overflights', *Quarterly Journal of Military History*, 9/3 (1997), pp. 24–39.
58 Ibid.
59 NAS IGY Archive, Drawer 32, Minutes, 5th Meeting, Arctic Committee, Press Release from US Department of State, No. 496, 20 September 1956, US Note to the Soviet Embassy on Exchange of Flights over the Arctic Ocean during the International Geophysical Year.
60 Sullivan, *Assault on the Unknown*, p. 34.
61 Hoinkes, Herfried C., 'Glacial Meteorology' in Hugh Odishaw (ed.), *Research in Geophysics, Volume 2: Solid Earth and Interface Phenomena* (Cambridge, MA, 1964), pp. 391–424.
62 'Notes on a Glaciology Program' August 1962 Draft, in William O. Field Papers, Series 17, Box 109, Folder 'Correspondence – CPR Glacier Panel'.
63 Kasser, Peter, *Fluctuations of Glaciers, 1959–1965*. See also *Perennial Ice and Snow Masses: A Guide for Compilation and Assemblage of Data for a World Inventory; Variations of Existing Glaciers: A Guide to International Practices for their Measurement*. All publications were part of the UNESCO series 'Technical Papers in Hydrology' and were produced out of the Paris UNESCO office between 1967 and 1970.
64 ACIA Secretariat, *Arctic Climate Impact Assessment* (Cambridge, 2005).
65 Sturm, Matthew, 'The Spirit of the Arctic and the Next Generation of Arctic Researchers', *Arctic* 53/3 (2000), pp. iii–iv.

NOTES

CHAPTER 7

I would like to thank the editors for inviting me to contribute this chapter in the first place and for the helpful comments of Christy Collis, Alan Hemmings, James R. Ryan and Simon Naylor. I am also indebted to the Leverhulme Trust for the award of a Philip Leverhulme Prize (2005), which enabled me to enjoy extended research leave. I wish to thank Jenny Kynaston for redrawing the figures in this chapter.

1. Anon, 'Antarctica: The Sleeping Beauty', *The Evening Post* (Wellington), 11 June 1955.
2. Archives of New Zealand PM 208 10/1 Part 1, C. Bowden 'New Zealand's Party's Program in Antarctica', 15 September 1957.
3. Sullivan, Walter, *Assault on the Unknown* (New York, 1961).
4. For some of the most important analyses published in the midst or immediate wake of the IGY, see *Guide to the IGY (1957): With a Foreword Written by Sir James Wordie and Contributions by Members of the British National Antarctic Committee for IGY* (London, 1957) and *The Geophysical Monograph Number 1. Antarctica in the IGY* based on a symposium on the Antarctic, co-sponsored by the US National Committee for IGY (Washington, 1956). Other relevant publications include Fraser, R. *Once Round the Sun* (London, 1957).
5. Pyne, Steven, *The Ice: Journey to Antarctica* (London, 2003).
6. Wexler, Harry, 'Antarctic Research in Connection with the International Geophysical Year' *Geophysics* 21 (1956), pp. 681–90. The quote is taken from p. 682.
7. Wilson, E., *The Spiritual History of the Ice* (Basingstoke, 2003) p. 4.
8. Goodrick-Clarke, N., *Black Sun: Aryan Cults, Esoteric Nazism and the Politics of Identity* (New York, 2003), pp. 152–4.
9. For further details, see Dodds, K. *Geopolitics in Antarctica: Views from the Southern Ocean Rim* (Chichester, 1997).
10. Cloud, John, 'Crossing the Olentangy River: The Figure of the Earth and the Military–Industrial–Academic Complex, 1947–1972', *Studies in the History and Philosophy of Modern Physics* 31 (2000), pp. 371–404. The phrase military–industrial–academic complex is first used by Leslie, S., *The Cold War and American Science: The Military-Industrial-Academic Complex at MIT and Stanford* (New York, 2002).
11. Doel, Ronald. E., 'Constituting the Post-war Earth Sciences: The Military's Influence on the Environmental Sciences in the USA after 1945', *Social Studies of Science* 33 (2003), pp. 635–66.
12. Hemmings, A., 'Is Antarctica Demilitarized?' in R. Herr, R. Hall and M. Haward (eds), *Antarctica's Future: Continuity or Change?* (Hobart, 1990).
13. Doel, Ronald E. and Alan Needell, 'Science, Scientists and the CIA: Balancing International Ideals, National Needs, and Professional Opportunities', in R. Jeffrey-Jones and C. Andrew (eds), *Eternal Vigilance? 50 Years of the CIA* (London, 1997), pp. 59–81, p. 67. One area of obvious Communist Party interference with Soviet scientific endeavour was in the area of genetics and the destructive role of Trofim Lysenko.
14. This is discussed further in Dodds, Klaus, *Geopolitics in Antarctica* (Chichester, 1997) Chapter 3.
15. It is important to note that European governments responded differently to the news of Sputnik and most including the British admired rather than feared this achievement. It also came in the aftermath of the Hungarian Uprising of October 1956, which had disillusioned many about the nature of the Soviet regime. On the Sputnik moment and a contemporary assessment, see

Horelick, A., 'Outer Space and Earthbound Politics', *World Politics* 13 (1961), pp. 323–9.
16 Hall, R., 'The Eisenhower Administration and the Cold War: Framing American Astronautics to Serve National Security', *Prologue* 27 (1995), pp. 59–72.
17 Boczek, B., 'The Soviet Union and the Antarctic Regime', *American Journal of International Law* 78 (1984), pp. 834–58.
18 The last meeting of the Special Committee of the IGY (CSAGI) was held in Moscow between 30 July and 8 August 1958.
19 Cited in Dickson, P., *Sputnik: Shock of the Century* (New York, 2001), p. 103.
20 See, for example, Swithinbank, Charles, *Vodka on Ice: A Year with the Russians in the Antarctic* (London, 2001) and Dewart, G. *Antarctic Comrades* (Columbus, 1989).
21 Doel, Ronald, T. Levin and M. Marker, 'Extending Modern Cartography to the Ocean Depths: Military Patronage, Cold War Priorities, and the Heezen-Tharp Mapping Project, 1952–1959', *Journal of Historical Geography* 32 (2006), pp. 605–26.
22 Doel, Ronald E., 'The Earth Sciences and Geophysics', in J. Krige and D. Pestre (eds), *Science in the Twentieth Century* (Amsterdam, 1997), pp. 391–426. The quote is taken from p. 404.
23 Beck, P., *International Politics of Antarctica* (New York, 1986).
24 Mawson, D., *The Home of the Blizzard* (New York, 1998 [1914]).
25 Jones, Max, *The Last Great Quest* (Oxford, 2005).
26 Dodds, Klaus, *Pink Ice: Britain and the South Atlantic Empire* (London, 2002).
27 Seed, P., *Ceremonies of Possession* (Cambridge, 1993) contains important insights into European explorers and their sponsoring nations employed different modes of claiming and colonial settlement.
28 Beck, P., *The International Politics of Antarctica* (New York, 1986); Klotz, F., *America on Ice* (Washington DC, 1990) and Joyner, C. and E. Theis, *Eagle Over the Ice* (Hanover, 1997).
29 The phrase belongs to Hunter-Christie, E., *The Antarctic Problem* (London, 1951).
30 Bertrand, K., *Americans in Antarctica 1775–1948* (New York, 1971); Lovering, J., and J. Prescott, *Last of Lands: Antarctica* (Melbourne, 1979).
31 See Weissburg, G., 'Maps as Evidence in International Boundary Disputes: A Reappraisal', in M. Shaw (ed.), *Titles to Territory* (Aldershot, 2005), pp. 399–421.
32 Cited in Dodds, Klaus, *Pink Ice: Britain and the South Atlantic Empire* (London, 2002), p. 55.
33 See Beck, *International Politics of Antarctica*, for further details on Anglo-Argentine-Chilean rivalries.
34 Dodds, Klaus, 'The Great Game in Antarctica: Britain and the 1959 Antarctic Treaty', *Contemporary British History* 22 (2008), pp. 43–66.
35 See, Needell, Alan, *Science, Cold War and the American State: Lloyd V. Berkner and the Balance of Professional Ideals* (Washington, DC, 2000).
36 Hall, R., 'Casey and the Negotiation of the Antarctic Treaty', in J. Jabour-Green and M. Hawards (eds), *The Antarctic: Past, Present and Future* (Hobart, 2002), pp. 27–33.
37 See Moore, J., 'Tethered to an Iceberg: United States Policy towards the Antarctic 1939–1949', *Polar Record* 35 (1999), pp. 125–34, for further information on the context surrounding events in the 1950s and the United States and the IGY.
38 Moore, J., 'Thirty Seven Degrees Frigid: US–Chilean Relations and the Spectre of Polar Arrivistes, 1950–59', *Diplomacy and Statecraft* 14 (2003), pp. 69–93.

39 Cromley, R., 'We are Losing the Antarctic', *American Mercury* 87 (1958), pp. 5–11.
40 Cited in Elzinga, Aant, 'Antarctica: The Construction of a Continent by and for Science', in E. Crawford, T. Shinn and S. Sorlin (eds), *Denationalising Science* Dordecht, 1993), pp. 73–106. The quote is taken from pages 85–86.
41 Australian Archives A 1838/2 1495/3/2/1 Part 3 JIC Issued Report (November 1956).
42 Petrov, V., 'Soviet Participation in the International Geophysical Year', *Professional Geographer* 13 (1957), pp. 11–14.
43 The literature is substantial but includes Lewis, R., *Continent for Science* (New York, 1965); Briggs, P., *Laboratory at the Bottom of the World* (New York, 1970); and Dickson, P., *Sputnik: The Shock of the Century* (New York, 2001).
44 Kevles, D., 'Cold War and Hot Physics: Science, Security and the American State, 1945–1956', *Historical Studies in the Physical Sciences* 20 (1990), pp. 239–64.
45 Kirsch, Scott, 'Experiments in Progress: Edward Teller's Controversial Geographies', *Ecumene* 5 (1998), pp. 267–86.
46 Sullivan, Walter, 'Antarctica in a Two Power World', *Foreign Affairs* 36 (1957), pp. 154–66.
47 Spiller, J., 'Re-imagining United States Antarctic Research as a Defining Endeavour of a Deserving World Leader: 1957–1991', *Public Understanding of Science* 13 (2004), pp. 31–53, 34.
48 See Point 4 of President Truman's inaugural address delivered in January 1949 and quoted in Hamblin, Jacob, 'Visions of International Scientific Cooperation: The Case of Oceanic Science, 1920–1955', *Minerva* 38 (2000), pp. 392–423.
49 Needell, Alan, 'From Military Research to Big Science: Lloyd Berkner and Science-Statesmanship in the Postwar Era', in P. Galison and B. Hevly (eds), *Big Science* (Stanford, 1992), pp. 290–311.
50 Doel and Needell, 'Science, Scientists and the CIA: Balancing International Ideals, National Needs, and Professional Opportunities', in R. Jeffrey-Jones and C. Andrew (eds), *Eternal Vigilance? 50 Years of the CIA* (London, 1997), pp. 59–81.
51 Cloud, John, 'Imaging the World in a Barrel: CORONA and the Clandestine Convergence of the Earth Sciences', *Social Studies of Science* 31 (2001), pp. 231–51.
52 Sullivan, *Assault on the Unknown*, p.20, and McDougall, W., *The Heavens and Earth: A Political History of the Space Age* (Baltimore, 1985), p. 118.
53 Belanger, Dian, 'The International Geophysical Year in Antarctica: Uncommon Collaborations, Unprecedented Results', *Journal of Government Information* 30 (2004), pp. 482–9. On Lloyd Berkner, see Needell, *Science, Cold War and the American State*.
54 Hall, R., 'The Eisenhower Administration and the Cold War', *Prologue* 27 (1995), pp. 59–72.
55 Farish, Matthew, 'Frontier Engineering: From the Globe to the Body in the Cold War Arctic', *The Canadian Geographer* 50 (2006), pp. 177–96.
56 Elzinga, Aant, 'The Antarctic as Big Science', in E. Hicks and W. van Rossum (eds), *Policy Development and Big Science* (Amsterdam, 1991), pp. 15–25.
57 Sullivan, 'Antarctica in a Two Power World', p. 160.
58 Korsmo, Fae, 'Shaping up Planet Earth: The International Geophysical Year and Communicating Science through Print and Film Media', *Science Communication* 26 (2004), pp. 162–87.

59 Sullivan, *Assault on the Unknown*.
60 See, for further reflections on this issue, Livingstone, David, *Putting Science in its Place* (Chicago, 2002).
61 Buedeler, W., *International Geophysical Year* (Paris, 1957), p. 60.
62 Robin, Gordon, 'Norwegian–British–Swedish Expedition, 1949–52', *Polar Record* 6 (1953), pp. 608–14.
63 'History Ice hounds: UW's Charles Bentley Team, Blazed Antarctic trail', 7 January 2001. Available at: www.jsonline.com/news (accessed 30th November 2006).
64 Wexler, H., 'Antarctic Research in Connection with the International Geophysical Year', *Geophysics* 21 (1956), pp. 681–90, 683.
65 See, for further analysis, Dean, Katrina, Simon Naylor, Martin Siegert and Simone Turchetti, 'Data in Antarctic Science and Politics', *Social Studies in Science* 38 (2008), pp. 571–604.
66 See the review in Lewis, R., *A Continent for Science* (London, 1965).
67 There is an interesting parallel to be made between this mapping and recent Australian attempts to map the ocean floor so that it can claim the seabed off the Australian Antarctic Territory as an Australian continental shelf under UNCLOS.
68 Wexler, 'Antarctic Research in Connection with the International Geophysical Year', p. 690.
69 Royal Society archives CMB 106a Letter from Sir David Brunt to D Martin, 12 May 1960.
70 Burns, Robin, 'Stories about place: The Antarctic as an International Reserve for Science', in Christopher Houston et al. (eds), *Imagined Places: The Politics of Making Space* (Melbourne, 1998), pp. 159–68. On Australia and the Antarctic see Hains, B. *The Ice and Inland* (Melbourne, 2002).
71 Elzinga, 'Antarctica: The Construction of a Continent by and for Science', p. 88.
72 Statement made by Director of the British Survey, Professor Chris Rapley (June 27 2006). Available at: www.antarcticconnection.com (accessed 23 November 2006).

CHAPTER 8

My thanks to Jane Gregory, Michael Kandiah and the editors for their comments on an earlier version of the text. The early part of this chapter builds on a brief survey article by the author published on the *History in Focus* website: http://www.history.ac.uk/ihr/Focus/cold/articles/godwin.html.

1 The term 'Britnik' was used in the tabloid press: see 'Britnik Won't Take Animals' in *The Daily Sketch*, 30 July 1959.
2 Bulkeley, Rip, *The Sputniks Crisis and Early United States Space Policy* (London, 1991), also the articles in Launius, Roger et al. (eds), *Reconsidering Sputnik* (Amsterdam, 2000).
3 The complex, often seemingly contradictory, nature of civil/military interactions has been identified by a number of scholars in relation to various fields of cold war science, most notably by Ronald Doel, 'Earth Sciences and Geophysics', in John Krige and Dominique Pestre (eds), *Twentieth Century Science* (Amsterdam, 1997), pp. 402–3. Joel Hagen gives an account of the incongruous way in which the field of systems ecology was essentially founded and sponsored by the US Atomic Energy Commission in Hagen, J. B., in *An Entangled Bank* (New Jersey, 1992), pp. 100–21. For discussion of civil/military interactions in relation to early British space activities, see Whyte, Neil, 'United Kingdom Space Policy, 1955–1960', unpublished PhD thesis,

NOTES

University of London, 1996; also Godwin, Matthew, *The Skylark Rocket, British Space Science and the European Space Research Organisation, 1957–1972* (Paris, 2007). Fraser MacDonald (in this volume) develops this theme in relation to the Corporal missile, noting the interchange of the terms 'rocket' and 'missile' and extending the analysis to include the assimilation of the military Corporal missile into popular culture.

4   Bulkeley, *The Sputniks Crisis*, p. 89.
5   Ibid., pp. 92–4.
6   Needell, Alan, *Science, Cold War and the American State* (Amsterdam, 2000), p. 299.
7   Massey, Harrie and Malcolm Robins, *History of British Space Science* (Cambridge, 1980), p. 2.
8   Bulkeley, *The Sputniks Crisis*, pp. 90–2.
9   Needell, *Science, Cold War*, pp. 298–9.
10 Ibid., pp. 3–4, 298; Berkner was even advising the Central Intelligence Agency (CIA) on UFOs in the early 1950s. See Needell, *Science, Cold War*, p. 306.
11 Needell, *Science, Cold War*, p. 328.
12 The RAND Corporation was an American military think-tank which conducted studies on behalf of the US military. See Needell, *Science, Cold War*, p. 329.
13 Needell, *Science, Cold War*, p. 334.
14 Quoted in Needell, *Science, Cold War*, p. 340.
15 Ibid., p. 341.
16 Bulkeley, *The Sputniks Crisis*, pp. 104–6.
17 Osgood, Kenneth, 'Before Sputnik: National Security and the Formation of US Outer Space Policy', in Launius, Roger et al. (eds), *Reconsidering Sputnik* (Amsterdam, 2000), pp. 179–229, 211.
18 The following contemporary study looks at the analogy between space and the Antarctic in trying to devise a legal framework for international control: Jessup, Philip and Taubenfeld, Howard, *Controls for Outer Space* (London, 1959).
19 See Krige, John, 'Technology, Foreign Policy and International Co-operation in Space', in Dick, Stephen and Roger Launius (eds), *Critical Issues in the History of Spaceflight* (Washington, DC, 2006), pp. 239–60, 241.
20 America (and to some extent Britain) were reluctant to set over-bearing restrictions on activities in space in case this undermined their own military programmes. In so doing it was realised that the Soviets would also be unlikely to want to discuss restrictive laws which curtailed their own space interests. See The National Archives, Kew [henceforward TNA] FO 371/163359: jkt IAS71/6: From JAC Gutteridge to FA Vallat. 30/01/1962.
21 For an account of the European response to Sputnik, see Krige, John, 'Building a Third Space Power: Western European Reactions to Sputnik at the Dawn of the Space Age', in Launius, Roger et al. (eds), *Reconsidering Sputnik* (Amsterdam, 2000), pp. 289–307.
22 TNA CAB 128/31: CC(57) 72 Conclusions.
23 TNA CAB 124/2811: JIC (57) 119, Some Reasons for Soviet Technological Success. 15/11/1957. For further details on the JIC and Sputnik see Cradock, Percy, *Know Your Enemy: How the Joint Intelligence Committee Saw the World* (London, 2002).
24 For details of Anglo-American nuclear co-operation, see Simpson, John, *Independent Nuclear State: The United States, Britain and the Military Atom* (Basingstoke, 1986).
25 Quoted in Whyte, Neil, and Philip Gummett 'The Making of the United Kingdom's First Space Policy', *Minerva* 35 (1997), pp. 139–69,142.
26 Whyte, 'United Kingdom', p. 34.

27 TNA FO 371/157317: jkt IAS61/68: Arnold. W. Frutkin, 'International Programs of NASA'.
28 Massey and Robins, *History of British*, p. 67.
29 See Krige, John, *American Hegemony and the Postwar Reconstruction of Science in Europe* (Cambridge, Mass, 2006); also Krige, 'Technology, Foreign Policy'.
30 For details of the Skylark programme, see Godwin, *The Skylark Rocket*.
31 Massey and Robins, *History of British*, p. 62.
32 For details of the first British space policy, see Whyte and Gummett, 'The Making'; also Godwin, *The Skylark Rocket*.
33 Massey and Robins, *History of British*, p. 71; for more detail on the early phases of Anglo-American space interactions and on this agreement, see Whyte, 'United Kingdom', pp. 107–13, 127–34.
34 TNA DSIR 23/32776: Aeronautical Research Council: The Ariel I Satellite Project and Some Scientific Results. M. O. Robins. October 1963, p. 1.
35 Massey and Robins, *History of British*, p. 86.
36 HC Deb, 29 July 1959, vol. 610, no. 157, c86W.
37 'British Satellites in Two Years' in *The Manchester Guardian*, 30 July 1959.
38 TNA CAB 124/2273: From unknown to Henry Billingsley, 30 July 1959.
39 TNA DSIR 49/1: Publicity for Launching S51. Meeting Notes. 18 April 1962.
40 TNA DSIR 23/28491: Progress of the Joint US/UK Satellite Programme using NASA Scout Vehicles. 03 February 1961.
41 For technical details of the Scout rocket see TNA DSIR 23/28488: Note on Project Scout. 08 March 1961.
42 Massey and Robins, *History of British*, pp. 82–4.
43 TNA AVIA 92/148: From Foreign Office to Washington Embassy. 06 April 1962.
44 TNA CAB 124/2265: The probable geophysical and astronomical effects of the high-altitude explosion [Paper by Lovell sent to Prime Minister]. 21 May 1962.
45 'Sir Bernard Criticises US' in *The Guardian*. 30 May 1962.
46 TNA PREM 11/4449: From Harold Macmillan to Sir Harry Legge-Bourke. 25 June 1962.
47 An indictment of the United States at the Hague International Court was considered by several governments and which Legge-Bourke indicated to Macmillan he would support.
48 TNA CAB 124/2265: From Roger Quirk to Langdon et al. Proposed US High Altitude Nuclear Explosion. 04/06/1962.
49 TNA FO 371/163344: jkt IAS11/69: Statement by the Soviet Government dated 3 June 1962 on the United States high-altitude nuclear explosions.
50 TNA FO 371/163133: jkt IAD 29/7: Press Release: AEC and DOD Announce High Altitude Tests. 28 May 1962.
51 'Space Bomb was of 1.4 Megatons' in *The Yorkshire Post*, 22 September 1962.
52 'Nuclear Explosion 200 Miles High' in *The Times*, 10 July 1962.
53 TNA FO 371/165244: jkt GP101/1: From Foreign Office to Washington Embassy. 18 July 1962.
54 TNA FO 371/165244: jkt GP101/2: From Washington Embassy to Foreign Office. 18 July 1962.
55 TNA FO 371/165244: jkt GP101/3: From Foreign Office to Washington Embassy. 21 August 1962.
56 TNA FO 371/165244: jkt GP101/3: From RC Hope-Jones to P Wilkinson. 21 August 1962.
57 TNA FO 371/165244: jkt GP101/4: From Washington Embassy to Foreign Office. 21 August 1962.
58 TNA FO 371/165244: jkt GP101/14: C. Herzig to TJ Bligh. 20/09/1962; From Foreign Office to Washington Embassy. 20 September 1962.

NOTES

59   In the following years several reports were published on the scientific results obtained by Ariel on the nuclear explosion. In particular, Massey and his colleagues published a special series of papers: *Proceedings of the Royal Society: Series A Mathemetical and Physics Sciences* 218/1387 (1964).
60   TNA FO 371/165244: jkt GP101/17: Draft File Note. 30 October 1962.
61   TNA FO 371/171044: jkt GP1152/9: Discussion with Mr Richard N Gardner Deputy Assistant Secretary of State for International Organisation Affairs State Department. June 28 1962.
62   TNA DSIR 23/32776: Aeronautical Research Council: The Ariel I Satellite Project and Some Scientific Results. M. O. Robins. October 1963, p. 1.
63   Booda, Larry, 'Wiesner, Charyak Ordered Starad Secrecy' in *Aviation Week*. 15 April 1963.
64   Massey and Robins, *History of British*, p. 82.
65   TNA FO 371/165244: jkt GP101/6: From Foreign Office to Washington Embassy. 29 August 1962.
66   TNA FO 371/165244: jkt GP101/6: From Foreign Office to Washington Embassy. 29 August 1962.
67   TNA FO 361/165244: jkt 101/8: From JF Hosie to RN Quirk. 04 September 1962.
68   Comment in the *New Scientist*. 06 September 1962.
69   TNA PREM 11/3967: From Hailsham to Macmillan. 10 September 1962.
70   'Please Leave this Space as You Would Wish to Find It ... ' in *The Economist*. 25 May 1963.
71   TNA FO 371/165244: jkt GP101/8: From JF Hosie to RN Quirk. 04 September 1962.
72   See TNA CAB 124/2265: From F. Graham Smith to Hailsham. 01 October 1962; From Martin Ryle to Hailsham. 01 October 1962.
73   TNA CAB 124/2263: Notes of a lecture on West Ford. 14 November 1960.
74   Ibid.
75   Ibid.
76   Levin, Tanya, 'Contaminating Space: Project West Ford and Scientific Communities, 1958–1965', unpublished MA thesis, University of Alaska Fairbanks, 2000, p. 79. See Levin for a detailed discussion of the West Ford project.
77   Both incidents were grouped together and condemned by veteran space journalist Patrick Moore (now Sir) in his book, *Space in the Sixties* (Harmondsworth, 1963), pp. 75–81.
78   Levin, 'Contaminating Space', pp. 5–9.
79   Ibid., p. 13.
80   Stubbs, Peter, 'May Rockets Disturb the Weather', *New Scientist*, 01 August 1963, pp. 230–3.
81   Godwin: *The Skylark Rocket*, p. 152.
82   For details of the outcome of West Ford, see Levin, 'Contaminating Space'.
83   The working party members were: Dr J. A. Ratcliffe (Director of Radio Research, DSIR) (chair); Prof D. E. Blackwell (Oxford); Dr J. V. Dunworth (National Physical Laboratory); Prof Sir Bernard Lovell (Manchester); Prof Sir Willis Jackson (Imperial); D. G. King-Hele (Royal Aircraft Establishment); Prof Martin Ryle (Cambridge); H. Stanesby (General Post Office); C. Williams (Royal Aircraft Establishment); Dr R. Wilson (Atomic Energy Research Establishment). There were two consultants: Prof H. Elliot (Imperial College London); Dr AP Willmore (University College London). The terms of reference were 'a). to consider, on the basis of available unclassified information, the effects of high level nuclear explosions on scientific experiments; b). to report their views to the Minister, through the Steering Group.'

84 Extract from a speech by Senator Albert Gore, as United States representative to the First Committee of the United Nations General Assembly, 3 December 1962, cited in 'The Effects of High Altitude Nuclear Explosions on Scientific Experiments', cmnd. 2029. (London, 1963).
85 TNA CAB 124/2265: Roger Quirk to Frank Turnbull. 11 February 1963.
86 Published as 'The Effects of High Altitude Nuclear Explosions on Scientific Experiments', cmnd. 2029. (London, 1963).
87 TNA CAB 124/2266: From Zuckerman to Minister of Defence. 29 April 1963.
88 For example, see HC Deb 26 March 1963, Vol. 674 c. 1119–1120.
89 TNA PREM 11/4449: From P de Zulueta to Harold Macmillan. 03 May 1963.
90 TNA PREM 11/4449: From Sir Harry Legge-Bourke to Harold Macmillan. 14 September 1962; In a similar side-swipe at least one official in Whitehall had noted that a proportion of the scientists opposed to the Starfish test were 'probably prejudiced because they were in a priori sympathy with the CND [Campaign for Nuclear Disarmament]' see TNA FO 371/165244: jkt GP101/7: File note by ADF Pemberton-Pigott. 23 October 1962.
91 For example see TNA FO 371/163344: jkt IAS11/69: Statement by the Soviet Government dated 3 June 1962 on the United States high altitude nuclear explosions.
92 TNA CAB 124/2266: From MW Hodges to JF Hosie. 28 June 1963.
93 For details of the Marshall plan and American plans for post-war science in Europe, see Krige, *American Hegemony*.
94 Freedman, M, 'A Shabby Test' in *The Guardian*, 1 January 1963.

CHAPTER 9

1 Bragg, James W., *Development of the Corporal: The Embryo of the Army Missile Programme*, Historical Monography no. 4 (Redstone, Alabama, 1961), p. x.
2 See Graham, Stephen, 'Vertical Geopolitics: Baghdad and After', *Antipode* 26/1 (2004), pp. 12–23.
3 Virilio, Paul, 'Interviewed by James der Derian', *Speed: Technology, Media, Society*, 1/4 http://proxy.arts.uci.edu/~nideffer/_SPEED_/1.4/articles/derderian.html, accessed 7 March 2002.
4 Cosgrove, Denis, *Apollo's Eye: A Cartographic Genealogy of the Earth in the Western Imagination* (Baltimore, 2001).
5 Cosgrove, Denis, 'Contested Global Visions: *One-World, Whole-Earth*, and the Apollo Space Photographs', *Annals of the Association of American Geographers* 84/2 (1994), pp. 270–94.
6 Redfield, P. *Space in the Tropics: From Convicts to Rockets in French Guinana* (Berkeley, 2000), p. 115.
7 Sorrenson, Richard, 'The Ship as a Scientific Instrument in the Eighteenth Century', *Osiris* (Chicago, 1996), pp. 221–36, 221. See also DeVorkin, D., *Science with a Vengeance : How the American Military Created the Space Sciences in the V-2 Era* (New York, 1992).
8 Driver, Felix, *Geography Militant: Cultures of Exploration and Empire* (Oxford, 2001); Ryan, James, 'Our Home on the Ocean: Lady Brassey's Voyages on the Sunbeam, 1874–1887', *Journal of Historical Geography* 32/3 (2005), pp. 579–604; Ogborn, Miles, 'Writing Travels: Power, Knowledge and Ritual on the English East India Company's Early Voyages', *Transactions of the Institute of British Geographers* NS 27 (2002), pp. 155–71; Lambert, David, Martins, Lucianna, and Ogborn, Miles, 'Currents, Visions and Voyages: Historical Geographies of the Sea', *Journal of Historical Geography* 32 (2006), pp. 479–93.

9   Bille, M. and E. Lishock, *The First Space Race: Launching the World's First Satellite* (College Station, 2004); Siddiqi, Asif, *Sputnik and the Soviet Space Challenge* (Gainesville, 2003).
10   Following most of the military usage, I refer to the 'Corporal missile' throughout.
11   DeVorkin, *Science with a Vengeance*, p. 154.
12   It does not merit a single mention in the Walter McDougall's otherwise authoritative work: McDougall, Walter, *The Heavens and the Earth: A Political History of the Space Age* (Baltimore, 1997).
13   Strictly speaking, it was the WAC Corporal in combination with a V-2 that held this distinction.
14   Livingstone, David, *The Geographical Tradition: Episodes in the History of a Contested Enterprise* (Oxford, 1992), p. 77.
15   Driver, *Geography Militant*; Smith, Neil, and Godlewska, Anne, *Geography and Empire: Critical Studies in the History of Geography* (Oxford, 1994).
16   Benjamin, M., *Rocket Dreams: How the Space Age Shaped Our Vision of a World Beyond* (London, 2003), p. 46.
17   Turner, Frederick Jackson, 'The Significance of the Frontier in American History', in *The Frontier in American History* (New York, 1920). I am grateful to Innes Kieghren for this observation. See also Nye, David E., *The American Technological Sublime* (Cambridge, Mass., 1996).
18   Redfield, P., 'The Half-Life of Empire in Outer Space', *Social Studies of Science* 32/5–6 (2002), pp. 791–825, 795.
19   MacDonald, Fraser, 'Geopolitics and the Vision Thing: Regarding Britain and America's First Nuclear Missile', *Transactions of the Institute of British Geographers* 31/1 (2006), pp. 53–71.
20   Clark, I., *Nuclear Diplomacy and the Special Relationship: Britain's Deterrent and America, 1957–1962* (Oxford, 1994).
21   MacDonald, Fraser, 'Anti-Astropolitik: Outer Space and the Orbit of Geography', *Progress in Human Geography* 31/5 (2007), pp. 592–615.
22   Redfield, 'The Half-Life of Empire in Outer Space', p. 792.
23   The converse is also true; the development of Earthly geographies was necessary for missile development, the geodetic measurement of the Earth being required for missile accuracy. See Warner, D. J., 'Political Geodesy: The Army, the Air Force and the World Geodetic System of 1960', *Annals of Science* 59 (2002), pp. 363–89.
24   Bragg, *Development of the Corporal*, p. ix.
25   Formerly called the Guggenheim Aeronautical Laboratories, California Institute of Technology (GALCIT).
26   Interview of William H Pickering II, former director of JPL, by Shirley K Cohen, Caltech Archives Oral Histories, http://oralhistories.library.caltech.edu/86/, accessed 26 March 2007.
27   In engineering terms, the 'attitude' of a body is its orientation as perceived in a certain frame of reference.
28   Previously named Operation Overcast and renamed Operation Paperclip in March 1946.
29   None were delivered from Germany in flyable condition; General Electric won the contract to re-build and upgrade the V-2s.
30   This claim was contested. Earlier high-altitude balloons had reached over 13 miles high in 1935; Holliday, Clyde T., 'Seeing the Earth from 80 Miles Up', *National Geographic* 98 (1950), pp. 511–28, 511.
31   Holliday, 'Seeing the Earth from 80 Miles Up', p. 512.
32   Ibid.

33 Dahlquist, John E., 'Foreword', in Nels A. Parsons Jnr, *Guided Missiles in War and Peace* (Cambridge, Mass., 1956), p. 6.
34 Johnson, S. B., *The Secret of Apollo: Systems Management in American and European Space Programs* (Baltimore, 2002), p. 84.
35 Bragg, *Development of the Corporal*, p. 176.
36 See MacDonald, 'Geopolitics and the Vision Thing'.
37 Michael Neufeld, *Von Braun: Dreamer of Space, Engineer of War* (London, 2007), p. 351.
38 Ó Tuathail, Gerard, *Critical Geopolitics: The Politics of Writing Global Space* (Minneapolis, 1996); Dalby, Simon, 'Critical Geopolitics: Discourse, Difference and Dissent', *Environment and Planning D: Society and Space* 9/3 (1991), pp. 261–83.
39 Smith, Neil, 'Is a Critical Geopolitics Possible? Foucault, Class and the Vision Thing', *Political Geography* 19 (2000), pp. 365–71; Heffernan, Michael, 'Balancing Visions: Comments on Gerard Ó Tuathail's Critical Geopolitics', *Political Geography* 19 (2000), pp. 347–52; Thrift, Nigel, 'It's the Little Things', in Klaus Dodds and David Atkinson (eds), *Geopolitical Traditions: A Century of Geopolitical Thought* (London, 2000), pp. 380–87.
40 See for instance: Sharp, Joanne, 'Hegemony, Popular Culture and Geopolitics: The Reader's Digest and the Construction of Danger', *Political Geography* 15 (1996), pp. 557–70; Sharp, Joanne, *Condensing the Cold War: The Reader's Digest and American Identity* (Minneapolis, 2000); Dittmer, J., 'Captain America's Empire: Reflections on Identity, Popular Culture, and Post-9/11 Geopolitics', *Annals of the Association of American Geographers* 95 (2005) pp. 626–43; Dodds, Klaus, 'Licensed to Stereotype: Popular Geopolitics, James Bond and the Spectre of Balkanism', *Geopolitics* 8 (2003) pp. 125–56; Power, M., and Crampton, J., 'Reel Geopolitics: Cinemato-Graphing Political Space', *Geopolitics* 10 (2005), pp. 193–203.
41 Thrift, 'It's the Little Things'.
42 Hughes, J., 'Deconstructing the Bomb: Recent Perspectives on Nuclear History', *British Journal for the History of Science* 27 (2004), pp. 455–64, 456.
43 Canaday, John, *The Nuclear Muse: Literature, Physics and the First Atomic Bombs* (Madison, 2000); Boyer, Paul, *By the Bomb's Early Light: American Thought and Culture at the Dawn of the Atomic Age* (New York, 1985).
44 Canaday, The Nuclear Muse, p. 223.
45 Taylor, Bryan C., 'Our Bruised Arms Hung Up as Monuments: Nuclear Iconography in Post-Cold War Culture', *Critical Studies in Media Communications* 20 (2003), pp. 1–24, 6.
46 Carter, D., *The Final Frontier: The Rise and Fall of the American Rocket State* (New York, 1988).
47 Fleming, Ian, *Goldfinger* (London, 1959).
48 Dodds, Klaus, 'Screening Geopolitics: James Bond and the early Cold War Films', *Geopolitics* 10 (2005), pp. 266–89; Dodds, Klaus, 'Popular Geopolitics and Audience Dispositions: James Bond and the Internet Movie Database (IMDb)', *Transactions of the Institute of British Geographers* 31 (2006), pp. 116–30; Dodds, Klaus, 'Licensed to Stereotype: Geopolitics, James Bond and the Spectre of Balkanism', *Geopolitics* 8/2 (2003), pp. 125–56.
49 See for instance Der Derian, James, 'War as Game', *The Brown Journal of World Affairs* 10/1 (2003), pp. 37–48; Huizinga, J., *Homo Ludens: A Study of the Play-Element in Culture* (London, 1971).
50 Philo, C. and Smith, F. 'Guest Editorial: Political Geographies of Children and Young People', *Space and Polity* 7/2 (2003), pp. 99–115.
51 Holloway, Sarah, and Valentine, Gill, *Children's Geographies: Playing, Living, Learning* (London, 2000).

52 Harker, C., 'Playing and Affective Time-Spaces', *Children's Geographies* 3/1 (2005), pp. 47–62; Fleming, D., *Powerplay: Toys as Popular Culture* (Manchester, 1996); Sutton-Smith, B., *The Ambiguity of Play* (Boston, 1997); Winnicott, D. W., *Playing and Reality* (London, 1971).
53 Thrift, Nigel, 'Closer to the Machine? Intelligent Environments, New Forms of Possession and the Rise of the Supertoy', *Cultural Geographies* 10 (2003), pp. 389–407.
54 Thrift, 'Closer to the Machine?', p. 390.
55 The Toyman, Dinky Toys News, *Meccano Magazine* 44/11 (1959), p. 498.
56 See MacDonald, 'Geopolitics and the Vision Thing'; MacDonald, Fraser, 'The Last Outpost of Empire: Rockall and the Cold War', *Journal of Historical Geography* 32 (2006), pp. 627–47.
57 Van Cleemput, M., *The Great Book of Corgi, 1956–1983* (London, 1989).
58 Fleming, *Powerplay*, p. 68.
59 Ibid.
60 Benjamin, Walter, 'Toys and Play: Marginal Notes on a Monumental Work', in Michael Jennings, Howard Eiland and Gary Smith (eds), *Walter Benjamin Selected Writings. Volume II* (Cambridge, 1999).
61 Sutton-Smith, B., *Toys as Culture* (New York, 1986), p. 204.
62 Fleming, *Powerplay*, p. 33.
63 Richardson, Mike, *Collecting Dinky Toys* (London, 2001), p. 6.
64 Fleming, *Powerplay*, pp. 67, 90.
65 Thrift, 'Closer to the Machine?', p. 395.
66 A mint condition Dinky Corporal might fetch US $800.
67 Sutton-Smith, *The Ambiguity of Play*, p. 192.
68 Oldenziel, R., 'Boys and Their Toys: The Fisher Body Craftsman's Guild, 1930–1968, and the Making of a Male Technical Domain' in R. Horowitz (ed.), *Boys and Their Toys? Masculinity, Technology and Class in America* (New York, 2001), pp. 139–68.
69 Haber, Heinz, 'Space Satellites: Tools of Earth Research', *National Geographic* 104/4 (1956), pp. 486–509, 494.
70 See Kirsch, Scott, *Proving Grounds: Project Ploughshare and the Unrealized Dream of Nuclear Earth-Moving* (New Jersey, 2006).
71 See MacDonald, 'Anti-Astropolitik'.
72 See Cervino, M., S. Corradini, and S. Davolio, 'Is the Peaceful use of Outer Space Being Ruled Out?', *Space Policy* 19 (2003), pp. 231–7.
73 Redfield, *Space in the Tropics*, p. 814.
74 Lane, K. Maria D., 'Geographers of Mars: Cartographic Inscription and Exploration Narrative in Late Victorian Representations of the Red Planet', *Isis* 96 (2005), pp. 477–506; Lane, K. Maria D., 'Mapping the Mars Canal Mania: Cartographic Projection and the Creation of a Popular Icon', *Imago Mundi: The International Journal for the History of Cartography* 58/2 (2006), pp. 198–211; Dittmer, J., 'Colonialism and Place Creation in Mars Pathfinder Media Coverage', *Geographical Review* 97/1 (2007), pp. 112–30.
75 Cosgrove, Denis, 'Moon', in S. Harrison, S. Pile and N. Thrift (eds), *Patterned Ground: Entanglements of Nature and Culture* (London, 2004), pp. 222–3.

CHAPTER 10

1 Muir, Peter, 'Desert Tracks', in Ronele and Eric Gard, *Canning Stock Route: A Traveller's Guide* 2nd ed. (Wembley Downs, WA, 1995).
2 Glover, Ian and Allan Whiting, 'Where the Blazes?', *Experience* 15 (1996), pp. 8–16, 11.

3 Glover, Ian and Allan Whiting, 'Salt on the Tale', *Experience* 16 (1997), pp. 8–16, 14.
4 Glover, Ian and Allan Whiting,, 'Desperation Well', *Experience* 18 (1997), pp. 8–15, 11.
5 Glover and Whiting: 'Desperation Well', p. 11.
6 Ibid., p.14.
7 Ibid., p.13; This phrase invokes David Carnegie's 1898 Gibson Desert exploration narrative, *Spinifex and Sand: A Narrative of Five Years' Pioneering and Exploration in Western Australia* (Melbourne, 1973).
8 Glover and Whiting, 'Desperation Well', p. 14.
9 Ibid.
10 The capitalization will be used throughout this study in order to signal Footsteps expeditions as a distinct phenomenon.
11 Cresswell, Tim, 'Imagining the Nomad: Mobility and the Postmodern Primitive', in George Benko and Ulf Strohmayer (eds), *Space and Social Theory: Interpreting Modernity and Postmodernity* (Oxford, 1997), pp. 360–82, 360.
12 Lefebvre, Henri, *The Production of Space* Trans. Donald Nicholson-Smith (Oxford, 1984); de Certeau, Michel, *The Practice of Everyday Life*, Trans. Steven F. Randall (Berkeley, 1984).
13 Ryan, Simon, *The Cartographic Eye: How Explorers Saw Australia* (Cambridge, 1996), p. 3.
14 Haynes, Roslynn, *Seeking the Centre: The Australian Desert in Literature, Art, and Film* (Cambridge, 1998).
15 Dyer, Richard, *White* (London, 1997).
16 While people other than white Australians go on Footsteps expeditions, all Footsteps accounts discussed here are written by Australians who identify themselves as Anglo-Australian or white.
17 The term 'Indigenous' refers to all of Australia's indigenous inhabitants, both Aboriginal and Torres Strait Islander. Because Aboriginal people and groups are the inhabitants and original owners of Australia's deserts, the term 'Aboriginal' will be used through much of this chapter.
18 McInerney, Graham and Alec Mathieson, *Across the Gibson* (Adelaide, 1978), p. 29.
19 Eriksen, Ray, *West of Centre* (London, 1972), p. 159.
20 Rothwell, Nicolas, 'Ride of Rediscovery', *The Weekend Australian*, 6–7 May 2000, 'Books' section, p. 13.
21 Gebicki, Michael, 'Exploring the Past', *The Australian Way*, March 2001, pp. 100–6, 102.
22 *Conquering the Continent* Videotape (South Australia, 1990).
23 McInerney and Mathieson, *Across the Gibson*.
24 Kelly, Kieran, *Hard Country Hard Men: In the Footsteps of Gregory* (Sydney, 2002).
25 Eriksen, *West of Centre*.
26 McClintock, Anne, *Imperial Leather: Race, Gender and Sexuality in the Colonial Contest* (London: Routledge, 1995), p. 45.
27 McClintock, *Imperial Leather*, p. 45.
28 Morris, Meaghan, *Too Soon, Too Late: History and Popular Culture* (Bloomington, 1998), p. 98.
29 Glover and Whiting, 'Salt on the Tale'.
30 *The Madigan Line* Videotape (Melbourne, 1981).
31 Flannery, Tim, *The Explorers* (Melbourne, 1998), p. 3.
32 Carter, Paul, *The Road to Botany Bay: An Essay in Spatial History* (London, 1987), p. 51.

33 Certeau, *Practice of Everyday Life*, p. 143.
34 Frost, Alan, 'New South Wales as Terra Nullius: The British Denial of Aboriginal Land Rights', in Susan Janson and Stuart Macintyre (eds), *Through White Eyes* (Sydney: Allen & Unwin, 1990), pp. 65–76, 66.
35 Seed, Patricia, *Ceremonies of Possession in Europe's Conquest of the New World 1492–1640* (Cambridge, 1995).
36 Frost, 'New South Wales as Terra Nullius', p. 67; Seed, *Ceremonies of Possession*.
37 For instance, *New South Wales Land Rights Act* (1983), South Australian *Pitjantjatjara Land Rights Act* (1981), South Australian *Maralinga Tjarutja Land Rights Act* (1984), Western Australian *Aboriginal Heritage Act* (1972).
38 Gelder, Ken, and Jacobs, Jane, *Uncanny Australia: Sacredness and Identity in a Postcolonial Nation* (Melbourne, 1998), p. 81.
39 Rowse, Tim, *After Mabo: Interpreting Indigenous Traditions* (Melbourne, 1993), p. 246.
40 Rowse, *After Mabo*; Maddock, Kenneth, *Anthropology, Law, and the Definition of Australian Aboriginal Rights to Land* (Nijmegan, 1980); Peterson, Nicholas, and Marcia Langton, *Aborigines, Land, and Land Rights* (Canberra, 1983).
41 Read, Peter, 'Northern Territory' in Ann McGrath (ed.), *Contested Ground: Australian Aborigines Under the British Crown* (Sydney, 1995), pp. 269–305, 293.
42 Hawke, Steve, and Michael Gallagher, *Noonkanbah: Whose Land, Whose Law* (Fremantle, 1989), p. 28.
43 Rowse, Tim, 'Mabo and Moral Anxiety', *Meanjin* 52/2 (1993), pp. 229–52, 232.
44 *The Madigan Line*.
45 *Conquering the Continent*.
46 McInerney and Mathieson, *Across the Gibson*, p. 5.
47 Ibid., p. 24.
48 Ibid., p. 30.
49 Ibid., p. 21.
50 Carter, *The Road to Botany Bay*, p. 267.
51 McNaughton, Howard, 'The Speaking Abject: The Impossible Possible World of Realized Empire', in Chris Tiffin and Alan Lawson (eds), *De-Scribing Empire: Post-Colonialism and Textuality* (London, 1994), pp. 218–29, 225.
52 Foster, Jim, and Cheryl, 'Sturt's Country', *4x4 Australia* July 1990, pp. 70–6, 75.
53 Gebicki, 'Exploring the Past', p. 100
54 McInerney and Mathieson, *Across the Gibson*, p. 7.
55 Ibid.
56 Ibid.
57 Ibid.
58 Eriksen, *West of Centre*, p. 39.
59 Ryan, *The Cartographic Eye*.
60 Ibid., p. 91.
61 McInerney and Mathieson, *Across the Gibson*, pp. 14–15.
62 Glover and Whiting, 'Salt on the Tale', p. 12.
63 Ibid., p. 12.
64 Ibid., p. 14.
65 Carter, *Road to Botany Bay*, p. 335.
66 Glover and Whiting, 'Salt on the Tale', p. 14.
67 McInerney and Mathieson, *Across the Gibson*, p. 23.
68 Ibid., p. 23.
69 Ibid., p. 64.
70 Ibid., p. 24.

CHAPTER 11

1 See also special issue on 'Science and Politics: The International Geophysical Year, 1957-8', *Journal of Historical Geography* 34 (2008), pp. 555–657.
2 The Cold War provides only one context of course. In some key respects the representation of the Apollo missions, as the name suggests, drew on older ways of seeing and imagining the whole earth, see Cosgrove, Denis E., *Apollo's Eye: A Cartographic Genealogy of the Earth in the Western Imagination* (Baltimore, 2001).
3 See especially Peter Hansen's exemplary study of the geopolitics of the Everest ascent: 'Confetti of Empire: The Conquest of Everest in Nepal, India, Britain and New Zealand', *Comparative Studies in Society and History* 42 (2000), pp. 307–32.
4 'Sir Ranulph Fiennes OBE, keynote speaker and motivational speaker', http://www.nyt.co.uk/sir.htm, accessed 27 October 2008.
5 Quoted in Stafford, Robert A., *Scientist of Empire: Sir Roderick Murchison, Scientific Exploration and Victorian Imperialism* (Cambridge, 1989), p. 59.
6 Endersby, J., *Imperial Nature: Joseph Hooker and the Practices of Victorian Science* (Chicago, 2008), pp. 20–8.
7 For various examples, see Camerini, Jane, 'Evolution, Biogeography, and Maps: An Early History of Wallace's Line', *Isis* 84 (1993), pp. 700–27; Kohler, Robert E. *Landscapes and Labscapes: Exploring the Lab–Field Border in Biology* (Chicago, 2002); Bravo, M. and S. Sörlin (eds), *Narrating the Arctic: A Cultural History of Nordic Scientific Practices* (Sagamore Beach, 2002); Lane, K. M., 'Geographers of Mars: Cartographic Inscription and Exploration Narrative in Late Victorian Representations of the Red Planet', *Isis* 96 (2005), pp. 477–506.
8 Barnes, Trevor and Matthew Farish, 'Between Regions: Science, Militarism and American Geography from World War to Cold War', *Annals of the Association of American Geographers* 96 (2006), pp. 807–26.
9 Sörlin, S., 'Narratives and Counter-Narratives of Climate Change: North Atlantic Glaciology and Meteorology, c. 1930–1955', *Journal of Historical Geography* 35 (2009), pp. 237–55.
10 Gieryn, T.,'Boundary-Work and the Demarcation of Science from Non-Science: Strains and Interests in Professional Ideologies of Scientists', *American Sociological Review* 48 (1983), pp. 781–95. For thoughts on the relations between 'professionals' and 'amateurs' in contemporary natural history, see Ellis, R. and C. Waterton, 'Caught Between the Cartographic and the Ethnographic Imagination: The Whereabouts of Amateurs, Professionals, and Nature in Knowing Biodiversity', *Environment and Planning D: Society and Space* 23 (2005), pp. 673–93.
11 Endersby, *Imperial Nature*.

Select Bibliography

Adams, Percy, *Travelers and Travel Liars 1660–1800* (Berkeley, 1962).
Akerman, James R. (ed.), *Cartographies of Travel and Navigation* (Chicago, 2006).
Anderson, W., *The Cultivation of Whiteness: Science, Health and Racial Destiny in Australia* (Melbourne, 2002).
Arnold, Harry J. P., *Photographer of the World: The Biography of Herbert Ponting* (London, 1969).
Barczewski, Stephanie, *Antarctic Destinies: Scott, Shackleton, and the Changing Face of Heroism* (London, 2008).
Barnes, Trevor J. and Farish, Matthew, 'Between Regions: Science, Militarism, and American Geography from World War to Cold War', *Annals of the Association of American Geographers* 96 (2006), pp. 807–26.
Barth, Kai-Henrik, 'The Politics of Seismology: Nuclear Testing, Arms Control, and the Transformation of a Discipline', *Social Studies of Science* 33 (2003), pp. 743–81.
Baughman, T.H., *Before the Heroes Came: Antarctica in the 1890s* (Lincoln, 1994).
Bayliss-Smith, Tim, 'Papuan Exploration, Colonial Expansion and the Royal Geographical Society: Questions of Power/Knowledge Relations', *Journal of Historical Geography* 18 (1992), pp. 319–29.
Beck, P., *The International Politics of Antarctica* (New York, 1986).
Belanger, Dian, 'The International Geophysical Year in Antarctica: Uncommon Collaborations, Unprecedented Results', *Journal of Government Information* 30 (2004), pp. 482–9.
– *Deep Freeze: The United States, the International Geophysical Year, and the Origins of Antarctica's Age of Science* (Colorado, 2006).
Bell, Morag, Robin Butlin, and Michael Heffernan (eds), *Geography and Imperialism 1820–1940* (Manchester, 1995).
Benjamin, M., *Rocket Dreams: How the Space Age Shaped Our Vision of a World Beyond* (London, 2003).
Benko, George and Ulf Strohmayer (eds), *Space and Social Theory: Interpreting Modernity and Postmodernity* (Oxford, 1997).
Berman, Morris, '"Hegemony" and the Amateur Tradition in British Science', *Journal of Social History* 8 (1974–5), pp. 30–50.
Bertrand, K., *Americans in Antarctica 1775–1948* (New York, 1971).
Bickell, Lennard, *In Search of Frank Hurley* (Melbourne, 1980).
– *Shackleton's Forgotten Men: The Untold Tragedy of the Endurance Epic* (London, 2001).
Bille, M. and Lishock, E., *The First Space Race: Launching the World's First Satellite* (College Station, 2004).

Black, Jeremy, *Visions of the World: A History of Maps* (London, 2003).
Bloom, Lisa, *Gender on Ice: American Ideologies of Polar Expeditions* (Minnesota, 1993).
Blunt, Alison, *Travel, Gender and Imperialism: Mary Kingsley and West Africa* (London, 1994).
Boczek, B., 'The Soviet Union and the Antarctic Regime', *American Journal of International Law* 78 (1984), pp. 834–58.
Boddington, Jennie and Vivian Fuchs, *Antarctic Photographs, 1910–1916: Herbert Ponting and Frank Hurley* (London, 1979).
Bourguet, Marie-Noèelle, Christian Licoppe and Heinz Otto Sibum, *Instruments, Travel, and Science: Itineraries of Precision from the Seventeenth to the Twentieth Century* (London, 2002).
Bowd, G. and D. Clayton, 'Fieldwork and Tropicality in French Indochina: Reflections on Pierre Gourou's Les Paysans Du Delta Tonkinois, 1936', *Singapore Journal of Tropical Geography* 24 (2003), pp. 147–68.
Boyer, Paul, *By the Bomb's Early Light: American Thought and Culture at the Dawn of the Atomic Age* (New York, 1985).
Bravo, Michael, and Sörlin Sverker (eds), *Narrating the Arctic: A Cultural History of Nordic Scientific Practices* (Canton, Mass., 2002).
Briggs, P., *Laboratory at the Bottom of the World* (New York, 1970).
Brockway, Lucile, *Science and Colonial Expansion: The Role of the British Royal Botanic Gardens* (New York, 1979).
Brosse, J., *Great Voyages of Discovery: Circumnavigation and Scientists, 1764–1843*, translated by S. Hochman (New York, 1983).
Bulkeley, Rip, *The Sputniks Crisis and Early United States Space Policy* (London, 1991).
Bullis, Harold, *Science, Technology, and American Diplomacy: The Political Legacy of the International Geophysical Year* (Washington, DC, 1973).
Burnett, D. Graham, *Masters of All They Surveyed: Exploration, Geography, and a British El Dorado* (Chicago, 2000).
Burns, Robin,'Stories about Place: The Antarctic as an International Reserve for Science' in Christopher Houston et al. (eds), *Imagined Places: The Politics of Making Space* (Melbourne, 1998), pp. 159–68.
Camerini, Jane, 'Evolution, Biogeography, and Maps: An Early History of Wallace's Line', *Isis* 84 (1993), pp. 700–27.
– 'Wallace in the Field', in Kuklick, H. and R. Kohler (eds), *Science in the Field* (Chicago, 1996), pp. 44–65.
Cameron, Ian, *To the Farthest Ends of the Earth: The History of the Royal Geographical Society, 1830–1980* (London, 1980).
Carter, D., *The Final Frontier: The Rise and Fall of the American Rocket State* (New York: Verso, 1988).
Carter, Paul, *The Road to Botany Bay: An Essay in Spatial History* (London, 1987).
Cervino, M., S. Corradini and S. Davolio, 'Is the Peaceful Use of Outer Space Being Ruled Out?' *Space Policy* 19 (2003), pp. 231–7.
Chapman, Walker, *The Loneliest Continent: The Story of Antarctic Discovery* (Connecticut, 1964).
Chipman, Elizabeth, *Women on the Ice: A History of Women in the Far South* (Carlton, Vic., 1986).
Clark, I., *Nuclear Diplomacy and the Special Relationship: Britain's Deterrent and America, 1957–1962* (Oxford, 1994).
Clayton, Daniel W., *Islands of Truth: The Imperial Fashioning of Vancouver Island* (Vancouver, 2000).
Cloud, John, 'Imaging the World in a Barrel: CORONA and the Clandestine Convergence of the Earth Sciences', *Social Studies of Science* 31 (2001), pp. 231–51.

SELECT BIBLIOGRAPHY

Cloud, John, 'Crossing the Olentangy River: The Figure of the Earth and the Military-Industrial-Academic Complex, 1947–1972', *Studies in the History and Philosophy of Modern Physics* 31 (2000), pp. 371–404.

Collier, P. and R. Inkpen, 'The RGS, Exploration and Empire and the Contested Nature of Surveying', *Area* 34 (2002), pp. 273–83.

– 'The Royal Geographical Society and the Development of Surveying 1870–1914', *Journal of Historical Geography* 29 (2003), pp. 93–108.

Cosgrove, Denis, 'Contested Global visions: One-World, Whole-Earth, and the Apollo Space Photographs', *Annals of the Association of American Geographers* 84 (1994), pp. 270–94.

Cosgrove, Denis (ed.), *Mappings* (London, 1999).

– *Apollo's Eye: A Cartographic Genealogy of the Earth in the Western Imagination* (Baltimore, 2001).

– *Geography and Vision* (London, 2008).

Cosgrove, Denis and Veronica della Dora (eds), *High Places: Cultural Geographies of Mountains, Ice and Science* (London, 2008).

Cradock, Percy, *Know Your Enemy: How the Joint Intelligence Committee Saw the World* (London, 2002).

Crary, Jonathan, *Techniques of the Observer: On Vision and Modernity in the Nineteenth Century* (Massachusetts, 1992).

Dalby, S., 'Critical Geopolitics: Discourse, Difference and Dissent', *Environment and Planning D: Society and Space* 9 (1991), pp. 261–83.

Daston, Lorraine and Peter Galison, *Objectivity* (New York, 2008).

David, Robert, *The Arctic in the British Imagination 1818–1914* (Manchester, 2000).

Deacon, Margaret, *Scientists and the Sea, 1650–1900: A Study of Marine Science* (London, 1971).

Dean, Katrina, Simon Naylor, Simone Turchetti and Martin Siegert, 'Data in Antarctic Science and Politics', *Social Studies of Science* 38 (2008), pp. 571–604.

DeVorkin, D. *Science with a Vengeance: How the American Military Created the Space Sciences in the V-2 era* (New York, 1992).

Dewart, G., *Antarctic Comrades* (Columbus, 1989).

Dewsbury, J. D. and Simon Naylor, 'Practising Geographical Knowledge: Fields, Bodies and Dissemination', *Area* 34 (2002), pp. 253–60.

Dick, Stephen and Roger Launius (eds), *Critical Issues in the History of Spaceflight* (Washington, DC, 2006).

Dickson, P., *Sputnik: Shock of the Century* (New York, 2001).

Dittmer, J., 'Captain America's Empire: Reflections on Identity, Popular Culture, and Post-9/11 Geopolitics', *Annals of the Association of American Geographers* 95 (2005), pp. 626–43.

– 'Colonialism and Place Creation in Mars Pathfinder Media Coverage', *Geographical Review* 97 (2007), pp. 112–30.

Diubaldo, Richard J., *Stefansson and the Canadian Arctic* (Montreal, 1978).

Dodds, Klaus, *Geopolitics in Antarctica: Views from the Southern Ocean Rim* (Chichester, 1997).

– 'Putting Maps in Their Place: The Demise of the Falkland Islands Dependency Survey and the Mapping of Antarctica, 1945–1962', *Ecumene* 7 (2000), pp. 176–210.

– Klaus, *Pink Ice: Britain and the South Atlantic Empire* (London, 2002).

– 'Screening Geopolitics: James Bond and the Early Cold War films', *Geopolitics* 10 (2005), pp. 266–89.

– 'Post-Colonial Antarctica: An Emerging Engagement', *Polar Record* 42 (2006), pp. 59–70.

– 'The Great Game in Antarctica: Britain and the 1959 Antarctic Treaty', *Contemporary British History* 22 (2007), pp. 43–66.

- 'Icy Geopolitics', *Environment and Planning D: Society and Space* 26 (2008), pp. 1–6.
Doel, Ronald, 'Constituting the Post-War Earth Sciences: The Military's Influence on the Environmental Sciences in the USA after 1945', *Social Studies of Science* 33 (2003), pp. 635–66.
- 'The Earth Sciences and Geophysics', in J. Krige and D. Pestre (eds), *Science in the Twentieth Century* (Amsterdam, 1997), pp. 391–426.
- and Alan Needell, 'Science, Scientists and the CIA: Balancing International Ideals, National Needs, and Professional Opportunities', in R. Jeffrey-Jones and C. Andrew (eds), *Eternal Vigilance? 50 Years of the CIA* (London, 1997), pp. 59–81.
- T. Levin and M. Marker, 'Extending Modern Cartography to the Ocean Depths: Military Patronage, Cold War Priorities, and the Heezen-Tharp Mapping Project, 1952–1959', *Journal of Historical Geography* 32 (2006), pp. 605–26.
Domosh, Mona, 'Toward a Feminist Historiography of Geography', *Transactions of the Institute of British Geographers* 16 (1991), pp. 95–101.
Drayton, Richard H., *Nature's Government: Science, Imperial Britain, and the 'Improvement' of the World* (New Haven, 2000).
Driver, Felix, 'Geography's Empire: Histories of Geographical Knowledge', *Environment and Planning D: Society and Space* 10 (1992), pp. 23–49.
- 'Making Space', *Ecumene* 1 (1994), pp. 386–90.
- 'Sub-Merged Identities: Familiar and Unfamiliar Histories', *Transactions of the Institute of British Geographers* 20 (1995), pp. 410–13.
- 'Editorial: Fieldwork in Geography', *Transactions of the Institute of British Geographers* 25 (2000), pp. 267–8.
- *Geography Militant: Cultures of Exploration and Empire* (Oxford, 2001).
- 'The Active Life: The Explorer as Biographical Subject', in Matthew, H. C. G., Brian Harrison and Lawrence Goldman (eds), *Oxford Dictionary of National Biography (Oxford DNB)* (Oxford, 2004–), online edition.
Driver, Felix and Luciana Martins (eds), *Tropical Visions in an Age of Empire* (Chicago, 2005).
Dyer, Richard, *White* (London, 1997).
Edney, Matthew H., *Mapping an Empire: The Geographical Construction of British India, 1765–1843* (Chicago, 1997).
Edwards, Elizabeth (ed.), *Anthropology and Photography, 1860–1920* (New Haven, 1992).
- *Raw Histories: Photographs, Anthropology and Museums* (Oxford, 2001).
- and Janice Hart, *Photographs Objects Histories: On the Materiality of Images* (London, 2004).
Ellis, R. and C. Waterton, 'Caught Between the Cartographic and the Ethnographic Imagination: The Whereabouts of Amateurs, Professionals, and Nature in Knowing Biodiversity', *Environment and Planning D: Society and Space* 23 (2005), pp. 673–93.
Elsner, Jaâs and Joan-Pau Rubiâes (eds), *Voyages and Visions: Towards a Cultural History of Travel* (London, 1999).
Elzinga, A., 'The Antarctic as Big Science', in E. Hicks and W. van Rossum (eds), *Policy Development and Big Science* (Amsterdam, 1991), pp. 15–25.
- 'Antarctica: The Construction of a Continent by and for Science', in E. Crawford, T. Shinn and S. Sorlin (eds), *Denationalising Science* (Dordecht, 1993), pp. 73–106.
Eriksen, Ray, *West of Centre* (London, 1972).
Evans, E. G. R. G., *South with Scott* (London, 1921).
Fabian, Johannes, *Out of Our Minds: Reason and Madness in the Exploration of Central Africa* (Berkeley, 2000).

Farish, Matthew, 'Frontier Engineering: From the Globe to the Body in the Cold War Arctic', *The Canadian Geographer*, 50/2 (2006), pp. 177–96.
Fernândez-Armesto, Felipe, *Pathfinders: A Global History of Exploration* (New York, 2006).
Flannery, Tim, *The Explorers* (Melbourne, 1998).
Fogg, G. E., 'The Royal Society and the South Seas', *Notes and Records of the Royal Society of London* 55 (2001), pp. 81–103.
Fraser, R., *Once Round the Sun* (London, 1957).
Freeman, T. W., *One Hundred Years of Geography* (London, 1961).
French, Patrick, *Younghusband: The Last Great Imperial Adventurer* (London, 1994).
Galison, Peter and Bruce Hevly (eds), *Big Science* (Stanford, 1992).
Gieryn, T., 'Boundary-Work and the Demarcation of Science from Non-Science: Strains and Interests in Professional Ideologies of Scientists', *American Sociological Review* 48 (1983), pp. 781–95.
Godwin, Matthew, *The Skylark Rocket, British Space Science and the European Space Research Organisation, 1957–1972* (Paris, 2007).
Goetzmann, William H., *Army Exploration in the American West, 1803–1863* (New Haven, 1959).
– *Exploration and Empire:The Explorer and the Scientist in the Winning of the American West* (New York, 1966).
– *New Lands, New Men: America and the Second Great Age of Discovery* (New York, 1986).
Goren, H., 'Scientific Organizations as Agents of Change: The Palestine Exploration Fund, the Deutsche Verein Zur Erforschung Palastinas and Nineteenth-Century Palestine', *Journal of Historical Geography* 27 (2001), pp. 153–65.
Goudie, Andrew, *Immensity: Exploration of the Western Desert by Motorcar* (Oxford, 2006).
Gregor, Gary C., *Swansea's Antarctic Explorer: Edgar Evans, 1876–1912* (Swansea, 1995).
Grosz, Elizabeth, *Time Travels: Feminism, Nature, Power* (London, 2005).
Guelke, Jeanne Kay and Karen M. Morin, 'Gender, Nature, Empire: Women Naturalists in Nineteenth Century British Travel Literature', *Transactions of the Institute of British Geographers* 26 (2001), pp. 306–26.
Guest, Harriet, *Empire, Barbarism, and Civilisation: James Cook, William Hodges, and the Return to the Pacific* (Cambridge, 2007).
Hagen, Joel B., *An Entangled Bank* (New Brunswick, 1992).
Hains, B., *The Ice and Inland* (Melbourne, 2002).
Hall, R., 'The Eisenhower Administration and the Cold War: Framing American Astronautics to Serve National Security', *Prologue* 27 (1995), pp. 59–72.
Hall, R. Cargill, 'The Truth about Overflights', *Quarterly Journal of Military History* 9 (1997), pp. 24–39.
Hall, R., 'Casey and the Negotiation of the Antarctic Treaty', in J. Jabour-Green and M. Hawards (eds), *The Antarctic: Past, Present and Future* (Hobart, 2002), pp. 27–33.
Hamblin, Jacob, 'Visions of International Scientific Cooperation: The Case of Oceanic Science, 1920–1955', *Minerva* 38 (2000), pp. 392–423.
Hamblin, Jacob, 'The Navy's 'Sophisticated' Pursuit of Science: Undersea Warfare, the Limits of Internationalism, and the Utility of Basic Research, 1945–1956', *Isis* 93 (2002), pp. 1–27.
– *Oceanographers and the Cold War* (Seattle, 2005).
Hansen, Peter, 'Confetti of Empire: The Conquest of Everest in Nepal, India, Britain and New Zealand', *Comparative Studies in Society and History* 42 (2000), pp. 307–32.

Hattersley-Smith, G., *The Norwegian with Scott: Tryggve Gran's Antarctic Diary 1910–1913* (London, 1984).
Hauser, Kitty, *Shadow Sites: Photography, Archaeology, & the British Landscape 1927–1955* (Oxford, 2007).
Haynes, Roslynn, *Seeking the Centre: The Australian Desert in Literature, Art, and Film* (Cambridge, 1998).
Heffernan, Michael, 'The Limits of Utopia: Henri Duveyrier and the Exploration of the Sahara in the Nineteenth Century', *Geographical Journal* 155 (1989), pp. 342–52.
– '"A Dream as Frail as Those of Ancient Time": The In-Credible Geographies of Timbuctoo', *Environment and Planning D: Society and Space* 19 (2001), pp. 203–25.
– 'The Science of Empire: The French Geographical Movement and the Forms of French Imperialism, 1870–1920', in Godlewska A. and N. Smith (eds), *Geography and Empire* (Oxford, 1994), pp. 92–114.
Hevly, Bruce, 'The Heroic Science of Glacier Motion', in Kuklick, H. and E. Kohler (eds), *Science in the Field* (Chicago, 1996), pp. 66–86.
Holt, Richard, J. A. Mangan and Pierre Lafranchi (eds), *European Heroes: Myth, Identity, Sport* (London, 1996).
Horelick, A., 'Outer Space and Earthbound Politics', *World Politics* 13 (1961), pp. 323–9.
Hughes, J., 'Deconstructing the Bomb: Recent Perspectives on Nuclear History', *British Journal for the History of Science* 27 (2004), pp. 455–64.
Hulme, Peter and Russell McDougall (eds), *Writing, Travel and Empire* (London, 2007).
Huntford, Roland, *Scott and Amundsen* (London, 1979).
– *The Shackleton Voyages* (London, 2002).
Jeal, Tim, *Stanley: The Impossible Life of Africa's Greatest Explorer* (New Haven, 2007).
Jessup, Philip and Howard Taubenfeld, *Controls for Outer Space* (London, 1959).
Johnson, Anthony M., *Scott of the Antarctic and Cardiff* (Cardiff, 1984).
Johnson, S. B., *The Secret of Apollo: Systems Management in American and European Space Programs* (Baltimore, 2002).
Jones, A. G. E., *Polar Portraits: Collected Papers* (Whitby, 1992).
Jones, Max, *The Last Great Quest: Captain Scott's Antarctic Sacrifice* (Oxford, 2003).
– 'Introduction', in Scott, Robert F., *Journals: Scott's Last Expedition* (Oxford, 2005).
Joyce, Ernest Edward Mills, *The South Polar Trail: The Log of the Imperial Trans-Antarctic Expedition* (London, 1929).
Joyner C. and E. Theis, *Eagle Over the Ice* (Hanover, 1997).
Kelly, Kieran, *Hard Country Hard Men: In the Footsteps of Gregory* (Sydney, 2002).
Kelly, Saul, *The Hunt for Zerzura: The Lost Oasis and the Desert War* (London, 2002).
Kennedy, Dane, *The Highly Civilized Man: Richard Burton and the Victorian World* (Harvard, 2005).
– 'British Exploration in the Nineteenth Century: A Historiographical Survey', *History Compass* 5/6 (2007), pp. 1879–1900.
Kevles D., 'Cold War and Hot Physics: Science, Security and the American State, 1945–1956', *Historical Studies in the Physical Sciences* 20 (1990), pp. 239–64.
Kirsch, Scott, 'Experiments in Progress: Edward Teller's Controversial Geographies', *Ecumene* 5 (1998), pp. 267–86.
– *Proving Grounds: Project Ploughshare and the Unrealized Dream of Nuclear Earth-Moving* (New Jersey, 2006).
Klotz F., *America on Ice* (Washington, DC, 1990).

Kohler, Robert E., *Landscapes and Labscapes: Exploring the Lab–Field Border in Biology* (Chicago, 2002).
Kohler, Robert, 'Place and Practice in Field biology', *History of Science* 40 (2002), pp. 189–210.
Korsmo, Fae, 'Shaping up Planet Earth: The International Geophysical Year and Communicating Science through Print and Film Media', *Science Communication* 26 (2004), pp. 162–87.
– 'The Early Cold War and US Arctic Research', in Benson Keith R. and Helen M. Rozwadowski (eds), *Extremes: Oceanography's Adventures at the Poles* (Sagamore Beach, 2007), pp. 173–99.
Krige, John, *American Hegemony and the Postwar Reconstruction of Science in Europe* (Cambridge, Mass., 2006).
Kucklick, Henrika and Kohler, Robert (eds), *Science in the Field* (Chicago, 1996).
– *The Savage Within: The Social History of British Anthropology, 1885–1945* (Cambridge, 1991).
Lagerbom, Charles, *The Fifth Man: Henry R. Bowers* (Whitby, 1999).
Lambert, Andrew D., *The Foundations of Naval History: John Knox Laughton, the Royal Navy, and the Historical Profession* (London, 1998).
Lane, K. Maria D., 'Geographers of Mars: Cartographic Inscription and Exploration Narrative in Late Victorian Representations of the Red Planet', *Isis* 96 (2005), pp. 477–506.
– 'Mapping the Mars Canal Mania: Cartographic Projection and the Creation of a Popular Icon', *Imago Mundi: The International Journal for the History of Cartography* 58 (2006), pp. 198–211.
Larsen, A., 'Equipment for the Field', in N. Jardine, J. Secord and E. Spary (eds), *Cultures of Natural History* (Cambridge, 1996), pp. 358–77.
Launius, Roger et al. (eds), *Reconsidering Sputnik* (Amsterdam, 2000).
Leach, Hugh, with Susan Maria Farrington, *Strolling about on the Roof of the World: The First Hundred Years of the Royal Society for Asian Affairs (formerly Royal Central Asian Society)* (New York, 2002).
Legg, Frank and Toni Hurley, *Once More on My Adventure* (Sydney, 1966).
Leslie, S., *The Cold War and American Science: The Military-Industrial-Academic Complex at MIT and Stanford* (New York, 1992).
Lewis, R., *A Continent for Science* (London, 1965).
Limb, Sue and Patrick Cordingley, *Captain Oates: Soldier and Explorer* (London, 1995).
Livingstone, David N., *The Geographical Tradition: Episodes in the History of a Contested Enterprise* (Oxford 1992).
– *Putting Science in its Place: Geographies of Scientific Knowledge* (Chicago, 2003).
Lorimer, H. and N. Spedding, 'Locating Field Science: A Geographical Family Expedition to Glen Roy, Scotland', *British Journal for the History of Science* 38 (2005), pp. 13–34.
Lovering J. and J. Prescott, *Last of Lands: Antarctica* (Melbourne,1979).
Lowerson, John, *Sport and the Middle Classes* (Manchester, 1993).
MacDonald, Fraser, 'The Last Outpost of Empire: Rockall and the Cold War', *Journal of Historical Geography* 32 (2006), pp. 627–47.
MacDonald, Fraser, 'Geopolitics and the Vision Thing: Regarding Britain and America's First Nuclear Missile', *Transactions of the Institute of British Geographers* 31 (2006), pp. 53–71.
– 'Anti-Astropolitik: Outer Space and the Orbit of Geography', *Progress in Human Geography* 31 (2007), pp. 592–615.
Mackenzie, John (ed.), *Imperialism and Popular Culture* (Manchester, 1986).
MacLeod, R., and P. E. Rehbock (eds), *Nature in its Greatest Extent: Western Science in the Pacific* (Honolulu, 1988).

MacNaughton, Howard, 'The Speaking Abject: The Impossible Possible World of Realized Empire', in Chris Tiffin and Alan Lawson (eds), *De-Scribing Empire: Post-Colonialism and Textuality* (London, 1994), pp. 171–84.
Markham, Clements. R., *The Fifty Years Work of the Royal Geographical Society* (London, 1881).
Martin, G., *Ellsworth Huntington: His Life and Thought* (Connecticut, 1973).
Martins, Luciana, 'A Naturalist's Vision of the Tropics: Charles Darwin and the Brazilian Landscape', *Singapore Journal of Tropical Geography* 21 (2000), pp. 19–33.
Massey, Harrie and Malcolm Robins, *History of British Space Science* (Cambridge, 1980).
Matless, David, 'Regional Surveys and Local Knowledges: The Geographical Imagination in Britain, 1918–39', *Transactions of the Institute of British Geographers* 17 (1992), pp. 464–80.
Mayewski, Paul A. and Frank White, *The Ice Chronicles: The Quest to Understand Global Climate Change* (Hanover, 2002).
McClintock, Anne, *Imperial Leather: Race, Gender and Sexuality in the Colonial Contest* (London, 1995).
McDougall, Walter, *The Heavens and the Earth: A Political History of the Space Age* (Baltimore, 1997).
McElrea, Richard and David Harrowfield, *Polar Castaways: The Ross Sea Party of Sir Ernest Shackleton, 1914–17* (Christchuch, 2004).
McEwan, Cheryl, 'Gender, Science and Physical Geography in Nineteenth-Century Britain', *Area* 30 (1998), pp. 215–23.
– *Gender, Geography, and Empire: Victorian Women Travellers in West Africa* (Aldershot, 2000).
McGrath, Ann (ed.), *Contested Ground: Australian Aborigines Under the British Crown* (Sydney, 1995).
McInerney, Graham and Alec Mathieson, *Across the Gibson* (Adelaide, 1978).
McKernan, Luke, 'The Great White Silence: Antarctic Exploration and Film', in Van Der Merwe, P. (ed.), *South: The Race to the Pole* (London, 2000), pp. 91–103.
Mill, Hugh R., *The Record of the Royal Geographical Society, 1830–1930* (London, 1930).
Moore J., 'Tethered to an Iceberg: United States Policy towards the Antarctic 1939–1949', *Polar Record* 35 (1999), pp. 125–34.
– 'Thirty Seven Degrees Frigid: US–Chilean Relations and the Spectre of Polar Arrivistes, 1950–59', *Diplomacy and Statecraft* 14 (2003), pp. 69–93.
Moorehead, Alan, *The White Nile* (New York, 1960).
– *The Blue Nile* (New York, 1963).
Moore, Patrick, *Space in the Sixties* (Harmondsworth, 1963).
Morrell, Margot and Stephanie Capparell, *Shackleton's Way: Leadership Lessons from the Great Antarctic Explorer* (London, 2001).
Morris, Meaghan, *Too Soon, Too Late: History and Popular Culture* (Bloomington, 1998).
Naylor, Simon, '"That Very Garden of South America": European Surveyors in Paraguay', *Singapore Journal of Tropical Geography* 21 (2000), pp. 48–62.
– 'Discovering Nature, Rediscovering the Self: Natural Historians and the Landscapes of Argentina', *Environment and Planning D: Society and Space* 19 (2001), pp. 227–47.
– 'Exploration and Field Work', in Heilbron, John (ed.), *Oxford Companion to the History of Modern Science* (New York, 2003), pp. 288–91.
– Katrina Dean and Martin Siegert, 'The IGY and the Icesheet: Surveying Antarctica', *Journal of Historical Geography* 34 (2008), pp. 574–95.
– Martin Siegert, Katrina Dean and Simone Turchetti, 'Science, Geopolitics and the Governance of Antarctica', *Nature Geoscience* 3 (2008), pp. 143–45.

Needell Alan, *Science, Cold War and the American State: Lloyd V. Berkner and the Balance of Professional Ideals* (Washington, 2000).
Ó Tuathail, Gerard, *Critical Geopolitics: The Politics of Writing Global Space* (Minneapolis, 1996).
Outram, Dorinda, 'New Spaces of Natural History', in Jardine. N., J. Secord and E. Spary (eds), *Cultures of Natural History* (Cambridge, 1996), pp. 249–66.
Pálsson, Gísli, *Travelling Passions: The Hidden Life of Vilhjalmur Stefansson* (Manitoba, 2003).
Pang, Alex Soojung-Kim, *Empire and the Sun: Victorian Solar Eclipse Expeditions* (Stanford, 2002).
– 'Gender, Culture, and Astrophysical Fieldwork: Elizabeth Campbell and the Lick Observatory-Crocker Eclipse Expeditions', in Kucklick Henrika and Robert Kohler (eds), *Science in the Field* (Chicago, 1996), pp. 17–43.
Peterson, Nicholas and Marcia Langton, *Aborigines, Land, and Land Rights* (Canberra, 1983).
Powell, J. M., 'Griffith Taylor and "Australia Unlimited"', *The John Murtagh Macrossan Memorial Lecture 1992* (Brisbane, 1992).
– 'The Cyclist on the Ice: Griffith Taylor as Explorer', *Proceedings of the Royal Geographical Society of Australasia* 80 (1979), pp. 1–28.
– *An Historical Geography of Modern Australia: The Restive Fringe* (Cambridge, 1988).
Power, M. and J. Crampton, 'Reel Geopolitics: Cinemato-Graphing Political Space', *Geopolitics* 10 (2005), pp. 193–203.
Pratt, Mary Louise, *Imperial Eyes: Travel Writing and Transculturation* (London, 1992)
Pyne, S., *The Ice: Journey to Antarctica* (London, 2003).
Quilley, Geoff and John Bonehill (eds) *William Hodges 1744–1797: The Art of Exploration* (London, 2004).
Redfield, P., *Space in the Tropics: From Convicts to Rockets in French Guinana* (Berkeley, 2000).
– 'The Half-Life of Empire in Outer Space', *Social Studies of Science* 32 (2002), pp. 791–825.
Rice, Tony, *Voyages of Discovery: Three Centuries of Natural History Exploration* (London, 2000).
Riffenburgh, Beau, *The Myth of the Explorer: The Press, Sensationalism, and Geographical Discovery* (London, 1993).
Riffenburgh, Beau and Liz Cruwys, *The Photographs of H. G. Ponting* (London, 1998).
Ritvo, Harriet, *The Animal Estate: The English and Other Creatures in the Victorian Age* (Cambridge, MA, 1989).
Robinson, Michael F., *The Coldest Crucible: Arctic Exploration and American Culture* (Chicago, 2006).
Rose, Gillian, *Feminism and Geography: The Limits of Geographical Knowledge* (Cambridge, 1993).
Rotberg, Robert I. (ed.), *Africa and its Explorers: Motives, Methods, and Impact* (Cambridge, 1970).
Rowse, Tim, *After Mabo: Interpreting Indigenous Traditions* (Melbourne, 1993).
Rozwadowski, Helen, 'Science, the Sea, and Marine Resource Management: Researching the International Council for the Exploration of the Sea', *The Public Historian* 26 (2004), pp. 41–64.
– *Fathoming the Ocean: The Discovery and Exploration of the Deep Sea* (London, 2005).
Rozwadowski, Helen and David Keuren (eds), *The Machine in Neptune's Garden: Historical Perspectives on Technology and the Marine Environment* (Sagamore Beach, 2004).
Ryan, James R., *Picturing Empire: Photography and the Visualisation of the British Empire* (London, 1997).

Ryan, Simon, *The Cartographic Eye: How Explorers Saw Australia* (Cambridge, 1996).
Said, Edward W. *Orientalism* (New York, 1979).
Sanderson, M., *Griffith Taylor: Antarctic Scientist and Pioneer Geographer* (Carlton, 1988).
Savours, Ann (ed.), *Scott's Last Voyage: Through the Antarctic Camera of Herbert Ponting* (London, 1974).
Schumaker, Lynette, 'A Tent with a View: Colonial Officers, Anthropologists, and the Making of the Field in Northern Rhodesia, 1937–60', in Kucklick, Henrika and Robert Kohler (eds), *Science in the Field* (Chicago, 1996), pp. 237–58.
Schwartz, Joan M. and James R. Ryan (eds), *Picturing Place : Photography and the Geographical Imagination* (London, 2003).
Scott, Robert F., *The Voyage of the 'Discovery'* (London, 1905).
Seaver, George, *'Birdie' Bowers of the Antarctic* (London, 1938).
– *The Faith of Edward Wilson* (London, 1948).
Seed, Patricia, *Ceremonies of Possession in Europe's Conquest of the New World 1492–1640* (Cambridge, 1995).
Sfraga, Michael P., *Bradford Washburn: A Life of Exploration* (Corvallis, 2004).
Sharp, J., 'Hegemony, Popular Culture and Geopolitics: The Reader's Digest and the Construction of Danger', *Political Geography* 15 (1996), pp. 557–70.
– *Condensing the Cold War: The Reader's Digest and American Identity*, (Minneapolis, 2000).
Sheets-Pyenson, Susan, *Cathedrals of Science: The Development of Colonial Natural History Museums During the Late Nineteenth Century* (Kingston, Ont., 1988).
Siddiqi, Asif, *Sputnik and the Soviet Space Challenge* (Gainesville, 2003).
Simpson, Donald, *Dark Companions: the African Contribution to the European Exploration of East Africa* (London, 1975).
Simpson, John, *Independent Nuclear State: The United States, Britain and the Military Atom* (Basingstoke, 1986).
Siple, Paul, *90° South: The Story of the American South Pole Conquest* (New York, 1959).
Smith, Bernard, *European Vision and the South Pacific* (New Haven, 1985).
Smith, Michael, *An Unsung Hero: Tom Crean, Antarctic Survivor* (London, 2000).
– *I am Just Going Outside: Captain Oates – Antarctic Tragedy* (Staplehurst, 2002).
Smith, Neil, *American Empire: Roosevelt's Geographer and the Prelude to Globalization* (California, 2003).
Smith, Neil and Anne Godlewska (eds), *Geography and Empire: Critical Studies in the History of Geography* (Oxford, 1994).
Solomon, Susan, *The Coldest March* (London, 2001).
Sorrenson, Richard, 'The Ship as a Scientific Instrument in the Eighteenth Century', in Kucklick, Henrika and Robert Kohler (eds), *Science in the Field* (Chicago, 1996), pp. 221–36.
Sparke, Matthew, 'Displacing the Field in Fieldwork: Masculinity, Metaphor and Space' in Duncan, Nancy (ed.), *Bodyspace: Destabilizing Geographies of Gender and Sexuality* (London, 1996), pp. 212–33.
Spufford, Francis, *I May be Some Time: Ice and the English Imagination* (London, 1996).
Stafford, Robert A., *Scientist of Empire: Sir Roderick Murchison, Scientific Exploration and Victorian Imperialism* (Cambridge, 1989).
– 'Scientific Exploration and Empire' in Porter, Andrew (ed.), *The Oxford History of the British Empire, Vol. 3, The Nineteenth Century* (Oxford, 1999), pp. 294–319.
Staum, M. S., 'The Paris Geographical Society Constructs the Other, 1821–1850', *Journal of Historical Geography* 26 (2000), pp. 222–38.
Steel, Robert W., *The Institute of British Geographers: The First Fifty Years* (London, 1984).

Stoddart, D. R., 'The RGS and the "New Geography": Changing aims and Changing Roles in Nineteenth Century Science', *Geographical Journal* 146 (1980), pp. 190–202.
– *On Geography: and its History* (Oxford, 1986).
Stoddart, D. R. (ed.), 'The Institute of British Geographers 1933–1983', *Transactions of the Institute of British Geographers* 9 (1983), pp. 1–124.
Sturm, Matthew, 'The spirit of the Arctic and the Next Generation of Arctic Researchers', *Arctic* 53 (2000), pp. iii–iv.
Swan, R. A., *Australia in the Antarctic* (Melbourne, 1961).
Swithinbank, C., *Vodka on Ice: A year with the Russians in the Antarctic* (London, 2001).
Synder, Joel, 'Territorial Photography', in W. J. T. Mitchell (ed.), *Landscape and Power* (London, 1994), pp. 175–202.
Thomas, Nicholas, *Colonialism's Culture: Anthropology, Travel, and Government* (Princeton, 1994).
Thomas, Nicola. J., 'Broadening the Boundaries of Biography and Geography: Lady Curzon, Vicereine of India 1898–1905', *Journal of Historical Geography* 30 (2004), pp. 496–519.
Tucker, Jennifer, *Nature Exposed: Photography as Eyewitness in Victorian Science* (Baltimore, 2005).
Turchetti, S., K. Dean, S. Naylor and M. Siegert, 'Accidents and Opportunities: A History of the Radio Echo-Sounding of Antarctica, 1958–79', *British Journal for the History of Science* 41 (2008), pp. 417–44.
Tyler-Lewis, Kelly, *The Lost Men: The Harrowing Saga of Shackleton's Ross Sea Party* (London, 2006).
Waller, D. J., *The Pundits: British Exploration of Tibet and Central Asia* (Kentucky, 1990).
Warner, D. J., 'Political Geodesy: The Army, the Air Force and the World Geodetic System of 1960', *Annals of Science* 59 (2002), pp. 363–89.
Welch, David F., *Operation Highjump II: An Exercise in Planning* (Washington, DC, 1970).
Wexler, H., 'Antarctic Research in Connection with the International Geophysical Year', *Geophysics* 21 (1956), pp. 681–90.
Whyte, Neil and Philip Gummett, 'The Making of the United Kingdom's First Space Policy', *Minerva* 35 (1997), pp. 400–4.
Wilson, D. M. and D. B. Elder, *Cheltenham in Antarctica: The Life of Edward Wilson* (Cheltenham, 2000).
Wilson, E., *The Spiritual History of the Ice* (Basingstoke, 2003).
Withers, Charles W. J., 'Travelling and Credibility: Towards a Geography of Trust', *Geographie et Cultures* 33 (2000), pp. 3–17.
– 'Authorizing Landscape: 'Authority', Naming and the Ordnance Survey's Mapping of the Scottish Highlands in the Nineteenth Century', *Journal of Historical Geography* 26 (2000), pp. 532–54.
Wråkberg, Urban, *The Centennial of S. A. Andrée's North Pole Expedition: Proceedings of a Conference on S. A Andrée and the Agenda for Social Science Research of the Polar Regions* (Stockholm, 1999).
– 'The Politics of Naming: Contested Observations and the Shaping of Geographical Knowledge', in Bravo, Michael and Sverker Sörlin (eds), *Narrating the Arctic: A Cultural History of Nordic Scientific Practices* (Cambridge, Mass., 2002) pp. 155–97.
Wylie, John, 'Becoming-Icy: Scott and Amundsen's South Polar Voyages, 1910–1913', *Cultural Geographies* 9 (2002), pp. 249–66.

Wyse Jackson, P. N. (ed.), *Four Centuries of Geological Travel: The Search for Knowledge on Foot, Bicycle, Sledge and Camel* (London, 2007).

Young, Wayland, 'On the Debunking of Captain Scott', *Encounter* 54 (1980), pp. 8–19.

Yusoff, Kathryn, 'Antarctic Exposure: Archives of the Feeling Body', *Cultural Geographies* 14/2 (2007), pp. 211–33.

Index

Aboriginal Land Rights (NT) Act (1976), 230
Across the Gibson, 227, 234, 237, 240
'Acts of exploration,' 7
Adventurous exploration, 247
Aerial archaeology, 20
Age of exploration, end of, 241
Ahlmann, Hans W., 130, 131, 135, 136
Amundsen, Roald, 25, 40, 42, 48, 69
Antarctica
   changing geopolitical condition of, 153
   'coast,' 52
   conference on the future of, October 1959, 170
   effect of Cold War, 150
   films on
      newpapers on, 67
      and their effect on audience, 66
   first aerial photograph of, 53
   first photograph on, 53
   fragmentary knowledge of, 163
   fundamental re-evaluation of, 150
   geographical context for naval officers/ scientists/ political leaders, 164
   increasing visiblity of exploration and scientific investigation, 159
   intention of research in, 149
   as 'laboratory' for science, 165–166
   major area of geophysical interest, 163
   mineral potential of, 170
   'opening up' through photographic image to audiences, 61
   photographic moment, 75
   photography in, 55
   role played by print media, 159
   seismic soundings and traverse research, 169
   sub-glacial, 168
   territorial claim on, 154
   two sorts of models of exploration, 158
Antarctic Adventure, 27
Antarctic exploration, 58
   ethnographic focus on everyday activities of, 57
   historical importance of configuring through photography, 54
   pre-photographic period in, 59
Antarctic painting, first (William Hodges), 52
Antarctic photographs, 63–64
Antarctic Treaty and practices of international scientific cooperation, 13
'Anti-environment,' 72
Arctic
   Army's 'defeatist' attitude, 132
   comparative/quantitative science of glaciology, 127
   environmental change, 125
   glaciology and exploration, 126
   research, 127
Arctic Climate Impact Assessment, 145
'Ariel,' 180
   disrupted transmission after nuclear destruction, 186
   nuclear destruction of, 182–186
   in orbit, 183
   origins of, 178–182
'Armchair geographers,' 247
Army Ballistic Missile Agency, officials of, 207
Assault on the Unknown, 17
'Assault on the unknown,' *see* International Geophysical Year (IGY) of 1957–8
Australia, A Geographical Reader, 108
Australia, T. Griffith Taylor and exploration of, 105–108
   contesting scientific expertise, 120–123
   fieldwork and geographical career, 108–113
   fieldwork and geographical knowledge, 113–118
   geographical performance, 119–120
Australian Antarctic Territory (AAT), 158
Australian desert exploration
   generically classic narrative, 222
   twentieth-century, genealogical filiation, 228
Australian exploration spatiality, 225–226
Australian interior scenery, 121
Australia Twice Traversed: the Romance of Exploration, 226
Australia Unlimited, 117
Autobiography by explorers, 25

Baigent, Elizabeth, 23, 107, 246
Barnes, Trevor J., 126
Benjamin, Walter, 60, 63
Biographies of explorers, 7–8, 27
   aim, 8
Bioscope, 64
'Blaze trees,' 234
The Book of Hidden Pearls, 86
'British Antarctica,' 155

British geography, Nineteenth-century, 24
British National Antarctic Expedition of 1901-4, 53
British Natural History Museum, 3
Britnik: how America made/destroyed Britain's first satellite, 173-174
  Ariel functioning intermittently after nuclear bombing, 186-189
  damages of Starfish, 189-193
  origins of Ariel, 178-182
  'sputnik shock,' 174-177
  'Starfish' and nuclear destruction of Ariel, 182-186
Bumper WAC launch from Cape Canaveral, 208
Burton, Richard, 8
By Rocket to Planetary Space, 206

The Cadastral Survey of Egypt, 1892-1907, 86
Cairo Scientific Journal, 86
Camerini, Jane, 88
Campbell, Victor, 28
Canada, 108
Carter, Paul, 1, 224, 229, 249
The Cartographic Eye, 224
Cartography, 6
'Ceremonies of possession,' 155
Chinese flag waving in outer space (28 September 2008), 242
Chipman, Elizabeth, 45
Chronophotography, 56-57
Cloud, John, 150, 162
Cold War
  effect on Antarctic, 150
  funding/organisation of physical/life sciences, 161
  and IGY, 138-144
Cold-weather clothing, 132-133
Collis, Christy, 222
Conquering the Continent, 227, 234, 236, 238, 240
Contemporary exploration spatiality, 224
'The Contribution of Polar Expeditions to the Science of Glaciology,' 131
Conventional models of 'the explorer,' 246
Conventional models of 'the explorer,' 246
Corporal missile, 200, 203, 213, 218
COSPAR, 179, 184, 191
The Course of Empire, 224

Crary, Jonathan, 54, 55, 56, 60, 76
CSAGI, 139, 140, 141, 142
Currents of the Atlantic Ocean, 15

'The Dakhla-Owanat Road,' 98
Dalby, S., 210
Darwin, Charles, 248
Deacon, Margaret, 11
'Deeds not words,' 23
'Defenders of America,' 218
Department of Scientific and Industrial Research (DSIR), 181
Desert trip, itineraries, 226
DeVorkin, D., 190, 285, 286
Dictionary of National Biography (DNB), 32
The Diminishing Paradise, 224
Dinky Supertoy no. 666, advert for, 214
Disappearance during exploration. *see* Fossett, Steve
Dodds, Klaus. J., 148, 243
Doel, Ronald, 127, 151, 153
Driver, Felix, 4, 7, 10, 54, 80, 81, 241

Edney, Matthew H., 84
Egyptian Survey Department, 86, 90, 94
Ellis, R., 291
Elzinga, A., 164, 171
Encounter/epistemology, processes of, 5
Endurance, 29
Environment, Race and Migration, 108
'Environmental determinism,' 106
Environment and Nation, 108
Environment and Race, 108
Eriksen, Ray, 227, 236
European explorers, trustworthiness/credibility of, 3
Expeditionary photography, 77
Exploration
  academic study of, 1
  Antarctic, ethnographic focus on the everyday activities of, 57
  'art' and 'science,' 6
  Duveyrier's view of, 5
  foci of recent academic enquiry, 2
  geopolitical significance of, 21
  modernity of, 241
  as process of physical/material contact and exchange, 5
  and production of knowledge, 2
  promotion of, 3
  satellites in, 20

scientific knowledge and, 4
ship as scientific instrument of, 198
Stanley's view of, 4-5
success in, 245
texts and issues of textuality and, 2
Explorer biography, *see* biographies of explorers
Explorers
  charges, 4
  organisations providing support, 3
  physical environments role in, 6
  training in field observation, 4
  vs. geographers, 30

Falklands Islands Dependencies Survey (FIDS), 19, 153, 156
Farish, Matthew, 126, 127, 247
Fernández-Armesto, Felipe, 21
Field, 54
  importance in geographical knowledge, 113
  photography, 55
Field, William O.
  and IGY, 136-138
Fieldworker
  reputations of, 107
  usefulness of photography and motorcar to, 120
Fiennes, Ranulph, 244, 245
Film, *see* chronophotography
"Flags, trio of," 242
Flannery, Tim, 229
Footsteps expeditions, 226-227, 233-240
'Footsteps of explorers' expeditions and contest for Australian desert space, 222-226
  crises, 230-233
  empire's exploration spatiality, 228-230
  footsteps, 226-228
  footsteps expeditions, 233-240
Fossett, Steve, 245
Fraser, R., 196, 243
French, Patrick, 12
From the Earth to Moon, 197

Geodesy, 20
Geographers *vs.* explorers, 30
The Geographical Journal, 88, 94, 95, 96, 97, 98, 99, 101
Geographical knowledge
  centrality of exploration and fieldwork in, 106
  constructing, 4
  relationship between forms of power and, 4

306

INDEX

exploration and science of, 196
importance of field in, 113
travel as means of acquiring, 118
The Geographical Laboratory, 108
Geographical media, 29
Geography in the Twentieth Century, 108
'Geography Militant,' 9, 105
'Geography Triumphant,' 10, 105
Geopolitical frameworks for exploration, 12
Geopolitics, 196, 210
Geopolitics, Antarctic science and International Geophysical Year (1957–8), 148–154
exploration, geopolitics and territorial claims, 154–161
geophysics, seismic sounding and over-snow traverses of Antarctica, 165–170
US science, IGY and cold war, 161–165
Glacial regime, atmosphere on, 130
Glaciers, melting of, 125
Glaciology, 137, 166
Arctic, and US Military, 1945–58, 125–127
Arctic and US military, 127–129
glaciology, Arctic, IGY, 144–147
IGY and cold war, 138–144
Paul Siple and poles, 129–135
William O. Field and IGY, 136–138
Global village and need for genuine travelling, 241
Godwin, Matthew, 173, 243
Goetzmann, William H., 10, 11
'Golden ages' of exploration, equivalents, 242
Great Trigonometrical Survey of India, 3
Great White Silence, 65, 68
Grosz, Elizabeth, 62

Hagen, Joel B., 296
Halley Hay, 157
Hamblin, Jacob, 15
Hauser, Kitty, 20
Haynes, Roslynn, 225
Heart of the Antarctic, 29
'The hegemonic ideal of the gentleman amateur,' 30
'Heroic Age' exploration, 166

Heroic Era' (1890s–1910s) of Antarctic exploration, 56
Highjump, Operation, 164
Hillary, Edmund, 12, 244
Hill, Jude, 5, 11, 78, 247
Hints to Travellers, 4
HMS *Challenger*, 11
Hodges, William, 52
Hydrography, 13–14

Iconographie photographique de la Salpêtrière, 71
IGY, *see* International Geophysical Year (IGY) of 1957–8
IGY glaciology program, 127, 135, 144
Imperial exploration, 229
Imperial spatiality, 225
The Imperial Trans-Antarctic Expedition of 1914–16, 56, 57
Indian flag on surface of Moon, 242–243
Institute of British Geographers (IBG), 27
Interior of darkroom, 24 March 1911, Antarctica, 76
International Council of Scientific Unions (ICSU), 162
International Geophysical Year (IGY) of 1957–8, 16, 243
and Cold War, 138–144
glaciology on agenda of, 137
map of major scientific stations during, 152
motivation and further development of, 174
on oceanography, 17
opportunity for polar scientists to accumulate new knowledge about Antarctic, 149
overland snow traverses during, 167
scientific exploration of ocean floors, 18
US bases, 167
William O. Field and, 136–138
International Hydrological Decade (IHD), 145
International polar year (1950), 146
'Isoiketes,' 116

Joint Research and Development Board (JRDB), 159
Jones, Max, 21
Journal of Glaciology, 126

Kew Gardens, 3
King, Harding, 5, 11, 79, 80

completion of his first field season, 90–91
exploration of Libyan desert, 78–102
field seasons in Egypt and Libyan Desert, 82
final season, 92
first journey and changing plan, 90
geopolitical context of his work, 91
map of routes taken on 1909 and 1911, 83
principal guides, *see* Qway; Qwaytin
'Remains of the Dakhla–Owanat Road,' 99
role played by local employees in exploration, 88
second season, 91
Korsmo, Fae L., 13, 16, 125, 165

Land Rover's Calvert Centenary Expedition (1996), 224
Landscape photography, 60
Leica cameras from *Bryd Antarctic Expedition*, 62
Leichhardt, Ludwig, 235
Libyan desert, explorations in, 78–84
geopolitical context of Libyan desert, 84–89
making reputations, 93–102
making sense of Libyan desert, 90–93
Libyan desert, exploring, 79
geopolitical context of, 84
interior of vast desert sea, 84
King's exploration efforts to identify water sources/useful strategic information, 87
goal, 87
individuals concerned with, 94
Lyons' comments, 95
preparation prior to, 85
Life writing and early twentieth-century British polar exploration, 23–24
biography and geography at start of twentieth century, 24–30
making celebrities, making heroes, 30–49
'Living dangerously,' 244
Livingstone, David N., 4, 12, 81, 93, 94, 117, 202
'The Lost Oasis of the Libyan Desert,' 102

McClintock, Anne, 227
MacDonald, Fraser, 7, 196

McInerney, Graham, 234, 235, 239, 240
Manhattan Project, development, 161
Maps/charts, making of, 6
Markham, Clements. R., 26, 39, 43, 50
Massey, Harrie, 180, 184
Matless, David, 115
Mémoires sur l'Egypte, 85
Meteor, 15
Mill, Hugh R., 37, 38, 47
Missile, 199, 200, 203
Modern explorers, 241–249
Moon landing (20 July 1969), first, 244
Morris, Meaghan, 228
Mount Everest, conquest of, 12
Mysteries of Libyan Desert, 88, 99, 101, 104
  Rodd's review of, 99–100

National Aeronautics and Space Administration (NASA), 177, 179, 180, 181, 182, 186, 188, 194
National claims to Antarctic, 156
National security *versus* international cooperation in science, 131
'Native information,' 87, 98
'Natural history' model of science, 247
Naylor, Simon, 1, 81, 105, 248
Needell, Alan, 138, 151, 175
Norwegian– British–Swedish Antarctic Expedition of 1949–52, 131, 156
'Nothing is beyond your reach,' 244
Nuclear bomb, development, 161

Oates' 'thrilling' sacrifice, 65
Oceanography, 14–15
  history of, 11
  physical, 15
Orientalism, 1
Our Evolving Civilisation, 108
'Outlook geography,' 115

'Pacific Sector,' 155
Pathfinders: A Global History of Exploration, 21
Permafrost research, 129
Peterson, Nicholas, 231
Photography, 6–7
  in early twentieth-century antarctic exploration, 52–59
  dark rooms, white space and fields of vision, 76–77

first point of emergence: landscapes in transmission, 65–72
pre-photographic moment in 'moment' of discovery, 59–65
second point of emergence: close up and ethnographic, 72–75
multiple forms of visual practices accompanying, 54
Physical and life sciences, trends contributing to rise of, 162
The Physics of Blown Sand and Desert Dunes, 102
Place-based 'natural history' model, 246
Place names, 28
'Planet Earth,' 165
Polar exploration
  reputations of, 107
  and Royal navy, 31
Polar Sale, 72
"Political economy" of geography's publications, 24
Ponting, Herbert, 65, 66, 68, 69, 70, 76
Powell, J. M., 111, 119, 121
Pratt, Mary Louise, 1
'Problems in Exploration,' 78
Project Genetrix, 143

Qway, 88, 89, 92
Qwaytin, 88, 89, 92

Radio-echo sounding (RES), 20, 166
'Rainbow' bomb, 184
Redfield, P., 197, 202, 221
Research and Development Board under National Security Act of 1947, 128
'Rhetorical device of persuasion,' 117
Rice, Tony, 11
The Road to Botany Bay, 224
Rocketry, 209
Rocketry and popular geopolitics of space exploration, 1944–62, 196–201
  pioneering with vehicle-instrument-projectile, 204–210
  popular geopolitics of space exploration, 210–212
  rocketry as child's play, 212–217
  stockpiling and assembling, 217–219

towards historical geography of space exploration, 201–204
Rohlfs, Gerhard, 85
Ronne, Finn, 19
Royal Geographical Society (RGS), 3, 78
  'geography,' 25
Royal Geographical Society's 1896 Calvert Expedition, 223
Russian flag to bottom of Arctic Sea (2007), 242
Ryan, James R., 1, 81, 225, 237

S-51, 180
Said, Edward, 1
Savours, Ann, 45
Science and military power, associations between, 243
Science in the Field, 106
Scientifically motivated exploration, 11
Scientific exploration and Cold War military, 16
Scientific knowledge, 4
Scientific mission, state-sponsored, 243
Scientific Travel in Australia, 119, 120
Scott and Amundsen, 33
Seaver, George, 32
Seeking the Centre, 224
Senussi, 91, 92, 93, 103
Shackleton *versus* Scott, 30
Siple, Paul
  Lawrence's criticism of, 136
  and poles, 129–135
  on Stefansson, 134
  strategic guidance, 134–135
Siple, Paul, 126, 127, 129, 130, 131, 132, 133, 134, 135, 136, 137, 140, 146
Skylark, 179
Snow, Ice, and Permafrost Research Establishment (SIPRE), 135
Solomon, Susan, 45, 49, 69
Sorrenson, Richard, 198
90° *South*, 65, 68
South Pole, first photograph at, 70
Space exploration, historical geography of, 201–204
Space race, 243–244
  birth of, 173
'Speculative geography,' 25
Sputnik satellite, 174
  United Kingdom's reaction to, 178
'Sputnik shock,' 174–177
Stanley, Henry Morton, 8, 244
'Starad,' 187

INDEX

'Starfish,' 184
   controversy over, 193
   damages inflicted by, 189–190
Stefánsson, Vilhjálmur, 41, 108, 120, 121, 122, 126
   cold-weather clothing, 132
   Taylor's criticism of fieldwork in Australia, 123
Stories of Scott's Last Expedition, 27
Strachey, Richard, 26
Study of Environmental Arctic Change (SEARCH), 125
Sturm, Matthew, 147
Survey Notes, see Cairo Scientific Journal
Sydpolen, 26
Synder, Joel, 60

Taylor, T. Griffith, 4
   Australian fieldwork, 112–113
   'block diagrams,' 113, 114
   cartographic claims, 117
   exploration of Australia, 105–108
   contesting scientific expertise, 120–123
   fieldwork and geographical career, 108–113
   fieldwork and geographical knowledge, 113–118
   geographical performance, 119–120
   fieldtrips, forms of conveyance, 119
   fieldwork, 118
   geographical training, 109
   map, 116
   map of northern Queensland and the Northern Territory, 114
   pencil caricature of, 110
   physiographer to Weather Service, 111
   shift from geology to geography, 109
   on Stefánsson, 121–122
   theories, 116–117
   unpopularity, 117
   town of Duchess upon working out of town's mine, 118
   on usefulness of photography, 120
Tenzing, norgay, 12, 244
Terra Nova Expedition, 56, 68
   camera activated by string by various members of expedition, South Pole, 70
Terra nullius, 59, 229–230, 231, 232, 236, 239
Thomas, Nicola J., 5, 11, 78, 247
'To the ends of the earth,' 244
'Transculturation,' 5
'Travel literature,' 2
'Travels in the Libyan Desert,' 95
Trieste (bathyscaphe), 16, 17
'Tropical Problems,' 114
Twentieth century, exploration and, 1–2, 9
   historiographies of exploration, 2–9
   new spaces of exploration, 13–19
   practices of exploration, mapping and surveying, 12
   reaching for skies, 19–20
   twentieth-century exploration, 9–13

Urban Geography, 108
USS Thresher, 16

Vision, 54
Visual representations, 7
Voyages of Discovery, 10–11

Wells, Lawrence, 223
West of Centre, 227
Wexler, H., 149, 168, 169
White Sands Missile Range, 199
The Whole Earth, Earthrise and *22727*, 197
Williamson, Carrie, 227
Windmill, Operation, 164

Younghuband, Francis, 8
Yusoff, Kathryn, 7, 52, 241

'The Zerzura Problem,' 102